STUDIES IN EVANGELICAL HISTORY AND THOUGHT

When Streams Diverge

John Murdoch MacInnis and the Origins of Protestant Fundamentalism in Los Angeles

STUDIES IN EVANGELICAL HISTORY AND THOUGHT

A complete listing of all titles in this series
will be found at the close of this book.

STUDIES IN EVANGELICAL HISTORY AND THOUGHT

When Streams Diverge

John Murdoch MacInnis and the Origins of Protestant Fundamentalism in Los Angeles

Daniel W. Draney

Foreword by
James Bradley

MILTON KEYNES · COLORADO SPRINGS · HYDERABAD

Copyright © Daniel W. Draney 2008

First published 2008 by Paternoster

Paternoster is an imprint of Authentic Media
9 Holdom Avenue, Bletchley, Milton Keynes, MK1 1QR, UK
1820 Jet Stream Drive, Colorado Springs, CO 80921, USA
OM Authentic Media, Medchal Road, Jeedimetla Village,
Secunderabad 500 055, A.P., India

www.authenticmedia.co.uk
Authentic Media is a Division of IBS-STL UK, a company limited by guarantee
(registered charity no. 270162)

14 13 12 11 10 09 08   7 6 5 4 3 2 1

British Library Cataloguing in Publication Data
A catalogue record for this book is available from the British Library

ISBN 978-1-84227-523-8

Typeset by Susan Carlson Wood, Pasadena, CA, USA
Printed and bound in Great Britain
for Paternoster

STUDIES IN EVANGELICAL HISTORY AND THOUGHT
SERIES PREFACE

The Evangelical movement has been marked by its union of four emphases: on the Bible, on the cross of Christ, on conversion as the entry to the Christian life and on the responsibility of the believer to be active. The present series is designed to publish scholarly studies of any aspect of this movement in Britain or overseas. Its volumes include social analysis as well as exploration of Evangelical ideas. The books in the series consider aspects of the movement shaped by the Evangelical Revival of the eighteenth century, when the impetus to mission began to turn the popular Protestantism of the British Isles and North America into a global phenomenon. The series aims to reap some of the rich harvest of academic research about those who, over the centuries, have believed that they had a gospel to tell to the nations.

Series Editors

David Bebbington, Professor of History, University of Stirling, Stirling, Scotland, UK

John H. Y. Briggs, Senior Research Fellow in Ecclesiastical History and Director of the Centre for Baptist History and Heritage, Regent's Park College, Oxford, UK

Timothy Larsen, McManis Professor Christian Thought, Wheaton College, Illinois, USA

Mark A. Noll, McAnaney Professor of History, University of Notre Dame, Notre Dame, Indiana, USA

Ian M. Randall, Senior Research Fellow, International Baptist Theological Seminary, Prague, Czech Republic

Contents

List of Illustrations

FOREWORD

This study of John Murdoch MacInnis is a well-written, sensitive, and yet empirically rigorous assessment of a neglected religious leader that takes us considerably beyond the life of a single individual, or the examination of a passing crisis within fundamentalism. Daniel Draney's research is wonderfully comprehensive, drawing as it does on manuscript and unpublished sources and demonstrating wide reading in the more popular periodical publications. He advances the historiography of fundamentalism in important new ways and provides an excellent survey of the secondary literature on the broader controversy. The author adopts a sophisticated comparative historical method that demonstrates the importance of weighing the local, regional, and national contexts of early-twentieth-century American Protestantism.

Beginning with MacInnis himself, the book brings a great deal of new research to bear on his life and the rancorous debate he provoked at Biola in the 1920s. The documentation of MacInnis' life is superb, and Draney's study is the first to examine the MacInnis papers in detail. The book devotes attention to the social, intellectual, and cultural forces that shaped MacInnis' life, and in this broader context as well, the author excels in the use of sources and insightful analysis. For example, Draney examines the size and composition of the congregations that MacInnis pastored, and his survey of archival materials from Syracuse, Chicago, and Montrose, Pennsylvania, combined with the examination of local newspapers in the cities where MacInnis ministered, is fresh and revealing. The book provides us with important insights into the education and temperament of MacInnis, and the subject's background in turn reveals important aspects of his denominational loyalty. The study is characterized throughout by vivid descriptions, for example, of the stark, physical appearance of fundamentalist institutions. The administration buildings of these conservative institutions help reveal something of the true ethos of fundamentalism.

The study reaches beyond MacInnis, however, and offers us the best available survey of fundamentalism in Los Angeles and especially at Biola. The work provides very important insights into the corporate and business mentality of Lyman Stewart, the founder of Biola. We find here, as well, valuable new material on the conflict between fundamentalism and Pentecostalism. Draney gives special attention throughout to Christian schools and colleges with a sensitive handling of the educational context of the Bible School movement. He demonstrates a clear awareness of the theological world in which MacInnis moved, and in describing this larger world, the work illuminates many obscure corners of fundamentalism. The discussion, for example, of Billy Sunday's campaigns is judiciously integrated into the larger story with telling effect.

In yet broader terms, the study is crucial for helping us understand several puzzles in the historiography of fundamentalism that have heretofore remained unsolved. For example, the book provides clear evidence for why there was an absence of denominational commitment among many fundamentalists. Draney shows how the doctrine of the church (or, in effect, its absence) was central to the emergence and growth of fundamentalism. More importantly, the dissertation fits into a broad range of recent studies that show a growing interest in the conflict between moderate and radical fundamentalists. Draney's work provides the best documentation yet for the existence of a wide "middle ground of moderate mainline clergy." By examining the support for MacInnis, the author uncovers a moderate conservative cohort of leaders that is crucial for understanding how the streams of conservative Protestantism diverged and how fundamentalism was thus a radical departure from the earlier, more unified, nineteenth-century evangelicalism.

In brief, this work is especially helpful in the ongoing attempt to understand and define fundamentalism, both regionally and nationally. The study is characterized throughout by the compelling attention it gives to historical context, not only in relation to conservative religion in Los Angeles, but from the perspective of the national fundamentalist movement generally. The carefully nuanced distinctions between the educational ideals of the leaders of the Bible School movement and the doctrinal matters that were the purported cause of the local crisis sheds important new light on the whole period. The study demonstrates the author's fine ability in sensitive historical analysis and shows creative and imaginative gifts in historical comparison. By uncovering an important group of "evangelical inclusivists" who supported MacInnis, Draney significantly challenges the prevailing "two-party" understanding of the fundamentalist-modernist controversy. This is an important, well-written work of intellectual and cultural history that deserves to be widely read.

James E. Bradley
Geoffrey W. Bromiley Professor of Church History
Fuller Theological Seminary

PREFACE

When I first began to delve into the origins of Protestant fundamentalism in Los Angeles the field was still young and few scholars were dedicating much more than cursory looks at the subject. But world events over the last twenty years have forced scholars to focus greater attention on fundamentalist religious movements, if only to better understand their resurgence and significance in the modern world. Since the destruction of the World Trade Center in New York, "9/11" has become a virtual code word for the unanticipated power and terror of religious fundamentalism. Although that event could be construed as a consequence of particular attitudes and beliefs of radical Islamic fundamentalism, it is widely perceived that religious fundamentalism is a common force affecting all religions, and that the growth of these "fundamentalisms" is not likely to abate any time soon. The fundamentalism described in this book is removed by almost a century from the images and stereotypes of fundamentalism that we hear about in today's popular media. The term "fundamentalism" was coined originally by mainline Protestants who had little in common with the negative stereotypes of today's "religious fundamentalist." While it is probably impossible to recover that original use of the word without the overlay of events that have radically altered our contemporary images of religious fundamentalism, it is my hope that this study will at least contribute to a greater understanding of how and why Protestant fundamentalism became a potent force in American religious history. If there are any affinities between the "fundamentalism" of this study and that of other "fundamentalist movements," those observations will have to be made by other scholars of religion more competent than myself.

I began this study with less lofty goals than contributing to a better understanding of global trends in religion. Actually, it began with my own past, in a quest to make sense of the religious roots of my own family. I had long known that my grandparents were Protestant fundamentalists, and that they might have worn that label proudly. Indeed, as migrants to Los Angeles from Ireland and Nebraska in the early 20th century, they became involved in many of the events and knew many of the people described in this book. It never occurred to me as I was growing up that the religious views and attitudes of people like them would become the topic of scholarly study. It wasn't until I began a doctoral program in American religious history in the 1990s that I realized the growing scholarly interest in the topic. This, combined with my own social proximity to the movement, led me to explore the subject with an interest and zeal that would be needed to get through the arduous requirements of a Ph.D. while working full time and beginning a family. It has not been without sacrifices, as all graduate students know, but its rewards have also been gratifying.

One might well wonder if having a personal connection to the subject of this study has rendered my conclusions less than objective. Of course, one can never completely escape the problem of personal bias. But I have tried to avoid the pitfalls of social proximity to these events through rigorous self-criticism and sound historical method. It will remain for the reader to decide if I have been a fair interpreter of the complexities of Protestantism in the early 20th century. What I have lacked in objectivity, I hope will be made up by insights from my own life experience. But any shortcomings are mine alone; not from those who have helped me along this road of discovery.

There are so many that helped me with this project who deserve special mention. First, I must thank Gordon MacInnes, son of John M. MacInnis, for providing me with so much information and source material to complete this work. (John MacInnis had apparently encouraged his sons to change the spelling of their last name to reflect its original Scottish spelling). Gordon carried the mantle of family historian and preserved his father's personal papers. He also gave me two original editions of *Peter the Fisherman Philosopher*, which must now be very rare given that most were destroyed in 1929. I am deeply grateful to him. Sadly, he did not live to see this project completed.

I also owe thanks to the many librarians, archivists, and research assistants who gave of their time to help me locate source materials for this study. I can only name them here, but they deserve much more: Walter Osborne, Diane Gerow, Sara Ely, W. Leng, Barbara Frame, John Witmer, Dana Porter, Noelle Melito, Kelly Bilderback, Karen Sundland, Gari-Anne Patzwald, and Roy Dodge. Special thanks to Patty Peffall who read through three years of Presbyterian periodicals to find a mere handful of useful articles, but as every historian knows, words are to be weighed not counted, and silence may speak louder than many words. I also thank Susan Carlson Wood for her amazing editorial assistance in preparing this manuscript for publication.

Although few are likely to read this book, it is always especially gratifying to receive encouragement and comments from scholars who share your interests. Regarding Canadian evangelicalism, I received helpful comments from James Cameron, John Stackhouse Jr., David Elliott, and Robert K. Burkinshaw. Peter Lineham of Massey University provided valuable comments on fundamentalism in New Zealand, and David Bebbington offered some helpful insights on British fundamentalism at an ISAE conference in Wheaton, Illinois. Glen Spann of Asbury University provided helpful information on Leander Munhall and the Methodist connections. One item of special note: through a circuitous route I found the son of G. Campbell Morgan, Dr. Richard Morgan, living in Lenoir, North Carolina. He told me, much to my disappointment, that all of Morgan's diaries and correspondence, which would have been invaluable for early 20th century Protestantism, were destroyed by well-meaning family members.

A special word of appreciation is due to Dr. George Marsden at the University of Notre Dame and Dr. Robert K. Johnston of Fuller Theological Seminary for their reading of the original academic manuscript of this book. I was honored to have their fair-minded criticisms, but I especially enjoyed their words of affirmation. To Dr. James Bradley, mentor, scholar, and friend, I can only express my deepest appreciation. Without his meticulous guidance and constant encouragement this project would never have been completed. When G. Campbell Morgan dedicated his book, *Categorical Imperatives of the Christian Faith*, to John MacInnis, his words could well describe James Bradley: a "Saint and Scholar," a "Revealer of the Truth that the Spiritual and Intellectual are not Incompatible."

Finally, I want to thank my family and friends during this long season of study, writing, and research. My wife and daughter attended many gatherings without me, and endured many lonely evenings as I worked late into the night. I can say that even if not everyone understood my determination to finish this project, everyone encouraged me nonetheless. I am especially grateful to my mother, Ruth Wynola, who never failed to support and encourage me in almost anything I did—whether deserved or not. Toward the end of completing my Ph.D. she began to experience symptoms of Alzheimer's Disease, and much to my sorrow, she did not live to see this work break into print. I dedicate this book to her.

CHAPTER 1

Introduction

In 1928 a book entitled *Peter the Fisherman Philosopher* became the subject of a protracted and bitter controversy. The author, John Murdoch MacInnis, was dean of the Bible Institute of Los Angeles, a fundamentalist Bible school, then located in downtown Los Angeles. Although MacInnis did not intend to create a controversy, his book quickly became something of a fundamentalist cause célèbre, dividing evangelical Protestants and leaving in its wake a legacy of emotional bitterness and tragedy.

Few today know the extent of the controversy. Taking place mostly among self-professed fundamentalists, it affected some of the top Protestant leaders of the 1920s, including William B. Riley, Charles Erdman, G. Campbell Morgan, Reuben Torrey, Charles Trumbull, and James Gray. It involved not only leaders from the United States, but also from England, New Zealand, and Canada. Several emerging fundamentalist leaders found their career plans dramatically changed by the MacInnis controversy. Alva McClain, a teacher at Biola during the crisis, felt constrained to leave Biola due to his support of MacInnis, but this did not seem to tarnish his fundamentalist reputation, for he later founded the fundamentalist Grace Seminary in 1937. The career of Charles Fuller gained a significant boost from the episode, lifting him into a fundamentalist spotlight that greatly enhanced his influence and prestige.

Few, however, acquired any personal benefit from the crisis. More common were the longtime friendships, strained or broken by its bitterness. "The wounds of a friend," mused Riley, "are far deeper and harder to bear than those of an enemy."[1] So it was, friend against friend, often to the point of an irrevocable breach. By any account, MacInnis suffered the most. A lifetime of friendships were lost, but none so great as his split with Reuben Torrey, a friend of more than twenty years. Others too, like the widows of Lyman and Milton Stewart, though sisters-in-

---

[1] Quoted in Charles Hurlburt to W. B. Riley, 26 November 1926, MacInnis Papers, Presbyterian Historical Society, Philadelphia, Pennsylvania.

law, refused to speak to each other on account of the controversy. So devoted was Mrs. Milton Stewart to MacInnis that, when she died, she was buried by his side. Such emotional intensity was not the exception.

The controversy also affected institutions. Aside from the calamity it precipitated at Biola, its impact could be seen in other ways. In Los Angeles, it caused the formation of new fundamentalist organizations, such as French Oliver's fundamentalist tabernacle. At Moody Bible Institute, it led to the adoption of a statement of doctrine.[2] At the Evangelical Theological College, it influenced Lewis Sperry Chafer to reorganize management of the school.[3] But nowhere did it have greater consequences than in the Presbyterian and Baptist churches of Los Angeles. For many denominational clergy, the crisis would be remembered for many years and have a continuing impact on the future relations of mainline churches with interdenominational evangelical enterprises. Thus, more than twenty years later, the crisis would reemerge as a spectre, haunting the efforts of Fuller Seminary to establish itself in the domain of Protestant denominationalism.[4]

From the perspective of Bible school fundamentalists who looked to Moody Bible Institute as their flagship institution, the MacInnis controversy was the greatest crisis of the 1920s. It is very difficult for the contemporary historian, familiar with the anti-evolution campaigns in the state legislatures, or the political struggles of the Baptist and Presbyterian denominations, to appreciate how seriously the MacInnis controversy was regarded. True, it received nowhere the attention of the Scopes Trial or Harry Emerson Fosdick, but to the typical Bible school fundamentalist, these episodes were distantly felt, removed from his psyche and personal sphere of influence. But to many fundamentalists, the MacInnis controversy felt much closer to home, because it occurred in a prominent American Bible school. This fact has been rightly emphasized by one historian.

> From Torrey's perspective and from the perspective of other fundamentalists, the MacInnis episode was the major religious controversy of the 1920s (not the Fosdick case or the Scopes trial), because of the perceived

---

[2] "Doctrinal Statement of the Moody Bible Institute of Chicago (Adopted at the Annual Meeting of the Board of Trustees, October 1928)," February 1929, 273.

[3] John David Hannah, "The Social and Intellectual History of the Origins of the Evangelical Theological College" (Ph.D. diss., University of Texas, Dallas, 1988), 322.

[4] George M. Marsden, *Reforming Fundamentalism: Fuller Seminary and the New Evangelicalism* (Grand Rapids: Eerdmans, 1987), 87, 95.

threat to fundamentalist Christianity from within its own ranks and not from the outside.[5]

In spite of this fact, no major study has been written on the MacInnis controversy. There are several reasons for this. First, historians have noted that fundamentalists have largely failed to write their own history. Perhaps if they had, they would have given greater attention to the episode. Oddly, however, two works written by historians at the fundamentalist Bob Jones University have not changed the situation,[6] though this may be because they missed the import of a controversy that occurred primarily in the Northeast, Midwest, and western United States, but was largely ignored in their native South. A second reason may be the general lack of attention to the religious history of the American West.[7] Ever since Sandeen, it has become common to believe that real fundamentalist influence was born in the Northeast, with an occasional nod to Lyman Stewart, Biola, and the *Fundamentals*. Probably this has caused some interpreters to neglect fundamentalism in the West.

Other factors too may account for its historical demise. Until the rise of contemporary religio-cultural analysis of Protestant fundamentalism, most interpreters of the phenomenon, such as Norman Furniss, focused exclusively on either its political aspects as an anti-evolution movement, or on its role in the Protestant denominations.[8] Consequently, an intra-fundamentalist crisis did not adequately fit the paradigm, and therefore, did not merit any greater attention. This bias is seen vividly in Furniss' comment that the magazine of the Bible Institute of Los Angeles, *The King's Business*, "is of no value" for the history of fundamentalism.[9] Related to this denominational bias is the fact that the controversy never resulted in the formation of a major institution. The controversy at

---

[5] Kermit Staggers, "Reuben A. Torrey: American Fundamentalist" (Ph.D. diss., Claremont Graduate School, 1986), 301.

[6] David O. Beale, (Greenville, South Carolina: Unusual Publications, 1986); George W. Dollar, *A History of Fundamentalism in America* (Greenville, South Carolina: Bob Jones University, 1973). Dollar's bias is seen in his exclusion of MacInnis from a lengthy list of fundamentalist and non-fundamentalist leaders, while including many others of less importance.

[7] Eldon G. Ernst. "American Religious History from a Pacific Coast Perspective," in *Religion and Society in the American West*, ed. Carl Guarneri and David Alvarez (Lanham, MD: University Press of America, 1987), 8; Ernest R. Sandeen, *The Origins of Fundamentalism: Toward a Historical Interpretation*, Facet Books Historical Series (American Church), ed. Richard C, Wolf, vol. 10 (Philadelphia: Fortress Press, 1968), 26.

[8] Sandeen, *The Origins of Fundamentalism*, 1–2.

[9] Norman Furniss, *The Fundamentalist Controversy, 1918–1931* (New Haven: Yale University Press, 1954), 186.

Princeton Seminary led to the formation of Westminster Seminary. The
schism in the Fundamentalist Fellowship led to the organizing of the
Baptist Bible Union. But the split at the Bible Institute of Los Angeles
resulted in no new institution. Hence, it has been too easily ignored.

There are, as well, positive reasons to undertake a study of this kind.
With scholarly interest in fundamentalism continuing to expand, a study
of this crisis will fill crucial gaps in our understanding of inter-denominational evangelical Protestants, their beliefs, attitudes, activities, and
the social and cultural realities that shaped their perceptions.[10] Many of
the key figures discussed in this study have never been the focus of
scholarly attention: for example, G. Campbell Morgan, Charles Hurlburt, leader of the African Inland Mission, and Charles Trumbull, editor
of the influential *Sunday School Times*. Second, recent discussions in
the problems of neo-evangelical historiography have pointed to a need
for more specialized studies to test and critique the current models of
historical interpretation.[11] Third, as new sources become available, it is
necessary to ask how they will affect a current understanding of the
history. Hence, this study will explore documents from the MacInnis
papers, that have never been extensively studied.

MacInnis and the Historiography of Fundamentalism

Although there has been no significant monograph written about the
MacInnis controversy, the crisis has been summarily discussed in a
number of published books, dissertation literature, and unpublished
works. Prior to 1980, references to the controversy were few and largely
unreliable. But in the last few years, as studies of various aspects of
Protestant evangelicalism have increased, so too have discussions of this
topic. Important information about the controversy is found in both
scholarly and popular sources, so it is necessary to review each of these
respectively.

---

[10] For the growing interest in evangelicalism see the excellent bibliographies
now available on the subject. Norris A. Magnuson and William G. Travis, eds.
American Evangelicalism: An Annotated Bibliography (Locust Hill Press: West
Cornwall, CT, 1990); also Edith L. Blumhofer and Joel A. Carpenter, eds.
Twentieth Century Evangelicalism: A Guide to the Sources (New York: Garland Publishers, 1990). See too the Fundamentalism Project, which examines
"fundamentalisms" as a modern socio-religious phenomenon: Martin E. Marty
and R. Scott Appleby, eds., *Fundamentalisms Observed*, The Fundamentalism
Project 1 (Chicago: University of Chicago Press, 1991).

[11] Joel A. Carpenter, "The Scope of American Evangelicalism: Some Comments on the Dayton-Marsden Exchange," *Christian Scholar's Review* 23
(September 1993): 57; Donald W. Dayton, "Rejoinder to Historiography Discussion," *Christian Scholar's Review* 23 (September 1993): 70.

Scholarly Sources

The MacInnis controversy was ended, for all intents and purposes, by March 1929. Only two years later, historians began to reflect on the birth of the fundamentalist movement in the 1920s. Comprised mostly of observers, and in some cases participants in the Fundamentalist Modernist Controversy, these writers attempted to offer an historical understanding of the causes of Protestant fundamentalism. Three significant writings of this period include H. Richard Niebuhr's influential study of fundamentalism, Frederick Allen's retrospective of the 1920s, and the first book length treatment of the subject by a professor at Crozier Theological Seminary, Stewart Cole, all published in 1931.[12] These and other writings immediately following the 1920s initiated what William E. Ellis has called the "liberal school" of interpretation.[13] A key theme of this "school," which was partly influenced by the interpretations of the Scopes Trial by literary media elites like H. L. Mencken and Joseph Wood Krutch, was that fundamentalism was caused by social conflict between rural and urban values, or the remains of an outmoded worldview in conflict with modern enlightened culture. During this early period of reflection, Stewart Cole was the only one to mention the MacInnis controversy, when he stated that the crisis was caused by "moderate views" applied to fundamentalism, a view that reflected his own mainline denominational perspective more than a particular theory of social conflict.[14]

A period of twenty three years passed before another major work on fundamentalist history appeared. In 1954, Norman Furniss published a Yale dissertation on the fundamentalist modernist controversy during the 1920s. This book, stimulated by the McCarthy era of American politics, constituted a resurgence of the earlier social interpretations of fundamentalism. Furniss, for example, discounted Niebuhr's rural urban conflict theory, but still stated that fundamentalism was essentially a reaction of fear and insecurity caused by rapid intellectual progress.[15] Although his book provides some important information about the fundamentalist controversies of the 1920s, it is not a consistently reliable

---

[12] H. Richard Niebuhr. "Fundamentalism," in *The Encyclopedia of the Social Sciences,* vol. 6 (New York, 1931), 526–27; Frederick Lewis Allen, *Only Yesterday: An Informal History of the Nineteen Twenties* (New York: Harper and Brothers, 1931), 195–206; Stewart Cole, *The History of Fundamentalism* (New York: Harper & Row, 1931; repr. Hamden, CT: Archon Books, 1963).

[13] William E. Ellis, "Evolution, Fundamentalism, and the Historians: An Historiographical Review," 44 (November 1981): 17.

[14] Cole, *History of Fundamentalism,* 248.

[15] Furniss, *The Fundamentalist Controversy,* 28–29, 35.

guide. His characterization of fundamentalists as simple minded and ignorant may have some basis in fact, but fails to offer a useful model of
interpretation. Moreover, his failure to distinguish various degrees of
conservative and liberal opinion in the 1920s led him to use terminology
uncritically, as if fundamentalism were only another name for
orthodoxy.[16]

Although Furniss wrote a paragraph on the MacInnis controversy, his
treatment of the crisis suffers from factual errors and biased interpretation. His assertions that MacInnis interjected "heresy" at the Bible Institute of Los Angeles, or that *Peter the Fisherman Philosopher* was a
series of "modernist lectures," reveal that he read fundamentalist
sources uncritically. Also, his statement that the Biola Board of Directors had conducted a "purge," not only of MacInnis but of four other
board members, is incorrect.[17]

Beginning in the late 1950s, hints of a revisionist perspective on the
fundamentalist modernist controversy began to appear. No longer satisfied with exclusively social or economic explanations of fundamentalism, scholars began to re-examine the theological issues which domi-
nated the period. The same year that Furniss published his monograph,
Lefferts Loetscher offered a historical study of the theological issues in
the Presbyterian fundamentalist controversy, and the following year
Robert Handy attempted to explain the controversy as an instance of
conflict between faith and reason: using this paradigm, he identified five
different theological parties in the 1920s.[18] But the best bellwether of the
new self-conscious revisionism appeared in 1968, when a chastened
historian, Paul Carter, wrote that he and other historians had erred in describing fundamentalism as a dying force. If fundamentalism were only
the result of "cultural lag" and rural urban conflict, how could one explain its continuing growth and vitality? That problem led Carter to begin serious questioning of the prevailing social interpretations, and several of his initial questions subsequently provided fruitful directions of
research for a revisionist historiography.[19]

These early revisionist impulses finally came to fruition in the work
of Ernest Sandeen, who attempted to reconstruct the origins of funda-

---

[16] Ibid., 22.

[17] Ibid., 73–74.

[18] Lefferts A. Loetscher, *The Broadening Church: A Study of Theological
Issues in the Presbyterian Church Since 1869* (Philadelphia: University of
Pennsylvania Press, 1954); Robert Handy, "Fundamentalism and Modernism in
Perspective," *Religion in Life* 24 (Summer 1955): 385–94.

[19] Paul A. Carter, "The Fundamentalist Defense of the Faith," in *Change and
Continuity in Twentieth Century America: The 1920s,* ed. John Braeman,
Robert H. Bremner, and David Brody (Columbus: Ohio State University Press,
1968), 179–214.

mentalism as a distinctly theological movement. In his 1968 article, and later in a book length treatment entitled *The Roots of Fundamentalism,* Sandeen challenged the beliefs of earlier historians, that fundamentalism was mostly a rural and Southern phenomenon, by demonstrating that its real strength in the 1920s lay in the large cities of the Northeast. In addition, Sandeen argued that the fundamentalist movement could not be understood properly through a study of the fundamentalist controversy; rather, one must study its roots, which he identified as an alliance of two 19th century traditions, the biblical literalism of the so-called "Princeton theology," and a separate but parallel tradition of Protestant millennialism. Although his interpretation was widely discounted, Sandeen's work effectively turned back the earlier social theories and paved the way for broader, religio-cultural interpretations of fundamentalism.[20]

If Sandeen weakened one leg of the earlier social interpretations, the work of C. Allyn Russell weakened another, namely, that fundamentalists of the 1920s were all of one stripe. To the contrary, Russell has shown through his biographical portraits of fundamentalists that they were a more diverse group than commonly supposed.[21] His work, however, has focused primarily on the best known fundamentalist leaders and has not paid attention to the grass-roots, or to mid-level leaders such as MacInnis.

The year 1980 marked an important transition in the historiography of American Protestant fundamentalism. First, the election of Ronald Reagan stimulated a renewed scholarly interest in the origins of the religious right in American politics.[22] Although the socio-political perspective of these studies precluded any treatments of the MacInnis controversy, the renewed interest in American fundamentalism encouraged other related studies. For example, a work by Leo Ribuffo examining the "old Christian right" and the role of the radical fundamentalist, Gerald Winrod, briefly mentioned the controversy.[23] Ribuffo empha-

---

[20] Ernest R. Sandeen, *The Roots of Fundamentalism: British and American Millenarianism, 1800–1930* (Chicago. University of Chicago Press, 1970; repr. Grand Rapids: Baker Books, 1978), 248; for criticism of Sandeen's position see LeRoy Moore Jr., "Another Look at Fundamentalism: A Response to Ernest R. Sandeen," *Church History* 37 (June 1968):195–202; and George M. Marsden, "Defining Fundamentalism," *Christian Scholar's Review* 1 (Winter 1971): 141–51. Also see Sandeen's response, "Defining Fundamentalism: A Reply to Professor Marsden," in *Christian Scholar's Review* 1 (Spring 1971): 227–32.

[21] C. Allyn Russell, *Voices of American Fundamentalism* (Philadelphia: Westminster Press, 1976).

[22] For a bibliographical essay see Richard V. Pierard, "The New Religious Right in American Politics," in *Evangelicalism and Modern America,* ed. George M. Marsden (Grand Rapids: Eerdmans, 1984), 161–74.

[23] Leo Ribuffo, *The Old Christian Right: The Protestant Far Right from the Great Depression to the Cold War* (Philadelphia: Temple University Press,

sized Winrod's paradoxical role in the MacInnis crisis, noting that he chose to defend the more moderate MacInnis from the attacks of his own militant fundamentalist colleagues. Second, the historiography greatly advanced with the publication of George M. Marsden's *Fundamentalism and American Culture*. This work continued to develop the new historiography of Sandeen, but also tried to correct some of its shortcomings. In particular, Marsden argued that Sandeen's definition of fundamentalism as a theological alliance was too narrow, and that he underemphasized other significant roots in 19th century American evangelicalism, including revivalism, pietism, and "variant orthodoxies."[24] Although Marsden has been faulted for finding too much continuity between fundamentalism and its 19th century forebears,[25] this work still remains the standard text for students of American Protestant fundamentalism, and, moreover, it also represents a *tour de force* of the new school of evangelical historians, attempting to analyze and critically evaluate their own religious history.[26]

Ironically, in spite of growth in the historiography of fundamentalism, there were no significant scholarly examinations of the MacInnis controversy between 1960 and 1980. One reason for this was a lack of studies examining the period 1925 to 1935, ten years that Robert Handy considered a "religious depression."[27] Handy's epithet reflected the earlier widely held opinion that fundamentalism after 1925 was "fading into obscurity,"[28] and, therefore, did not merit further historical investigation. This idea, though partially true if one considers that Bryan was gone, the anti-evolution struggle had collapsed, and fundamentalist leaders were in disarray, nevertheless, ignored the fact that fundamentalists continued to develop an institutional infrastructure and attract new adherents during this period. Though a few historians have now adequately overturned this earlier perception, their works have emphasized the growth of fundamentalism after 1930.[29] In the same vein,

---

1983), 89.

[24] George M. Marsden, *Fundamentalism and American Culture: The Shaping of Twentieth-Century Evangelicalism, 1870–1925* (New York: Oxford University Press, 1980), 200–201.

[25] Timothy Smith, "Historical Fundamentalism," *Fides et Historia* 14 (Fall–Winter 1981): 70–71.

[26] Leonard I. Sweet, "Wise as Serpents, Innocent as Doves: The New Evangelical Historiography," 56 (Fall 1988): 397–416.

[27] Robert T. Handy, "The American Religious Depression, 1925–1935," *Church History* 29 (March 1960): 3–16.

[28] See, for example, the often cited editorial, "Fading Fundamentalism," *Christian Century,* 6 June 1927, 742–43.

[29] Louis Gaspar, (The Hague, Paris: Mouton & Co, 1963); Joel A. Carpenter, "Fundamentalist Institutions and the Rise of Conservative Protestantism, 1929–

the works of Sandeen, Marsden, and several others, explored the roots of fundamentalism to the 1920s, but did not extend the history beyond 1925.[30]

One exception to this scholarly gap was a dissertation written in 1969, which surveyed various fundamentalist sects in Los Angeles between 1910 and 1930, from the Peniel Mission to Aimee Semple McPherson and "fighting Bob Shuler." Edmondson offered a lengthy description of the Bible Institute of Los Angeles, focusing mostly on Lyman Stewart and the *Fundamentals*. A four page description of the MacInnis controversy, however, became the first real analysis of the controversy in a scholarly medium.[31] Unfortunately, his treatment relied too heavily on Furniss and repeated a number of his errors. Even so, Edmondson advanced his own thesis about the controversy, arguing that MacInnis had been "too congenial to the social gospel." Although there is some truth in this assertion, opposition to MacInnis was far more complex and varied than Edmondson believed.

Since the resurgence of interest in fundamentalism after 1980, several scholarly works have commented on the MacInnis controversy, thus lifting it from its earlier obscurity. Three recent biographical dissertations now offer researchers a broader acquaintance with the controversy. Brian McKenzie's 1985 study of Rowland Bingham, the Canadian founder of the Sudan Interior Mission, stated that Bingham rejected the philosophical method of MacInnis, in spite of their close friendship.[32] A year later, Kermit Staggers completed a study of Reuben Torrey, which

---

1942," 49 (March 1980): 62–74; Douglas E. Herman, "Flooding the Kingdom: The Intellectual Development of Fundamentalism, 1930–1941" (Ph.D. diss., Ohio University, 1980).

[30] Carroll Edwin Harrington, "The Fundamentalist Movement in America, 1870–1920" (Ph.D. diss., University of California, Berkeley, 1959); Paul C. Wilt, "Pre-Millennialism in America, 1865–1918, With Special Reference to Attitudes Toward Social Reform" (Ph.D. diss., American University, 1970); and Nelson Hodges Hart, "The True and the False: The Worlds of an Emerging Evangelical Protestant Fundamentalism in America" (Ph.D. diss., Michigan State University, 1976).

[31] William Edmondson, "Fundamentalist Sects of Los Angeles, 1900–1930" (Ph.D. diss., Claremont University, 1969), 166–70; there is also a brief review of the crisis in a thesis written by a nephew of MacInnis: Donald MacInnes, "Leadership Training in the Synod of California, Southern Area: Inception, Formative Years, the Present" (Master's Thesis, San Francisco Theological Seminary, 1960), 26–32.

[32] Brian A. McKenzie, "Fundamentalism, Christian Unity, and Premillennialism in the Thought of Rowland Victor Bingham (1872–1942): A Study of Anti-Modernism in Canada" (Ph.D. diss., University of Toronto, 1985), 139–40.

traced the friendship of MacInnis and Torrey to 1907, when they jointly founded the Montrose Bible Conference. Staggers claimed that Torrey's death was partly caused by his rupture with MacInnis, but this idea was not original—some savvy fundamentalists had discovered much earlier that blaming Torrey's deathbed illness on MacInnis made effective anti-MacInnis propaganda.[33] A third dissertation, completed in 1988, noted that the crisis influenced Lewis Sperry Chafer to reorganize Dallas Theological Seminary in an effort to avoid the type of controversial schism that occurred at Biola.[34] Taken together, these studies reveal the diverse responses of fundamentalist leaders to the MacInnis crisis.

When Sandeen first offered his interpretation of fundamentalism, he charted two important aspects of fundamentalist origins—premillennialism and Bible schools. The former received greater attention in Timothy Weber's book on the history of premillennialism in America.[35] Though Weber did not comment on MacInnis, who played a minor but not insignificant role in the Bible prophecy conference movement, his book is vital to understanding the controversy, because premillennialism and dispensationalism were at the heart of the issues dividing pro and anti-MacInnis factions. The other aspect of Sandeen's work, which is also vital, has now received definitive treatment in Virginia Brereton's analysis of the American Bible school. Brereton's book began as a dissertation, and in its original form it did not include a study of the Bible Institute of Los Angeles. Her published revision, however, included a study of Biola in order to achieve greater balance. Brereton commented on the MacInnis controversy very briefly, arguing that it was a good example of how Bible schools imposed a "middle class conventionality" on one another.[36] Ironically, though she was correct that Bible schools attempted to control the boundaries of Bible school identity, the MacInnis controversy was not a good example of middle class conventionality, because as this study argues, it was really a radicalization of the Bible school movement rather than a movement toward conventionality.

The best scholarly treatment of the MacInnis controversy, however, is found in Marsden's history of Fuller Seminary and the new evangelicalism.[37] This work is a continuation of Marsden's earlier book, tracing the movement of mostly Baptist and Presbyterian fundamentalists of the

---

[33] Staggers, "Reuben A. Torrey," 306; T. C. Horton, "An Open Letter to the Members of the Southern California Premillenial Association," (December 1928), MacInnis Papers.

[34] Hannah, "Origins of the Evangelical Theological College," 320–22.

[35] Timothy P. Weber, *Living in the Shadow of the Second Coming: American Premillennialism, 1875-1982* (Chicago: University of Chicago Press, 1979).

[36] Virginia Lieson Brereton, *Training God's Army: The American Bible School, 1880–1940* (Bloomington: Indiana University Press, 1990), 147.

[37] Marsden, *Reforming Fundamentalism,* 39–40, 87, 95.

1920s to the neo-evangelicals of the 1980s. Two features of Marsden's discussion are helpful: first, he showed that the controversy had a continuing life in the presbytery of Los Angeles, when leaders at Fuller Seminary discovered, to their chagrin, that memories of the crisis still hindered their acceptance by the presbytery. Second, Marsden emphasized that the lack of a denominational authority in Protestant fundamentalism forced fundamentalists to depend on an informal authority of prominent Bible teachers and leaders. His conclusion that the crisis was "a classic intra-fundamentalist struggle that revealed the tensions within the movement," is a useful starting point for historical understanding.

Popular Sources

In addition to those scholarly works that have discussed the MacInnis controversy, another important source of information has come from popular biographies of fundamentalist leaders, and institutional histories of Biola and the Church of the Open Door. Though most fundamentalists were reluctant to accept critical historiography, they reveled in popular hagiography, and thus many biographies have been written about fundamentalist leaders, including many of those who participated in the MacInnis controversy. Unfortunately, because these works tended to celebrate their heroes rather than to analyze them, there is almost no trace of the controversy in this literature.

An exception, however, occurs in biographies of G. Campbell Morgan, a popular British itinerant Bible teacher, who unwittingly found himself caught up in the crisis. An early biography of Morgan, written while he was still an active Bible teacher, only briefly mentioned the controversy even though its author, John Harries, was ostracized from fellow ministers in the presbytery of Philadelphia because of his outspoken support of Morgan and MacInnis.[38] Another Morgan biography, written by his daughter-in-law, also mentioned the controversy, commenting that some "extreme fundamentalists" disagreed with Morgan on fine points of doctrine.[39] Few of MacInnis' opponents would have agreed, however, with that assessment. To the contrary, Trumbull and his co-belligerents described the controversy as "one of the greatest dangers of this generation," and several leaders expressed the opinion

---

[38] John Harries, *G. Campbell Morgan: The Man and His Ministry* (New York: Fleming H. Revell Co., 1930), 146. For Harries' exclusion from pulpits in Philadelphia see John Harries to MacInnis, 15 March 1930 and 24 March 1930, MacInnis Papers.

[39] Jill Morgan, *A Man of the Word: Life of G. Campbell Morgan* (London: Pickering & Inglis, 1951), 274–75.

that the entire Bible institute movement in America was threatened.[40] Thus, so-called "fine points" of doctrine often became broad lines of division.

More interesting is the extensive discussion found in Dan Fuller's book on his father, Charles E. Fuller. His account of the crisis has been a significant source of information for other interpreters, and it also includes the author's own analysis of *Peter the Fisherman Philosopher*. In general, it is a reliable outline of the main events of the controversy, but it is weakened by personal bias and tendentious argument. For example, Fuller displays a tendency, like other popular reconstructions of the controversy, to portray Charles Fuller as the hero of a tragic drama, saving Biola from disaster.[41] There is no hint that Fuller and other anti-MacInnis board members threatened the stability of Biola in their attempts to appease fundamentalist critics. But a more significant weakness is the lack of historical context. Fuller's account is a chapter in the life of Charles Fuller, not of the fundamentalist movement as a whole. While this is, of course, suitable for a biography, its singular focus does not offer a sufficiently broad perspective for historical interpretation.

Three other books treating the crisis from an institutional perspective have, perhaps, been most influential in shaping contemporary understanding of the crisis among heirs of Biola and Southern California fundamentalism. A manuscript history of Biola was written by James O. Henry, erstwhile teacher of history at Biola, but this work has not been published. Henry devoted an entire chapter to the theological controversies which rocked Biola from 1910 to 1930, and reserved the bulk of his discussion for the MacInnis crisis. His treatment is a valuable contribution to an understanding of the controversy, principally because he provides much useful information which has not been previously known.[42] A more readable and less detailed history of Biola was written by Robert Williams and Marilyn Miller on the occasion of Biola's 75th anniversary.[43] Interestingly, whereas Henry's account tended to accept too uncritically the judgements of anti-MacInnis fundamentalists and concluded that MacInnis was out to change and reorder the school's direction, Williams and Miller provided a more sympathetic view, writing

---

[40] See John MacInnis to Charles Trumbull, 10 May 1928; W. B. Riley to Alexander MacKeigan, 21 March 1928; P. B. Fraser to MacInnis, 10 July 1928, MacInnis Papers.

[41] Daniel P. Fuller, *Give the Winds a Mighty Voice: The Story of Charles E. Fuller* (Waco, Texas: Word Books, 1972), 68–74.

[42] James O. Henry, History of Biola, TMs, n.d., Biola University, La Mirada, CA.

[43] Robert Williams and Marilyn Miller, *Chartered for His Glory: Biola University, 1908–1983* (La Mirada, CA: Associated Students of Biola University, 1983), 48–51.

that MacInnis was a brilliant scholar whose statements were "grossly misconstrued," and describing his opponents as "ultra-fundamentalists," who did much damage by their "judgmental attitudes."[44] Finally, because of the close ties between the Church of the Open Door and the Bible Institute of Los Angeles, a history of that church also provided a discussion of the MacInnis controversy.[45] Though all three of these works depict the MacInnis crisis as a cause of Biola's subsequent financial calamity, a claim that lacks sufficient evidence, and although they fail to document their sources, a fact that limits their usefulness, they represent a largely dispassionate attempt of the heirs of the crisis to explain their own history.

Goals of This Study

The lack of scholarly attention to the MacInnis controversy, as well as its apparent merit as a topic of scholarly investigation in the now burgeoning field of fundamentalist historiography, constitute the principal reasons for a new academic study of the MacInnis controversy. Three questions, however, must first be considered. First, what kind of work is this? Second, how will it relate to critical issues in current scholarly discussions of fundamentalism? Third, how will it advance or revise our understanding of fundamentalism in America?

The Nature of This Work

First, this study will describe and analyze the origins of the MacInnis controversy, and based on this analysis, ascertain its historical significance in fundamentalism and American Protestantism in general. This approach will differ from earlier discussions by beginning not with the controversy itself, but with its root causes. Previous treatments of the controversy, which have focused on the events of 1928, have tended to see the controversy simply as a response to the publication of MacInnis' book. But this picture distorts the fact that many other elements contributed to the controversy and influenced its outcome. It is, therefore, frankly assumed that the controversy of 1928 cannot be adequately understood apart from an examination of its historical antecedents.

But how will these antecedents be determined? First, the main figure of the controversy, John MacInnis, must be considered an important starting point for analysis. Although his book precipitated the year long

---

[44] Henry, History of Biola Manuscript, 90; Williams and Miller, *Chartered for His Glory,* 48, 49, 51.

[45] G. Michael Cocoris, *70 Years on Hope Street: A History of the Church of the Open Door* (Los Angeles: Church of the Open Door, 1985), 43–47.

controversy, and he did more than anyone else to shape its direction and outcome, he has remained virtually unknown to historians of fundamentalism. Consequently, this study will begin with a biographical analysis of his life and thought with a special focus on his formative religious experiences. Moreover, because he eventually became the leader of an important fundamentalist institution, his life and thought will be examined in relation to the origin of fundamentalism in the early 20th century. A second part of this monograph will analyze the educational goals and ideals of Bible school leaders, as they were envisioned by founders of the Bible Institute of Los Angeles. Considerable tensions and contradictions inhered in the aspirations of Bible school leaders, and it is the contention of this study that organizational conflicts arising from these ideas contributed significantly to the final collapse of the MacInnis administration. This aspect of the controversy has also been overlooked by an overemphasis on doctrinal issues surrounding MacInnis' book. Third, and closely related to the study of Biola's educational goals, is the local ethos of fundamentalism in Los Angeles. Previous discussions have tended to interpret the controversy as an internecine theological struggle with little or no awareness of the ways that regional factors may have influenced the crisis. This analysis, however, will seek to place the development of the controversy in a particular regional context, by emphasizing the roles of important Los Angeles fundamentalists, and how their unique regional history and circumstances impacted the crisis. Finally, no understanding of the controversy would be adequate without a study of the issues surrounding MacInnis' theological opinions. Although his book was the primary catalyst for attacks on his orthodoxy, questions were raised much earlier. Hence, problems of evolution and premillennialism are treated first, primarily in their local context, while doctrinal issues emerging from discussions of his book are analyzed in two subsequent chapters. This analysis of doctrinal controversy will seek to "contextualize" MacInnis' ideas in the complex theological currents of early 20th century America.

The scope of this work will require the interweaving of at least three types of historical literature: biography, intellectual history, and institutional history. But given the preceding summary, it should be clear that this work is not, strictly speaking, any one of these. It is not, for instance, a biography of MacInnis, although it includes considerable biographical analysis. There is no attempt to portray his life either as a hero in American religious history, or as a victim of tragic circumstances. His biography is studied only insofar as his beliefs and actions contributed to the origin of the controversy, not as the organizing theme of this monograph. Neither is this work exclusively an intellectual history of MacInnis or the controversy, although this constitutes a major part of its focus. Instead, ideas are interpreted in relation to events which significantly influenced the lives of participants in the controversy, or in relation to changing social and cultural realities of 20th century America. Finally, although this study involves extensive discussion of a fundamentalist institution, the Bible Institute of Los Angeles, it is not institutional history, in that it does not make the life of that institution its central concern.

Defining Fundamentalism

Recent scholarly discussions on defining fundamentalism indicate that there remains considerable diversity of opinion about how fundamentalists ought to be understood and described.[46] Because this study does not seek to draw any conclusions about the nature of fundamentalism as a cross-cultural religious and sociological phenomenon, but rather is concerned to explain the religious issues that emerged in a single subgroup of American Protestants, fundamentalism will be described in reference to its character as a religious movement. Perhaps a useful starting point, therefore, is George Marsden's broad description of fundamentalism as a coalition of militant anti-modernist Protestant evangelicals.[47] But beneath that general definition there lies an ocean of unresolved questions. Were all fundamentalists militant? Perhaps most of them were, but militancy came in many varieties, and in the case of MacInnis and his fundamentalist defenders, it was no badge of honor. Or, in another unresolved question, what did it mean to be "anti-modernist," and to what extent did fundamentalists share a common notion of anti-modernism? Here too, aside from the symbolic function of a few Christian doctrines, there was a greater diversity of anti-modernist attitudes than has previously been realized.[48]

A need for greater specificity has led scholars to construct longer lists of beliefs and attitudes which characterize fundamentalists. But at the same time, historians frequently admit that for every fundamentalist belief there is a fundamentalist somewhere who has dissented. Probably the most conspicuous example of this was the fundamentalist attempt to

---

[46] Compare, for example, the basically sociological approach of James Davison Hunter versus the religious history approach of George Marsden in Norman J. Cohen, ed., *The Fundamentalist Phenomenon: A View from Within, A Response from Without* (Grand Rapids: Eerdmans, 1990).

[47] Marsden, *Fundamentalism and American Culture*, 4. Also "Defining American Fundamentalism," in *The Fundamentalist Phenomenon*, 22–24.

[48] Grant Wacker's study of A. H. Strong is a fine example of the complex nature of evangelical anti-modernism; see Grant Wacker, *Augustus H. Strong and the Dilemma of Historical Consciousness* (Macon, GA: Mercer University Press, 1985). See also William R. Hutchison, *The Modernist Impulse in American Protestantism* (New York: Oxford University Press, 1976), 193–206.

expunge the teaching of evolution from America's schools. Even if anti-evolutionism was the most trenchant characteristic of 1920s fundamentalism, it certainly was not the most common. Many prominent leaders of fundamentalism disliked the anti-evolution crusade, as this study of the MacInnis controversy will show. In a more theological vein, however, since Sandeen identified inerrancy and premillennialism as basic building blocks of fundamentalism, historians have tried to expand and modify the list of essential beliefs. Among those usually considered important is dispensational theology, because by most accounts it became a major fundamentalist preoccupation in the 1920s and is often tied to sectarian predilections. Other beliefs that have received attention include revivalism, Common Sense philosophy, radical biblicism, and a commitment to Keswick-type holiness.[49]

Most historians argue that fundamentalism emerged as a distinctly self-conscious popular religious movement shortly after World War I, though it is readily acknowledged that militant anti-modernism characterized many evangelicals long before Curtis Lee Laws coined the term "fundamentalist" in 1920. Defined as a popular religious movement, fundamentalism possessed a distinctive set of symbols and symbolic actions, such as the use of a specific cluster of beliefs and attitudes, in order to define the symbolic boundaries of the movement.[50] But fundamentalism was more than a patchwork of beliefs and mental attitudes, because fundamentalists also worked to institutionalize their movement through particular schools, committees, conferences, mission boards, independent churches, and a variety of other organizations.[51] Hence, though exact lines cannot be drawn between the "insiders" and "outsiders" of the movement, a distinct identity characterized fundamentalists, sometimes based on their beliefs and attitudes, and sometimes based on their affiliation with fundamentalist organizations.

As in any social movement, there were those who tried to control the ideological and institutional boundaries of fundamentalism. In W. B. Riley's grandiose vision, fundamentalists would be defined by their affiliation to the best known fundamentalist organization, the World's Christian Fundamentals Association. But from the beginning the dynamic entrepreneurial character of the movement, and its variegated

---

[49] Joel A. Carpenter, "The Fundamentalist Leaven and the Rise of an Evangelical United Front," in *The Evangelical Tradition in America,* ed. Leonard I. Sweet (Macon GA: Mercer University Press, 1984), 259; Marsden, *Fundamentalism and American Culture,* 4; Brereton, *Training God's Army,* 1–38.

[50] Peter W. Williams, *Popular Religion in America: Symbolic Change and the Modernization Process in Historical Perspective* (Urbana: University of Illinois Press, 1989), 160–61.

[51] Carpenter, "Fundamentalist Institutions," 64.

theological and social roots, determined that the movement would never be defined by a single organization. Rather, the movement became a loosely affiliated network of individuals and groups, seeking to advance one or more aspects of fundamentalist concerns. A basic tension emerged, therefore, between those who saw in the WCFA and related organizations a defining authority over fundamentalism, and others who saw the WCFA as only one voice among many, and not even representative of the majority of fundamentalists.[52]

Closely linked with the lack of a central authority in fundamentalism was its transdenominational character. Like all evangelicals, fundamentalists came from a variety of Protestant denominations, but most did not consider their denominational affiliation the most important element of their religious identity. Fundamentalism was, in fact, pulled in two directions: in its efforts to purge the Protestant denominations of "creeping liberalism," it was, in the words of Martin Marty, a reactionary and revanchist movement.[53] But for a good many fundamentalists in the 1920s, their real religious identity lay not in the denominations, which already seemed a lost cause, but in the growing network of transdenominational evangelical organizations. Within this arena of activity, however, fundamentalists are sometimes distinguished from their evangelical kin by their unwillingness to tolerate a broad church tradition, in which there is, in the interests of comity and culture status, more theological latitude than rectitude. What Joel Carpenter called the militant separatist or evangelical inclusivist positions, and John Stackhouse has called a "churchish" or "sectish" *mentalité,* well describes the ambivalence of evangelicals toward mainline religion.[54] Though fundamentalists of the 1930s and 40s tended to be more sect-like in their behavior, seen in their almost limitless capacity for group divisions and multiplication, in the 1920s most fundamentalists were still linked, albeit loosely, to their mainline denominations, and some of them held distinctly strong feelings of loyalty to churchly traditions. Nevertheless, it is generally agreed that most fundamentalists in the 1920s were becoming increasingly alienated from their mainline denominations.[55]

---

[52] William V. Trollinger, *God's Empire: William Bell Riley and Midwestern Fundamentalism* (Madison: University of Wisconsin Press, 1990), 41–43.

[53] Martin E. Marty, *Modern American Religion, Volume 2, The Noise of Conflict, 1919–1941* (Chicago: University of Chicago Press, 1991), 159.

[54] Carpenter, "Fundamentalist Leaven," 286; John G. Stackhouse Jr., *Canadian Evangelicalism in the Twentieth Century: An Introduction to Its Character* (Toronto: University of Toronto Press, 1993), 16–17.

[55] Cole, Cole, *History of Fundamentalism,* 235, 315; Sandeen, *Roots,* 239–41; Weber, *Living in the Shadow,* 171–73; Trollinger, *God's Empire,* 43, 151; Douglas W. Frank, *Less Than Conquerors: How Evangelicals Entered the Twentieth Century* (Grand Rapids: Eerdmans, 1986), 70; Joel A. Carpenter,

The foregoing observations all play important roles for understanding
the MacInnis controversy. Although many of MacInnis' opponents construed the debate as a classic struggle between fundamentalism and
modernism, in fact, it was far more complex than a simple two-party
paradigm will allow.[56] Was MacInnis a fundamentalist? In W. B. Riley's
narrowly conceived sense of the word, the answer is clearly, he was not:
he lacked the requisite criteria of militant separatism and anti-modernist
feelings that characterized Riley's WCFA. But in the sense that he held
important organizational and personal ties to the fundamentalist movement, and shared important theological ideas and goals with many fundamentalists, rooted in a shared heritage of holiness and revivalism, he
was, as he himself claimed, a fundamentalist. But neither of these self-
descriptions is very helpful in describing the antagonists in the MacInnis
controversy; on the one hand, Riley's analysis fails to account for a considerable variety of attitudes still present in fundamentalism in 1928; on
the other hand, MacInnis' self-description appears disingenuous, given
that by 1928 the streams of fundamentalist separatism and evangelical
inclusivism had already diverged.

How then should the MacInnis controversy be construed? In the first
place, it must be affirmed that the MacInnis controversy was really an
intra-fundamentalist debate. It was a struggle for authority to define the
limits of who was, and who was not, a fundamentalist. It was not, therefore, a debate between liberals and conservatives, but a debate between
two very different kinds of conservatives, who defined fundamentalism
differently. Those who opposed MacInnis were mostly united in their
militant anti-modernism and argued for various reasons that MacInnis
lacked the needed fundamentalist credentials to lead a Bible school.
Those who defended MacInnis constituted a wider cross section of religious perspectives and are, therefore, not as easy to classify. A few
were fundamentalist militants, members of Riley's WCFA. Some were
recognized fundamentalists who, for various reasons, objected to the
attacks on MacInnis. Still others may be described by Kenneth
Cauthen's classification as evangelical liberals. But most were "evangelical inclusivists," seeking to balance the twin threads of doctrinal
orthodoxy and a cooperative Christian spirit. Among the latter were
many who still laid claim to the title fundamentalist.[57]

"From Fundamentalism to the New Evangelical Coalition," in *Evangelicalism
and Modern America,* ed. George M. Marsden (Grand Rapids: Eerdmans,
1984), 5–6.

[56] For a critique of a two-party model of interpretation see Douglas Jacobsen
and William V. Trollinger Jr., "Historiography of American Protestantism: The
Two-Party Paradigm and Beyond," *Fides et Historia* 25 (Fall 1993): 4–15.

[57] Kenneth Cauthen, *The Impact of American Religious Liberalism* (New

Given the complex and subtle distinctions between fundamentalists, it is necessary to adopt some qualifying adjectives in order to distinguish their respective positions. MacInnis' opponents, for instance, are best identified as radical or militant fundamentalists, to denote that they were often linked to an extreme emphasis of particular elements of evangelicalism, such as a use of militant rhetoric to oppose theological modernism, or an extreme reliance on premillennialism as a criterion of orthodoxy. Because so many of his critics were committed to dispensationalism, it is also possible to describe them as dispensational fundamentalists, but one should be careful to note that a few, like T. T. Shields, were not dispensationalists. Finally, another term which is helpful is Bible school fundamentalist, because the majority of his opposition was centered in Bible schools, but this too must be balanced by the fact that there were some Bible school leaders who did not support the anti-MacInnis crusade.

More difficult is how to describe MacInnis' position. Sydney Ahlstrom excluded from fundamentalism any person who "speaks to the issues, is well informed, and is in communication with those from whom he dissents."[58] By these criteria, MacInnis appears altogether out of sorts with fundamentalism. But following Ahlstrom too slavishly might well obscure important affinities that MacInnis shared with some fundamentalists, like Alva McClain, who was an ardent, but well informed fundamentalist. Nevertheless, it is necessary to use another term which better distinguishes him from the dominant traits of his opponents. Here one is tempted to adopt the usage of the fundamentalist historian, George Dollar, who distinguished true fundamentalists from simply "orthodox" Christians.[59] In his as well as other fundamentalist interpretations, the real fundamentalists were recognized by their militant separatism, which distinguished them from an earlier, anti-modernist coalition of conservatives who were orthodox, but unwilling to separate from apostate denominations. Dollar's terminology has the advantage of emphasizing the confessional basis of MacInnis' position, and was, actually, a term that MacInnis himself used. But, in light of recent criticisms by Donald Dayton, the too facile identification of evangelicalism with orthodoxy may distort some aspects of evangelicalism which are really anti-orthodox. Dayton's analysis is, therefore, helpful if

---

York: Harper & Row, 1962), 27–29.

[58] Sydney E. Ahlstrom, "Continental Influence on American Christian Thought Since World War I," *Church History* 27 (September 1958): 257, n. 3.

[59] Dollar, *History,* 175–76; for a similar assessment see Beale's treatment of the Winona Lake Bible Conference, in which he argues that the conference was not really fundamentalist until 1920, in spite of its orthodox roots (*In Pursuit of Purity,* 94–95).

one considers that MacInnis was more like a "classical evangelical" than a strictly observant Presbyterian confessionalist.[60] His commitment to revivalism, for example, in his support of Billy Sunday, underscores the broader New School and "anti-orthodox" orientation that characterized his perspective. A better alternative, therefore, is to adopt Dayton's distinction of classical evangelical, to distinguish MacInnis' position from either the orthodox confessionalism of Presbyterian traditionalists, or the militant separatism of fundamentalists in Bible schools and independent churches.[61] Yet other terms such as moderate fundamentalist, or broad church evangelical, also indicate a centrist tone that characterized this type of evangelicalism, which in the 1920s was still mostly committed to denominational cooperation. Sometimes, however, descriptions of these variant positions become stylistically tedious and cumbersome; thus, if MacInnis is sometimes referred to in this study as simply evangelical in contrast to fundamentalist critics, it is not to obscure important differences or similarities, but to avoid taxing the reader any more than necessary.

Primary Arguments and Issues

The final question to consider is the contribution that this monograph will make to our understanding of Protestant fundamentalism in the 1920s. There are several aspects of the MacInnis controversy which have important bearing on current issues in the historiography of fundamentalism. First, the controversy is not only important in its own right, but is also a good foil for understanding fundamentalism in the neglected years between the Scopes Trial and the beginning of the Great Depression. If, as historians have claimed, there inhered in fundamentalism profound tensions and contradictions, these became more pronounced in the ideological conflicts between pro-MacInnis and anti-MacInnis factions. Hence, a study of the MacInnis controversy will shed additional light on important tensions within fundamentalism: intellect versus piety, the Bible versus traditionalism, scholarship versus pragmatism, Victorian individualism versus progressive social thought.

---

[60] Donald W. Dayton, "'The Search for the Historical Evangelicalism': George Marsden's History of Fuller Seminary as a Case Study," *Christian Scholar's Review* 23 (September 1993): 15.

[61] Timothy Weber, however, uses the term "classical evangelical" to refer to the evangelicals of the reformation, i.e., Lutherans. See Timothy Weber, "Fundamentalism Twice Removed: The Emergence and Shape of Progressive Evangelicalism," *New Dimensions in American Religious History: Essays in Honor of Martin E. Marty,* ed. Jay Dolan and James P. Wind (Grand Rapids: Eerdmans, 1993), 264.

Second, this study of the MacInnis controversy will confirm the much discussed point that the Fundamentalist Modernist Controversy of the 1920s was much more complex than a simple two-party paradigm allows. Though primarily emphasizing subtle distinctions among evangelicals, this study will also demonstrate that "liberals" and "conservatives" often shared important assumptions and attitudes, making it increasingly difficult to draw bold lines of demarcation between them. If one considers, for example, that William Rainey Harper was a vigorous proponent of lay Bible education, then one is less likely to repeat stereotypes that depict only conservatives as worried about a decline in biblical literacy and control of religious education by experts. When one adds to this point the fact that some evangelicals, like MacInnis, received biblical training from Harper's lay correspondence course, the confluence between opposing "parties" becomes more apparent.

Finally, this study will argue that the MacInnis controversy was not an isolated theological struggle, but instead, symptomatic of the radicalization of the fundamentalist movement, in which moderate thinkers became alienated from the goals and purposes of more radical fundamentalists. Although this study does not purport to examine the ideas of all moderate fundamentalists, it will situate MacInnis in the context of others like him, who identified with fundamentalism, but were estranged from its censorious methods. Within a denominational setting the formation of the Baptist Bible Union represented a similar process of schism between moderate and radical fundamentalists of the Northern Baptist Convention.[62] But little is known about the disaffection of moderates outside of a denominational context. Almost from the inception of the WCFA, for example, there were many evangelicals who garnered some fundamentalist identity, but felt estranged from the movement. Criticisms of Moody Bible Institute, which appeared in the *Christian Century* in the 1920s, also revealed an outsider perspective on the tensions between moderate and radical fundamentalists.[63] But these tensions began to widen after 1925, not only because of the Scopes debacle, but because many moderates found that fundamentalism had become a narrow and ill-conceived version of a broader evangelical tradition. Hence, intra-fundamentalist arguments over E. Stanley Jones' orthodoxy, or Philip Mauro's anti-dispensational polemics, represented further alienation between moderate and radical elements of the movement. But of the many disagreements between fundamentalists, the

---

[62] Marsden, *Fundamentalism and American Culture,* 181–82; Ferenc M. Szasz, The *Divided Mind of Protestant America, 1880–1930* (Alabama: University of Alabama Press, 1982), 96.

[63] See the editorial, "Where Would Mr. Moody Stand?" in the *Christian Century,* 12 July 1923, 870–72.

MacInnis crisis became the most bitter and divisive, because it occurred in the middle of the fundamentalist camp—a revered Bible school. While fundamentalists could increasingly afford to ignore or deprecate the apostasy of the denominations, they could ill-afford to ignore a threat of the same from their own backyard. Radical fundamentalists attacked MacInnis because his moderate position in a recognized fundamentalist institution threatened the integrity and viability of the entire movement. Therefore, the crusade to oust MacInnis from Biola became the last major struggle of the 1920s between radical and moderate fundamentalists outside of a denominational setting.

Two aspects of this thesis require explicit mention. First, the growing alienation of fundamentalists from the mainline denominations resulted in their increasing dependence on trans-denominational organizations, such as Bible schools, to achieve their religious goals and identity.[64] Hence, while the fundamentalist movement became increasingly radicalized, the Bible schools also came under similar pressures, and this reality made it quite difficult for MacInnis to adopt a moderate position at Biola. Although this study does not examine how these pressures influenced other Bible schools, it does focus on how they influenced the Bible Institute of Los Angeles. Second, an important assumption of this thesis is the view that there was a significant transition in the nature of evangelicalism, as it went from being primarily a revivalist and holiness movement in the 19th century, to a loose coalition of co-belligerents in the 20th century, united more by their anti-modernism than their shared revivalist heritage. Most historians have argued for such a transition, and if there is a difference of opinion about the nature of this evangelicalism, it is a consensus, nevertheless, that fundamentalism after World War I had become more or less a narrow and constricted version of an earlier evangelicalism.[65]

The disaffection of moderate fundamentalists from the more extreme elements of the fundamentalist movement gradually led to its dissipation as a diverse movement. If fundamentalists in 1920 still regarded leaders like G. Campbell Morgan and J. Stuart Holden as men of their own kind, by 1929 that was no longer possible: indeed, as a result of the MacInnis controversy, both Morgan and Holden became disenchanted with fundamentalism, and the loss of their association, even if never at the center of the organized movement, represented yet another step toward the increasing marginalized position of organized fundamental-

---

[64] Carpenter, "From Fundamentalism to the New Evangelical Coalition," 3–16.

[65] Trollinger, *God's Empire*, 8; Weber, *Living in the Shadow*, 173; Sandeen, *Roots*, 241–42; also C. Norman Kraus, *Dispensationalism in America: Its Rise and Development* (Richmond, VA: John Knox Press, 1958), 109.

ism in American religious life. Yet, in spite of the withering of an organized center, fundamentalism did not disappear, as liberal critics were too eager to believe, but found in its capacity for entrepreneurial growth and business-like pragmatism new ways of adapting.[66] That story is best told elsewhere, however, for the MacInnis episode ended in 1929, when the final token of a resurgent moderate evangelicalism, *Peter the Fisherman Philosopher,* was destroyed by radical fundamentalists.

---

[66] Grant Wacker, "The Holy Spirit and the Spirit of the Age in American Protestantism, 1880–1910," *Journal of American History* 72 (June 1985): 45–46; George Marsden, "Fundamentalism and American Evangelicalism," in *The Variety of American Evangelicalism,* ed. Donald W. Dayton and Robert K. Johnston (Downers Grove, IL: InterVarsity Press, 1991), 23–24; Bradley Longfield, *The Presbyterian Controversy: Fundamentalists, Modernists, and Moderates,* Religion in America Series (New York: Oxford University Press, 1991), 132.

CHAPTER 2

John Murdoch MacInnis:
Higher Fundamentalist

Today there are few, even among historians of fundamentalism, who would recognize the name John Murdoch MacInnis. Compared to many other fundamentalist leaders of the 1920s his influence was relatively minor. His writings were few compared to the prolific W. B. Riley. He acquired no fame as a pulpit orator, as did Clarence Macartney and John Roach Straton. He did not rise to prominence in fundamentalist circles either as a Bible conference speaker like Lewis Sperry Chafer, or as an evangelist like Reuben A. Torrey. Neither did he achieve recognition as a pastor of a large metropolitan church, like Mark Matthews or J. Frank Norris. Finally, unlike fundamentalist Gerald Winrod or Harry Rimmer, he did not begin an independent organization with a fundamentalist constituency. Yet in spite of his relative obscurity, a study of his religious development may yield valuable insights into fundamentalist origins, which are less apparent in the lives of his more famous colleagues.

For example, although W. B. Riley was a prolific writer, having written more than thirty books and pamphlets and hundreds of articles, his work, on the whole, is rather predictable. From a survey of his books, one would find it difficult to discover any tensions or ambiguities in fundamentalist thought. MacInnis' writings, however, fairly bristle with ambiguities, which reveal the complex nature of early 20th century anti-modernism. Likewise, though he did not exhibit a charismatic personality, which helped some fundamentalist ministers build huge congregations, in many ways his unique blend of irenic feeling, scholarly detachment, and pragmatic attitudes illustrates far better the diversity of personality types within fundamentalism, than depictions of belligerent, dogmatic, and ignorant "fighting fundamentalists." Moreover, if he did not achieve prominence through the usual means of Bible conferences, itinerant evangelism, foreign missions, or by following the well-trodden path of beginning an independent fundamentalist organization, nevertheless, the intersections of his religious and professional life with all of these traditional fundamentalist endeavors provide exceptional insights into the complexities of fundamentalist identity. Here, what is often interesting to the historian is less the center of the stream, where the movement is vigorous and uniform, but the side streams, where the flow becomes attenuated and disturbed. In this regard, MacInnis is a particularly interesting subject, for his career took him in and out of the emerging fundamentalist movement at strategic times: Moody's 1893 World's Fair campaign, the *Fundamentals* project of 1910, the Philadelphia Prophetic Conference of 1918, which gave birth to the WCFA in the following year, and his appointment as dean of the Bible Institute of Los Angeles only months before John Scopes challenged the anti-evolution law of Tennessee—at these significant junctures, MacInnis' career illustrates better than most the ambiguities of early 20th century Protestant conservatism.

Early Life and Influences

Canadian Roots

There is little in MacInnis' plain and mostly rural upbringing which could have led anyone to predict his eventual rise to prominence as a Bible school leader and educator. John Murdoch MacInnis was born into a small Scottish Highlander community on Prince Edward Island, Canada, on August 6, 1871. There his grandparents had settled in 1841, having left the rugged and bleak moors of Skye, an Island in the Hebrides near the northwest coast of Scotland. His grandparents were just one of a great many Highland Scots who emigrated between 1760 and 1860. Those who arrived in the 1830s and 1840s, in particular, were often faced with the grim choice of emigration or starvation. Most of these poor rural emigrants settled throughout Prince Edward Island, Nova Scotia, and New Brunswick, often forming communities where no other language but Gaelic was spoken. By the 1880s, settlers from Scotland became the dominant ethnic group on the Island comprising at least 38% of the population.[1]

Most of these settlers were farmers. While growing urbanization was changing the character of Victorian life in Canada, Prince Edward Island held stubbornly to rural life well into the 20th century. In the last decades of the 19th century immigration slowed, so that by the 1880s

---

[1] Ian Ross Robertson, "Historical Writing on Prince Edward Island Since 1975," *Acadiensis* 18 (Autumn 1988): 168; Alan Brooks, "The Exodus: Migration from the Maritime Provinces to Boston During the Second Half of the 19th Century" (Ph.D. diss., University of New Brunswick, 1978), 63; A. H. Clark, *Three Centuries and the Island* (Toronto: University of Toronto Press, 1959), 125–28.

more than 90% of the Island's population was native born.[2] MacInnis, like so many Highlanders on the Island, grew up in a poor farming community. In Sir Andrew Macphail's classic account of life in 19th century Prince Edward Island, poor Highlander immigrants struggled to earn a meager living from the land, and the children were put to work on the farm at an early age.[3]

Farm life was dull and difficult. The typical farming income on the Island allowed for little more than subsistence. "Rural Island communities," commented one historian, were "often characterized by a certain element of conventionality, restraint, and drabness, as well as the harshness demanded by hard work."[4] Another historian noted that the difficulty of inland travel and a traditional decentralized economy contributed to ethnic and religious fragmentation in the Maritime Provinces.[5] In the rural ethnic community of MacInnis' youth, the church occupied a dominant role in village social life. A close community cohesion was engendered by "church associations, common ethnic origins, kinship ties, geographic proximity, and shared agricultural vocations."[6] As might be expected in such insular circumstances, Highlander life on the Island was highly provincial. Macphail, for example, humorously wrote that his first cup of coffee, which was prepared by the minister's wife, "a foreigner" from Nova Scotia, introduced him to an exotic new world. This provincialism, however, varied among Highlanders, some being more insular than others. The immigrants who arrived from the Isle of Skye in the 1840s, for example, among whom were MacInnis' own grandparents, acquired a reputation for remaining aloof from other Highlanders who had migrated to the Island in the 1790s.[7] Something of this extreme provincialism is seen in a comment that MacInnis made years later when he wrote to a friend that as far back as he could trace his family, "they had never as much as married outside of the Highlanders and the Presbyterian Church."[8]

---

[2] Clark, *Three Centuries and the Island*, 121, 128–32; Brooks, "Migration from the Maritime Provinces," 65.

[3] Sir Andrew Macphail, *The Master's Wife* (Toronto: McClelland and Stewart Ltd., 1939), 117.

[4] James Donald Cameron, "The Garden Distressed: Church Union and Dissent on Prince Edward Island, 1904–1947" (Ph.D. diss., Queen's University, 1989), 21–24.

[5] Brooks, "Migration from the Maritime Provinces," 61.

[6] Cameron, "The Garden Distressed," 27.

[7] John Macleod, *History of Presbyterianism on Prince Edward Island* (Chicago, IL: Winona Publishing Company, 1904), 116; for the reputation of settlers from the Isle of Skye see Macphail, *Master's Wife*, 13–14, 72.

[8] John MacInnis to James D. McGregor, 4 July 1908, MacInnis Papers.

The insulated provincialism of Scottish communities on Prince Edward Island was accompanied by a distinctly cultural and religious traditionalism. MacInnis, for example, first spoke Gaelic and probably did not learn English until he was twelve years old.[9] Religious services in the Presbyterian church at Valleyfield, where MacInnis spent his early years, were given in Gaelic as well as English.[10] As late as 1895, while a student at Moody Bible Institute, MacInnis was sought out for religious work in Cape Breton because he could speak Gaelic, and many Highland folk continued to use Gaelic in worship well into the 20th century).[11] William MacInnes later captured the traditionalism of his father's Highland Presbyterian upbringing when he said that "he was reared on porridge, the shorter catechism, the Book and the Gaelic tongue."[12] To this list, MacInnis himself might have added "Pilgrim's Progress, Baxter's Saint's Rest and Robert Burns' Poems."[13] Life was everywhere permeated by a sense of religious duty, and perhaps there was no higher duty than to keep the Sabbath. "In Orwell," observed Macphail of his native village, "the test of righteousness was the scrupulosity with which the Sabbath day was kept."[14] Yet there was much of that "Kirk" traditionalism that MacInnis later rejected. In a self-critical moment, for example, he said that his "cold Highland Scotch Church" had failed to lead him into the kingdom because no one spoke to the children about Christ.[15]

Though there is little known of any specific formative experiences in his childhood, it is at least certain that his family suffered financial hardship. In 1879 the "Leadville excitement" overtook the Maritimes, when the news spread that gold was discovered in Colorado. A local newspaper touted that "Colorado fever" was so great that "some of the boys were bound to go even if they had to walk all the way."[16] With fi-

---

[9] William MacInnes, "A Son's Appreciation," TMs, November 1957, MacInnis Papers. This reminiscence by MacInnis' son contains valuable biographical insights.

[10] Garland C. Brooks, *Challenged to Be the Church in Unity: An Historical Review of the United Church of Canada on Prince Edward Island, 1925–1985* (Sherwood PEI: PEI United Church History Committee, 1988), 16.

[11] David Sutherland to MacInnis, 25 November 1895, MacInnis Papers; Macleod, *History of Presbyterianism on Prince Edward Island,* 116.

[12] MacInnes, "A Son's Appreciation."

[13] John MacInnis, *Peter the Fisherman Philosopher* (Los Angeles: Biola Book Room, 1927), 33.

[14] Macphail, *Master's Wife,* 104.

[15] John MacInnis, "Our Responsibility for the Salvation of the Children," Sermon Delivered at Macalester Presbyterian Church in 1901, MacInnis Papers.

[16] Brooks, "Migration from the Maritime Provinces," 85.

nancial difficulty weighing heavily on him, MacInnis' father decided to leave for Colorado in search of gold. His family never saw him again. Hence, at around the tender age of nine or ten, MacInnis, the oldest of four sons, assumed some burden of providing for his family. To earn what meager income he could, he left the farm and began an apprenticeship in tailoring with his uncle in nearby Charlottetown, which at that time numbered about ten thousand, the largest city on the Island. This early responsibility prevented him from acquiring any more than a common school education.[17]

While in Charlottetown, MacInnis probably developed his first firmly held religious convictions under the influence of David Sutherland, the pastor of Zion Presbyterian Church. Zion was the largest Presbyterian congregation in Charlottetown, having a seating capacity of nearly one thousand. Its roots were in the Free Church tradition, and therefore it was at once more pietistic and revivalistic than the Church of Scotland.[18] Sutherland deeply influenced the young MacInnis, for their later correspondence indicates a close fatherly relationship: indeed, MacInnis later named his first son after him. Although it is not known when MacInnis first began to consider the ordained ministry as a profession, it is likely that his attitudes about the ministerial calling and his early evangelical feelings were first nurtured by Sutherland. During the brief tenure of Sutherland at Zion Church, when MacInnis himself was still a member, the church moved in a distinctly evangelical and pietistic direction. For example, it might be noted that Sutherland substituted grape juice for wine in the communion service, which was quite contrary to MacInnis' early childhood experience where temperance was not a concern.[19] Other signs of evangelical pietism include Sutherland's emphasis on prayer meetings, which were well attended, and his encouragement of revivalism, which in one case was conducted by evangelists from the United States.[20]

---

[17] MacInnes, "A Son's Appreciation"; and MacInnis to James D. McGregor, 4 July 1908, MacInnis Papers.

[18] Suzanne MacKinnon, *History of the Zion Presbyterian Church, 1860–1985* (Privately printed booklet, 1985), held in the Robertson Library, University of Prince Edward Island; Macleod, *History of Presbyterianism on Prince Edward Island,* 139–53.

[19] MacKinnon, *History of Zion Church,* 11; for MacInnis' early experience of religious attitudes about drinking alcohol, see *Peter the Fisherman Philosopher,* 103.

[20] John MacInnis, a typewritten document describing the last evening he saw David Sutherland, not dated but probably written sometime in 1898, MacInnis Papers; also see MacKinnon, *History of Zion Church,* 11.

A Cleansing of Ways

After MacInnis had learned his trade in Charlottetown he left Prince Edward Island, probably in the early 1890s, and made his way to Boston to continue as a tailor and further his education. Leaving the Island and going to Boston became a common trend in the 1890s, as economic hardship on the Island continued to worsen. As Alan Brooks has documented, the Maritimes declined in population by forty percent between 1871 and 1901:

> Countless numbers of young and old, single and married men and women left declining rural areas and small towns, even the new expanding cities to seek livelihoods elsewhere.[21]

Unfortunately, there is nothing known about his time in Boston except that it was short, for he soon traveled to Chattanooga, Tennessee. There his life took a dramatic turn when he contracted scarlet fever and feared that he would die.[22] Whether or not this near death experience influenced his sense of religious need is unknown, but a second event, which was remembered by his son as a religious conversion, occurred one evening as he heard a sermon preached on the subject, "Wherewith Shall a Young Man Cleanse His Ways."[23] Although his son later identified this incident as the primary motivation for his father's decision to enter the ministry, the experience does not appear to have played a major role in his religious self-consciousness, for unlike other evangelicals, who often repeated their experiences of salvation and recorded them for posterity, MacInnis did not leave a written record of his conversion. But whatever its importance, it seems from this time on he steeled his heart toward one goal—to enter a religious vocation.

MacInnis and Moody Bible Institute

As a young man in his early twenties, with little education or money, it seemed unlikely that he would be anything but a skilled tradesman. But a new school in Chicago gave him, and many others like him, a new chance for religious education and possible upward social mobility. It is not known how MacInnis first learned of Dwight Moody's Bible school, which had only begun four years earlier, but with an unyielding desire

---

[21] Brooks, "Migration from the Maritime Provinces," 9.
[22] Angus MacInnis to William MacInnes, 23 December 1957, MacInnis Papers.
[23] MacInnes, "A Son's Appreciation."

to enter religious work and with little possibility of completing a college or seminary education, the new type of school seemed a perfect starting place. In fact, Moody's Chicago Bible Institute was specifically designed for people like MacInnis. Advertisements from 1889 described exactly his situation: "There are also many men called of God into Christian work at too late a period of life to take a regular college and seminary course, but who would, with such an opportunity of study as our Institute affords, be qualified for great usefulness."[24]

Studies have shown that students who entered Bible schools between 1890 and 1920 tended to share several characteristics. First, most students came from the ranks of middle class occupations, including farmers, teachers, clerks, salespeople, secretaries, mechanics, tradespeople, and small business owners. Second, because so many students left their occupations to train for a full time religious vocation, they tended to be older, usually in their mid to late twenties. Many continued to work in their fields while attending classes at the Bible school. Third, early students often had no more than a common school education. Fourth, many Bible students were drawn from the wave of rural migrants to America's cities in the late nineteenth century.[25] MacInnis obviously fit this profile rather well. Quite probably he worked as a tailor in Chicago while attending classes at the Bible Institute. If, as he once asserted, he was a member of a labor union and participated in labor strikes, it would probably have taken place during this period, as Chicago tailors, who took up to fifty hours to make a dress coat, were being undermined by the "sweating system" of large wholesale clothing merchants.[26] But this latter picture is difficult to reconcile with the white Protestant middle class profile that characterized most Bible school students.

Although it is not certain how he supported himself while a student at the new Bible institute, he remained in Chicago for about four years. Official records indicate that MacInnis began his studies at Moody Bible Institute on July 6, 1893, just before his twenty-second birthday. He attended classes for only 9 months. A second enrollment occurred

---

[24] Quoted in Gene Getz, *MBI: The Story of Moody Bible Institute* (Chicago: Moody Press, 1969), 62.

[25] For these observations see Virginia Lieson Brereton, "The Bible Schools and Conservative Evangelical Higher Education, 1880–1940," in *Making Higher Education Christian,* ed. Joel A. Carpenter and Kenneth W. Shipps (Grand Rapids: Eerdmans, 1987), 114; also see Brereton, *Training God's Army,* 80, 126.

[26] For MacInnis' comment on labor unions see his sermon "Why Men Do Not Attend Church," 27 November 1904, MacInnis Papers; for labor conditions of clothing workers in Chicago in the early 1890s see Ray Ginger, *Altgeld's America: The Lincoln Ideal Versus Changing Realities* (New York: Funk & Wagnalls Co., 1958; repr. Chicago: Quadrangle Books, 1965), 26–30.

more than two years later on October 31, 1896, when he was twenty-five, and this time he remained only four months, leaving the Institute on March 2, 1897.[27] Though it may seem that his attendance was short and infrequent, his pattern was apparently not unusual. The Institute was structured to make religious training possible for working people: this meant flexible class schedules, part-time study, a year round program, and the ability to enroll at any time. Often students left the school without completing the full two year program. If extant records are complete, therefore, his schooling lasted only about one year.

There is nothing known of his experiences at the Moody school. Most likely he first met Reuben Torrey, the dean of the institute, during this time. Although he certainly heard Dwight L. Moody preach, there is no evidence he ever knew the celebrated evangelist personally. But it is very likely that he assisted Moody as a student helper during the six month revival campaign at the Chicago World's Fair. The World's Fair began on May 1, 1893, and Moody made the institute his campaign headquarters for a major outreach directed toward the estimated twenty-seven million visitors that would pass through the city. MacInnis enrolled at the institute barely two months after the fair opened, and almost certainly he joined the more than two hundred students who assisted Moody and many other evangelists, by distributing pamphlets, visiting homes and prisons, organizing meetings, and praying for the visitors pouring into the city every day.[28]

As a student during this campaign, MacInnis was introduced for the first time to a plethora of evangelical leaders. Aside from Moody himself, others who preached during the campaign included Reuben Torrey, Amzi C. Dixon, J. Wilbur Chapman, A. J. Gordon, James Brookes, William G. Moorehead, Cyrus I. Scofield, Charles Blanchard, Arthur T. Pierson, Robert Speer, David Breed, A. P. Fitt, A. B. Simpson, A. F. Gaylord, and Leander W. Munhall. Two leaders who had the unique distinction of remaining with Moody throughout the entire campaign were Ralph Atkinson and John McNeill; both would later become colleagues of MacInnis at the Bible Institute of Los Angeles. McNeill was remembered as the most popular speaker of the campaign. Although he was relatively unknown in America, the Scottish evangelist was acclaimed in Britain for his oratorical abilities.[29] Sensing his popularity with the Chicago crowds, Moody invited him to stay for the length of the campaign, and as his reputation spread, he attracted thousands of

---

[27] Mr. Walter Osborn, Moody Bible Institute Reference Librarian and Archivist to Daniel Draney, 14 November 1991.

[28] H. B. Hartzler, *Moody in Chicago or The World's Fair Gospel Campaign* (New York: Fleming H. Revell Company, 1894), 158–76.

[29] "John McNeill," TD, n.d., Biola University Archives, La Mirada, CA.

people to the tents and rented halls throughout the city. Ralph Atkinson, who later became a close friend of MacInnis, took charge of a nightly tent meeting. Finally, one other leader of minor note in the campaign was Robert A. Hadden, who years later would be a significant fundamentalist opponent of MacInnis.[30] Although the extent of MacInnis' involvement is unknown, the Moody Bible school experience made a significant impact on his personal identification with evangelicalism.

Moody Bible Institute and the Evangelical Experience

By attending the Moody Bible Institute, MacInnis was exposed to a religious ethos quite different from his youth. As a child, MacInnis learned the Calvinist confessions of Scottish Presbyterianism and a liturgical tradition that was governed more by psalter hymnody than gospel tunes, by reasoned sermonic exposition than heartwarming emotionalism. Some years later he encountered a more revivalist tradition at Zion Presbyterian Church, but this experience still lacked the warm enthusiasm and sentimental piety of a Moody revival. When he arrived at the Moody Bible Institute, however, MacInnis experienced a religion that emphasized piety more than orthodox confessionalism, action more than thought, a God of love and sentiment more than a God of wrath and the creed.[31]

The Moody Bible Institute was part of a diffuse movement which by the end of the 19th century had emerged as a distinctly self-conscious form of conservative evangelicalism: conservative because its proponents resisted the encroachments of theological liberalism, and evangelical because it tried to preserve the classic tenets of American revivalism. Although evangelicals in the 19th century still belonged to the mainline Protestant denominations, they increasingly tended to find their real identity in some commonly shared values and beliefs, as well as in many institutional associations which served to implement evangelical concerns outside of denominational structures. The dominant concerns of evangelicals included salvation, which comes through a personal experience of conversion, the necessity of living a holy life, and an emphasis on evangelism. These concerns were implemented through Bible conferences, such as the Niagara Bible Conference, which began as an annual summer conference in 1875, as well as many other

---

[30] For these leaders see Hartzler, *Moody in Chicago,* 36, 55, 65, 86–87, 95, 213.

[31] Bernard Weisberger, *They Gathered at the River: The Story of the Great Revivalists and their Impact upon Religion in America* (Boston: Little, Brown and Co., 1958), 211–12; James F. Findlay Jr., *Dwight L. Moody: American Evangelist, 1837–1899* (Chicago: University of Chicago Press, 1969), 227–61.

voluntary associations of evangelicals, including faith mission boards, rescue missions, Sunday school unions, reform societies, prayer meetings, and holiness conventions.[32]

But MacInnis' experience at Moody Bible Institute can be defined even more precisely, for by the 1890s it was becoming increasingly evident that leaders of the Chicago Bible school would represent a more narrow group of associations and concerns than, for instance, the Evangelical Alliance, which in 1887 still included leaders as diverse as Washington Gladden and Arthur T. Pierson.[33] Responding to the growth of religious liberalism in the mainline Protestant denominations, evangelicals at Moody Bible Institute began to emphasize biblical infallibility, and earlier evangelical commitments to social reform were weakened as leaders of the social gospel became identified with theological progressives. Consequently, evangelicals after 1890 increasingly began to preserve 19th century laissez-faire economic views, in opposition to a perceived link between theological liberalism and the social gospel.[34] A. J. Gordon, a Baptist pioneer of the Bible school movement, noted the emphasis on the Bible as early as 1883, when he observed that the new generation of evangelical leaders emphasized the testimony of scripture more than earlier revivalists, who had appealed more to the emotions.[35] But nowhere was this new biblicism more pronounced than in the curriculum that Reuben Torrey established at the Chicago Bible school. As its first superintendent, and the principal architect of the study program, Torrey made the foundation of the curriculum his series of lectures on Bible doctrine, which was later published as *What the Bible Teaches*. It is difficult to underestimate the importance of this decision for the future development of Protestant fundamentalism, for in making Bible doctrine the fulcrum of his curriculum, Torrey took a major institutional step toward what Virginia Brereton has called the "apotheosis of American Protestant Biblicism."[36] As a student, MacInnis thus encountered a world in which all aspects of life were thought to be governed by discrete biblical facts.

Closely related to this new emphasis were two themes which came to characterize the ethos of Bible school evangelicalism: premillennialism and an emphasis on personal holiness. These concerns of Bible institute

---

[32] Marsden, *Fundamentalism and American Culture,* 27–39.

[33] Wacker, "The Holy Spirit and the Spirit of the Age," 45–46.

[34] Findlay, *Dwight L. Moody,* 405–9; George Marsden, "The Gospel of Wealth, the Social Gospel, and the Salvation of Souls in Nineteenth-Century America," *Fides et Historia* 5 (Fall and Spring 1972–1973): 17–18.

[35] Bruce Shelley, "A. J. Gordon and Biblical Criticism," *Foundations* 14 (January–March 1971): 72–73.

[36] Brereton, "Bible Schools and Conservative Evangelical Higher Education," 118.

evangelicals are readily apparent in extant documents from the Moody Bible Institute. In 1897, for example, such venerable premillennialists as W. G. Moorehead, A. T. Pierson, A. C. Dixon, C. I. Scofield, George C. Needham, A. J. Gordon, and James Gray were listed as instructors.[37] Of the speakers associated with Moody at the Chicago World's Fair, more than half of them were premillenarians who achieved prominence in the prophetic conference movement of the late 19th century.[38] Holiness teaching also received a strong emphasis at the institute, especially after 1894, when American premillenarians became reconciled to the Keswick version of holiness.[39] After that, noted Keswick leaders Andrew Murray and H. W. Webb-Peploe were listed as instructors, and other Keswick leaders frequently lectured at the institute, such as G. Campbell Morgan and F. B. Meyer. Moreover, given Torrey's twin commitment to premillennialism and the second blessing of the Holy Spirit, these particular evangelical views became an established part of the Moody Bible school curriculum.[40]

In spite of MacInnis' formal, liturgical, and confessional upbringing, he appears to have imbibed these evangelical distinctives rather well. His later career as a Presbyterian minister yields abundant evidence of his acceptance of revivalism, personal piety, and Keswick holiness. It is not known when he embraced premillennialism. As a young person he may have been exposed to a revivalist and millenarian sect which took root among the Highland Scots of Prince Edward Island, but it is doubtful that he received anything more than a mere acquaintance with their teachings. Yet the widespread nature of such teachings, even in geographically remote areas, makes it likely that MacInnis already had some awareness of millenarian ideas and was, therefore, open to an acceptance of premillennialism at Moody Bible Institute.[41]

---

[37] *Catalogue of the Bible Institute for Home and Foreign Missions of the Chicago Evangelization Society* (1897), 8, Moody Bible Institute Archives.

[38] Hartzler, *Moody in Chicago,* 36, 55, 65, 86–87, 95, 213; Sandeen, *Roots,* 132–61.

[39] Bruce L. Shelley, "Sources of Pietistic Fundamentalism," *Fides et Historia* 5 (Spring 1973): 73.

[40] *Catalogue* (1897), 8.

[41] David Weale, "The Time Is Come! Millenarianism in Colonial Prince Edward Island," *Acadiensis* 7 (1977): 35–48; for additional revivalist influences in Prince Edward Island see Terrence Murphy, "The Religious History of Atlantic Canada: The State of the Art," *Acadiensis* 15 (1985): 158–59.

A Presbyterian Parson

Ordination

While a student in Chicago, MacInnis hoped to become a missionary. He therefore offered himself for service, but when the mission board learned that his intended wife did not feel similarly inclined, they recommended that he choose another vocation.[42] So he turned instead to a clerical profession in the Presbyterian Church. Having received a call for assistance from a distant church in northern Minnesota, MacInnis left Chicago in the spring of 1897 to begin a brief stint as a student pastor. After about six months of successful work, and having no doubts that he had discovered God's calling, he returned to Prince Edward Island temporarily to marry his long-time sweetheart, Ida Coffin.[43] Shortly after they were married MacInnis and his wife returned to Minnesota to begin what became a twenty-five year career in the ministry. In spite of his lack of education, which could have prevented his ordination in the Presbyterian church, there were two demographic trends that enabled him to choose this course: an oversupply of mission churches with no pastor, and a shortage of Presbyterian clergy to fill vacant rural pulpits.

The need for ministers in rural churches provided a starting place for many Bible school students to enter the ministry. Although it was never the original intention of leaders at Moody Bible Institute to provide a ministerial education, it was recognized *de facto* that many Moody Bible school students were becoming ordained pastors. By 1895, more than two-hundred former students were employed in churches, and in 1901 the institute reported that nineteen of its students that year became pastors of rural churches.[44] That this fact embarrassed school officials, who worried about opposition from the denominational seminaries, is seen in the fact that they attempted to justify this situation by printing a statement of a home missions board, which noted that the needs of frontier fields could not be met without Bible students.[45]

The northern Midwest to which MacInnis turned was hit particularly hard by a shortage of ministers. In Minnesota, for example, there were 175 Presbyterian ministers in 1898, but there were 266 churches, leav-

---

[42] Ida MacInnis to Gordon MacInnes, 22 July 1945, MacInnis Papers.

[43] John MacInnis, "Possessed by the Word of Christ," Sermon Manuscript, dated 23 October 1904, MacInnis Papers.

[44] Getz, *MBI: The Story of Moody Bible Institute,* 188.

[45] Ibid., 190.

ing many congregations without an installed pastor.[46] Other denominations suffered a similar shortage in this region.[47] More difficult still,
many of these churches were small struggling congregations, incapable
of supporting a minister: that same year sixty three percent of Presbyterian churches in Minnesota showed fifty members or less.[48] Given
these circumstances, MacInnis had no trouble finding a church that
needed his services, especially when most Bible school graduates were
willing to endure hardships that a typical seminary graduate would not.
Records show that he was ordained by the Red River Presbytery on
April 6, 1898, and installed as the pastor of the First Presbyterian
Church of Hallock Minnesota on May 25, 1898.[49] Though his qualifications fell short of denominational standards he was not the only one, for
there were others too, better known than MacInnis, who were ordained
with little or no formal theological training. Billy Sunday, for example,
was ordained by the Chicago Presbytery in 1903, having had little more
than his reputation for success on the "kerosene circuit." Charles
Stelzle, the Presbyterian advocate for a social Christianity, was also a
contemporary of MacInnis. He attended Moody Bible Institute for one
year in 1895 and with these credentials was ordained at the turn of the
century. Finally, the famous fundamentalist Presbyterian, Mark
Matthews, was ordained in 1887 even though he lacked any formal
college education.[50]

Pastorates: The Early Years, 1897–1909

Apparently MacInnis' assignment to the First Church of Hallock was
partly a crisis motivated decision because his son recalled that prior to
his arrival this church was "in real danger of being lost to the Denomination."[51] It is not known what threatened this small congregation, located in the far northwest corner of Minnesota near the Canadian bor-
der, but MacInnis was apparently able to preserve the church's unity
with the presbytery because he remained with the church for two and a

---

[46] *Minutes of the General Assembly of the Presbyterian Church in the United
States of America* (Philadelphia, 1898), 732.

[47] Trollinger, *God's Empire*, 92.

[48] *Minutes of the General Assembly*, 484–95.

[49] Letter of Certification signed by Eliot H. Moore, Crookston, Minnesota,
n.d., MacInnis Papers; also Jo Montgomery, Secretary of First Presbyterian
Church, Hallock, Minnesota, to Daniel Draney, 10 December 1991.

[50] Daniel G. Reid, Robert D. Linder, Bruce L. Shelley, and Harry S. Stout,
eds., *Dictionary of Christianity in America* (Downers Grove, IL: InterVarsity
Press, 1990), s.v. "William Ashley Sunday," by L. W. Dorsett; "Mark Allison
Matthews," by C. A. Russell; and "Charles Stelzle," by L. W. Japinga.

[51] MacInnes, "A Son's Appreciation."

half years, during which time the membership increased from twenty-five to fifty-seven.[52] Once, recalling his experience at Hallock, MacInnis claimed that the field had been "split up and practically lost to the Presbytery," but through his efforts two new churches were built and the field became united.[53]

Showing a marked aptitude for ministry, MacInnis was next invited to fill a one year assignment as a college pastor at Macalester College in St. Paul, Minnesota. During this year he led chapel services at Macalester College and organized a Christian student group, which became his first real contact with collegiate life. When this assignment ended, MacInnis next accepted a call in Santa Clara, California, to guide a church of about two hundred members, but this lasted only two years and, with the exception of a great earthquake, was uneventful.[54] There is little known about these early years of ministry; they were, no doubt, years of small but important lessons in the art of leadership, which served him well in the challenging roles of later years. His assessment of this period of his life, written in 1908, provides some interesting insights. First, MacInnis displayed a strong sense of loyalty to the Presbyterian Church. As he indicated in his own family history, he was virtually purebred Presbyterian, but it seemed to him that his religious inheritance was now not only a matter of birth, but of personal choice: "I am Presbyterian," he wrote, "not only by birth and training but by conviction."[55] Although his loyalty to the Presbyterian church is hardly surprising given his Scottish heritage, it is noteworthy that MacInnis differed from most of his American evangelical counterparts who were gradually weakening their denominational ties in the early 20th century.[56] Second, his brief tenure as college pastor at Macalester College appears to have sparked an interest in ministry among students and educators. About this he wrote: "While God has graciously owned my work among the common people my strongest friends and admirers are among the college men and women."[57] By 1908 then, MacInnis had expressed a strong preference to work with college educated people, if not students themselves, rather than "common people." This comment provides an important insight into his later career decisions, such as his efforts to obtain higher education, his interests in academic teaching, his intellectually oriented writings aimed at students and an educated reading public, and his acceptance of a teaching post in a Bible school.

---

[52] *Minutes of the General Assembly* (1898–1900).

[53] MacInnis to James D. McGregor, 4 July 1908, MacInnis Papers.

[54] For the earthquake see his handwritten notes, n.d., MacInnis Papers.

[55] MacInnis to James D. McGregor, 4 July 1908, MacInnis Papers.

[56] Sandeen, *Roots*, 239–40.

[57] MacInnis to James D. McGregor, 4 July 1908, MacInnis Papers.

From Santa Clara, MacInnis moved to Montrose, Pennsylvania, a small community in the Blue Ridge Mountains of northeastern Pennsylvania. Here in 1904, he began a pastorate at the Montrose Presbyterian Church, a church of nearly four hundred members. This transition marks a new phase of his ministry, for the events and characteristics of his ministry that brought him into the fold of premillennial evangelicalism, not only as a participant but as a minor leader in the movement, became more visible. He stayed in Montrose only five years, but fruitful years they were. As a pastor he was much loved and successful, and to this day the church has never attained a membership greater than under his leadership. Even so, his most important contribution was not really his work as a pastor, but his efforts in founding the Montrose Bible Conference.

MacInnis, Torrey, and the Montrose Bible Conference

A new Bible conference in a small American town might not have attracted much of anyone's attention in 1908. Many such conferences met all over North America. What made the Montrose conference unique was its founding luminary, Reuben A. Torrey. Torrey's fame as an evangelist, Bible teacher, writer, and superintendent of the Moody Bible Institute was well established by 1908, and so his presence attracted immediate interest from evangelicals. In addition, because he had so many personal connections with evangelical leaders throughout the country, Torrey was able to attract other prominent names and aspiring leaders who were eager to share his platform.

But Torrey's leadership of the conference was largely titular. The real work of administration was done by others, and it is accurately said that the organizational leadership and early success of the conference was largely the result of MacInnis' efforts. Today the story is told that MacInnis first began to think about organizing a Bible conference in the summer of 1906, after he attended the famous Northfield Conference.[58] A short time later he learned of Torrey's plans to begin a similar conference, so MacInnis contacted Torrey in the hope that Torrey would consider locating the conference in Montrose. Then, in October 1907, Torrey visited Montrose, and MacInnis took him to an idyllic setting overlooking the town and surrounding mountain dales. Torrey was so impressed by this serene idyll that he immediately decided to make Montrose the sight of the conference. Together they made plans for its first meeting to be held in August 1908.[59]

---

[58] *Montrose Bible Conference 50th Jubilee, 1908–1958*, Pamphlet, n.d., MacInnis Papers.

[59] Jill Torrey Renich, *A Dream That Refused To Fade: The Montrose Bible*

Although MacInnis has not been remembered as a major figure in the Montrose Bible Conference, his contributions have been understated by the organization's official literature, probably because the MacInnis controversy in 1928 proved to be an embarrassment to conference leaders. As its first general secretary, however, he filled its most important administrative post. A remark by Torrey in 1916 indicated his significant role: "I do not suppose you need a definite invitation to come to the Montrose Bible Conference," he wrote, "for it is your conference, if anything, more than it is mine."[60] Both as a speaker and as a secretary of the conference, MacInnis continued to be an active participant through 1926.

The Montrose Bible Conference placed MacInnis for the first time in a role of evangelical leadership. Of course, prior to Montrose he was already closely identified with premillennial evangelicalism. But now, through a close association with Torrey, he acquired new friendships with other evangelical leaders. As its primary correspondent, for example, MacInnis came to know the first speakers of the conference, which included A. C. Dixon, pastor of the Moody Church, and soon-to-be editor of the *Fundamentals,* William Erdman, the well known speaker at the Niagara and Northfield conferences, and Louis Meyer, a Jewish Christian missionary who would later take over the editorial work of the *Fundamentals.* Other premillennial evangelical leaders that came to the 1908 conference included Henry Frost, director of the North American Branch of the China Inland Mission, and Harris Gregg, who succeeded James Brookes as pastor of the Washington Street Presbyterian Church of St. Louis, Missouri. In following years, MacInnis became acquainted with many other evangelical speakers at Montrose including W. H. Griffith Thomas, William Evans, Leander Munhall, J. C. Massee, Charles Hurlburt, James Gray, J. Stuart Holden, and A. P. Fitt. With the success of the first conference, which official literature claimed was better attended than any Bible conference in America (except Northfield and Winona Lake), MacInnis was suddenly propelled into leadership of an organization of conservative premillennial evangelicals, many of whom would later be called fundamentalists.[61]

Conference Story (Montrose, PA: Montrose Bible Conference, 1978), 9. This booklet by Torrey's granddaughter is an abbreviated version of a more detailed history by a Dr. Walter Vail Watson. Watson's manuscript could not be located.

[60] Reuben Torrey to MacInnis, 28 November 1916, MacInnis Papers.

[61] For the size of the conference see Renich, *A Dream That Refused To Fade,* 14; for the conference speakers see the collection of Montrose Bible Conference programs located in the Moody Bible Institute Archives.

Pastorates: The Later Years, 1910–1922

MacInnis left Montrose in April 1909 to accept a call from the Gaston Presbyterian Church of Philadelphia, a congregation of over one thousand members. This post was brief, however, because only nineteen months later he fulfilled his long held desire to return to Canada by accepting a call to the Park Street Presbyterian Church of Halifax, Nova Scotia.[62] This congregation was the largest Presbyterian church in the city, and therefore his reputation and prestige had grown considerably. Very little is known about these years in Halifax. As pastor of a large and influential church he probably joined in critical Presbyterian debates over a proposed union of mainline Protestants into a single church. MacInnis supported union, as did most Presbyterians in Canada in 1912.[63] His support did not imply any particular theological view, however, because liberals and conservatives could be found on both sides of the issue. When union finally occurred on June 10, 1925, MacInnis, who by this time was dean of the Bible Institute of Los Angeles, supported it because he claimed that the opposition to union came mostly from liberals, in spite of the fact that many of his conservative friends also opposed the union.[64] Few other traces remain of his ministry at Halifax, but it is known that he spoke out against prostitution in the city, and perhaps his criticisms contributed to his resignation after less than two years.[65] In a departing sermon, MacInnis made special note of his denunciation of sin.

> I do not for one moment regret having been outspoken in my denunciation of sin. I never spoke without knowing what I was speaking about, nor without facts to warrant what I said. If I have regrets at all it is that I was not faithful in bringing men face to face with the sins that are standing between them and God.[66]

---

[62] MacInnis to Park Street Presbyterian Church, n.d., MacInnis Papers.

[63] N. Keith Clifford, *The Resistance to Church Union in Canada, 1904–1939* (Vancouver: University of British Columbia Press, 1985), 52.

[64] MacInnis to George S. Carson, 14 July 1926, MacInnis Papers. George Carson was editor of the *New Outlook,* the official periodical of the United Church of Canada; for his awareness of conservatives who stayed out of the union see MacInnis to Dr. Robert Johnson, 21 October 1926, MacInnis Papers. Johnson was a minister who stayed out of the union.

[65] W. H. Matheson et al., *History of St. John's United Church, Halifax, Nova Scotia, 1793–1975* (St. John's United Church Historical Committee, [1975]), 26, in the Maritime Conference Archives of the United Church of Canada, Halifax, Nova Scotia.

[66] John MacInnis, "A Gospel that Needs No Apology," Sermon Manuscript

MacInnis left Halifax to accept a position at South Presbyterian Church of Syracuse, New York. Later he remembered these years in Syracuse as the happiest of his ministry, and he once claimed with pride that he had won the church away from its earlier liberalism under an Auburn Affirmation leader, Murray Shipley Howland.[67] There he spent the war years and, like most of his fellow clergy, when the United States entered the war in 1917, MacInnis supported it and worked with the YMCA to aid the war effort.[68] During this period he also became involved in a civic campaign to ban liquor sales from public places.[69] Hence, like many other clergy during the Progressive Era, he joined specific efforts to reform society, such as his opposition to prostitution and support of Prohibition. Until recently the participation of evangelicals in Progressive Era social reforms has largely been ignored. But this lacuna has been filled to a great extent by the awareness that many evangelical clergy prior to World War I and the so-called "great reversal" were quite active in fighting civic corruption and social ills.[70] MacInnis was, therefore, not out of step with other evangelicals of this period.

In spite of these activities, however, MacInnis did not appear to be an avid social reformer and to the contrary, there is evidence that he preserved conservative 19th century social views in spite of his putative sympathy for the laboring man. As previously noted, for example, MacInnis claimed to be a former union member, and he sympathized with union demands for better wages.[71] But when he advocated a half-holiday on Sundays for workers, his principal motive was to encourage the

---

dated 28 September 1913, MacInnis Papers.

[67] For the happiness comment see South Presbyterian Church Bulletin, 26 March 1922; for "liberalism" at South Church under Howland see MacInnis to O. M. Edwards, 30 December 1926, both in the MacInnis Papers.

[68] A YMCA certificate signed by John R. Mott indicates that MacInnis was a volunteer speaker for the United War Work Drives from February 1917 to March 1917. This certificate was retained in the possession of Gordon A. MacInnes, Pasadena, CA.

[69] Francis Chadwick, South Presbyterian Church Archivist, Syracuse, New York, to Daniel Draney, 19 February 1992.

[70] Szasz, *Divided Mind of Protestant America,* 58–62; for W. B. Riley's Progressive Era reforming activities see Trollinger, *God's Empire,* 62–67; also see Dale E. Soden, "In Quest of a City on a Hill: Seattle Minister Mark Matthews and the Moral Leadership of the Middle Class," in *Religion and Society in the American West,* ed. Carl Guarneri and David Alvarez (Lanham, MD: University Press of America, 1987), 355–73. For the "great reversal" idea see David Moberg, *The Great Reversal: Evangelism versus Social Concern* (Philadelphia: J. B. Lippincott Co., 1972), 30–33.

[71] *Syracuse Post-Standard,* 14 February 1916, 6.

working class men to attend church.[72] In the same sermon, he once claimed that the poor and working classes were shown the same consideration as anyone else in the Presbyterian church. At the same time that he made this claim, however, his own church still utilized pew rents, a practice that discriminated against the poor. Evangelicals had often worked to end pew rents, but the Montrose church did not do so until five years after MacInnis had left.[73] On another occasion, MacInnis voiced a typical 19th century laissez-faire, hard work, honesty, and self-improvement attitude toward social problems: It is not society that goes to hell, he claimed, but the individual. "If the individual is bad, then society is bad; if the person is good, then society will be good."[74] Given such sentiments, it would appear that MacInnis did, as Marsden argued of most evangelicals, continue to stress a 19th century capitalist ethic, but there is no evidence in MacInnis' life that he did so as a reaction to links between theological modernism and the social gospel. Rather, in later years MacInnis discovered in the social gospel much that enriched a Christian view of society, but these insights never displaced his life-long Republican ideals of individualism and personal responsibility.[75]

Perhaps most interesting in his nine year ministry at Syracuse was his outspoken support of Billy Sunday. In December 1915, Billy Sunday arrived in Syracuse to conduct one of his well orchestrated and highly publicized evangelistic campaigns. This particular campaign took place at the height of Sunday's career, when he was preaching to large urban audiences: just prior to Syracuse, Sunday claimed to have received more than forty-one thousand "trail hitters" in Philadelphia, and at the close of the Syracuse campaign he added another twenty-one thousand.[76] MacInnis joined with other clergy in extending an invitation to Sunday, but not without some personal doubts. "I must confess," he stated after the campaign ended, "I was prejudiced against Mr. Sunday." But, he added, after seeing Billy Sunday and the results of his campaign, all doubts were dispelled.[77] His support of Sunday, however, was not well received by "conservative" members of his own congregation, who doubted the value of "quick converts" acquired through revivalistic

---

[72] MacInnis, "Why Men Do Not Attend Church."

[73] Untitled Xerograph of a History of Montrose Presbyterian Church, n.d. sent to this author by D. L. Birchard, Montrose Presbyterian Church archivist.

[74] *Syracuse Post-Standard,* 14 February 1916, 6.

[75] Marsden "The Gospel of Wealth, The Social Gospel, and the Salvation of Souls," 18; for MacInnis' Republicanism see his tribute to Theodore Roosevelt in the *Syracuse Post-Standard,* 13 January 1919, Onondaga Historical Association, Syracuse, New York.

[76] Lyle W. Dorsett, *Billy Sunday and the Redemption of Urban America* (Grand Rapids: Eerdmans, 1991), 85–107.

[77] *Syracuse Herald,* 14 February 1916, 11.

methods. Therefore, in order to satisfy these skeptics, MacInnis requested that every trail-hitter seeking membership in his church be interviewed and that none receive membership until five weeks after the close of the campaign.[78]

MacInnis' support of the campaign resulted in a large influx of new members for the South Presbyterian Church. Three hundred and forty-five people joined the church in February 1916, the largest gain of any church in Syracuse.[79] The reports of increased church membership became a regular feature of Sunday's publicity, and so the growth of South Church became one more example of Sunday's evangelistic success. But some writers have been skeptical of the numbers bandied about by the Sunday organization. William McLoughlin, for example, gives a different view of Sunday's success stories.

> The explanation for the tremendous success of three or four churches out of the hundreds which co-operated in every big city campaign lay in the important, but not usually mentioned, facts that they were invariably among the largest churches in the city even before the campaign and that their ministers, almost without exception, possessed the aggressive, salesman-like personality which made the most out of the opportunities offered by the revival crowds and publicity.[80]

McLoughlin used membership statistics from MacInnis' church as well as others to support his argument that the large and successful congregations obtained the greatest results. South Presbyterian Church had 978 members before the campaign began, which truly was the largest congregation in the presbytery. But it does not follow that other smaller churches failed to show similar increases of membership. Actually, four other churches in the same presbytery registered higher rates of growth, and these began the campaign with approximately 200 members or less.[81] Overall, congregations with less than 400 members received 53% of the new growth from 1915 to 1916, and the congregations which grew more than 20% were, except for South Church, smaller than the 653 average size church cited by McLoughlin.[82] This data, therefore, at

---

[78] John MacInnis to J. W. Hopkins, 15 October 1925, MacInnis Papers.

[79] Unidentified Newspaper Clipping, 6 February 1916, MacInnis Papers.

[80] William G. McLoughlin, *Billy Sunday Was His Real Name* (Chicago: University of Chicago Press, 1955), 205.

[81] *Minutes of the General Assembly* (1916), 727–28. The rates of growth for each church were: Westminster, 42%; Liverpool, 109%; Elmwood, 101%; Otisco, 78%.

[82] McLoughlin, *Billy Sunday,* 205. The numbers are: 14 churches, representing 32% of the churches in the Syracuse Presbytery, grew by 20% or more

least among Syracuse Presbyterians, does not support the view that Sunday's campaigns did little to boost memberships of smaller churches. But neither does it upset the fact that large metropolitan churches received the biggest and most publicized increases.

If McLoughlin's criticism needed some refinement, his comments on the "aggressive, salesman-like personalities," of the big church clergy seem gratuitous. Were most big church clergy aggressive and salesman-like, and small church clergy passive and unassuming? Although this picture appears more stereotypical than real, McLoughlin erred in linking MacInnis to such a characterization. Actually, he was quite the opposite. He was not a tall or imposing figure, nor was he particularly striking in his appearance, although as a former tailor he always dressed with meticulous distinction. He lacked the stentorian voice that characterized some of his well known colleagues, and his preaching was a somewhat tepid and rational exposition of scripture, often illustrated by quaint images of Scottish home life or daily experiences. A balding head and round wire rimmed glasses presented more a stereotype of a scholar than a dramatic titan of the pulpit. It seems, therefore, contrary to McLoughlin, that an "aggressive salesman-like personality" had nothing at all to do with the large membership gains at MacInnis' church.

In spite of his success with the Sunday campaign, and the recognition of Sunday himself,[83] there were still many in his own church that found the revival distasteful. It may seem odd that the reserved Canadian Scot pastor enjoyed, even participated, in an event which sometimes reminded one more of a vaudeville show than a religious gathering. But MacInnis was not alone in his position, for Sunday received support from many mainline Protestants who believed that the results outweighed any untoward considerations. One minister, for example, when asked about Sunday replied:

> Why, my dear sir, the man has trampled all over me and my theology. He has kicked my teachings up and down that platform like a football. He has outraged every ideal I have had regarding my sacred profession. But what does that count against the results he has accomplished?[84]

In a similar fashion, MacInnis defended the theatrical methods of Sunday on pragmatic grounds—he believed that Sunday's showmanship,

---

from 1915–1916. Excluding MacInnis' church, their average size was 216 members.

[83] *Syracuse Herald,* 6 November 1915.

[84] William G. McLoughlin, *Modern Revivalism: Charles Grandison Finney to Billy Graham* (New York: Ronald Press, 1959), 419–20.

crass though it could be, successfully got people into the church; to prove it, five years after the campaign he looked up every trail-hitter that had joined his church and found that all but nine were still active in the church.[85]

At the close of the campaign, Billy Sunday invited MacInnis to assist him in an upcoming Trenton, New Jersey campaign. But this offer he did not accept, because he believed that he ought to remain at home to help the new church members get established.[86] Yet close on its heels, as the excitement of revival waned, controversy flared. Not all Syracuse clergy had welcomed the revival. In particular, Frederick Betts, a Universalist minister, published a series of critical articles on the campaign, which subsequently appeared as a book.[87] Betts openly criticized Billy Sunday and charged that the Syracuse ministers had invited Sunday because they felt "a dismal sense of failure" in their churches.[88] Not surprisingly, his criticism of Sunday so nettled some of his ministerial colleagues that at one point Betts feared they might hang him to the nearest lamp post. The ministers, however, apparently found a more charitable solution, because at a subsequent meeting MacInnis introduced a motion to suspend Betts from the Syracuse Ministerial Association. Not long after, however, MacInnis withdrew this motion when a conference with Betts convinced him that the controversy was based on a misunderstanding.[89]

Educational Advancement

Keenly aware of his lack of education, MacInnis worked to improve his academic standing during his years as a pastor. We cannot be sure when he first contemplated advanced degree work, but perhaps he first discovered an aptitude for the academic life while a pastor at Macalester College. A survey of his correspondence and writings reveals that he was a voluminous reader, and that he was especially interested in philosophy, theology, history, and in the newer expanding fields of psy-

---

[85] MacInnis to J. W. Hopkins, 15 October 1925, MacInnis Papers.

[86] Francis Chadwick, South Presbyterian Church Archivist, Syracuse, New York, to Daniel Draney, 19 February 1992.

[87] Frederick W. Betts, *Billy Sunday: The Man and Method* (Boston: Murray Press, 1916).

[88] McLoughlin, *Billy Sunday,* 198; *Syracuse Post-Standard,* 14 February 1916, 6; *Syracuse Herald,* 14 February 1916, 11.

[89] Betts makes only a brief mention of the incident in an autobiography, *Forty Fruitful Years* (Boston: Murray Press, [1929]), 224; for MacInnis' role see the *Syracuse Herald,* 28 February 1916, 6.

chology and sociology.[90] His Bible training at Moody Bible Institute
hardly touched these subjects.

Figure 1: Photograph of MacInnis

This photograph of MacInnis was probably taken in 1927 before the outbreak
of the controversy over *Peter the Fisherman Philosopher*. Having been trained
as a tailor, MacInnis was known for his well-fitted clothing.

---

[90] An indication of his extensive reading is suggested by the fact that in
1938, after he donated most of his library to his sons, he still had about eight
hundred volumes left to give to San Francisco Theological Seminary; see Mac-
Innis to William MacInnes, 2 December 1938, MacInnis Papers.

Though MacInnis clearly had a proclivity for learning and scholarship, his formal education was inconsistent. By 1908 he had completed further education through correspondence, both from William Rainey Harper's School of Sacred Literature, a popular course for lay Bible education, and through a correspondence school in Oskaloosa, Iowa, called the Iowa Christian College.[91] The latter institution claimed to emphasize Bible study in its correspondence program, as well as a regular college course. Although MacInnis completed a Ph.D. from this college, there is nothing known of his academic work, and the school appears to have had no academic credibility.[92]

The most firm datum in his educational experience is the Bachelor of Divinity degree awarded on June 3, 1911.[93] Soon after he came to Montrose in 1904, MacInnis enrolled in a correspondence course given by the Temple University School of Theology. This course fit his needs precisely, because as a full time minister he could complete the required coursework according to his own schedule. The theological school designed their program for persons such as MacInnis, who had been "forced into the ministry before acquiring a theological education." Although the university normally required a college degree for theological study, exceptions were made for ministerial students who could demonstrate academic competence.[94]

Temple University had been founded only sixteen years earlier as a part of Russell Conwell's innovative institutional Grace Baptist Church, but in that brief time it had experienced remarkable growth. Its theological school, claiming to be nonsectarian, took students from all Protestant denominations. It professed to teach students the "full gospel ministry," which emphasized the "best methods for securing redemption and holiness of soul, sanity of the mind and health of the body." The five year program, therefore, covered not only the traditional subjects of divinity—theology, ethics, practical theology, church history, exegesis, and biblical languages—but also progressive courses such as sociology, psychology, and educational methods.[95]

Though his theological education at Temple was customary, there was a marked emphasis on philosophy, which is consonant with MacInnis' later interest in this subject. Most theological schools only taught philosophy as a prolegomenon to the study of theology or often as a course in apologetics. A typical class, for example, might bear the title

---

[91] MacInnis to James D. McGregor, 4 July 1908, MacInnis Papers.

[92] On this school see Manoah Hedge, *Past and Present of Mahaska County, Iowa* (Chicago: S. J. Clarke, 1906), 110–11.

[93] Temple University Catalog (1912–1913), 89, Temple University Archives.

[94] Ibid., 76, 81.

[95] Ibid., 76, 82–83.

"Evidences of Christian Belief" or "Philosophy of the Christian Religion." But Temple's program, besides the typical apologetics courses, emphasized the study of philosophy as "distinct movements of systematic thought."[96] Given the philosophical orientation of Temple's program, it is probable that this is where his philosophical interests were first developed.

The style of MacInnis' seminary education is probably best described as a moderately progressive evangelicalism. The school made an attempt to attract students of all denominations and provide them with a broad enough education for ordination. It was not a dogmatically conservative education like that of Princeton Seminary, because an openness to biblical criticism and curriculum innovation is evident in the books and subjects of seminars. The course reading materials, for example, varied from A. T. Pierson's book, *Keys to the Word,* to Hodge's *Systematic Theology:* and advanced students studied works by modern critical scholars like Johannes Weiss and Marcus Dods, and subjects that ranged from English Bible to advanced topics on the "Messianic Consciousness of Jesus" and the "Authorship of the Fourth Gospel." Hence, a survey of the curriculum indicates a moderately progressive education, open to critical scholarship but still oriented toward Protestant evangelicalism.

This assessment supports MacInnis' own description of his education recorded in 1908: "These courses have given me a broader view point than if I had continued in one groove and have made it possible for me to the more intelligently appreciate the good things in Presbyterianism."[97] Although he did not explain what "groove" he was talking about, one may well guess that MacInnis was referring to the strict Presbyterian orthodoxy then regnant at Princeton Seminary. In any case, his intent is not lost on the careful reader: having received a broader, more progressive education, he was better able to appraise and appreciate his own tradition—not merely as a traditionalist, but as a critical observer and loyal participant. One may see in this statement an early indication of his commitment to a moderate Presbyterian conservatism. When twenty years later, during the fundamentalist controversy, MacInnis supported moderates like Robert Speer and Charles Erdman, he was showing a similar but matured sentiment, namely, that theological education should be broader than the tightly drawn definitions of Princeton orthodoxy.

Though MacInnis used the title "doctor" based on his Ph.D. from Iowa Christian College, there is scanty evidence that he may have completed some work toward a higher degree in theology at Temple Univer-

---

[96] Ibid., 78.
[97] MacInnis to James D. McGregor, 4 July 1908, MacInnis Papers.

sity, which would have required three additional years of study and a dissertation.[98] But, for unknown reasons, MacInnis never finished this work. Thus, he never really earned a doctorate from a recognized institution. In 1920, however, while a minister at South Presbyterian Church, MacInnis was awarded the honorary Doctor of Letters degree from Syracuse University. But, unfortunately, there remains no official record of the occasion for this award.[99]

A mere recitation of his academic degrees, however, would not give an adequate picture of MacInnis as an intellectual. His sermons, letters, lectures and published writings reveal a mind sensitive to the intellectual currents of his day. Some of his peers, who later became known as fundamentalists, had superior academic credentials. Reuben Torrey, for example, studied at Yale, Leipzig, and Erlangen. W. B. Riley, not having enjoyed the advantages of New England privilege like Torrey, nevertheless, completed a degree at Hanover College and a divinity degree at Southern Baptist Theological Seminary. Yet both these writers seem to have been untouched by advances in history and criticism, except for the flinty determination to assert traditional Protestant orthodoxy with greater force.

MacInnis, however, seemed more sensitive to the challenges posed by modern thought. He took them seriously and attempted to understand them with some degree of disinterested concern, unlike some fundamentalists who appeared to exhibit a radical either/or type of thinking.[100] Indeed, it may be noted that sometimes he even appeared naive, as though he believed that everyone else shared his intellectual openness and curiosity. Once, in 1918, MacInnis wrote a lengthy letter to James Gray arguing against the idea of an imminent rapture of the church. In a nervous reply, Gray felt it necessary to warn MacInnis against using any of the materials in William Rainey Harper's American Institute of Sacred Literature, because as Gray put it, the institute was a "powerful opponent of revealed and evangelical religion."[101] In Gray's closure he expressed concern for MacInnis' "mental and spiritual crisis." This brief exchange, crisis or not, illustrates MacInnis' sometimes naive openness to people who were suspect among conservative evangelicals. For addi-

---

[98] Ibid. See the scribbled note, "S. T. D. work," on his copy of the article, John MacInnis, "Calvinism and Modern Thought," *Book News Monthly,* December 1909, 270, in the MacInnis Papers.

[99] Mary O'Brien, Syracuse University Archives, to Daniel Draney, 4 November 1991. Donald MacInnes, however, stated that *Peter the Fisherman Philospher* had been written as a thesis for the D.Litt. degree; MacInnes, "Leadership Training in the Synod of California," 30.

[100] Richard Hofstadter, *Anti-Intellectualism in American Life* (New York; Alfred A. Knopf, 1963), 135.

[101] James Gray to John MacInnis, 17 December 1918, MacInnis Papers.

tional evidence of his willingness to comprehend modern theological problems, one should also consider his broad reading of modern theology and philosophy, a basically irenic personality, and a passion for objectivity and fairness.

In the 1920s, when MacInnis began broadcasting sermons over Biola's radio station, a listener accused him of being narrow minded and intolerant. Feeling affronted, MacInnis replied:

> The fact is that I have invested practically all the spare cash I have been able to get in my lifetime in books, and the most of these books written by people with whom I do not at all agree, in order that I might have a rounded tolerant conception of life and history.[102]

His defense, though overstated, described his reading habits accurately. In addition to his regular reading of periodicals like *Christian Century* and the *British Weekly,* records indicate that he was familiar with works by authors of differing religious perspectives, such as Ernst Troeltsch, Albert Schweitzer, Josiah Royce, Walter Rauschenbusch, Bertrand Russell, and William James.[103] MacInnis' openness to reading divergent opinions was matched by an irenic disposition and a desire for fairness and objectivity. There is much in his extant correspondence, for example, that suggests he disliked theological argument. Once as a young pastor fresh out of Bible school, MacInnis had an opportunity to offer his church building to a Roman Catholic priest for use in a funeral mass. Recalling this incident, MacInnis declared that he was "ready to cooperate with any man who honors Jesus Christ and the Word of God."[104] His bravado, however, was not an admission that he lacked conviction, for in the same address he exhorted his listeners to embrace a spirit of loyalty to the gospel, but without a "revival of narrow sectarianism." If his cooperation with Roman Catholics departed from the norm of most evangelicals, certainly his openness to liberals in the 1920s was out of step with his fundamentalist associates. MacInnis' openness to dialogue with liberals can be contrasted to Torrey's tendency to disparage and dismiss them altogether. Torrey's steely frame-of-mind can be seen, for example, in his assessment of Harry Emerson Fosdick. Writing in 1922,

---

[102] MacInnis to Dana L. Teague, 12 January 1926, MacInnis Papers.

[103] Gordon A. MacInnes, interview by author, 10 June 1992, Pasadena, CA: for his wide reading see G. A. Johnston Ross to MacInnis, 17 December 1918; "Lecture Notes on Comparative Religion," 29 January 1924, MacInnis Papers; also see *Peter the Fisherman Philosopher,* 102, 137, 159, 164.

[104] John MacInnis, Address Presented to the Society of Graduate Endeavorers at the Meeting of the Synod of California, Presbyterian Church, U.S.A., San Francisco, CA, TMs, 25 October 1903, MacInnis Papers.

Torrey commented that Fosdick spoke in "skillfully phrased sentences" that were "mere verbiage" instead of "substantial truth." Torrey's opinions were strengthened nine days later, when Fosdick preached his famous sermon, "Shall the Fundamentalists Win?"[105] MacInnis, however, displayed a different attitude toward Fosdick, when he wrote to suggest that Fosdick had been unfair to fundamentalists. This charge prompted Fosdick's pained reply:

> I am sorry that you think I was not altogether fair to the Fundamentalists. I would rather be fair than almost anything else. Of course, a term like Fundamentalist covers all sorts of people and it is impossible to comprehend them all in one characterization. I feel sure, however, both from the information which I had before preaching the sermon and from the information that has come to me from all parts of the country since, that I was substantially correct in my picture of the great body of Fundamentalists in the present campaign of intolerance.[106]

To further solidify this contrast, MacInnis had also asked Fosdick to provide a list of books that would adequately explain the modern position. Although Fosdick listed several books, he cautioned MacInnis that liberalism was still in the process of being wrought out. Here too, MacInnis' dialogical approach is evident, in contrast to the determined Torrey, who would never have been so meek or inquisitive in his approach to Harry Emerson Fosdick.

MacInnis' ideal of the intellectual life matured under the pressures of radical fundamentalist opposition in the late 1920s. Shortly after his ordeal at the Bible Institute of Los Angeles was ended, he sought to give expression to this ideal, which he summarized as four virtues: an open mind, an honest mind, a critical mind, and a venturesome mind.[107] In a moment of personal reflection, he contrasted these virtues with intolerance and dogmatism. The opposite of dogmatism, he stated, was the ability to grow and change. "Some people boast that they stand where they stood thirty years ago," he said, in a backward glance at his former fundamentalist friends, but "any man that has stopped seeing new things in God's world and word is to be profoundly pitied." Although his former fundamentalist opponents were not in principle against growth, dis-

---

[105] Reuben Torrey to James Gray, 12 May 1922, Moody Bible Institute Archives; for Fosdick's sermon see Halford R. Ryan, *Harry Emerson Fosdick: Persuasive Preacher* (New York: Greenwood Press, 1989), 79–89.

[106] Harry Emerson Fosdick to MacInnis, 8 September 1922. MacInnis Papers.

[107] John M. MacInnis, "The Beroean Nobility—An Aristocracy of Truth," a Typed Manuscript of a Lecture Given in Pasadena, ca. 1929, MacInnis Papers.

covery, and intellectual honesty, they defined these ideas differently, tolerating growth within the limits of specific community beliefs and behaviors. If truth is from God, reasoned the fundamentalist, one could not grow beyond truth. Perhaps so—but from MacInnis' point of view, still feeling the pain of having been shunned by his former companions, this idea had been twisted into a staid unthinking traditionalism. "The man I am most afraid of," he later declared, "is the man who is satisfied with things as they are."[108] The stridency with which he came to embrace virtues of intellectual growth and discovery represented not only his defensive response to former fundamentalist critics, but also his personal growth beyond the fold of mere evangelicalism. Although there is no evidence that MacInnis abandoned the evangelical religion that had nurtured him throughout his life, his movement back into the denominational fold and his enthusiastic embrace of a tolerant perspective was strengthened by his painful experiences in fundamentalism. His later association with Robert Freeman, for example, a well known liberal minister of Pasadena Presbyterian Church, exemplified his growing openness and movement away from theological dogmatism.[109] Echoing the sentiments of a progressive theologian like Lymon Abbott, who described religion as the "life of God in the soul of man," and Newman Smyth, who defined modernism as a "vitalizing spirit making all things new rather than a body of doctrines," MacInnis preferred to think of Christianity in poetic terms, as a "venture of faith on the way of love."[110]

Conclusions

Until recently it has been difficult to assess the significance of various life experiences and socio-economic realities that affected an individual like MacInnis, because few studies had been done on other leaders who, like him, identified themselves as fundamentalists in the 1920s. But, as mentioned in the introduction, this situation has greatly improved since the 1970s, and so there is now much more information by which to interpret his life in relation to specific cohorts and social trends.

One obvious social trend that influenced MacInnis was the great rural migration to cities during the late 19th and early 20th centuries. There

---

[108] MacInnis to William MacInnes, 30 April 1935, MacInnis Papers.

[109] Charles Erdman to MacInnis, 31 March 1934, MacInnis Papers. Erdman notes that MacInnis had been preaching at the Pasadena Presbyterian Church.

[110] MacInnis, "The Beroean Nobility"; Lyman Abbott, *The Theology of an Evolutionist* (Boston: Houghton, Mifflin and Co., 1897), 1; for Newman Smyth see Ferenc Szasz, "Three Fundamentalist Leaders: The Roles of William Bell Riley, John Roach Straton, and William Jennings Bryan in the Fundamentalist-Modernist Controversy" (Ph.D. diss., University of Rochester, 1969), 35.

were many fundamentalists in the 1920s who, early in life, had left small villages and impoverished farming communities in order to find more prosperity and security in the city. Historians who identified these rural transplants as core participants in a later urban fundamentalist phenomenon were not mistaken, though it is no longer possible to argue that rural attitudes were an essential characteristic of fundamentalism, or that liberalism was a sure sign of urban sophistication. MacInnis, for example, though hailing from a poor and rural social ethos, nevertheless, displayed many qualities of intellectual curiosity and literary interest. For him, as for countless other rural migrants, literary culture, even if it came through the avenue of a Bible school, was often seen as a way to escape the drudgeries of rural existence and a means to achieve enhanced social status.[111] It is not surprising, therefore, that he discovered a pathway to social advancement through a school of Dwight L. Moody's that attracted mostly conservative white middle class Protestants then moving to America's growing cities. In the context of Chicago's "cosmopolitan frontier," MacInnis formed his first ties to other transplanted Anglo-Protestants, many of whom would later make up the fundamentalist movement.

More significant than rural origins, however, was the strongly ethnic and traditional Scottish Presbyterian confessionalism of his youth. Because his self-identity was tied deeply to his ethnic and religious roots in Scotland, MacInnis maintained a basically conservative Victorian social temperament throughout his life. He never questioned the need for a social order based on principles of Victorian morality or the necessary harmony between interests of state and religion. Hence, like most fundamentalists, MacInnis believed in traditional 19th century concepts of personal morality. His commitment to a basically Christian society influenced his shallow participation in Progressive reforms, but his strong social and religious conservatism prevented him from becoming either predominantly a social crusader or a radical premillenarian, looking only to save souls from a collapsing social order. Rather, having won a large degree of social esteem through enlarging ministerial responsibilities, MacInnis very often sought to preserve the status quo.

The most important aspect of his ethnic and religious roots, however, which separated him most strikingly from his fundamentalist colleagues, was his strong loyalty to Presbyterian denominationalism. Even though MacInnis identified with evangelical revivalism from an early age, this

---

[111] For MacInnis' status motivation see MacInnes, "A Son's Appreciation"; for the problems of a rural versus urban explanation of fundamentalism see Paul A. Carter. "Fundamentalist Defense of the Faith," 202–6; for the desire to escape rural hardship through education or a ministerial career see Macphail, *Master's Wife*, 117.

identity did not seem to weaken his sense of Presbyterian loyalty and identity. But this was not the case for most evangelicals who became leaders in the fundamentalist movement. A comparison of MacInnis and Lewis Sperry Chafer, for example, reveals some interesting similarities and differences. Both men were born in 1871 and followed similar career paths; around 1908, as MacInnis worked to launch the Montrose Bible Conference, Chafer was making his transition to a career as a Bible conference speaker; both men participated in the prophetic conferences of 1918 which stimulated the formation of the WCFA; and in the early 1920s, both Chafer and MacInnis entered full time teaching careers in fundamentalist institutions. But, in spite of these and other similarities, they differed significantly in their denominational stances. Chafer displayed very little preference or loyalty for one denomination, and although he eventually settled with the Southern Presbyterian Church, his career depended far more on nondenominational evangelical networks than did MacInnis' career. What Chafer lacked, like many American evangelicals, was a strong ethnic link to a particular liturgical tradition, and it was primarily this aspect of MacInnis' religious identity that preserved his strong tie to Presbyterianism, in spite of countervailing tendencies in popular American evangelicalism.[112]

MacInnis' educational background exemplifies some of the differences that William Hutchison found between liberal and conservative leaders from 1875 to 1915.[113] First, Hutchison reported that liberals were more likely to have come from a family of educators or professionals than conservatives: in this, MacInnis certainly followed the pattern of many conservatives who not only came from rural or laboring class roots, but as a result also experienced economic privation and early adult responsibilities. While the religious ideas of many liberals were being formed during the crucial undergraduate years, conservatives were more often forced into some other work, hence depriving them of the influence of a "mind-opening" teacher.[114] Second, conservatives were more likely to have deviated from the customary pattern of college and seminary education by omitting college in favor of a Bible school or seminary education alone. Here too, MacInnis more nearly fits a conservative profile: he did not attend a college prior to his seminary training, but he received his adult education first through a Bible school and later by correspondence. His formative years, therefore, were more in-

---

[112] For Chafer see Hannah, "Social and Intellectual History of the Evangelical Theological College," 90–144.

[113] William R. Hutchison, "Cultural Strain and Protestant Liberalism," *American Historical Review* 76 (April 1971): 386–411.

[114] Ibid., 399.

fluenced by pastors and Bible school teachers than "mind-opening" professors.

Another facet which Hutchison studied was the experience of religious conversion. Very few liberals recorded a conversion experience, while about two thirds of conservatives described sharply defined and usually dramatic conversions. But here, as previously noted, MacInnis' experience is unclear. Like many fundamentalists, he experienced a conversion, but it did not seem to form a major part of his religious self-consciousness. Two other aspects of liberal/conservative differences which Hutchison studied, namely, the home environment and a tendency to shun controversy, present some affinities to MacInnis, but raise questions as well. There is not enough known about his early life to ascertain whether or not it was similar to the home environment of many liberals, orthodox but nonrepressive. But if so, this trait as well as a basically non-acerbic personality has more affinity for liberal patterns. The data, therefore, indicate that MacInnis shared certain important traits with both liberals and conservatives.

A very significant point that emerges from this study is that MacInnis received his formative religious ideas and experiences before ever having to really face the challenges of modern theology. Whereas many liberals stated that they were influenced by a family member who was somewhat heretical but admired, no such person appears to have influenced MacInnis.[115] To the contrary, the most influential person in his early life was David Sutherland, a fairly conservative Scottish Free Church minister. When he finally entered a Bible school, this experience only served to reinforce conservative ideas, and it was not until his early thirties that he finally received a higher theological education, but this experience was by no means a liberal education.

The fact that MacInnis formed his primary associations before he had the chance to encounter the full implications of liberalism explains a great deal about the direction of his career. In spite of his moderate Presbyterian theology and denominational loyalty, he kept active in trans-denominational evangelical circles, because this is where he began his religious career, and it seemed to him that his views were most compatible with evangelical causes. Indeed, when the Stewart brothers began the *Fundamentals* project in 1910, MacInnis, seeing himself as part of the evangelical establishment, submitted an article to A. C. Dixon for consideration. Though Dixon replied favorably, it was never published in that famous collection of essays, because a little later Louis Meyer became editor, and he was less favorably disposed to MacInnis' proposed subject. Perhaps given his identity with popular evangelical-

---

[115] Ibid., 400.

ism, it is not surprising that years later MacInnis would accept a teaching position in a fundamentalist Bible school. He, just as much as W. B. Riley, looked to a generation of Niagara Bible conference leaders as his religious forebears. But the Bible school of the 1920s had changed dramatically from his early days at Moody Bible Institute, and these changes were to have a profound impact on his experience at the Bible Institute of Los Angeles.[116]

---

[116] For MacInnis' article see A. C. Dixon to MacInnis, 5 October 1909, and Louis Meyer to MacInnis, 21 November 1911, MacInnis Papers.

CHAPTER 3

Biola: The Origins and Educational Ideology
of an American Bible School, 1908–1918

Having examined the major religious and social influences in MacInnis' life, it is necessary to turn to a study of the Bible Institute of Los Angeles in order to fully comprehend the factors which led to the MacInnis controversy. This order of study seems reasonable in light of the apparent dissonance that MacInnis experienced between his own beliefs and attitudes and those of his Bible school associates. The principal question, therefore, that this portion of the study will seek to answer is: To what extent did MacInnis share or reject cardinal ideas of Bible school education, and how did his views contribute to the opposition which emerged during his deanship of Biola?

A study of Biola's educational ideology, however, soon reveals that the goals of Bible school leaders were in flux between the years of 1908 and the end of MacInnis' administration in 1928. No single set of beliefs or attitudes, therefore, can be precisely fixed as the charter of Biola's self-understanding; rather, the rhetoric of Bible school leaders reflected changing and often very different conceptions of what a Bible school should be. Hence, it is important to begin with the earliest expressions of Bible school self-understanding, and then trace these evolving and usually overlapping conceptions of Bible school leaders through the period of MacInnis' own administration. The plan of this chapter, therefore, is to begin with the idea of a Bible school as conceived by Dwight L. Moody and his associates at the Chicago institute, and relate this to Biola's formative years from 1908 to 1918. This method commends itself for two reasons: first, Moody Bible Institute was the principal model upon which leaders of Biola patterned their school; second, the early idealism of the Bible school movement was most fully realized at Biola during this period, before a world war ended America's so-called innocence, and theological changes soon erupted into a full-fledged Modernist Fundamentalist Controversy. With the new social and religious climate of post-war America, beginning about 1918 and extending through the tumultuous decade of the 1920s, came pressures to alter some of the original ideas of Bible school training, and these changes, not surprisingly, relate significantly to fundamentalist criticisms of MacInnis and his administration. Hence, a subsequent chapter will study the changing character of Bible school training and examine to what extent MacInnis tried to modify or conserve the original idealism of Bible school education.

The Bible Institute Idea

Dwight L. Moody and the Origins of an Idea

The concept of creating an institution for the purpose of training lay Christian workers in Bible and missionary methods did not originate with the founders of the Bible Institute of Los Angeles. Rather, they were the heirs of a twenty year tradition dating from the founding of Moody Bible Institute in 1889. Although not the first Bible school, Moody Bible Institute was by far the most influential. Sometimes this influence was spread by leaders of the institute who showed others how to begin a Bible school. This is how Torrey influenced the formation of the Bible Institute of Los Angeles. On other occasions, a former teacher, evangelist, or graduate of the school would begin a similar school somewhere else. One student, for example, "Brother J. C. Crawford," after leaving Moody Bible Institute for the small town of Boone, Iowa, began a Bible school, which by 1911 enrolled one hundred students.[1]

But what was the founding generation of Bible school leaders trying to accomplish? Although regional circumstances may have influenced the goals of different Bible schools, all of them shared a basic commitment to lay Bible training for missions and Christian service. The widespread influence of the Moody Bible Institute can be explained partly by Moody's articulation of this well-defined vision for lay Bible training, even though Moody himself never filled the role of a Bible school educator. This was left to other leaders more adept than Moody at educational endeavors, but, nevertheless, his rhetoric continued to dominate the thinking of Bible school leaders well into the next century, especially at the Bible Institute of Los Angeles.

Moody's earliest interest in lay Bible training grew out of his practical need for assistants in revival work. In the inquiry rooms, which Moody had devised as an integral part of his revivals, inquirers were in-

---

[1] For the influential role of Moody Bible Institute see Brereton, *Training God's Army*, preface; George M. Marsden, *Understanding Fundamentalism and Evangelicalism* (Grand Rapids: Eerdmans, 1991), 40–41; for Torrey's advice see *The King's Business*, August–September 1911, 174; for the J. C. Crawford illustration see Charles Blanchard to Lyman Stewart, 25 September 1911, Lyman Stewart Papers, Biola University Archives.

vited and coaxed gently into an experience of Christ, not in the public "anxious seat" of Finney, but in an intimate atmosphere of a small gathering. Hence, this method also required a large number of revival helpers to personally assist the penitents who gathered for prayer and salvation. Lacking ministerial help to fill these needs, Moody relied on trained lay helpers, and often he trained the workers himself. This revival context of lay Bible training continued to influence the language of later Bible school leaders: the term "personal work," for instance, became a staple of Bible school training. Moreover, the training that Moody himself gave his personal workers still informed Bible school curricula many years later, with topics like "How to Conduct a Prayer Meeting."[2]

A growing consciousness of urban crisis in the 1880s, motivated by a massive influx of immigrants into America's cities and growing labor unrest among the working classes, added yet another dimension to Moody's concept of lay Bible training. In the year that Josiah Strong published *Our Country,* a critique of America's social crisis and the failure of the church to adapt to the problems of urban life, Moody began to emphasize lay Bible training for city mission workers.

> Every city mission in this country and Europe has been almost a failure. It is a fact. I have looked into it. I have been in all the great cities of Great Britain, and I have investigated this matter, and there is not a city mission started in these countries that is not almost a failure, because the men are not trained.[3]

What Moody had so successfully done in a revival context—training Christian workers—could now be done to fill the needs of city missions. James Findlay has argued convincingly that Moody's call for the new type of training school was motivated by fears of increasing labor unrest, which in 1886 culminated in the bloody Haymarket riot.[4] Noting the growing tensions among Chicago's laboring classes after 1884, when the economy again suffered severe decline, Findlay portrayed Moody's new school as a movement of social conservatism designed to Christianize (and Americanize) working immigrant classes, which seemed to threaten Anglo-Protestant cultural hegemony. Although Moody's rhetoric appealed to the social conservatism of wealthy

---

[2] Findlay, *Dwight L. Moody,* 265–66; Weisberger, *They Gathered at the River,* 208.

[3] Dwight L. Moody, Speech at Farwell Hall, 22 January 1886, quoted in Getz, *MBI: The Story of Moody Bible Institute,* 36.

[4] James F. Findlay Jr., "Moody, 'Gapmen,' and the Gospel: The Early Days of Moody Bible Institute," *Church History* 31 (September 1962): 322–25.

Chicago businessmen, it was not his only motive, nor even a primary one. With typical impeccable timing, Moody sensed the concerns and worries of his old business friends in Chicago and framed his appeal for funds in language they would easily hear. But Moody's purpose was more religious than social, broader than the urban problems of the 1880s. As a force for stabilizing social unrest in Chicago, it is doubtful that the institute made much of any contribution. But as a religious training school, Moody's idea went further than probably he ever envisioned. Yet the social context in which Moody began his school was not forgotten, for years later Bible school leaders could still claim that they were training God's workers not only to reach the poor and the immigrant with the gospel, but to Americanize them as well.[5]

One should not assume that Moody's idea of lay Christian training was without precedent. Actually, Protestant denominations had already invested resources in various lay training schools, and a general trend toward greater lay leadership of religious activities was widely evident. Moody himself was not an ordained minister, and many significant movements of the period, for example, the Student Volunteer Movement, were led by lay people.[6] But the idea of creating an institution to train lay religious workers was not met with universal acclaim. Even though Moody thought of his students as "gap-men," that is, as lay men and women assisting the clergy, some Protestant religious leaders worried that the new school would compete with the denominational seminaries. Anxious to allay such fears and to gain support from Protestant clergy, Moody emphasized that the institute would not train students for the ordained ministry, but only as assistants for the clergy.[7] Most Bible institute leaders prior to World War I tried to preserve Moody's vision of cooperation with the mainline Protestant denominations, sometimes describing their role as a handmaid of the church.[8] Such an attitude was characteristic of Biola in 1908, when it declared that Bible schools were not designed to compete with theological seminaries, but to be a "blessing to every evangelical church."[9]

In spite of Moody's public insistence on church cooperation, the Bible school movement did represent an implicit critique of theological

---

[5] See the unsigned editorial entitled "The Americanization of the Foreigner," in *The King's Business*, March 1920, 243.

[6] Brereton, *Training God's Army*, 55–60.

[7] Dwight Moody, Interview in San Francisco, California, ca. 1889, quoted in Getz, *MBI: The Story of Moody Bible Institute*, 36.

[8] Ronald. G. Sawatsky, "'Looking for that Blessed Hope': The Roots of Fundamentalism in Canada, 1878–1914" (Ph.D. diss., University of Toronto, 1985), 278.

[9] "A Short Story of the Los Angeles Bible Institute," *The King's Business*, November 1910, 171–72.

education in America. One problem that Moody emphasized was the lack of clergy to reach the large number of immigrant laborers living in America's industrial cities. According to Moody, seminaries could not produce enough graduates to keep up with the burgeoning influx of immigrants.[10] Twenty years later Biola leaders still pointed to the same problem:

> Many large seminaries are destitute of students. Hundreds of small churches are without pastors. Other hundreds are closed entirely. There are thousands of unoccupied fields throughout the land, and more than half of the earth's inhabitants have never heard the gospel. There are constant calls for men and women who can do things for God. The Church needs Sunday School teachers, helpers, evangelists, and leaders who know the Bible, and it is to meet this demand that God has raised up in different sections of the land Bible schools where men and women can be trained in a knowledge of the Bible and practical work in the saving and sanctifying of souls.[11]

Yet beyond the shortage of clergy, Moody's critique pointed to a basic inadequacy in 19th century theological education: the academic thrust of the seminary curriculum, which emphasized language studies to the exclusion of Bible training and practical methods. This, thought Moody, tended to remove the seminary graduate from an awareness of the needs of average workers. "The ministers are educated away from these classes," he noted, adding that it was not too much education, but the kind of education they received. He proposed, therefore, that Bible schools reject the classical thrust of seminary education: "Never mind the Greek and Hebrew," he groused, "give them plain English and good scripture." Moody's call for more English Bible instruction and practical training was not unique in late 19th century Protestantism, but reflected a widespread dissatisfaction with traditional theological education. Yet Moody's clear formulation of the problems, and his role as a spokesman for evangelicalism, made his ideas foundational to American Bible schools.[12]

---

[10] Getz, *MBI: The Story of Moody Bible Institute*, 43.

[11] "A Short Story of the Los Angeles Bible Institute," 171.

[12] Getz, *MBI: The Story of Moody Bible Institute*, 36–37; Brereton, *Training God's Army*, 61–63; and Gary Moncher, "The Bible College and American Moral Culture" (Ph.D. diss., University of California at Berkeley, 1987), 54–105.

From Moody to Biola: Changing Perspectives

Although Moody's ideas formed the basis of Biola's self-understanding, there were some significant differences. One important difference was a lack of emphasis at Biola on the urban social crisis. When Biola president Lyman Stewart dedicated Biola's new buildings in 1913, he barely mentioned urban problems of Los Angeles and said nothing about the need to reach a growing class of poor immigrant workers: his theme, rather, was the opportunity that would come from the opening of the Panama Canal and the need for workers to spread the gospel. Absent from his speech was the language of aiding the poor and needy of society, a fact that reinforces Stewart Cole's observation that the second generation of Bible school founders neglected Moody's earlier social concerns.[13]

But Stewart's simple optimism and lack of emphasis on the problems of urban growth partly reflected a different social context. When the Moody Bible Institute began in 1889, Los Angeles numbered only fifty thousand, in comparison to Chicago's one million. And although Los Angeles continued to experience rapid growth, forming what some historians call a "cosmopolitan frontier," its delayed urbanization in comparison to East Coast cities, and its largely Anglo-Protestant immigration pattern, which gave the city a decided Protestant ethos after 1900, infused leaders of Biola with a breezy optimism. While cities in the Northeast and Midwest were experiencing disruption of a traditional social order, Americans migrating into the Los Angeles basin were busily transforming the former Mexican pueblo into a socially homogeneous Anglo-Protestant culture.[14] In such a context, concerns about urban poverty naturally receded into the background, and labor disputes, though reaching a critical moment in 1910 with the bombing of the Los Angeles Times building, also failed to disrupt the optimism of Los Angeles community leaders.

If Stewart's attitude was less motivated by urban ethnic immigration and labor unrest, other factors had gained importance. For example, though Moody had mentioned the possibility that some students would

---

[13] Lyman Stewart, "The President's Address," *The King's Business,* July 1913, 322–24; for Stewart's worries about the Panama Canal see Lyman Stewart to John Willis Baer, 21 September 1910, Lyman Stewart Papers; for Cole see *History of Fundamentalism,* 42–43.

[14] Sandra Sizer Frankiel, *California's Spiritual Frontiers: Religious Alternatives in Anglo-Protestantism, 1850–1910* (Berkeley: University of California Press, 1988), 71; Gregory H. Singleton, *Religion in the City of Angels: American Protestant Culture and Urbanization, Los Angeles, 1850–1930* (Ann Arbor: UMI Research, 1979), 42–43, 68, 83.

go into the foreign missions field, his original emphasis began with the evangelization of Chicago. Interestingly, two years before his death, the institute's catalog still hardly mentioned foreign missions. But by 1910, Moody Bible Institute had become a major training center for foreign missionaries.[15] At Biola a similar development never occurred because training foreign missionaries was a central feature of the curriculum from the start. After only five years, Biola leaders claimed proudly that almost seventy-five former students had gone on to foreign mission fields in South America, Africa, and China.[16]

But most importantly, Biola's leaders intoned a different theological climate. When Moody was asked in 1889 what the new school would teach, Moody's response was predictable: the doctrines of the Bible and methods of practical work.[17] Opposition to liberalism was not a part of his answer. But the founders of Biola had little doubt that their school stood on the front line of a battle with theological liberalism. Anti-modernism characterized Biola from its beginning. Indeed, when Biola leaders reflected on the beginning of their own movement, they sometimes assumed that anti-modernism was the most important reason that the original Bible schools were founded.

> Bible Schools are a product of the times—an outgrowth of certain conditions; they are God's agency for an emergency. God foresees a need and supplies it. He laid the foundations over a quarter of a century ago, when the work of undermining the faith in the Word of God began to take definite shape in this country.[18]

In another article, editors of Biola's magazine repeated the claim that Bible schools were organized in part "to meet the present emergency," which was "the satanic assault upon the Scriptures."[19] Biola was at the vanguard of opposition to liberalism. Lyman Stewart, for example, alarmed by the rise of liberalism in mainline Protestant churches, began funding publication of *The Fundamentals* in 1910, with hopes of stemming the liberal tide. The project was finished in 1915, after more than three million copies of the books were mailed to religious leaders

---

[15] For the lack of emphasis on foreign missions in 1897 see the Catalogue of the Chicago Evangelization Society, Moody Bible Institute Archives; for the rapid growth in foreign missions programs at Moody by 1910 see Brereton, *Training God's Army*, 128.

[16] Lyman Stewart, "The President's Address," 324.

[17] Getz, *MBI: The Story of Moody Bible Institute*, 42.

[18] "A Short Story of the Los Angeles Bible Institute," 171; see also Getz, *MBI: The Story of Moody Bible Institute*, 48, 54.

[19] "The Multiplication of Bible Schools," *The King's Business*, October 1911, 205.

throughout the English speaking world. Feeling a sense of confidence from this auspicious beginning, Biola leaders stated that their magazine would continue the project started by "two Christian laymen," by publishing articles which were not included in the original volumes.[20]

Though only a generation had passed between the founding of Moody Bible Institute and Biola, nevertheless, a momentous change had taken place in the religious thinking of American Protestant church leaders. Although it is quite difficult to identify just when "the old orthodoxies were displaced by the crippling doubts of modern life," as Grant Wacker put it, many historians consider the last decade of the 19th century a watershed in the development of theological liberalism.[21] During the 1890s, due largely to several watched church trials and publications, a division emerged in the public consciousness between theological progressives and anti-modernists over issues of biblical criticism and evolution.[22] As the tide of liberalism increased, a conservative response began to take shape. In 1902, for example, evangelicals formed the Bible League of North America to oppose modernism. In spite of these early efforts, however, by 1910, when the Stewarts began the *Fundamentals,* most conservatives were feeling increasingly embattled in the mainline Protestant bodies. The northern Presbyterians reaffirmed five doctrinal points in 1910 with the hope of staying liberal advances.[23] But unlike the 1890s, when a few theological progressives were forced out of their church related positions for holding heterodox views, by 1910 such occurrences were rare.

The atmosphere of Biola, therefore, was from the start infused with a feeling of grandiose purpose—to safeguard the truth, the Bible, a worldview, from the onslaughts of modern unbelief. This fortress mentality was evident in Lyman Stewart's dedication address, when he emphasized the strength of the Bible as Biola's only foundation no fewer than six times. This foundation, said Stewart, is one that can never be shaken or removed.[24] The perception of Biola as defender of the Bible

---

[20] "Testimony of the Fundamentals to Be Continued," *The King's Business,* April 1915, 269.

[21] Grant Wacker, "Searching for Norman Rockwell: Popular Evangelicalism in Contemporary America," in *The Evangelical Tradition in America,* ed. Leonard I. Sweet (Macon, GA: Mercer University Press, 1984), 290; for the watershed analogy see Robert W. Funk, "The Watershed of American Biblical Tradition," *Journal of Biblical Literature* 95 (1976): 8–14.

[22] Hutchison, *Modernist Impulse in American Protestantism,* 111–44; Arthur M. Schlesinger, *A Critical Period in American Religion, 1875–1900,* Facet Books Historical Series (American Church), ed. Richard C. Wolf (Philadelphia: Fortress Press, 1967), 8–10.

[23] Loetscher, *Broadening Church,* 98.

[24] "The President's Address," *The King's Business* 4 (July 1913): 323, 325.

from its critics was, ironically, reinforced by the school's architecture. The building itself, massive, blocked, faced with an elaborate series of Italian arches guarded on either side by huge towers was symbolic of the new Bible school, God's fortress of truth.

Figure 2: Façade of Biola

The massive façade of the Bible Institute of Los Angeles resembles a fortress, a fitting architectural metaphor of fundamentalist attitudes in the early 20th century. (Source: *The King's Business,* April 1928, p. 205.)

Lyman Stewart and the Ideological Origins of Biola

Lyman Stewart was the man who brought both the means and the will to create the Bible Institute of Los Angeles. Although many others exercised considerable influence and control over the school's affairs, there is no doubt that Stewart took a personal and active interest in his "investment." A study of Stewart's ideas, therefore, provides important information about what the early leaders of Biola were trying to accomplish.

Stewart arrived in California in the early 1880s, just on the eve of the first great wave of migration to Southern California. Bringing with him skills of oil prospecting from Pennsylvania, he assiduously set out searching for oil, and by 1890 Stewart had managed to become a successful oil tycoon. Having been raised a pious Presbyterian, Stewart then emerged in the 1890s as an important benefactor and leader of Christian causes.[25]

When he first arrived in Los Angeles, Stewart had served as president of the YMCA, and when Los Angeles Protestants joined together to form the Pacific Gospel Union (later known as the Union Rescue Mission) for relief work among the poor and indigent, Stewart worked on its board of directors. In its early days the focus of the mission was not only to aid those who were homeless, but to act as a central organizing agency for city-wide missionary outreach. As such, in addition to providing food and shelter for the destitute, the mission also held revivals, distributed Christian literature, sent out teams of lay workers for outdoor preaching or home visitation, and provided Bible teaching. Interestingly, not long after Stewart joined the board in 1892, the Gospel Union began an "official" Bible institute, although nothing is known of its operations.[26]

When the United States acquired the Philippines in 1898, Stewart was alarmed at the lack of Protestant missions in the islands, so he commissioned Augustus B. Prichard, a newly installed minister of First Presbyterian Church of Los Angeles, to prepare Spanish Bibles and tracts to send to the territory. In connection with this work, which later became known as the Bible House of Los Angeles, Stewart and Prichard saw the need for training missionaries, and so sometime in 1901 Prichard began an informal Bible school which met in his home two or three evenings a week for Bible study. This work did not end after Prichard accepted the pastorate of the Central Presbyterian Church in 1903, but was eventually absorbed into the Bible Institute of Los Angeles under the leadership of Thomas C. Horton, with Prichard designated the vice-president, and Stewart the president.[27]

---

[25] James O. Henry, "Black Oil and Souls to Save," *BIOLA Broadcaster* 3 (December 1973): 8–12; also see "The Stewarts as Christian Stewards, the Story of Milton and Lyman Stewart," *Missionary Review of the World* 47 (August 1924): 595–602.

[26] Helga B. Henry, *Mission on Main Street* (Boston: W. A. Wilde Co., 1955), 21–24; Henry, "Black Oil," 11–12.

[27] For Stewart's concerns about Catholicism in the Philippines see Henry, "Black Oil," 12; also see Neeta Marquis, *Immanuel and the Fifty Years: 1888– 1938* (Los Angeles: Immanuel Presbyterian Church, 1938), 33–34; for Prichard's early Bible school see the typed biographical memoir by his son: William H. Prichard, "Augustus B. Prichard," TD, n.d., Presbyterian Historical Society, Philadelphia, Pennsylvania. This account differs from Henry's, in that it claims (as did Neeta Marquis) that Prichard's Bible class did not end in 1903, but continued, eventually coming under T. C. Horton's leadership in 1906.

During this early period Stewart had concluded that his "investments" could not achieve success without a greater supply of well-trained Christian workers. According to James O. Henry, Stewart reached this conclusion when he decided to purchase a houseboat for evangelistic outreach to "boat people" in Hunan, China: on learning that there were no qualified workers to manage the project, Stewart then turned his attention to training Christian workers.[28]

Although Stewart had already shown some interest in Bible training prior to this incident, the story nicely illustrates the changing nature of his thinking. In his earlier days, Stewart had been active in interdenominational charities such as the Pacific Gospel Union and the YMCA. And although he continued to support these organizations, after 1900 Stewart redirected the majority of his time and money toward specifically religious goals of evangelism and the training of missionaries. This transition was motivated by Stewart's growing dissatisfaction with the activities of the Union Rescue Mission and the YMCA, both of which became increasingly concerned with social relief after 1900.[29] Indeed, in spite of personal assurances from the YMCA in 1902 that it would give greater emphasis to the "religious features" of its work, in 1910 leaders were upset that Stewart did not want to serve on its advisory council.[30]

Another factor which influenced Stewart's changing thinking was his inability to control the outcome of his contributions. This character trait was all too evident to leaders like R. A. Torrey, who resented Stewart's excessive intrusions into institute affairs. But without even considering Torrey's cavils, it is clear that Stewart's giving pattern showed a preference for projects that he could control, because most solicitations for donations received only token responses.[31] This aspect of his giving was likely influenced by his business model of Christian benevolence. When the first issue of *The King's Business* exclaimed boldly that "Our Lord was a businessman" and then compared the school's work to that of a corporation, Biola leaders revealed their sources of inspiration.[32] The use of rhetoric such as "investing in the Lord's work," and "doing the Lord's business" were more than metaphors for Christian service; they reflected the character of Bible school training, which drew much of its

---

[28] Henry, Biola Manuscript, 37. Henry omitted this story in his article, "Black Oil and Souls to Save."

[29] Henry, "Black Oil," 12; for the activities of the YMCA see C. Howard Hopkins, *History of the Y. M. C. A. in North America* (New York: Association Press, 1951), 504–12.

[30] W. M. Parsons to Lyman Stewart, 18 March 1902, and Arthur Letts to Lyman Stewart, 15 February 1910, Lyman Stewart Papers.

[31] Sandeen, *Roots,* 190.

[32] *The King's Business,* January 1910, 1.

inspiration from the influence of the industrial corporation, concerned about production, efficiency, and return on investment. Bible schools were not the only Protestant organizations to adopt business methods, but they were very receptive to business influences, partly because of their frequently close ties to business leaders, and partly because their pragmatic leanings naturally fit a business model.[33] Likewise, Stewart's changing "investments" reflected the demands of a sound business strategy—an enterprise which he could control, which would produce a trained labor pool for Christian ministries, and whose outcome could be measured with facts and figures.

But probably the key element which finally led Stewart to commit the majority of his benevolence to Biola was the failure of his plan to provide Bible training through the aegis of Occidental College. Stewart's hope of providing practical Bible training through Occidental College proved to be a frustrating, but formative experience. In 1905, Stewart offered to pay a three-thousand-dollar stipend for Bible instruction at Occidental, apparently hoping that the college would become known as a "Christian school," rather than as a merely denominational school.[34] Stewart explained his intentions in a letter to John Willis Baer, the president of Occidental College.

> The Bible Department alone is to give the College its distinctive character as a Christian school. As merely a Presbyterian school, it will not appeal to me, and as a nominally religious school it will have nothing to characterize it from any other sectarian institution. The College occupies a strategic point on this Coast, and in order to maintain its rightful position and exert its proper influence every student graduating therefrom should go out as a trained Christian worker.[35]

At this time Stewart still believed that Bible training could be done in the Bible department of a liberal arts college. It is clear that Stewart had no interest in denominational education per se, but sought a nonsectarian Bible teaching according to conservative evangelical beliefs. In his view, this plan would distinguish the school from the longstanding 19th

---

[33] For the influence of business on religion see Louis Weeks, "The Incorporation of American Religion: The Case of the Presbyterians," *Religion and American Culture: A Journal of Interpretation* 1 (Winter 1991): 102–9; for business influence on Dwight Moody see Paul Heidebrecht, "Chicago Presbyterians and the Businessman's Religion," *American Presbyterians: Journal of Presbyterian History,* 64 (Spring 1986): 39–42.

[34] Nellie May Young, *William Stewart Young, 1859–1937: Builder of California Institutions* (Glendale: The Arthur H. Clark Co., 1967), 81.

[35] Lyman Stewart to John Willis Baer, 4 August 1906, Lyman Stewart Papers.

century tradition of classical liberal arts, which he considered nominally Christian at best.

From the start Stewart encountered difficulties with his plan. He was concerned, for example, about the Bible teaching at Occidental and expressed deep reservations about its dean, Professor Stevenson, who had failed to get his students to withdraw from "theatrical entertainments" after eight months of Bible study.[36] To Stewart's relief, Stevenson resigned. This occasion gave Stewart the chance to advise Baer on the responsibility of teaching the Bible.

First, Stewart believed that a Bible teacher should be a person of vital spirituality. Without this, "a man may be a great theologian and yet not be able to properly instruct students in the scriptures." Academic qualifications of Bible teachers were less important than evidence of spirituality. A second qualification was that a Bible teacher should be a Christian worker.[37] Again, Stewart's business pragmatism left little room for the pursuit of intellectual culture. Hence, in Stewart's viewpoint, W. R. Newell was the best teacher he had yet seen, "not excepting even Campbell Morgan," because he was always engaged in the Lord's work. Newell's commitment to Christian work was not seen in his teaching abilities, but in his willingness to engage people on their state of salvation.[38] Sometimes Stewart's anti-intellectualism could lead to trivial, even obscurantist criticism. When someone suggested a Dr. White to fill the new position at Occidental, Stewart interjected his strong disapproval.

We could not conceive of A. J. Gordon, James H. Brooks [sic] or A. C. Gaebelein filling up their magazines with secular and literary matter, and this is what Dr. White does to a very large extent. I do not think Dr. Torrey or Mr. Newell, in publishing a magazine, would waste any of its space in publishing such matter.[39]

Third, Stewart believed that the Bible should be given preeminence at Occidental. Between 1906 and 1910, Stewart increasingly worried that Bible instruction was being neglected and crowded out of the curriculum, and that doctrines were being ignored and compromised.

I sincerely trust that more time will be given to the Bible in all the departments, and that Christian evidences along the line of Dr. A. T. Pier-

---

[36] Stewart to Baer, 27 July 1906.
[37] Stewart to Baer, 4 August 1906.
[38] Stewart to Baer, 27 July 1906.
[39] Ibid. For other examples of Stewart's obscurantism see Szasz, *Divided Mind of Protestant America*, 77–78.

son's "Many Infallible Proofs" be required of all the college students; that this in no sense be made elective. I do not want to dictate in these matters, but the tendency is to crowd the Bible into a corner, and unless a very firm stand is taken to give it its rightful position, its study will be generally restricted and made unpopular. I think special care should be given to the character of the text books used, and that more emphasis be placed on the direct study of the Bible itself.[40]

Stewart's worries were exacerbated by reports that indicated some doctrinal laxity among Occidental teachers. For example, Stewart complained that the school was using a text by Rush Rhees, *The Life of Jesus of Nazareth,* which Stewart regarded as "full of poison." Stewart also complained about a talk given at a local YWCA that was not worthy of the college. Finally, these instances and others led Stewart to suggest that a declaration of doctrines be appended to the college's constitution, and subscription be made mandatory of all teachers.[41] In the end, Stewart hoped that these measures would lead to a more thoroughgoing Bible education, in which study of the English Bible would occupy a central place in the curriculum, and every student would be a "trained Christian worker."

In spite of Stewart's many efforts to give the Bible greater prominence at Occidental, his plan failed. The correspondence between Stewart and Baer reveals a pattern of increasing tension and misunderstanding. Only one year later, when Baer needed additional funds for a teacher of physical education, who would also teach a Bible study, Stewart would not provide the additional revenue.[42] More discord emerged when Stewart objected to paying a salary of a Bible teacher, who also taught philosophy. Said Stewart, disingenuously: "My conviction has been growing that, with my limited means, I should use them exclusively for Bible work."[43] The following year Stewart discontinued most of his support, not because of his "limited means," but in order to invest his money in a new gospel venture, the Bible Institute of Los Angeles.[44]

In retrospect, the strain between Baer and Stewart went deeper than the support of a teacher's salary. Rather, the dispute reflects a widening gap between Stewart and Baer on the essential goals they hoped to achieve. One writer, commenting on the changes at Occidental College

---

[40] Stewart to Baer, 21 January 1907.

[41] Stewart to Baer, 8 February 1907.

[42] Baer to Stewart, 12 October 1908.

[43] Stewart to Baer, 21 September 1910.

[44] William S. Young to Lyman Stewart, 7 December 1911, Lyman Stewart Papers.

during the tenure of John Willis Baer, noted that he added faculty with university degrees rather than ministerial backgrounds, thus giving the school a fuller appreciation of modern scholarship. His further observations are highly suggestive:

> Baer was probably most responsible for changing Occidental's church-oriented curriculum to one which was more academic. For his time, as he drew the college away from its church origins, Baer's philosophy seemed most liberal. . . . Baer's liberalism caused him some trouble with supporters of conservative mind. A few even withdrew their financial aid because the faculty insisted upon teaching the theory of evolution which led to the infusion of Darwinian premises into the curriculum.[45]

Ironically, John W. Baer shared much in common with Lyman Stewart. Once a secretary of a Christian Endeavor Society and the Presbyterian Board of Home Missions, Baer was a Presbyterian layman lacking in solid academic qualifications. Like Stewart, he achieved his success in business.[46] But here the similarity ends, for Baer was a man of broad taste and culture. When he accepted the presidency of Occidental, partly because Lyman Stewart agreed to guarantee his salary, his lack of academic training did not hinder his hope of moving the college away from its church based orientation and into a new model of university education, characterized more by research, professional scholarship and specialization.[47] Stewart's encounter with this new research oriented academic scholarship proved unsettling, because it went against his own pragmatic and anti-intellectual disposition. For Stewart, as for many of his fundamentalist ilk, scholarship only produced doubt and infidelity.[48] His statement that the teaching at Princeton Seminary would only un-

---

[45] Andrew Rolle, *Occidental College: The First Seventy-Five Years, 1887–1962* (Occidental College, 1962), 15–16. See also Robert G. Cleland, *The History of Occidental College, 1887–1937* (Los Angeles: Occidental College, 1937), 45–46. Cleland notes that the college severed its ties to the Presbyterian Church in 1910.

[46] Rolle, *Occidental College*, 14–15; Cleland, *History of Occidental College*, 39; for Baer's relation to Christian Endeavor see William M. Runyan, *Dr. Gray at Moody Bible Institute* (New York: Oxford University Press, 1935), 56.

[47] For these trends see Mark A. Noll, "The University Arrives in America, 1870–1930: Christian Traditionalism During the Academic Revolution," in *Making Higher Education Christian,* ed. Joel A. Carpenter and Kenneth W. Shipps (St. Paul: Christian University Press, 1987), 98–109; and Burton J. Bledstein, *The Culture of Professionalism: The Middle Class and the Development of Higher Education in America* (New York: W. W. Norton, 1976), 300–309, 318–31.

[48] Stewart to Baer, 21 January 1907.

dermine a student's faith not only showed his ignorance of the seminary, which at that time was still a guardian of orthodoxy, but also his basic animadversion of all academic scholarship.[49] In the end, the growing diversification of the college curriculum, and the demand for academic specialization and higher academic standards, rendered Stewart's goals impracticable. But Stewart's hopes were not ended by his failure with Occidental College: rather, they were ignited by his realization that what he wanted to support was not a liberal arts college, but a Bible school.

Formation of the Bible Institute of Los Angeles

When the Bible Institute of Los Angeles was being organized, there were already several colleges founded by Protestants in Southern California, most of which had loose denominational connections.[50] But these fostered a liberal studies emphasis and, therefore, did not interest Lyman Stewart. The need for lay Bible training, however, was not adequately met in the area. A Bible training school was established by evangelical Quakers in 1899, but its association with holiness views led Stewart to reject any mutual cooperation. Another holiness institution associated with the Nazarene Church began with hopes of becoming a liberal arts university in 1902, but monetary problems and fundamentalist influences kept the school within the general framework of a Bible college well into the 1920s. But here too, the fragmentation of Los Angeles evangelicals into holiness, pentecostal, and fundamentalist enclaves contributed to the lack of cooperation between Presbyterian fundamentalists like Stewart, and holiness evangelicals at the Pasadena Nazarene College.[51]

With nowhere else to turn, therefore, Stewart decided to commit the bulk of his time and resources to a new endeavor that by 1910 was already showing remarkable success. Though only two years old, Biola was growing rapidly under the leadership of Thomas Corwin Horton, its primary organizer and instructor. Horton's association with Stewart began in 1906 after Horton was invited to Immanuel Presbyterian Church

---

[49] Stewart to Baer, 30 September 1910.

[50] William Ferrier, *Ninety Years of Education in California, 1846–1936* (Sather Gate Book Shop: Berkeley, CA, 1936), 257–80; Laurance Hill, ed., *Six Collegiate Decades: The Growth of Higher Education in Southern California* (Security First National Bank of Los Angeles, 1929).

[51] Charles Brackett, "The History of Azusa College and the Friends, 1900–1965" (M.A. Thesis, University of Southern California, 1967), 45–49; also see Ronald Kirkemo, *For Zion's Sake: A History of Pasadena/Point Loma College* (San Diego: Point Loma Press, 1992), 32–35, 53–56, 65–67; for the isolation of three evangelical groups see Carpenter, "Fundamentalist Leaven," 28.

in Los Angeles, where Stewart was a member and elder.[52] One of the first things Horton did as an energetic new associate minister was to begin a Bible class called the Fisherman's Club. This class, which grew so fast that it soon became independent of the church, later contributed many of the first students of the institute. Seeing the need for more Bible training in Los Angeles, Horton consulted with Stewart as well as Prichard and others to organize a new Bible school.[53]

Figure 3: Photograph of T. C. Horton
Thomas Corwin Horton, an important founding leader of Protestant
Fundamentalism in Los Angeles

---

[52] Henry, "Black Oil," 15; *Minutes of the General Assembly of the Presbyterian Church in the United States of America* (Philadelphia, 1906), 420.

[53] An early published account of the school's origin occurs in an article in *The King's Business,* probably written by Horton, entitled "The Story of the School," June 1911, 111–14; other similar accounts continued to appear in the magazine as well as in the school's catalogs; see Catalogue of the Bible Institute of Los Angeles [1913], 6–9; for secondary accounts, none of them documented, see Henry, "Black Oil," 15–24, as well as the more detailed account in his unpublished manuscript; also see Williams and Miller, *Chartered for His Glory,* 10–35; for a different view see Prichard, "Augustus B. Prichard."

The Bible Institute of Los Angeles was incorporated on February 25th, 1908, and commenced instruction in a former pool-hall the following month. Prior to the start of classes, Horton asked Torrey for advice on the structure and curriculum of the new school.[54] Drawing on his experience from Moody Bible Institute, Torrey recommended that the curriculum be confined to the Bible, because "literary work undertaken by other schools has not proved a real help to the student." In addition, Torrey suggested that the instruction be systematic and general and not dependent on "great lecturers or teachers that specialize."[55] Torrey's advice agreed with Stewart's goals rather closely: a pragmatic "result oriented" program based solely on Bible instruction, and a rejection of literary studies and academic specialization.

It seems odd, however, that Torrey would have been akin to Stewart's anti-intellectualism. No anti-intellectual himself, Torrey had studied at Yale University as well as in two German universities.[56] Why would Torrey have rejected specialized academic studies? Although the answer lies in the very complex psychology of Torrey's personality, it is at least likely that he, along with Lyman Stewart, distrusted the new influence of academic specialization based on scholarly research.

Torrey's education at Yale was strongly influenced by a conservative reaction against the rise of critical academic scholarship, which was then just becoming established at Harvard and Johns Hopkins University. Under Noah Porter, Yale University became a stronghold of opposition to German models of research scholarship and continued to advocate the traditional curriculum of classical studies even into the 20th century. Porter's academic philosophy was summarized in his comment that, "Better a simple hearted teacher with strong convictions than a dispassionate skeptic." This idea was reinforced by a curriculum that tried to "embrace all knowledge—while failing to develop a specialization."[57] Torrey graduated from Yale in 1875, the last year of the old required curriculum. Torrey's later studies in Germany seem to have made no

---

[54] Reuben Torrey, "Greetings from Dr. Torrey," *The King's Business,* August–September 1911, 174; Henry, "Black Oil," 16–17.

[55] Henry, Biola Manuscript, 42.

[56] *Dictionary of Christianity in America,* s.v. "Torrey, Reuben," by P. C. Wilt.

[57] George Wilson Pierson, *Yale College: An Educational History, 1871–1921* (New Haven: Yale University Press, 1952), 57–73; for Yale's role in the debate about higher education see Louise Stevenson, *Scholarly Means to Evangelical Ends: The New Haven Scholars and the Transformation of Higher Learning in America* (Baltimore: Johns Hopkins University Press, 1986), 58–66; George M. Marsden, *The Soul of the American University: From Protestant Establishment to Established Nonbelief* (New York: Oxford University Press, 1994), 123–33.

dent on his educational views. Like Porter, Torrey retained his belief in a generalist education, but in the context of a democratic Bible school ideology, Torrey's conservative views became even more truncated as he made the Bible itself the sole basis of lay Christian worker training.

It appears that Horton heeded Torrey's advice well, because the initial classes were all general systematic Bible classes taught by lay instructors or ministers of local Presbyterian and Baptist churches: the major classes were Horton's Practical Christian Work and R. A. Hadden's Outlines of Bible Books. Other occasional classes included Bible synthesis, homiletics, the Psalms, and the second coming of Christ, provided by the well-known Methodist layman, William E. Blackstone.[58] Two years later the following classes were listed in *The King's Business:* "Books of the Bible, The Great Doctrines, Chapter Studies, Homiletics, Church History, Practical and Personal Work, and Missions." This curriculum changed again the next year, however, because no church history was offered, but the Pauline epistles, Old Testament, Christian evidences, and music had entered the curriculum.[59]

Biola's changing curriculum became more established with the arrival of Reuben Torrey in 1912. In his statement published in *The King's Business,* Torrey announced that he would closely follow the methods of work adopted by Moody Bible Institute in his planning of Biola programs and curriculum.[60] Largely through his influence the curriculum was established and remained essentially unchanged for twenty years. Prior to his coming, the curriculum consisted mostly in Horton's practical work and a handful of Bible classes. In Torrey's curriculum, however, systematic doctrine classes were given greater emphasis. So-called "Bible doctrines" and personal work became the core of training at Biola.

Education at Biola

Biola leaders succinctly described the purpose of their curriculum as training in the knowledge and use of the English Bible. Before World War I, this ideal was fairly well held together; knowledge and use of the Bible were balanced components of Christian worker training. Of course, knowledge was always practically oriented—no veteran of the

---

[58] Henry, Biola Manuscript, 46.

[59] See "A Short Story of the Los Angeles Bible Institute," *The King's Business,* November 1910, 172; "The Work Within the Institute," *The King's Business,* May 1912, 117. It is difficult to identify the precise classes offered between 1908 and 1912. The article of November 1910 appears to conflate general categories of instruction with a listing of specific classes. For example, though church history was mentioned in 1910, no class of this topic was listed in the May 1912 article or the 1913 school catalog.

[60] Reuben Torrey, "Greetings from Dr. Torrey," 174.

Bible school movement would have separated knowledge of the Bible from its use, indeed, Bible knowledge apart from its use in Christian work was considered of little value. A balance was difficult to maintain, however, as various changes inside and outside the movement led to an erosion of personal worker training. At Biola, the early emphasis on practical training in the use of the Bible persisted well into the 1930s, but after World War II, this element of Bible training disappeared in the school's drive to achieve academic respectability.

Knowledge of the Bible

In the view of most Bible school leaders, what most distinguished the Bible school from the seminary was the use of the English Bible. Many Bible school leaders believed that seminaries had largely ignored the English Bible, and that preaching the Bible itself was rarely practiced. Frequently Bible school instructors expressed the view that seminaries only taught their students about the Bible, not the Bible itself. Another common criticism was that seminaries focused only on parts of scripture in the original languages, a view often reinforced by populist rhetoric.

> The "English Bible" is again coming into its own. The tendency of past years has been to neglect its study. Even in institutions for theological training has this fault been manifest. The Scriptures, in parts, have been studied in Hebrew and Greek, but the "English Bible," the Bible which "the people" have to read and study, has been sorely neglected.[61]

Although Bible school leaders were not the only ones to decry a lack of English Bible instruction, they focused their energies on the problem more than most.[62] One reason for their vigorous defense of the English Bible was their populist and democratic orientation. Fundamentalists objected to a domination of biblical knowledge by technical experts.[63] Sometimes in their ridicule of seminaries, for example, they argued that the right of the people to interpret scripture for themselves had been usurped by Bible scholars and professors, who had become, in effect, Protestant popes.[64] Another basis for English Bible instruction, which

---

[61] "Study of the English Bible," *The King's Business,* August 1915, 655.

[62] For similar attitudes elsewhere see, for example, the efforts of William Rainey Harper in Marsden, *The Soul of the American University,* 240–44; also see the similar efforts at Princeton Seminary in William K. Selden, *Princeton Theological Seminary: A Narrative History, 1812–1992* (Princeton, NJ: Princeton University Press, 1992), 97–98.

[63] Nathan Hatch, *The Democratization of American Christianity* (New Haven, CT: Yale University Press, 1989), 216; Szasz, *Divided Mind,* 40.

[64] See the editorial, "The Seminaries Settle It," *The King's Business,*

was intimately linked to their dispensational theology, was the ever present criticism that seminaries focused too much on narrow parts of scripture and consequently lost the meaning of the whole.

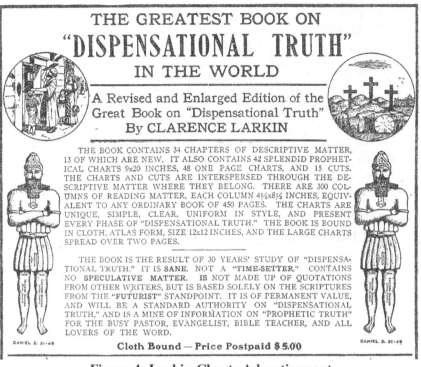

THE GREATEST BOOK ON
"DISPENSATIONAL TRUTH"
IN THE WORLD

A Revised and Enlarged Edition of the Great Book on "Dispensational Truth"
By CLARENCE LARKIN

THE BOOK CONTAINS 34 CHAPTERS OF DESCRIPTIVE MATTER, 13 OF WHICH ARE NEW. IT ALSO CONTAINS 42 SPLENDID PROPHETICAL CHARTS 9x20 INCHES, 48 ONE PAGE CHARTS, AND 15 CUTS. THE CHARTS AND CUTS ARE INTERSPERSED THROUGH THE DESCRIPTIVE MATTER WHERE THEY BELONG. THERE ARE 300 COLUMNS OF READING MATTER, EACH COLUMN 4½x8½ INCHES, EQUIVALENT TO ANY ORDINARY BOOK OF 450 PAGES. THE CHARTS ARE UNIQUE, SIMPLE, CLEAR, UNIFORM IN STYLE, AND PRESENT EVERY PHASE OF "DISPENSATIONAL TRUTH." THE BOOK IS BOUND IN CLOTH; ATLAS FORM, SIZE 12x12 INCHES, AND THE LARGE CHARTS SPREAD OVER TWO PAGES.

THE BOOK IS THE RESULT OF 30 YEARS' STUDY OF "DISPENSATIONAL TRUTH." IT IS SANE. NOT A "TIME-SETTER." CONTAINS NO SPECULATIVE MATTER. IS NOT MADE UP OF QUOTATIONS FROM OTHER WRITERS, BUT IS BASED SOLELY ON THE SCRIPTURES FROM THE "FUTURIST" STANDPOINT. IT IS OF PERMANENT VALUE, AND WILL BE A STANDARD AUTHORITY ON "DISPENSATIONAL TRUTH," AND IS A MINE OF INFORMATION ON "PROPHETIC TRUTH" FOR THE BUSY PASTOR, EVANGELIST, BIBLE TEACHER, AND ALL LOVERS OF THE WORD.

DANIEL 2: 31-45

Cloth Bound — Price Postpaid $5.00

DANIEL 2: 31-45

Figure 4: Larkin Charts Advertisement

So-called Larkin Charts, named for their author, Clarence Larkin, were used to help students properly interpret the Bible according to "dispensational truth."
(Source: *The King's Business*, February 1922, advertisement.)

Dispensationalism was, by its nature, a theology that depended on the "big picture" view of the Bible. Its complex scheme of dispensations, each of which was characterized by a distinctive test of human obedience, required a considerable grasp of the entire Bible in order to fit the pieces of the divine puzzle together. No wonder then, that Bible school students often memorized detailed charts of God's redemptive plan in order to "rightly divide the word of truth." Scofield's innovating introduction of marginal Bible notes became a sacrosanct guide for fundamentalist Bible readers. With Scofield's assistance, textual ambiguities

November 1920, 1016–1017, and W. H. Griffith Thomas, "Some Tests of Old Testament Criticism," *The King's Business*, January 1918, 12, also cited by Szasz in *Divided Mind*, 40.

could often be explained by placing every Bible event in its proper dispensation. Finally, for the diligent Bible student, using the right method was almost next to godliness.[65]

Virginia Brereton has made particular note of the emphasis that Bible school leaders gave to "whole Bible study," so much so, that such language in catalogs and advertising brochures became a buzz word of dispensationalism. Thus, when Torrey first came to Biola in 1913, a writer introduced his whole book approach in bold print: "He believes the whole book is inspired of God and he knows the whole Book as few living men know it."[66] Torrey's "whole book" approach included a comprehensive and systematic inductive study of Bible doctrine, and a general survey of all the books of the Bible. But several other Bible school leaders developed their own whole book methods. James Gray, for example, made a virtual career of his "Synthetic Method" and Biola touted a "Telescopic Method" that would "give the student a mental vision of the whole Bible."[67] Moreover, an emphasis on the whole Bible countered the tendency of liberals to emphasize one part of scripture over another, such as the Sermon on the Mount or the Lord's Prayer. No part of scripture could be ignored, for the whole Bible, even its mundane or obscure portions, bore the potential for some revelatory significance, if only seen in the correct light of interpretation.[68]

Ironically, however, the multiplication of Bible study methods showed that the English Bible was not always as easy to understand for the "common man" as their populist rhetoric implied. Moreover, when Bible school leaders added to this difficulty the finely tuned distinctions of dispensationalism, the task of reading the English Bible seemed more daunting than ever. A tension emerged, therefore, between the populist democratic instincts of Bible school leaders, and their tendency to make the Bible so complex that the "common man" was not very likely to understand it without help from Scofield's notes, special charts and diagrams, and the correct method of study.[69]

It is doubtful that dispensationalism contributed much of anything to the early emphasis on practical training for evangelism, other than pro-

---

[65] Timothy Weber, "The Two-Edged Sword: The Fundamentalist Use of the Bible," in *The Bible in America: Essays in Cultural History,* ed. Nathan O. Hatch and Mark A. Noll (New York: Oxford, 1982), 112.

[66] "Our New Dean," *The King's Business,* August–September 1911, 173; for the "whole book" emphasis see Brereton, *Training God's Army,* 87–88; also see Weber, "Two-Edged Sword," 114.

[67] *Bible Institute of Los Angeles, Bulletin,* October 1920, 70.

[68] Weber, "Two-Edged Sword," 106–10.

[69] Ibid., 114; also Kraus, *Dispensationalism in America,* 75; also see the criticisms along these lines in James Barr, *Fundamentalism* (London: SCM Press Ltd., 1977), 37, 195.

viding a rationale for the peculiar interest of fundamentalists in Zionism and Jewish missions.[70] To the contrary, the scholastic style of dispensationalism seemed better adapted to classroom lectures than practical methods training, and for this reason, it persisted in the curriculum long after personal worker training was abandoned. Moreover, dispensationalism had not been a very important reason for the founding of the first Bible schools. Not until Scofield's Bible in 1909 was there a popular standard of dispensational interpretation. Once wrought, however, it quickly became identified with American Bible schools. At Biola, unlike Moody Bible Institute, dispensationalism was an important reason for its founding.

Lyman Stewart, for example, had expressed frustration at the paucity of dispensational teaching in Los Angeles. Once, in an effort to influence the Bible teaching at Occidental College, Stewart sent a class syllabus of Scofield's "the Kingdom in Scripture" to an Occidental Bible teacher, Lorin Handley. To his dismay, however, Stewart received a mild rebuff from Handley: Scofield's "divisions are artificial," he wrote, "and some of his notions are arbitrary and unnatural."[71] Needless to say, Handley did not long remain a Bible teacher at Occidental! By this time, however, Stewart was already promoting Scofield's dispensational views at Biola with the help of Horton, a former associate of Scofield. For Horton, as for Stewart, the teaching of dispensational views was a major reason for starting Biola: "The need is now so definite for instruction along dispensational lines," he stated, "that I want to give it out."[72] Hence, from its beginning, Biola was characterized by a profound commitment to dispensationalism.

Another important facet of Bible knowledge at Biola was its "scientific" character. Perhaps to counter the impression that they were against science, fundamentalists often emphasized that their study methods were scientific, a claim which Reuben Torrey emphasized more than most. Torrey argued that his method was scientific because it was inductive: every doctrine is derived from the raw data of scripture, stated in succinct propositions and arranged in a systematic manner.[73]

In what sense was Torrey's method "scientific"? Scholars have argued in recent years that fundamentalism preserved an earlier tradition

---

[70] Cf. Ruth Mouly and Roland Robertson, "Zionism in American Premillenarian Fundamentalism," *American Journal of Theological Philosophy* 5 (September 1983): 98–102; and David A. Rausch, *Zionism Within Early American Fundamentalism, 1878–1918: A Convergence of Two Traditions* (New York: Edwin Mellen Press, 1979).

[71] Lorin Handley to Lyman Stewart, 23 September 1909, Lyman Stewart Papers.

[72] Quoted in Henry, Biola Manuscript, 41.

[73] *Biola Bulletin,* October 1920, 23.

of science based on Baconian principles of observation and classification, and Scottish Common Sense Realism, which affirmed the ability of the mind to apprehend reality directly and intuitively.[74] Torrey's method affords further evidence for this argument. Torrey believed that his method was scientific because it was based on the observation and systematic classification of Biblical "facts." When Torrey combined these discrete "facts" according to their content they yielded a proposition, which Torrey believed neither added to nor detracted from the texts themselves. In the classroom process, students were expected to know these propositions, and apply them as the fundamental principles of a "biblical science."

Torrey's method, however, did not always match his rhetoric. First, he insisted that his propositions contained only what is in the scriptures, but his orderly arrangement of propositions showed more dependence on traditional theological categories. When, for example, Torrey noted that God is love, and that "love is the essence of God's moral nature," it is certainly questionable, if not dubious, to claim that the latter idea is wholly contained in the former.[75] Second, it is difficult to see just how Torrey himself could avoid the charge of "proof-texting," because his method simply culled verses from the Bible with almost no regard for their literary or historical context. Finally, his inductive method was not self-critical. Rather, Torrey read the Bible as though it were a collection of data to be classified, after the fashion of a Baconian science, in ignorance of the assumptions which underlay his interpretation and selection of the biblical texts themselves.

Torrey's rigid uncritical method of extracting "Bible doctrines" from a scripture text was matched by an equally rigid emphasis on rote learning by memorization. Indeed, in the conservative ethos of a Bible school classroom there was little room for divergence of opinion, even less allowance for self-discovery.[76] Torrey's teaching method relied heavily on the student's ability to memorize and recite numerous propositions. One student remembered an experience in Torrey's class vividly:

---

[74] George M. Marsden, "Understanding Fundamentalist Views of Science," in *Science and Creationism,* ed. Ashley Montagu (New York: Oxford University Press, 1984), 97–100; for the 19th century background see Dwight Bozeman, *Protestants in an Age of Science: The Baconian Ideal and Antebellum American Religious Thought* (Chapel Hill: University of North Carolina Press, 1977).

[75] Reuben A. Torrey, *What the Bible Teaches* (New York: Fleming H. Revell Co., 1898), 42. Cf. Weber, "Two-Edged Sword," 110.

[76] Richard Dugan, "The Theory of Education Within the Bible Institute Movement at Selected Critical Times" (Ph.D. diss., New York University, 1977), 84.

Oi Ying had been called upon to recite in this class. At first she had been terribly frightened. Dr. Torrey had called suddenly, "Mrs. Wu, you may give the sixth proposition please." That had been a most unhappy experience.[77]

Although Torrey's stern and formal personality may well have influenced his choice of teaching methods, not all the instruction at Biola can be judged by a single approach. Actually, Torrey's style was probably an exception, because his reputation for formality and stern discipline was well known in contrast, perhaps, to the less formal style of T. C. Horton, who was often called "Daddy Horton" by the students. Nevertheless, most instruction consisted in routine memorization of principles and facts.

Figure 5: Photograph of Reuben Torrey

Reuben Archer Torrey was a principal architect of the Bible Institute curriculum. (Source: *The King's Business,* January 1929, p. 10.)

---

[77] "A Day in a Bible Institute," *The King's Business,* September 1921, 886.

Use of the Bible

Just as Bible schools upheld a distinctive approach to Bible knowledge, so too they developed a distinctive approach toward its use. Use of the Bible, in fact, was the self-conscious goal of Bible school teachers, who typically had little time or inclination to contemplate problems of a theoretical nature. For one student at Biola, the principles he learned in his Bible classes provided a specific plan for evangelistic outreach to seamen at the docks. First, when he boarded the ship against the demands of a dock foreman, this illustrated the principle of resisting the devil. Next, after boarding the ship his prayers for wisdom illustrated the principle of seeking God's guidance in every situation. Finally, having received guidance, he then led the ship's wireless operator to a decision for Christ, which illustrated the principle of sharing the gospel and asking for a decision.[78]

To learn to apply biblical principles, Biola required students to engage in some form of personal work or missions outreach. Ministry opportunities were abundant: teaching Sunday school, conducting home visits, preaching in missions or on street corners, distributing religious literature, relief work for indigents, visiting prisoners—these were only a few of the diverse ministries in which Biola students learned needed Bible skills. Far more than simply an educational institution, Biola maintained many programs of outreach, with an array of staff leaders to coordinate the activities of all the personal workers. Monthly reports occurred in *The King's Business* on the outreach to Mexicans, Jews, workers in the "car barns" and factories of Los Angeles, workers on the California Aqueduct, and to workers in the oil fields. Bible schools regularly published the number of meetings held, the number of tracts distributed, the number of sermons preached, the number of classes started, and the number of conversions registered. The recording of these statistics indicates not only the importance of practical work to the ideal of Bible school training, but also the businesslike pragmatism of Bible school leaders.

Just as Torrey's classes were the foundation course for training in the "knowledge of the English Bible," T. C. Horton's course on "the use of the Bible in personal work" formed the basis of practical training in the classroom. To help students learn the skills needed for personal evangelism, Horton wrote a training manual, which, like Torrey's approach, revealed a penchant for the systematic classification of facts. The first section gave in barest outline only the facts of theology which every worker must know. Unlike Torrey, Horton filled out his guide with many observations gained from personal experience. Hence, he listed sixteen reasons why Christians should be busy soul-winning, and twelve

---

[78] "The Harbor Work for Seamen," *The King's Business*, January 1914, 51.

useful tips for personal workers, such as don't put things off, and don't believe everything your told.[79]

Although Horton's course was a simplistic and formalized approach to "personal work," to the average student, many with no more than a common school education, his lessons provided valuable skills and useful information that enabled students to become acculturated to the ethos and requirements of polite society. Nothing seemed too mundane to address, from the personal appearance of a Christian worker to rules of etiquette and polite speech. For example, one former student recalled that she was gently corrected for using the word "lousy," because this was not a proper word for ladies to use.[80] In Horton's classes, many students first learned how to write a sermon and how to deliver a personal testimony. Consequently, interpersonal communication skills were acquired, which helped many students to advance their positions in society, either through religious work or secular employment. Leadership skills were also acquired by learning how to effectively organize groups. In addition to Horton's classes, other practical work classes provided training in methods of city and foreign missions work, teacher training, and organizing a Sunday school program for the local church. Thus, for some students, a Bible school provided basic skills useful for social and educational advancement.[81]

Transforming Ideals

From its founding in 1908 through World War I, Biola grew rapidly. In 1908 there were thirty five regular students, meeting in rented facilities with very meager resources. By the end of 1918, however, there were over two hundred and sixty-five students enrolled in day classes, and almost two hundred students enrolled in the evening school.[82] The rapid growth of the school brought new challenges and new opportunities. After the war, Biola sought to broaden its base even further by developing additional programs and upgrading some of its curriculum. But these developments raised new questions about the role of a Bible school. Should it train pastors? Should it upgrade its status to collegiate rank? And what was its primary purpose, to train students or to be an

---

[79] Thomas C. Horton, *Personal and Practical Christian Work* (Los Angeles: Biola Book Room, 1922), 28–29, 34.

[80] Rebecca Fuller, Interview by Author, 15 June 1991, Sepulveda, CA.

[81] See, for example, the influence of Biola on Virginia Draper, who founded the Draper Women's Clothing Stores: Virginia Draper and Jesse Heath McClendon, *Virginia Draper: An Autobiography* (Pasadena: Welsh Graphics, 1977), 44–50.

[82] "Bible Institute Happenings," *The King's Business,* December 1918, 1041, and "Bible Institute Happenings," December 1919, 1108.

evangelistic organizing society? These questions of self-understanding gradually became the subject of self-conscious reflection after the war. Some Bible school leaders supported changes which seemed to alter some of the basic principles of the early Bible school idea, while others, looking back nostalgically on the early ideals of Bible schools, opposed efforts to modernize or expand the traditional role of the Bible school. This division of opinion, however, did not openly surface at Biola until around 1925, when John M. MacInnis became dean and inaugurated an administration that some believed contradicted the basic ideals of a Bible school education.

CHAPTER 4

John Murdoch MacInnis and the Transformation of the Bible Institute Ideal, 1919–1929

It is usually a risky business to divide the flow of events into distinct periods, because doing so may exaggerate a supposed discontinuity between two spans of time, which participants themselves would hardly have noticed. Yet there seems to be some justification for making a distinction between the period of Biola's early growth years, when the Bible school idea held greatest sway over the programs and policies of the institute, and the period after the first world war. when changes in the curriculum and changing social realities began to threaten the early ideals of Bible school training.

It is relatively easy to fix the end of this period at 1929. There are at least two reasons. First, the second administration of the school, that of John MacInnis, ended December 31, 1928. His three and a half years represented a controversial period in the school's history, during which basic issues about the purposes of a Bible school were contested. Second, after his departure, a serious organizational and financial crisis ensued, which threatened the Bible institute's future viability. While Biola struggled to save itself from ruin, and economic depression overtook the nation, a new atmosphere of hardship and severity filled the air. Some of Biola's programs were cut back or eliminated, personnel were laid off, and the earlier period of financial prosperity was all but forgotten. The new economic reality forced Biola to examine its purpose, and when it finally emerged from the 1930s still in tact, the old vision of the Bible school, dedicated to training lay Christian workers, was not resurrected. In its place there stood a new goal of Christian liberal arts education. Thus, a changed set of social circumstances serves to distinguish the period of Biola's relative stability in the 1920s from the beleaguerment of the post-1929 era of severe financial crisis and organizational instability.

The beginning of this period of changing educational ideals may be set roughly around 1919, when Bible school leaders began a nationwide effort to coordinate and upgrade Bible school curricula and policies. But perhaps even more significant for Biola itself was the burning of its mortgage on November 30, 1919—an act which symbolized the strength and success of the new Bible school, then hardly more than ten years old.[1] That action seemed to presage the general mood of optimism and economic prosperity that swept the nation in the era of the "roaring twenties" and presents a striking symbolic contrast to the near financial collapse that came ten years later. During this period, it seems that Biola achieved a relatively stable enrollment as well as a general feeling of leadership and prestige among Bible schools, rivaled, perhaps, only by the Moody Bible Institute.

No less important to the character of this period, and its impact on the Bible schools, were the social changes taking place after the war. Even if one doubts Frederick Lewis Allen's observation that the post-war decade owed much of its character to habits of war-time thinking, it has often been stated that a new national temper emerged during the 1920s.[2] The end of the war meant that over three million military personnel would be returning to civilian life, and Bible school leaders eagerly planned to enroll some of them. On another front, ratification of the 18th Amendment on January 29, 1919, gave hope to many evangelical temperance supporters, like those at Biola, that the fight for public morals in America was not lost. Yet within two years of that victory, Biola leaders had seemingly given up any crusades for civic righteousness, focusing instead on problems of personal morality, anti-modernism, and anti-evolutionism.

Changing manners and morals also presented new challenges for Bible schools. While many Americans were fretting about the youth crisis, leaders at Biola believed along with most Protestants that they were safeguarding a Christian culture, in contrast to the new rising secular culture of jazz, movies, dancing, flappers, cigarettes, and loose morals.[3] In Southern California, as in other urban areas, the social and religious landscape was transformed by the automobile.[4] For the first time people

---

[1] *The King's Business,* January 1920, 26.

[2] Allen, *Only Yesterday,* 20; William E. Leuchtenburg, *The Perils of Prosperity, 1914–32* (Chicago: University of Chicago Press, 1958), 267–69.

[3] For the reaction of religious leaders to changing social mores in the twenties see Mary Patricia Thaman, *Manners and Morals of the 1920s: A Survey of the Religious Press* (New York: Bookman Assoc., 1954).

[4] Robert M. Fogelson, *The Fragmented Metropolis: Los Angeles, 1850–1930* (Cambridge: Harvard University Press, 1967), 147–48; James J. Coale, "Influence of the Automobile on the City Church," in *The Automobile: Its Province and Its Problems,* ed. Clyde L. King, Annals of the American Academy of Political and Social Science 116 (Philadelphia: American Academy of Political and Social Science, 1924), 81.

began to live in suburbs and travel to the city for work and entertainment. This situation contributed to the rise of the large downtown metropolitan church, which drew its membership partly from residents of suburban communities. Biola was closely associated with a church of this kind, the Church of the Open Door. Another development that transformed the older local culture was the development of radio. Biola was among the first to begin broadcasting sermons and radio Bible classes, giving the school a wider voice throughout metropolitan Los Angeles.

Hence, a new self-consciousness emerged in the twenties. At Biola the early days of the school could be remembered almost nostalgically as a time of growing pains, finally overcome with the burning of the mortgage in 1919. The old gospel wagons now seemed old-fashioned next to the modern gospel cars of the 1920s. New buildings and furnished dormitories, advertised with "all of the modern conveniences" contrasted sharply with the first rooms that Biola rented in 1908. Indeed, probably no other aspect of Biola's beginnings better symbolized the changed ethos of 1920 than the frequently told story that Biola had begun in a rented room that was once used as a poolhall. Here were all the elements of a growing mythic tradition: where once there was a poolhall, a symbol of modern urban iniquity, there now was a Bible institute, which soon grew to occupy most of a city block with an imposing edifice, and a veritable army of soul savers, fighting back the evils of modern life.[5]

Figure 6: A "Gospel Car" of the 1920s
(Source: *The King's Business,* December 1926, p. 715.)

---

[5] For an example of nostalgic reminiscence, in which a student describes the old leaky building on Main Street, where students kept warm by a wood-burning stove, see the *Biolan,* 1927, 50, Biola University Archives, La Mirada, CA.

Curriculum Transformation at
the Bible Institute of Los Angeles

The primary idea that determined the extent and limits of Bible school training was the Bible ideal. The Bible ideal was most frequently an implicit, self-defining assumption, but explicitly stated, it was the idea that the entire Bible school curriculum was based on study of the Bible, with a view to using the Bible in Christian work.[6] This ideal served to limit the growth of a Bible school curriculum by excluding courses of instruction that were not based on the Bible, or that did not contribute to the use of the Bible in evangelism. On a few occasions, especially after the Bible ideal began to decline in the 1920s, Biola leaders could defensively claim that their school taught the Bible alone. But these assertions were largely rhetorical, drawing upon the early ideals of Bible training. In reality, the growth and success of Bible schools in America, and changing social realities, were forcing Bible schools to move beyond that earlier idealism to embrace a wider vision of education.

How the Bible Ideal Functioned
to Limit Curricular Change

That which unified the Bible school curriculum, in the rhetoric of early Bible school leaders, was not the broad goal of character development, which inspired 19th century college teachers, nor was it, strictly speaking, the goal of Bible schools to develop in students a "biblical worldview," as interpreters of the later Bible college movement have assumed, if one means by the term "worldview" a comprehensive perspective on the arts, sciences, and culture.[7] Rather, Bible schools developed a narrow vision of education based solely on teaching the Bible. In theory, the entire curriculum was based simply on the Bible itself— practical methods and Bible doctrines were assumed to be taken directly from scripture in the form of classified facts and principles. Reuben Torrey, for example, boasted in the school's bulletin that the Bible was Biola's only text book.[8] In a similar vein, when the *Christian Century*

---

[6] For clear statements of this ideal see these editorials: "Why a Bible Institute?" *The King's Business,* October 1919, 899, and "News For the New Year," January 1923, 4.

[7] For the 19th century college ideal, see William C. Ringenberg, *The Christian College: A History of Protestant Higher Education in America* (Grand Rapids: Eerdmans, 1984), 60, 66; for a misapplication of the later Bible college ideal of "biblical worldview" to early Bible school training see Frank Gaebelein, *Christian Education in a Democracy: The Report of the N.A.E. Committee* (New York: Oxford University Press, 1951), 178.

[8] *Biola Bulletin,* October, 1920, 23.

attacked Bible schools for giving short courses in biblical proof texts, T. C. Horton responded with smug satisfaction that Bible schools did teach the Bible only:

> The Bible Institute of Los Angeles has not changed its standards, but confesses with real satisfaction that it does teach "just the Bible." Neither do these Institutes give merely "short courses in proof texts," but a two or three years' course in the Bible only.[9]

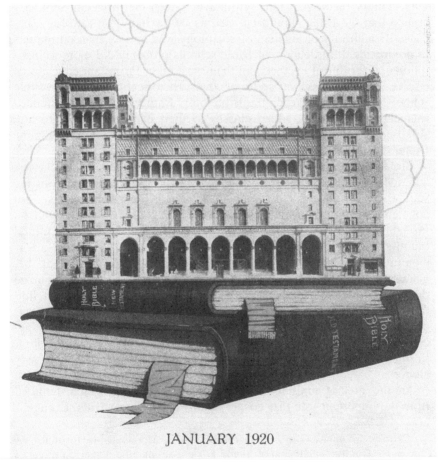

JANUARY 1920

Figure 7: Picture of Biola on the Bible

This picture, which appeared frequently in *The King's Business,* illustrates the idea that the curriculum would be based on the Bible alone.
(Source: *The King's Business,* January 1920, cover.)

---

[9] T. C. Horton, "Bothering the Brethren," *The King's Business,* May 1921, 423.

Statements of teaching the Bible only, while mostly rhetorical, gave leaders a criterion by which to limit the types of classes that a Bible school could offer, and also served to distinguish the Bible school's educational goals from other similar institutions, such as Gordon Bible College, which by 1918 was moving away from the Bible school ideal as Torrey perceived it.[10]

Bible school leaders were not the only evangelical Protestants to adopt such a biblical reductionism. Even a literate and well educated 19th century theologian like William B. Green of Princeton Seminary argued that the Bible should be used as the textbook of sociology, because its authority on matters of sociology was no less than on matters of dogmatics.[11] But leaders of Bible schools probably did more to institutionalize a biblical exclusivism than most other Protestant educational efforts. Nevertheless, in spite of their rhetorical aspirations, Bible schools did not really teach the Bible only. Rather, as they experienced financial growth, they added classes to their curricula that were not, strictly speaking, either studies of the Bible nor exclusively based on the Bible.

Biola, for example, began by offering only two main Bible classes, and special lectures on other biblical topics. But practically from the start, Biola introduced classes that were not Bible classes, per se, but augmented various aspects of practical worker training and evangelism. Probably the auxiliary course work most required was cross-cultural training for foreign missions. The first Biola student to become a foreign missionary departed for China in 1911, and thereafter students began entering foreign mission fields in great numbers.[12] Biola recognized that the cultural barriers faced by missionaries were significant hindrances to their success, and so in 1910 a class in foreign missions was offered, which studied "the great world fields and their needs," acquainting the student with countries, peoples, customs, and religions.[13] In this way, students received a broader training than just Bible study alone.

Another area of auxiliary growth was music training, which stemmed from the important role that gospel hymns played in revivals. Evangeli-

---

[10] Torrey to James Gray, 11 December 1918, Moody Bible Institute Archives; for Gordon's inclusion of liberal arts classes and the perceived threat of these to the Bible ideal see Brereton, "Bible Schools and Conservative Evangelical Higher Education," 119–20, and *Training God's Army,* 68, 103–5.

[11] Gary Scott Smith, "Conservative Presbyterians: The Gospel, Social Reform, and the Church in the Progressive Era," *American Presbyterians: Journal of Presbyterian History* 70 (Summer 1992): 103.

[12] "The Story of the School," *The King's Business,* June 1911, 119.

[13] "A Short Story of the Los Angeles Bible Institute," *The King's Business,* November 1910, 171.

cals since the early revivals of Moody had learned that simple gospel tunes were vital to a successful revival.[14] Hence, Moody himself had insisted on making gospel music part of the Bible school curriculum. At Biola, training in gospel music had entered the curriculum at least by 1912, in a class where students learned about "rudiments of music, the reading at sight of Gospel hymns, and their proper rendition."[15]

Following the pragmatic inclinations of Moody, who cared little about the aesthetic value of a piece of music, Biola leaders made clear the auxiliary purpose of music instruction. Students should not attend Biola for the intent of learning music alone—the primary purpose of every student was training in the Bible. The goal of the music course was: "To give the students such a working knowledge of music as will enable them to use this powerful agency in spreading the Gospel message."[16] Years later, this was put more directly:

> While the Institute music course prepares students for the work of the singing evangelist, it is not intended for any one who simply wishes education in music. The music work of the Institute is always made subordinate to the study of the Bible, and music is taught only as a means of qualifying one for more effective soul-winning service.[17]

Here the auxiliary purpose of music instruction was even more explicit. This pragmatism was so deeply a part of the Bible school psyche that, when Biola acquired chimes in 1919, some people worried that they would detract from the purpose of saving souls. To mitigate these worries, leaders published an account of how several people after hearing the chimes were actually led to salvation![18]

A third area of auxiliary growth came through the avenue of methods training. Horton's classes, although filled with personal anecdotes and bits of sage advise, still emphasized the Bible as the source for practical methods of evangelism. Bible instructors never tired of saying that Jesus demonstrated the best methods of teaching, or that Paul utilized the best methods of saving souls. But the need for better training led to the in-

---

[14] Sandra Sizer, *Gospel Hymns and Social Religion: The Rhetoric of Nineteenth-Century Revivalism* (Philadelphia: Temple University Press, 1978), 3–8: Findlay, *Dwight L. Moody*, 210–17; Weisberger, *They Gathered at the River*, 125, 148, 198.

[15] "The Work Within the Institute," 117.

[16] Catalogue of The Bible Institute of Los Angeles, [1913], 32; for Moody's lack of aesthetic music interest see Darrel M. Robertson, *The Chicago Revival, 1876: Society and Revivalism in a Nineteenth-Century City* (Metuchen: Scarecrow Press, 1989), 184, n. 32.

[17] *Biola Bulletin,* October 1920, 17.

[18] "Notes From the Bells," *The King's Business,* March 1919, 213–14.

clusion of methods classes which were not strictly based on so-called "Bible methods," but on the social sciences. In 1913, for example, Biola provided a teacher training course that was described as "a normal training class in which the students are taught the principles of teaching."[19] The normal schools had contributed to the rise of education as a profession, and by the 20th century teacher training was a well established part of American higher education.[20] Of course, Biola's class was intended to train Sunday school teachers, but the new expanding studies in social and educational methods could be adapted to the Bible ideal, if they contributed to the task of evangelism.

These areas of curriculum growth eventually developed into separate courses of study, allowing students to specialize in one area. By 1920, four courses were offered: the Regular Course, which emphasized Bible study, the Missions Course, the Music Course, and the Sunday School course. Although students could still complete the program in two years, they could now take a greater proportion of their studies in subjects other than Bible study alone. In spite of this growth, however, the curriculum still lay within the informal constraints of the Bible ideal.

Broadening the Vision of Bible School Training

As the world war in Europe was ending, Bible school leaders began to agitate for changes in the curriculum. There were several reasons. First, the explosive growth of high school education in America forced Bible schools to improve their educational standards. Between 1890 and 1930, as American Bible schools grew dramatically, the educational landscape also changed. The high school, for example, which had enrolled only about 200,000 students in 1890, moved from a peripheral role in society to an institution of huge social significance, in which 47 percent of teenage youths, or 4.4 million students in 1930 attended high school. Increasing literacy, therefore, became a principal factor motivating Bible schools to upgrade their curriculum to a level of post-high school education.[21]

A second factor, which may well have led Bible school leaders to muse about their unique brand of education, was a perception that revivalism was waning since 1910. As Torrey and James Gray discussed

---

[19] Catalogue of The Bible Institute of Los Angeles, [1913], 32.

[20] Lawrence Cremin, *American Education: The Metropolitan Experience, 1876–1980* (New York: Harper & Row, 1988), 498; Brereton, *Training God's Army*, 156–58.

[21] Cremin, *American Education*, 97–99; Joel H. Spring, *The American School, 1642–1985: Varieties of Historical Interpretation of the Foundations and Development of American Education* (New York: Longman, 1986), 194.

the issue of adding a third year of study to the institute curriculum, they agreed that a declining number of evangelists also made training in revival methods less exigent. A pensive Torrey blamed the decline on the rise of liberalism and the Men and Religion Forward Movement, but most interesting was his suggestion that the histrionic methods of Billy Sunday drew potential audiences away from more traditional evangelists. Whether or not Torrey's assessment was accurate, he nevertheless realized that a decline of revivalism would severely impact the future shape of Bible school training.[22]

The primary impetus for change, however, came from the decision of some Bible school leaders to add an additional year of study for pastors. The first rumblings of this change began not long after World War I, when James Gray of the Moody Bible Institute appointed a committee to recommend that Bible schools implement common educational standards.[23] Among the issues broached was how to coordinate Bible school programs and policies, the need to upgrade the level of instruction for Bible students, and the need to openly acknowledge that many students in Bible schools were preparing for pastoral ministry and, therefore, to make this an explicit goal. Some Bible schools had already taken the step of explicitly training pastors—the Northwestern Bible School, for example, which was founded by W. B. Riley in 1901.[24] But for the majority of Bible institutes, introducing a third year of study threatened the ideal of lay Christian worker training. Charily aware of this problem, leaders continued to uphold the Bible school ideal, but gradually they also started to assert that the Bible school could offer a slightly broader Christian education, wherein some classes would not be based on the Bible, such as the distinctly non-practical subjects of biblical languages, Christian history and philosophy, psychology and sociology.

When Torrey and Gray first began discussing the possibility of adding a theological course to the Bible school curriculum, they both were somewhat reluctant to do so, for fear that such a change would alienate mainline church leaders. Gray wrote to Torrey expressing his reticence to add the theological course in late 1919, but he acknowledged that they would soon have to do it, else the Riley "fundamentals propaganda" would lead other schools to it first. In spite of considerable dis-

---

[22] For Torrey's perception of a decline of revivalism see Torrey to James Gray, 2 June 1921, Moody Bible Institute Archives.

[23] *The King's Business*, May 1919, 412; *God Hath Spoken: Twenty-Five Addresses Delivered at the World Conference on Christian Fundamentals*, May 25 to June 1, 1919 (Philadelphia: Bible Conference Committee, 1919), 18–19; Gray to Torrey, 27 February 1919, and Torrey to Gray, 13 November 1919, Moody Bible Institute Archives.

[24] Trollinger, *God's Empire*, 92.

cussion about the matter, however, both Gray and Torrey waited until mid-1921 to implement the new course.[25]

Not unexpectedly, church leaders did notice the change. Though early soundings from several leading ministers of Chicago, including John Timothy Stone, who later became president of McCormick Theological Seminary, made Gray optimistic that a theological course would not rankle mainline churches, many clergy did object. Cleland McAfee, a professor at McCormick Seminary, penned his objections in an article in the *Christian Century*. Arguing that the Bible school's were ill-equipped to train students for the ministry, and that a proposal to do so would be impertinent, McAfee claimed to have the support of a majority of denominational ministers. From another quarter, however, a son of Dwight L. Moody also opposed the change. Following the addition of a third year at Moody, Will Moody requested that the institute cease using the Moody name, because by training ministers they had abandoned his father's ideals of lay Bible training.[26]

Hints of the new curriculum began to appear in 1920, when Biola gave a distinct class in church history. Church history was not easily explained in terms of the Bible school ideal. It was not Bible study, and it did not seem to augment the practical goals of training efficient personal workers. Moreover, strong biblicist and restorationist inclinations of Bible school fundamentalists often fostered the view that church history was of little value, being a record of the downward spiral of a corrupt church. Consequently, Biola leaders felt a need to explain how church history could be an appropriate subject for the Bible student.

> While the Bible is the only text book in the Bible Institute, yet a knowledge of the results of Bible teaching in the history of the church, and of the doctrines that have been taught, and the controversies that have taken place, and the declines and revivals that have occurred in the history of the church, is of great value.[27]

Explicitly relating it to the Bible ideal, church history could now find

---

[25] For the "Riley fundamentals propaganda" see Gray to Torrey, 19 November 1919; for the decision to add the theological course see Torrey to Gray, 25 May 1921, and Gray to Torrey, 28 June 1921, Moody Bible Institute Archives.

[26] For the support of Stone and others, see Gray to Torrey, 28 June 1921; for Will Moody's position see Torrey to Gray, 22 August 1922, Moody Bible Institute Archives; for McAfee's view see Cleland Boyd McAfee, "The Presbyterian Church Facing the Future," *Christian Century*, 9 November 1922, 1385–88; also see McAfee to MacInnis, 12 December 1922, MacInnis Papers; for notice of a third year course see "Moody Institute Now Offers Full Theological Course," *Christian Century*, 30 August 1923, 1115.

[27] *Biola Bulletin*, October 1920, 34.

a useful place in the curriculum as "the results of Bible teaching in the history of the church." A similar tension was also evident in the catalog's description of psychology, which had not yet become an independent class, but was still treated as a subsidiary topic in Bible classes and personal work classes.

> The best textbook on psychology is the Bible. The Bible sets forth man as he really is, and not as speculative philosophers imagine him to be.[28]

Though it is doubtful that Biola leaders taught psychology as a serious social science, nevertheless, the subject was beginning to gain recognition by Bible school leaders. Yet fundamentalists objected to the new psychology of Freud, which they believed was largely grounded in humanistic assumptions. Even so, they were able to appropriate an earlier tradition of psychology as a "practical science," which could help the student to better understand human nature and, therefore, make the student a more efficient personal worker.[29] This idea was expressed in the course catalog.

> The aim of the Institute is that the men and women who go out from it shall not only know their Bibles, but shall have a thorough, practical, working knowledge of men in their relation to themselves, to one another, to society, to the church, and to God.[30]

Interestingly, a tension between the Bible school ideal and its broader interpretation is hardly noticeable, until one compares this catalog statement with the usual motto, training and use of the Bible. The earliest motto united the study of the Bible with its practical use in personal work. But now, there was a subtle contrast in the catalog's description: not only the Bible, said the catalog's writer, *but also* a "practical, working knowledge of men." From here it was only a short step to teaching psychology as a separate subject, distinct from the Bible classes. But in this slight change of expression, there could be seen the seeds of a broader concept on which to build Biola's curriculum. To paraphrase a

---

[28] Ibid., 33.

[29] For fundamentalist objections to the new psychology, see the editorials: "Shall We Deal with Psychology," *The King's Business,* July 1928, 400–401; Ruby Burgess, "What Behaviorism and Freud Psychology Have Done," *Moody Bible Institute Monthly,* March 1928, 316. For a contemporary observation that prior to 1923, psychology in the church was mainly practical, see Edward L. Schaub, review of *Psychology and the Church,* ed. O. Hardman, in *The Journal of Religion* 6 (1926): 214–16; also cf. Brereton, *Training God's Army,* 103–4.

[30] *Biola Bulletin,* October 1920, 34.

famous saying, Biola would not live by the Bible alone, but by a new
goal of developing in students a Christian worldview.

John Murdoch MacInnis and the New Curriculum

The description of the new three year course added in 1922 extended
and formalized the changes that were taking place in the curriculum at
least since 1920. Much of the curriculum remained the same. For those
taking an additional year of study, however, various subjects were now
to be discussed in greater detail and depth, such as Bible, Bible criticism, Christian evidences, prophecy, and homiletics. Two new classes
for pastoral training were added, the "Work of the Pastor" and advanced
literary English. But the centerpiece of the new curriculum was the addition of an extensive course in the history and philosophy of the Christian religion. To teach this course, Biola enlisted a new faculty member,
John MacInnis.

Biola had first published its three year program in 1921, even though
the faculty was ill-equipped for the new teaching responsibilities. None
was prepared, with the exception of Torrey, to teach church history and
Christian philosophy. Hence, in November 1921, Torrey asked his
friend and longtime associate in the Montrose Bible Conference if he
would consider teaching the new course.[31] Torrey later described his anticipated role on the faculty: "you will be expected to teach Philosophy
of Religion," he said, but this description "is used in a large sense and is
expected to cover the study of Church History, questions of Biblical
Criticism, Christian Evidences, Comparative Religion."[32]

When MacInnis accepted the teaching offer, he had little experience
in education. He was leaving a comfortable and successful pastorate in
upstate New York, for an exciting promise of a second career in teaching at the age of fifty-one. Yet in many ways his temperament was
nicely suited for teaching. He was soft-spoken, scholarly but pious, and
a fit image of gentlemanly taste. He enjoyed learning and took personal
pride in keeping abreast of the latest developments in philosophy,
science, religion, and the social sciences. But he was also well suited for
a Bible school, because he was especially interested in the practical
work of evangelism and lay ministry. His years as a minister and Bible
conference organizer gave him a decidedly practical bent, which fit well
the needs of Biola students. In addition, he understood the Bible school
movement well, because he had been a student at Moody Bible Institute
and also an occasional instructor at the Practical Bible Institute during
his days in Montrose, Pennsylvania.

---

[31] Torrey to MacInnis, 15 November 1921, MacInnis Papers.
[32] Torrey to MacInnis, 13 March 1922, MacInnis Papers.

The 1922 catalog featured MacInnis' course in a prominent three page spread entitled, "A Course in the Philosophy of the Christian Religion."[33] The scope of the course was naively ambitious. In the first year alone, he would lead students through study outlines of Greek philosophy, Roman history and government, the Hebrew and popular religions of the ancient world, the life of Christ, the origin of the church, and the history of the church into the 12th century. In the second year, students would study the reformation, and the third year, the rise of the modern Church, including a study of the "complex and acute problems with which the church is now confronted in its thinking and activities."

Running parallel to this series of history classes, MacInnis would also seek to offer a philosophical interpretation of Christian history, or, in his own words, "to find the source, meaning and significance of the fact of religion as found in the history studies." In the first year:

This will be an endeavor to get a clear idea of the origin and meaning of our world with special regard to the origin, nature and meaning of religion. This will involve the different theories of evolution and the question of the possibility and nature of revelation.[34]

In the second year, MacInnis planned to focus on "Christ as the highest expression of life and the logical key to the final meaning of our world and the supreme authority in religion." This would include study of comparative religion, in order to discover the reason that Christianity is the universal and final religion. Finally, students would finish the third year with problems of supernatural and redemptive religion, including "modern Science, Philosophy and Criticism." Concluding his course description, MacInnis asserted that he would aim to give a true philosophy of religion based on history and human experience.

Therefore, a philosophical interpretation of the Bible as it centers and culminates in Christ involves a comprehensive and scientific interpretation of religion and of the world of which it is an essential part. That is why a course of this kind has a fundamental place in a "Bible Institute" which aims to thoroughly fit men and women to intelligently preach Christ and present His supreme claim to Lordship in life and its affairs.[35]

Here again a shift in language is perceptible. Philosophy was now said to have a "fundamental place" in the Bible school curriculum, as the old ideal of efficient personal workers was being supplemented by the

---

[33] *Biola Bulletin,* October 1922, 30–33.

[34] Ibid., 32.

[35] Ibid., 33.

newer ideal of "intelligently" preaching Christ and his lordship. Ironically, only a few years earlier Lyman Stewart had withdrawn his financial support of an Occidental philosophy instructor because he wanted to commit his resources to training missionaries and Bible workers. But now, philosophy was entering through the front door of Biola itself.[36]

The prominent way that Biola leaders featured the new course quickly linked MacInnis, in many fundamentalist minds, with progressive changes in Biola's educational focus, even though such changes were being arranged and slowly implemented by Torrey since 1919. Similar changes had been taking place at Moody Bible Institute too. Church history, for example, had entered Moody's curriculum in 1915; the third year pastor's course was implemented the same year that MacInnis came to Biola, and philosophy, psychology, and religious education all appeared in the 1924 Moody catalog.[37] But one major difference distinguished the changes at Moody and Biola. Where Biola made a conspicuous feature of the new program and linked it with the arrival of a new teacher, Moody did not highlight the distinctiveness of the changes. For many Biola alumni, therefore, it appeared that MacInnis had initiated radical changes in the ideals of Bible school training.

This perception of change was perhaps reinforced by a different style in the language of Torrey and MacInnis. While both men basked in the rays of "the scientific method," their understanding of it seemed to differ. Where Torrey emphasized finding and ordering biblical facts, MacInnis proposed to ground his philosophy of religion in "history and human experience." Where Torrey could assert that "the only sure and stable philosophy" is "philosophy revealed by an Omniscient God," MacInnis based his philosophy of religion in the "facts of experience."[38]

Another striking difference was the way that MacInnis distinguished between facts and their interpretation. His history course was an "objective" science based on observed facts, while his philosophy classes were a rational interpretation of the facts of history. Torrey's approach, however, tended to make no distinction between facts and their interpretation. He assumed that the Bible was a divine repository of doctrines, called "Bible doctrines," which were not "interpretations" of the Bible, but statements of revealed fact. This distinction was also accentuated by differences in their phraseology. Where Torrey never allowed any uncertainty to color his understanding of truth, as when he promised to

---

[36] Lyman Stewart to John Willis Baer, 21 December 1910, Lyman Stewart Papers.

[37] See the following bulletins of Moody Bible Institute: (1915), p. 24; (1922), p. 16; (1924–1925), pp. 27, 35, 37–38, in the Moody Bible Institute Archives.

[38] *Biola Bulletin,* October 1920, 24, and July 1922, 33.

give his students the "exact meaning" of a biblical text, and an "accurate and thorough knowledge of Bible truth," MacInnis tended to use phrases that conveyed an air of scientific investigation, such as: "we shall endeavor to find the source and meaning" and "we shall consider the validity of its claims." Torrey's distaste of tentative conclusions once led an admiring biographer to dub him, "the Apostle of Certainty," and another to specifically mention his "precise, calculating mind."[39]

But did their differing conceptions of scientific method influence their classroom teaching style? As earlier noted, rote learning, memorization, and intellectual conformity typified much of Bible school classroom learning. As in other classes, MacInnis lectured and students memorized. But his lectures reveal that there was room for some divergence of opinion. Rather than just giving the "correct" answer, MacInnis followed a dialogical and comparative approach to his subject. For example, when discussing the origin of religions, MacInnis presented first the opposing view, that monotheism evolved from a primitive animism, and then presented the arguments for his own view, that the world's religions had been degraded from an original pure religion.[40] He also cited authors of widely divergent perspectives, thus giving the student a broader acquaintance with intellectual life. Noting Albert Schweitzer's study on Christianity and the world's religions, MacInnis commented:

[Schweitzer] said that up to date we looked upon world religions as heathen religion that had nothing much to do with us, and those of us who were very earnest wanted to go to them as missionaries to convert them. He says we cannot do that now because they are being studied from another point of view, and we must seek to learn what they stand for because they are beginning to assert their right to be heard and recognized along certain lines.[41]

On this occasion MacInnis did not refute Schweitzer's contention, but simply noted that although he did not agree with everything that Schweitzer wrote, nevertheless, he had made some valuable contributions. But when he later described Schweitzer as an example of a great religious figure, who as a medical doctor in Africa had explained to an

---

[39] Roger Martin, *R. A, Torrey: Apostle of Certainty* (Murfreesboro, TN: Sword of the Lord Publishers, 1976); also Robert Harkness, *Reuben Archer Torrey: The Man, His Message* (Chicago: The Bible Institute Colportage Association, 1929), 36.

[40] John MacInnis, Lectures on Comparative Religion, TD, 4 March 1924, MacInnis Papers.

[41] Ibid., 29 January 1924.

African native how Jesus Christ saves us from sin and death, his students were probably exposed to a side of Schweitzer that they had never heard. It seems probable, therefore, that the classroom methods of MacInnis encouraged a greater degree of openness to divergent opinions than most Bible school classes in 1922.

Changes in Leadership, 1923–1924

The Passing of the Old Guard

Perhaps if the leadership of Biola had not suddenly changed in 1924, a new curriculum might never have created any problems. The courses which appeared unusual for a Bible school could probably have been assimilated in the growing Bible school tradition with little opposition. But the new courses came just as the founders of Biola were departing the scene. Within a period of sixteen months, Stewart, Torrey, and Horton were gone.

Lyman Stewart died on September 28, 1923. The loss was deeply felt, not only because he was the institute's primary financial benefactor, but also because he was its president and active policy maker. Only ten months later, Reuben Torrey resigned as the school's academic dean. This unexpected loss surprised and shocked many Biola supporters. Although he had become less involved in Biola's day-to-day operations at least two years earlier, his token presence, and his international reputation, gave Biola considerable stature in the eyes of conservative evangelicals.

Although the details of his resignation are uncertain, it is clear that his last few years at the institute were marred by personal difficulties. As early as 1921, Torrey considered resigning because of a strained relationship with Lyman Stewart. Though Stewart persuaded him to stay, personal differences between the two men did not abate.[42] When Stewart died in 1923, personal conflicts between Torrey and Horton, which had been squelched by Stewart's firm hand, now came to the surface.

A leadership conflict had long marred the relationship between Horton and Torrey. As Biola's founder and first superintendent, Horton had enjoyed administrative control of Biola, while Torrey had oversight of the faculty and academic policies. As long as they agreed on matters, they experienced little difficulty. But agreement was not always possible, and these situations led to brooding resentments between the two leaders. One irritant, for instance, occurred when Horton, claiming to be

---

[42] For Torrey's near resignation in 1921 see Torrey to MacInnis, 16 December 1921, MacInnis Papers; for Torrey's testy relations with Stewart see Staggers, "Reuben A. Torrey," 292–98.

short of money, refused to appropriate funds for Torrey's Montrose Ministerial Institute. Torrey was so piqued, that he considered moving the Ministerial Institute to Moody, because Horton had always been "loathe to get money for the Institute."[43]

Another aspect of Torrey's abrupt resignation was his opposition to a healing program. For several years, Lyman Stewart had insisted that Biola's leaders refrain from public criticism of other local ministries, such as Aimee Semple McPherson's Angelus Temple. Although fundamentalists like Torrey and Stewart had no fondness for the flamboyant McPherson and considered her pentecostal teachings of spirit baptism and divine healing with suspicion, Stewart had no desire to waste valuable time in divisive controversies. With his death, however, this policy quickly fell apart. Fundamentalist criticism of McPherson increased dramatically within months of Stewart's death, assisted by Robert Shuler, a local fundamentalist Methodist, who published his attack in a 1924 book titled *McPhersonism*. As fundamentalists around the country also joined the growing chorus of opposition to pentecostalism, Biola's silence began to attract attention.[44]

Although the details of the "healing program" are unknown, it is likely that Torrey's opposition was precipitated by students at Biola, who somehow had been influenced by McPherson's healing services. Contact with Angelus Temple was unavoidable, and some students even attended worship services in the evenings, when divine healing was practiced, even though Biola policy discouraged such student contacts. Only one of Torrey's biographers, Robert Harkness, noted an incident that may have led to Torrey's resignation. Brief and vague in his description, Harkness claimed that a student's participation in a "doubtful religious organization," which according to his earlier article in the *Sunday School Times* was a healing cult, caused a climactic division in the Biola faculty, some defending the dubious organization, and others taking the side of Torrey.[45] If this is the incident that provoked Torrey's

---

[43] Torrey to Gray, 18 March 1924, Moody Bible Institute Archives; the unhappy relations between Horton and Torrey later surfaced in connection with Torrey's death, but Horton himself denied any such discontent in, "An Open Letter to the Members of the Southern California Premillenial Association," Printed Pamphlet [December 1928], MacInnis Papers.

[44] Edith Blumhofer, *Aimee Semple McPherson: Everybody's Sister* (Grand Rapids: Eerdmans, 1993), 223–24, 257.

[45] Harkness, *Reuben Archer Torrey*, 48–49, and "Our Memories of Dr. Torrey as Personal Worker and Evangelist," *The Sunday School Times*, 17 November 1928, 680; for Biola's policy toward Angelus Temple note that students were cautioned not to take part publicly in services at Angelus Temple in the Faculty Minutes, Handwritten Document, 22 April 1925, Biola University Archives.

resignation, it seems that his views were opposed to those of Horton and the Biola board of directors, who chose to continue Stewart's policy of public neutrality. Torrey considered this view an unacceptable compromise, and through his extensive personal contacts, other fundamentalists began to openly criticize Biola's soft approach to pentecostalism. Among these were Cortland Myers, who was an outspoken fundamentalist, and a minister of the Immanuel Baptist Church of Pasadena, California; William P. White, connected with Moody Bible Institute; A. C. Gaebelein, fundamentalist editor of *Our Hope,* and French Oliver, a local militant fundamentalist evangelist. Horton's position on this matter caused a breach of relations between Biola and each of these individuals, which a few years later was still spoiling relations with Biola's fundamentalist friends.[46]

In response to increasing fundamentalist pressures, Biola finally chose to publicly declare its opposition to pentecostalism in a resolution passed on September 30, 1924. This broad statement was later deemed insufficient by some local Presbyterian fundamentalists, however, and so, deferring to their wishes, Biola reluctantly agreed to identify McPhersonism in their negations of pentecostalism, over the objections of Horton and a small contingent of the board. Seeing no other option, and feeling dejected by the board's resolution, Horton submitted his resignation, effective January 1, 1925, though he chose to continue as editor of *The King's Business.*[47]

A final aspect of Torrey's resignation may have been prompted by the developing academic orientation of the institute. Another Torrey biographer emphasized this point:

> . . . the fact that a majority of the administrators favored the expanding of the curriculum in the direction of a college or seminary, was to affect the future ministry of Dr. Torrey at the Institute. Dr. Torrey, with a firm conviction instilled by Moody, felt the need for a strictly *Bible* institute to meet a special need. Others in the administration felt that more could be accomplished with a liberal arts curriculum.[48]

---

[46] Henry, Biola Manuscript, 66–69. Note, however, that Henry incorrectly places the controversy over McPherson in early 1925.

[47] For fundamentalist pressures see the minutes of the Biola Board of Directors (hereafter Board Minutes); for Cortland Myers, 4 April 1924; for Walter E. Edmonds, H. N. Bunce, and Stewart MacLennan, 7 November 1924; for MacLennan, Torrey, Gaebelein, Pettinghill, and Gray, 24 November 1924; for the board's anti-pentecostal resolution see Board Minutes, 30 September 1924 and 7 November 1924, located in the Biola president's office, Biola University, La Mirada, CA; for the final published resolution see "Directors Statement," *The King's Business,* January 1925, 6.

[48] Martin, *Apostle of Certainty,* 248.

Oddly, no other biographers have corroborated Martin's assertion, and Stagger's recent biographical study suggested just the opposite, namely, that Torrey supported Biola's "new directions" in the 1920s, although the changes that Staggers noted, radio broadcasting and missionary expansion into China, were unrelated to changes in the curriculum. Staggers' account, however, is of limited use on this question, because he did not discuss either the tensions caused by changes in the institute curriculum, or more specifically, Torrey's views about these changes. To the contrary, in spite of Martin's observation, Staggers uncritically stated that "the Institute remained steadfastly devoted to its original purpose of educating young people," even though by the early 1920s, many suspected that Biola's original purpose was quickly fading into obscurity.[49]

Torrey's views, therefore, remain ambiguous. On the one hand, there is a clear indication that he opposed the trend of some Bible schools to adopt a broader liberal arts curriculum, which often became the first step toward a four year, degree granting, academic institution.[50] On the other hand, he was not a slavish traditionalist either, because it was he who implemented a new curriculum in 1922, which to many appeared to contradict the original ideals of a Bible institute. Ironically, few who later opposed MacInnis realized that it was really Torrey who had initiated the first major curricular changes.[51]

A New Administration

For the first time in its short history, Biola was faced with the task of finding a new president, dean and superintendent. For president, the board turned to Joseph Irvine, a real estate developer and prominent businessman, who had been associated with Biola since at least 1910.[52] Although he was a respected and judicious leader, moderate and conservative by temperament, he was less well known in fundamentalist circles outside of Los Angeles than Lyman Stewart.

Irvine's first challenge as president, apart from directing Biola through the troubled waters of the McPherson controversy, was securing a new dean. It seemed, in view of the heavy criticism that the institute

---

[49] Staggers, "Reuben A. Torrey," 291–92.

[50] Torrey to Gray, 11 December 1918, Moody Bible Institute Archives.

[51] A brief comment published in the Los Angeles *Evening Herald,* 5 December 1928, Section A, p. 20, that Torrey had resigned because of a controversy over evolution, could not be independently verified, although Torrey's variance with fundamentalists on the evolution issue did cause some fundamentalists to worry.

[52] For an early mention of Irvine at Biola see *The King's Business,* April 1910, 64.

had received over the McPherson episode, that a dean of impeccable fundamentalist credentials ought to be elected. With this consideration in mind, the board turned to the venerable but aged A. C. Dixon, who was not only a fundamentalist of worthy reputation, but had himself been an instructor at Biola in 1919.

Dixon expressed some interest in returning to Biola, and so he traveled to Los Angeles in December 1924 to explore the prospect of becoming Biola's new dean.[53] Discussions with the board, however, revealed that Dixon would not be a suitable candidate. Even though the board had already adopted its anti-pentecostal resolution, Dixon still felt constrained to press his vigorous opposition to Horton's position; only later did he report that Biola was not in sympathy with McPherson and her pentecostal teachings, in spite of one leader who was "captured by McPhersonism," an oblique reference to Horton. The primary barrier to cooperation, however, appeared to be his stipulations, which were rejected by the board on December 27. Dixon demanded that all departments of the institute be placed under a single head, presumably in an effort to avoid the kind of leadership conflict that had so affected Torrey. He also demanded a "dissolution," or perhaps a realignment of the Church of the Open Door, in order to avoid competition between the church and other local churches.[54]

Having rejected Dixon's conditions, the board again began to search for a suitable candidate. After consulting with Riley on February 6, they invited a Presbyterian minister from Berkeley, Lapsley A. McAfee, to consult with the search committee. Finally, on March 26, the board moved to call MacInnis as Biola's second dean, and this decision was ratified April 3, 1925, along with a request that McAfee take the position of superintendent. Although the latter did not accept, MacInnis warily but happily agreed to become the dean.[55]

His appointment came, no doubt, as a surprise to many of Biola's staff, students, and alumni, including Torrey himself, who apparently did not even know that MacInnis was being considered, or that he was elected on the first ballot by a unanimous vote. Even MacInnis himself was surprised.[56] He was not a nationally known figure. Neither was he a part of the World's Christian Fundamentals Association, which relied

---

[53] Board Minutes, 27 December 1924.

[54] For slightly different versions of what happened when Dixon met with Biola's board see the Board Minutes, 27 December 1924, and the bulletin of Dixon's University Baptist Church, Baltimore, Maryland, 11 January 1925, MacInnis Papers. Also compare Henry's account (Biola Manuscript, 67–68), which quotes from correspondence between Horton and Dixon, but fails to indicate the sources of these citations.

[55] Board Minutes, 6 February, 26 February, 26 March, and 3 April 1925.

[56] MacInnis to Torrey, 13 April 1925, MacInnis Papers.

on the support of many Bible school leaders. Moreover, he was not very well known to Biola alumni, having been at Biola barely more than two years. Ironically, for students and employees, he was probably best known for teaching the course in Christian philosophy and history, which was not a welcome innovation for some traditionalists.

Yet MacInnis was chosen for many reasons. First, he had been a long-time supporter of the Bible school movement and was a tireless advocate for lay Bible and missions training. Second, he was a popular teacher and quite well respected by his colleagues. Third, his academic background was likely seen as an important asset for the continuing development of the curriculum. Finally, because he was new to the faculty, he was probably a neutral choice, relatively free from the political stains of factionalism inspired by followers of Torrey and Horton.[57] With a solid academic reputation and a clear vision to upgrade Biola's standards, he seemed well equipped to lead the school.

John MacInnis: Liberal Arts Progressive or Bible School Idealist?

MacInnis had few doubts about what he hoped to accomplish at Biola: his published views were illuminating and indicate a moderately progressive agenda for the curriculum. One of his first actions which showed an interest in the school's curriculum was a request that all teachers submit a statement of the content and goals of their classes.[58] Shortly thereafter, he published a statement of his goals in *The King's Business*.

> In accepting this important position, involving so many interests, I wish to outline my understanding of the nature and purposes of the Bible Institute and the policies which shall govern me in carrying out my task and responsibility as the Dean.[59]

MacInnis' statement was carefully crafted to address the concerns of the variant "interests" at Biola. For those concerned about the expansion of

---

[57] For the existence of factions note that after Torrey's resignation a committee was formed to investigate if Horton had forced Torrey out of his position; see Horton's "An Open Letter to Members of the Southern California Premillenial Association." Also note Dixon's letter, which stated that Horton still controlled the school even though he had resigned; A. C. Dixon to MacInnis, 23 March 1925, MacInnis Papers.

[58] Faculty Minutes, 29 April 1925.

[59] John MacInnis, "A Declaration of Understanding, Policy and Motives in Accepting the Deanship of the Bible Institute of Los Angeles," *The King's Business*, June 1925, 242.

a non-traditional curriculum, MacInnis said that he would maintain the
course of study and continue the primary goal of training in soul winning and Bible study for those who did not have full educational advantages. Moreover, he noted that he would expand the courses for
youth work, Sunday school work, and Christian education. Finally, with
regard to the pastor's course, MacInnis spoke more cautiously: the
training would be the best possible, but primarily for those "who are
looking towards the ministry but cannot avail themselves of the courses
in the regular evangelical Institutions."[60] In other words, the stress
would now be placed on pastoral training only for those who could not
obtain a ministerial education at a denominational seminary. This point
was motivated by MacInnis' growing concern that Biola's pastoral
training would alienate mainline churches.

Two months later, at his installation ceremony, MacInnis again stated
his intention to carry out "the original purpose and intention of the Institute to its fullest possible realization."[61] At this early stage in his career, he gave no indications of transforming Biola into a four year Bible
college. Rather, he mentioned specific plans to expand the Sunday
School program and Christian education, which only continued the traditional emphasis on lay training. Coincidentally, while MacInnis was
reassuring Biolans of the continuity of his goals with the Bible school
ideal, James Gray was doing likewise. When he was promoted to president of Moody Bible Institute in 1925, Gray told his audience that there
was no change in the essential ideals of the curriculum. "The curriculum
was broadened," he avowed, "without violating the principle of giving
the English Bible and practical Christian work their chief place."[62]

In spite of such assurances, however, many were persuaded that Biola
was departing from its founding ideals. V. V. Morgan, the leader of the
Biola Club of Long Beach, submitted his resignation on August 7, 1925,
within days of MacInnis' installation. Although his reasons included
doctrinal criticism of MacInnis, he also argued that MacInnis was leading Biola away from its goals of training men and women for soul-sav-
ing evangelistic work.[63] An alumnus of Biola also perceived a transformation, but defended the changes. His view was that critics of the new
broader program of education were influenced by the anti-education attitudes of Biola's founders; therefore, they could not see that "knowledge of psychology and philosophy is not incompatible with zeal in

---

[60] Ibid., 243.

[61] "Installation of Dean, B.I.O.L.A.," *The King's Business,* August 1925,
372.

[62] Runyan, *Dr. Gray at Moody Bible Institute,* 147–48.

[63] V. V. Morgan to J. M. Irvine, 27 July 1925, MacInnis Papers.

soul-winning."[64] The most salient charges came in 1928, however, when a self-appointed committee of graduates claimed that the MacInnis curriculum replaced Bible study with psychology, philosophy, and religious education.[65] Such claims probably led Biola historian James Henry to argue that MacInnis really intended to transform Biola into a liberal arts college.

> MacInnis was convinced the time had come for Biola to become an "Institute of higher learning," meaning a change in status from a Bible Institute to a Liberal Arts College. He seemed totally unaware that it was a complete distrust of liberal arts academic institutions and their drift into liberalism that had prompted the founding of Biola.[66]

But in light of MacInnis' statements and actions, there is no evidence that he misunderstood the purpose of a Bible institute, or that he intended to change the institute into a liberal arts college. Although there were several changes in the policies and curriculum of Biola during his administration, none was a radical departure from basic Bible school training.

The most frequent criticism, of course, was that the introduction of a course in Christian history and philosophy constituted a departure from the Bible training ideal. Although it was certainly true that these subjects were not a part of early Bible school training, and, moreover, that they challenged the traditional self-understanding of Bible schools, it is clear that this process of transforming ideals began well before the MacInnis administration. Few, however, perceived the broadening interpretation of "Bible only" rhetoric, which began as early as 1920 under Torrey. Rather, with the rapid changes of administrative leadership in 1924, many assumed that MacInnis had changed the curriculum to include non-Bible classes.

The fact that MacInnis did not begin the process, however, would not affect the conclusion that he, nevertheless, sought to continue the movement away from Bible school idealism. But here, also, there is no evidence that he intended to transform Biola into a liberal arts college. When, for example, he sought to find a superintendent, MacInnis said that he was "carrying on with increased vigor," the study of the Bible

---

[64] David J. Donnan to J. H. Hunter, n.d., MacInnis Papers.

[65] Alumni Association Pamphlet, 13 June 1928, 6, MacInnis Papers. Also see the statement of the board, that his educational program was based primarily on "scholastic rather than spiritual" considerations: Los Angeles *Times,* 28 December 1928, Part II, 1.

[66] Henry, Biola Manuscript, 71. For the same claim by Roger Martin, in specific reference to Torrey's views already cited, see *Apostle of Certainty,* 248.

and methods of Christian work; a new emphasis was evident, however, in his expressed desire to train the students in Christian education.[67] Though MacInnis indicated that he was considering using "higher studies" in the course in March 1928, he added that the "major part of our work must be preparing native evangelists."[68] In spite of change in the curriculum under MacInnis, such as the implementation of a Christian Education Course, the faculty did not discuss a four year program until 1929, almost a year after his resignation, and this curriculum was approved by the faculty on April 29, 1930.[69] The lack of discussion on this question suggests that MacInnis did not advocate changing Biola into an academically oriented, four year liberal arts college. This point is reinforced by a comparison of the curriculum under MacInnis with the proposed curriculum of 1930. MacInnis added a formalized Christian education course and also offered classes in the Greek language and psychology. Apart from these changes, however, Biola's curriculum under MacInnis remained very similar to the 1922 program. But the proposed curriculum of 1930 radically altered the nature of Biola's Bible course. In that curriculum, many subjects were added that had never before been formally taught at Biola. These included Systematic Theology, Hebrew, Exegesis, Greek Exegesis, History of the English Bible, Child Development, and History of Doctrine.[70] These subjects often required advanced literary skills, which exceeded the abilities of most Bible school students.

It remains to be asked, however, if the changes that MacInnis wrought in the curriculum emphasized liberal arts to the diminution of Bible training. Neither the introduction of Greek in 1925, which was intended primarily for ministerial preparation, nor the development of a medical missions course in 1926, appeared to alter the general emphasis on Bible study.[71] The study of Greek and Hebrew had long been a minor element of the Bible classes, and so it became a natural progression in most Bible schools, when pastoral training was introduced, to offer separate instruction in the biblical languages. More questionable was the development of a distinct class in Christian psychology, which had ear-

---

[67] MacInnis to George F. Guy, 15 September 1925, MacInnis Papers.

[68] MacInnis to W. M. Hayes, 2 March 1928, MacInnis Papers.

[69] For the first faculty discussion about a four year curriculum see the Faculty Minutes, 15 October 1929; for its approval see the entry dated 22 April 1930, which includes a signed approval by MacInnis' successor, Elbert McCreery, dated 29 April 1929.

[70] Determined from a comparison of the Bulletin, July 1927, with the proposed curriculum of 1930 in the Faculty Minutes, 22 April 1929.

[71] For Greek see Henry, Biola Manuscript, 162; for a third year medical missions course see the *Biola Bulletin,* July 1927, 34–38.

lier only been treated as a topic in the personal work course.[72] But even here the Bible ideal was still pressed into service, when it was noted that applied psychology based on the Bible would be useful for all kinds of Christian work.

The change that generated the most controversy was the introduction of a Christian education course in 1925. Christian education was becoming a *cause célèbre* for many mainline Protestant church leaders during the 1920s, partly because of worries about the declining morals of young people, and as a response to the growing secularization of public education in America. The need for Christian educators, therefore, became a frequent theme of mainline periodicals. J. Armentrout, for example, stated in the *Presbyterian Magazine* what many ministers were feeling, that training Christian educators was one of the greatest needs of the church.[73] Seeing in this an opportunity for Bible schools, MacInnis made clear his goal of strengthening Christian education in his first public declarations as dean.[74] Soon thereafter, he sought permission to invite Florence Chaffee, a longtime friend and teacher at Gordon College, to direct a course in Christian education, which she began in September 1925.[75]

Chaffee showed signs of marked independence from the beginning. As a college teacher, she had used texts that were based on educational theories, rather than Bible methods. This practice at Biola, however, was considered a departure from Bible based teacher training. In self-conscious awareness of potential criticisms, MacInnis tried to relate the course in Christian education to the Bible ideal. Explaining the new course, MacInnis commented:

> We are trying to meet the issue at the Bible Institute of Los Angeles, in a way that will be true to the Bible ideal and also to the practical issues as they are raised in the Church life of our day.[76]

---

[72] Compare the Biola Bulletin, October 1920, 33, to the Bulletin, July 1927, 28.

[73] J. S. Armentrout, "Educational Leadership Important in Religious Life of Young People," *Presbyterian Magazine,* October 1928, 527. For an example of Christian education as a response to the secularization of public education, see William C. Covert, "Perils Threaten Church and Nation," *Presbyterian Magazine,* October 1928, 509–10.

[74] MacInnis, "A Declaration of Understanding, Policy and Motives," 242, and "Installation of Dean," 372.

[75] Board Minutes, 19 May 1925, and Faculty Minutes, 24 September 1925.

[76] John MacInnis and Florence Chaffee, "Our New Course in Christian Education," *The King's Business,* February 1926, 63.

For many Bible school fundamentalists, however, study of educational psychology and child development simply distracted students from their top priority of Bible learning and soul-winning. T. C. Horton voiced his objections to Christian education in *The King's Business.* In his view, Christian education was a meaningless term, because even Unitarians used it. What Bible schools needed was to return to the definite term "Biblical."

> The great need is not the need of more education, but the need of adding to the celebrated "Three R's"—Reading, 'Riting and 'Rithmetic, the other R—Regeneration.[77]

Expressing a similar view, Torrey complained that the institute had replaced soul-winning with Christian education.[78]

These concerns reflected deeply held fundamentalist suspicions about religious education. A stout emphasis on Christian education reminded many evangelicals of a 19th century debate about Christian nurture versus revival. Following in the tradition of Horace Bushnell, whom Chaffee had praised as a "great Christian educator," many religious romantics and liberals stressed the need of Christian nurture over the excesses of religious revivalism.[79] For the fundamentalist, however, nothing was more worthwhile than saving souls. A bias against religious education, therefore, suffused the fundamentalist mind. This bias was exacerbated by the gradual identification of religious education with theological liberalism. Hence, fundamentalists often attacked the liberal Religious Education Association, and under the leadership of Clarence Benson, who began Moody's Religious Education Course in 1924, they started the new Evangelical Teacher Training Association.[80] To avoid any misunderstanding, Biola leaders voted to use the term "Christian education," rather than the red flag term "religious education." Biola's fine reputation for orthodoxy was not helped, however, when it adver-

---

[77] T. C. Horton, "Religious Education? Regeneration? Revival?" *The King's Business,* December 1926, 704.

[78] Torrey to Gray, 24 December 1927, Moody Bible Institute Archives.

[79] For 19th century roots of revivalism versus nurture see Sydney Ahlstrom, *A Religious History of the American People* (New Haven: Yale University Press, 1972), 391, 610–11; for Chaffee's comment see "Our New Course in Christian Education," 63.

[80] See, for example, a repudiation of the Religious Education Association by the WCFA in 1922, reported in *The King's Business,* September 1922, 896–98. Also compare the widely read criticisms of religious education in Ernest Gordon's, *The Leaven of the Sadducees* (Chicago: Bible Institute Colportage Assn., 1926), 101–37, which specifically lambastes the International Council of Religious Education. For Benson see Brereton, *Training God's Army,* 143–44.

tised that its course met the requirements of the International Council of Religious Education, a point that Horton exploited in a widely circulated memo.[81]

In spite of the worries caused by the course in Christian education, its content did not differ greatly from the earlier Sunday School Work program, which it replaced. To be sure, more emphasis was placed on subjects such as pedagogy, child development, and educational psychology, which apparently relied less on the Bible ideal than on modern principles of education. The old two year program was extended to three years, which offered students more Bible classes than they would have had under the previous plan of study. In response to the widely repeated claim that students were learning less of the Bible under the MacInnis administration, John Hunter, a longtime teacher at Biola, argued that study of the English Bible had actually increased, while the hours of study in church history, philosophy, and psychology had declined.[82]

The greatest irony of the controversy over Christian education is seen in how far fundamentalists had strayed from their own roots in 1908. When Biola was founded, teacher training and Sunday school methods soon became an important part of the school's educational program. But now, exploiting a popular distaste for religious education, Horton was depicting the program as a violation of the Bible institute ideal. Probably to the degree that Christian education displaced the earlier "Bible methods" of the personal work classes, he was right. But the Bible ideal had always been just that—an ideal—a way of defining the distinctive nature of Bible school training. The new Christian education course, like other changes under MacInnis, stretched the ideal, but it did not break it. MacInnis did not attempt to displace Bible training with a liberal arts education. Rather, as he sought to upgrade and modify the Bible training courses, he allowed some progressive, non-traditional growth in the curriculum, but he also continued to use the Bible ideal, as had Torrey before him, to limit curricular change.

---

[81] Minutes of the Executive Committee of the Board of Directors (hereafter, the Executive Minutes), 6 October 1925, kept in the president's office, Biola University, La Mirada, CA. For the advertising see the Biola Bulletin, July 1927, 32; for the memo see the typed document, "Concerning Religious Education at Bible Institute of Los Angeles," n.d., MacInnis Papers. Also cf. "Religious versus Christian Education," *The Christian Fundamentalist,* February 1928, 12.

[82] Alumni Association Pamphlet, 13 June 1928, 6–7, 144.

Other Changes that Affected Bible Institute Ideals:
The Effects of Institutionalization

A changing curriculum, however, was not the only factor that caused Biolans to worry about the loss of the Bible school ideal. Under the MacInnis administration, numerous policy changes also influenced the perception that the old Biola, with its informal ethos, was being undermined by new uniform academic standards. As college education in America moved toward greater specialization and uniform educational standards, so too, Bible schools began to seek uniform standards, teaching expertise, and educational legitimacy. It appeared to some defenders of the Bible ideal, however, that these standards might erode certain organizational distinctives of the Bible school. Two areas of organizational changes were significant. First, there were changes in basic academic requirements, which impinged on the earlier informal and populist orientation of Bible schools. Second, and more significantly, there was a deep unresolved tension as to whether Biola was primarily a school for training, or a support agency for missionary outreach. Prompted by MacInnis' efforts to streamline the extensive ministry programs of the institute, this issue caused deep divisions in the Biola community, which severely eroded his support.

One policy that changed the quality of education at Biola was the new admission requirements that were gradually implemented in the 1920s. The only admission requirements in Biola's early days were a students' approved Christian character, and "the willingness to do hard work." This was a policy that gave real substance to their populist and democratic intentions.[83] But a growing literacy rate, and the need to set a minimum standard for those who would aspire to the training program, prompted leaders to require a common school education in 1921.[84] This trend continued under MacInnis, so that in 1927 the institute was strongly urging that prospective students have a high school education. Lacking that, students would still be admitted, but only by a vote of the faculty.[85] Though Bible school leaders felt constrained to define their academic standards in relation to the growing influence of high schools, there were some who worried that literary requirements would only squelch the call of God, which might come in spite of one's educational attainment. A former student, for example, recalled that most students were opposed to his suggestion in 1916, that remedial English be required of students lacking the requisite literary skills needed at Biola.

---

[83] Catalogue of The Bible Institute of Los Angeles, [1913], 26.
[84] Williams and Miller, *Chartered for His Glory*, 40.
[85] Biola Bulletin, July 1927, 45.

This attitude, he continued, was still prevalent among many alumni, who in earlier years had been encouraged to think that a lack of education was no hindrance to effective ministry.[86]

Other policy changes gradually eroded the informal and family ethos of the early days. In the 1920s, new procedures for taking class attendance, new rules about when students could enroll in a class, and standard grading policies, not only for classroom work but also for practical work assignments, created an increasingly rationalized institutional environment.[87] With these changes, some alumni expressed feelings of nostalgia for "the old B. I."[88] The large size of Biola, however, and the need for uniform standards between the Bible schools, fueled bureaucratic growth and complexity.

In his attempts to raise the academic standards of Biola, however, it is noteworthy that MacInnis did not seek to replace the mostly clerical Bible teachers with professional academics. Most of the teachers at Biola had ministerial or evangelism credentials, rather than an advanced academic education. Hence, the teaching level during the MacInnis years probably did not surpass a high school standard with the exception, perhaps, of three year students in pastor training and Christian education courses.

This fact, however, does not mean that academic expectations became languid. To the contrary, some teachers tried to raise the level of instruction in their classes and discovered that it was not always welcome, from faculty and students alike! When, for example, the famous British Bible expositor, G. Campbell Morgan, tried to enforce more rigorous standards of composition in his Bible classes, his American students began failing at an alarming rate—in one class forty students failed his examination, and in another, fifty. Student protest became so vociferous, that the faculty felt constrained to tell Morgan that his expectations were too rigorous for the average Bible student.[89]

Mission Agency or Training School?

The organizational issue that most divided Biola, however, was not the curriculum, but whether or not a Bible school should be primarily a school or an agency for missionary outreach. This issue, like that of the Bible ideal for the curriculum, was rooted in the earliest conception of

---

[86] David Donnan to J. H. Hunter, n.d., MacInnis Papers.

[87] Faculty Minutes, 3 December 1924, 19 January 1927, and 7 November 1928.

[88] See, for example, the expressions of nostalgia in Mrs. Stewart to MacInnis, 12 May 1927, MacInnis Papers.

[89] Faculty Minutes, 15 December 1927.

what a Bible institute should be. For some, especially those employed as evangelists by the school, Biola was a great missionary organization, sending workers into the field and maintaining a sizable infrastructure of support for local and foreign missions. To others, this vast array of activities was only an ancillary function of Bible schools, which were primarily intended to be institutions of training.

When MacInnis first declared his understanding of Biola's purpose, he made explicit his view that Biola was meant to be a school: "I understand the Institute to be primarily a school for the training of men and women," stated MacInnis, "and that all its activities are in accord with and supplementary to that great mission."[90] To those outside of the Biola community, his statement was probably not considered controversial. But to the Biola evangelistic staff his words carried ominous implications. If other activities were incidental to the great purpose of education, then those activities could also be dropped, if they were no longer considered meet or necessary. That implication became a reality during the next three years of his deanship, by a slow winnowing of evangelistic activities under the advice and consent of the board of directors. These actions proved immensely unpopular, however, and severely damaged his base of support in the Biola community, with the consequence that, when his fundamentalist orthodoxy came under intense criticism, his friends in the Biola community were too few to weather the storm.

The import of this issue was rooted in the very origins and identity of the American Bible school, which, as Sandeen cogently observed, functioned as a "denominational headquarters" for interdenominational fundamentalists. The Moody Bible Institute, for example, was first chartered as an evangelism society with the goal of not only training Christian workers, but maintaining them in active ministries as well, by providing in many cases their financial support. Biola, following closely the Moody pattern, and enjoying the largess of the Stewart brothers, also expressed this dual purpose. "The Institute has become a rallying center for the study of the Word," declared Biola's leaders, "and a radiating center for various forms of aggressive Christian work."[91] In its organizational structure, Biola also began as a society for evangelism with voting members.

During the years of Stewart's leadership, the twin threads of training and agency were held together, but after his death they began to unravel. A letter from A. C. Dixon, written shortly after his discussions with Biola, reveal that there was already an emerging division on the question.

[90] MacInnis, "A Declaration of Understanding, Policy, and Motives," 243.

[91] Sandeen, *Roots,* 242; Brereton, *Training God's Army,* xix; Getz, *MBI,* 61; for the Biola quotation see "A Short Story of the Los Angeles Bible Institute," 171.

The way in which the Bible Institute has been put into a corner and made only an educational department of a great complex mission is enough to make an angel weep. Lyman Stewart certainly never intended that such a thing should be done.[92]

Converging with this issue were the first attempts at reorganization of the institute due to financial constrictions, with a view toward discontinuing any work that was "not being done effectively."[93] It is difficult to determine whether program cut backs were the result of financial shortfalls, or because they were deemed ineffective or unnecessary. But in December 1926, a new policy was officially adopted, which made clear that Biola's goal was "training men and women for evangelistic work rather than engaging in that work."[94] The board later clarified this statement, noting that the practical work of the institute was for training purposes and not designed to compete with similar ministry programs of the churches.[95] This policy, which decidedly revealed the hope of MacInnis to position the institute as a training institution for the churches, appeared to transform the conception of "training *and* work," into a conception of "training *for* work."

The new policy brought several changes that disturbed many Biolans. A time-honored tradition of student preaching at Biola Hall came to an end in 1927, and the Biola Club of Long Beach was also closed.[96] But more difficult was opposition from Mrs. Lyman Stewart, who was now a full member of the board. Realizing that the policy threatened the continuing existence of many Biola evangelistic ministries, Mrs. Stewart began to express her unhappiness at the board's directions, especially when it became clear that the new policy would also affect her own ministry known as the Bible Women.

The "Bible Women" was an evangelistic ministry of Biola almost as old as the institute itself. Comprised mainly of older women who received some small compensation for conducting home visits and various ministry tasks, it had long been a special project of Lyman and Lula Stewart. Because of their singular interest in this ministry, the Stewarts established a distinct fund for its support, which was controlled by Mrs. Stewart herself. The Bible Women, therefore, enjoyed a greater degree of autonomy from the board of directors than other comparable ministries and tended to regard Mrs. Stewart as their primary authority. Their independent status, however, soon ran afoul of the board's goal to

[92] A. C. Dixon to MacInnis, 23 March 1925, MacInnis Papers.
[93] Board Minutes, 7 August 1925, 4 December 1925, 3 September 1926.
[94] Ibid., 3 December 1926.
[95] Ibid., 14 January 1927.
[96] Ibid., 2 September 1927.

streamline authority and to regulate the disparate ministries of the school.

Mrs. Stewart first began to express her doubts about the new policy in March 1927, when a Biola report omitted the work of the Bible Women. In a letter to MacInnis, she decried the curtailing of evangelistic work and also complained that *The King's Business* had reduced its column space for reports on the work of the Evangelistic Department.[97] These concerns began to boil, however, when she sent a telegram to J. M. Irvine, protesting the curtailment of evangelistic activities. "Evangelism has always distinguished us," she said, "and I am fearful of education superseding it."[98] At the next board meeting, Mrs. Stewart's concerns were heatedly discussed, and MacInnis was met by a volley of opposition from (as he put it) "narrow intolerant propagandists."[99]

Following this meeting, lengthy letters continued to pass between Stewart and MacInnis, as MacInnis attempted to assuage her worries about evangelistic cut backs, but with little success. She continued to remonstrate against the cut backs, and the board's decision to put the Bible Women under the personal supervision of Biola's new superintendent, Charles Hurlburt.[100] In spite of tense explanations and pleadings, however, Mrs. Stewart was not moved. Consequently, at the close of 1927, she successfully prevailed on the board to keep her personal leadership of the Bible Women without having to report to the superintendent.[101]

The discussion of the Bible Women deserves attention for two reasons. First, it became the most important incident in the debate over the essential purpose of a Bible school. Few in 1925 had much explicit awareness of the question, but by the end of 1927 the issues were well formulated, and lines of opposition had formed. Second, it also represented the addition of another layer of opposition in a shaky administration. Institutional changes, fears of a departure from the old Biola tradition, the loss of a shared vision: all these factors contributed to growing unrest and, for some, outspoken opposition. A few of MacInnis' most vocal critics were those displaced by the new policy, such as V. V. Morgan, the former leader of the discontinued Biola Club of Long

---

[97] Mrs. Lyman Stewart to MacInnis, 19 March 1927, and MacInnis' response, 30 March 1927, MacInnis Papers.

[98] Mrs. Lyman Stewart to J. M. Irvine, Telegram, 5 May 1927, MacInnis Papers.

[99] For Mrs. Stewart's letter see Board Minutes, 6 May 1927; for MacInnis' view of the meeting see MacInnis to William MacInnes, 7 May 1927, MacInnis Papers.

[100] See Mrs. Stewart to MacInnis, 12 May 1927; MacInnis to Stewart, 24 May 1927; Stewart to MacInnis, 25 May 1927; MacInnis to Stewart, 24 June 1927, MacInnis Papers.

[101] Board Minutes, 7 October 1927.

Beach. For others, like Mrs. Stewart and her Bible Women, it left hurt feelings and probably doubts about where MacInnis was leading them. But all these factors would probably not have broken MacInnis' personal support at Biola, had it not also been joined to perceptions of doctrinal irregularities.

Postscript

It is tempting to speculate whether or not MacInnis would have gone in the direction of many Bible schools and transformed Biola into a four year college, had controversy not intervened and forced his departure. Of course, this question lies beyond the purview of an historical study. But clearly it is true that many Bible schools did proceed with this transition, sometimes at a price of severe controversy. W. B. Riley's Northwestern Schools, for example, became a four year liberal arts college in 1944 against the desires of many, who believed that this was a betrayal of the Bible institute ideal. Ironically, that crisis contributed to the resignation of Billy Graham, who had succeeded Riley as Northwestern's president.[102] But it is also true that many institutes did not go through this transition, of which Moody Bible Institute is only the most conspicuous example.

What is, perhaps, more clear is that MacInnis did not change his focus from lay training after he left Biola in December 1928. In fact, his vision for lay training continued with great vigor, yielding no indication that he aspired to any other personal or professional goals. What did change, however, was the direction of his focus. Instead of lay Bible training in a Bible institute, he advocated with intense personal pathos that the church conduct its own lay leadership training. "The whole Bible Institute movement," he said bitterly, "is highly disturbing and divisive in the church and I believe that the sooner the church makes adequate provision for the training of its own lay workers the better for all concerned."[103] Consequently, after leaving Biola, he started a lay leadership training program in the Presbytery of Los Angeles.[104] Biola was not to remain a Bible institute, however, for not long after MacInnis left, steps were, taken by the new administration to change into a four year Bible college, a process which eventually led to the abandonment of the Bible ideal and an embrace of higher education based on the liberal arts.

---

[102] Trollinger, *God's Empire*, 153.

[103] MacInnis to William MacInnes, 23 November 1928, MacInnis Papers.

[104] For this work see MacInnes, "Leadership Training in the Synod of California, Southern Area: Inception, Formative Years, the Present" (Master's Thesis, San Francisco Theological Seminary, 1960), 26-32.

CHAPTER 5

The MacInnis Controversy in Los Angeles, 1925–1927

Introduction

The MacInnis controversy has usually been remembered as a religious conflict that began in 1928 over the significance of MacInnis' book, *Peter the Fisherman Philosopher*. This picture, however, ignores the extensive roots of controversy that were already growing in the rich fundamentalist soil of Los Angeles long before MacInnis published his book and, therefore, fails to give a satisfactory understanding of the controversy. Hence, a better approach is to begin with anti-MacInnis criticism that surfaced at least two years earlier, and seek to draw out the connections between local fundamentalist agitation over MacInnis and the subsequent national controversy that centered mostly on his book.

This approach is suggested by the need in historical literature, and in fundamentalist historiography in particular, to pay increased attention to the multiple levels of decision making and influence in any organized movement, from the local grass roots to regional and national levels of leadership. Since Samuel P. Hays pointed out the incongruities of describing a national political movement from its top level leadership alone, a few historians have become acutely aware of the shortcoming of writing fundamentalist history from the "top down," ignoring the significant ways that regional leaders influenced the movement from the "bottom up."[1] Although the MacInnis controversy was a national con-

---

[1] Samuel P. Hays, "The Social Analysis of American Political History, 1880–1920," *Political Science Quarterly* 80 (September 1965): 373–94. I am indebted to Trollinger's study of the "regional empire" of W. B. Riley for this approach to the analysis of social movements. Another historian calling for more regional analysis is Douglas Anderson: see his unpublished manuscript "California Protestantism, 1848–1935: Historiographical Explorations and Regional Method for a Nascent Field," (1983), in Graduate Theological Union

troversy, in so far as it involved the top levels of fundamentalist leadership, it began principally as a local controversy between mid-level and grass roots constituents of the Bible Institute of Los Angeles. The beginnings of the controversy in Los Angeles later shaped the character and intensity of the national controversy, especially as local anti-MacInnis groups influenced the actions and opinions of national figures like W. B. Riley, T. T. Shields, and other top level fundamentalist leaders.

John MacInnis was primarily a local and regional leader, providing an important link between higher levels of influence and the evangelical grass roots. Even though his position at Biola was somewhat comparable to James Gray's at Moody Bible Institute, he did not share Gray's influence or prestige. He knew through his involvement with the Montrose Bible Conference many top level fundamentalist leaders, but he never achieved the status and name recognition of Gray, Riley, or Torrey. On a few occasions, such as the Keswick Convention and the Philadelphia Prophetic Conference, he shared a platform with several of the top conservative evangelicals of his day, but his sphere of influence still remained primarily local. Not until his book became the focus of a national fundamentalist attack did he gain wide recognition, or infamy, but when the controversy eventually ended he left behind no organized following. Instead, he returned to local educational work under the guidance of the Presbyterian Church. It is important, therefore, to consider the extent to which the MacInnis controversy was a regional phenomenon, arising from social and religious factors peculiar to Southern California.

Assessing Fundamentalism in Southern California

"Heave an egg out of a Pullman window" quipped H. L. Mencken, "and you will hit a fundamentalist anywhere in the United States today."[2] Or so it seemed to Mencken in the 1920s; but his chances of hitting a fundamentalist in Southern California were probably better than just about anywhere else in America, if popular estimates were of any significance. The observation that fundamentalism was particularly strong in the West was echoed on different sides of the theological aisle. The president of Chicago Theological Seminary, Ozora S. Davis, for exam-

Library, Berkeley, CA. For an application of this method see Douglas Anderson, "San Francisco Evangelicalism, Regional Religious Identity, and the Revivalism of D. L. Moody," *Fides et Historia* 15 (Spring/Summer 1983): 44–66.

[2] Quoted in Gregory H. Singleton, "Fundamentalism and Urbanization: A Quantitative Critique of Impressionistic Interpretations," in *The New Urban History: Quantitative Explorations by American Historians,* ed. Leo F. Schnore (Princeton University Press, 1975), 205.

ple, stated that "as you travel westward the larger is the percentage of church members that are dedicating their all to it."

> By the time you reach Chicago fifty percent of the orthodox Protestants are Fundamentalists and on reaching the Pacific coast the percentage will climb almost to seventy five, and they are in earnest and stand ready to give everything they have to it.[3]

A few years later William B. Riley said much the same when he boasted that Los Angeles had more fundamentalist pastors and churches than most cities in America.[4]

Of course, the estimates of Davis and Riley were only impressions of a recent movement in America, but they nevertheless indicate a point of view that was sometimes shared by alarmist liberals and fundamentalist boosters, namely, that the fundamentalist movement enjoyed considerable popularity on the Pacific Coast and, in particular, Los Angeles. These estimates come as no surprise, however, given the regions' reputation as a center of radical and often esoteric religion. By the mid-1920s fundamentalism had shed its early mainstream roots and was increasingly being recognized as a radical offshoot of traditional evangelicalism, and this image was by no means out of place in Southern California's religious milieu.

Historians have often observed the regions' conservative tenor during the first three decades of this century, and fundamentalism has usually been lumped with the antics of Aimee Semple McPherson or her truculent rival in the cloth, Robert P. Shuler. It is also often observed that non-traditional churches held great appeal for many migrants to Southern California, most of whom were arriving from the American Midwest with their life savings and a complete stock of rural beliefs and attitudes. In this mobile social context, it is argued, traditional social expectations were heeded less, and the pursuit of leisure and novelty assumed greater importance, thus creating the kind of social environment in which radical sectarianism would thrive. According to Kevin Starr, therefore, migrations in the 1920s pushed to the edge a religious fundamentalism which had already become evident in the prewar period.[5]

---

[3] Quoted in W. B. Riley "The Christian Fundamentals Movement: Its Battles, Its Achievements, Its Certain Victory," in *Scriptural Inspiration versus Scientific Imagination*, ed. T. C. Horton (Los Angeles: Biola Book Room, 1922), 20.

[4] [W. B. Riley], "Los Angeles in 1930," *The Christian Fundamentalist*, December 1929, 444.

[5] For these arguments see Carey McWilliams, *Southern California: An Island on the Land* (Santa Barbara, CA, and Salt Lake City, UT: Peregrine Smith, Inc., 1973; first ed., 1946), 157–58, 181, 239, 261–62, 269; also Fogel-

The regions' reputation for radical sectarianism has provided grist for more than one scholar's mill, but hard statistical measures of fundamentalist prevalence in Los Angeles as compared to other cities in North America have been less forthcoming.[6] The only significant analysis to date has been the study of Gregory Singleton, which tried to measure the numerical strength of fundamentalists in Los Angeles from 1916 to 1936. His studies indicate that relative to the population, fundamentalism was stronger in Arizona, Nevada, California, and Oregon, than in any other region of the United States. He also argued that Protestant denominations that he classified as "sympathetic" to the organized fundamentalist movement, which were mainly millenarian and adventist groups, grew faster in Southern California than anywhere else.[7]

Singleton's conclusions, however, are based on his excessively narrow definitions of "fundamentalism," which consisted primarily in the millenarian and adventist sects. Hence, his conclusions are of little help in understanding those who considered themselves fundamentalist, but were identified with a mainline denomination. Nevertheless, the fact that there was an exceptional presence of radical evangelical sects in Los Angeles confirms the perceptions of social historians that there was a considerable degree of religious ferment on the periphery of mainline Protestant religion, and this activity potentially influenced some radically inclined mainline denominational fundamentalists.

Perhaps more illuminating, however, was Singleton's conclusion that a rural/urban conflict motif, so common in fundamentalist historiography, was less characteristic of Los Angeles fundamentalists than alienation from social and cultural influence. While this appears to have been true of non-mainline Protestant sects, it also seems to have been typical of some Presbyterian and Baptist fundamentalists who opposed MacInnis. If only about five percent of the members of Los Angeles Presbytery had any connection to Biola, not one held any significant position of leadership in the denomination, and a few of MacInnis' most vocal critics were members as non-parish clergy, evangelists and teachers, inured to the Presbyterian Church but alienated from its center of power and influence.[8]

---

son, *The Fragmented Metropolis: Los Angeles, 1850–1930,* 194, 197; and Kevin Starr, *Material Dreams: Southern California Through the 1920's* (New York: Oxford University Press, 1990), 131–36.

[6] For general descriptive studies see Edmondson, "Fundamentalist Sects of Los Angeles, 1900–1930," and James G. Lewis, "An Historical Survey of Radical Sectarianism in Los Angeles" (M.A. Thesis, Occidental College, 1950).

[7] Singleton, "Fundamentalism and Urbanization," 212–13.

[8] Determined from an accounting of Los Angeles Presbytery members known to have participated at Biola as teachers, guest speakers, evangelists,

If Singleton emphasized alienation as a significant religious element of Los Angeles fundamentalist sects, another historian has emphasized the role of personal fulfillment and inward spirituality in Southern California religion. Tamar Frankiel has argued that most Anglo-Protestant migrants to Southern California had already achieved some economic success in life, and therefore, were not as interested in financial enterprise as their Northern counterparts, but instead were seeking leisure and personal fulfillment. For these folk, she argued, traditional Protestant values of thrift and industry held less interest than messages of personal fulfillment and well being.[9]

Though Biola fundamentalists were not above adapting their message to a culture of personal fulfillment and mystical spirituality, they more often perceived religious pluralism in Southern California as a threat to traditional values and religious beliefs. Yet the prevalence of mystical religion and free thought no doubt heightened conservative fears and motivated a particularly strident anti-cult rhetoric after 1900.[10] Ironically, however, the atmosphere of religious experimentation, which Biola fundamentalists so abhorred, likely made it easier for some Biola teachers to introduce doctrinal innovations that were outside of the conservative mainstream and contributed to the growing perception that Biola fundamentalists too, like the metaphysical religions and mystical cults, were part of California's religious alternatives.

Increasingly after 1915, Biola itself was perceived by many Protestant clergy as another manifestation of Southern California's melange of sectarian religious movements. Singleton concluded that by the 1920s Biola had lost a real presence among the mainline churches of Los Angeles.[11] Although this overstates the matter, it is true that increasing divergence between mainline churches and Biola, especially after premillennialism was attacked in 1918 as aberrant and unpatriotic, left many members of the Biola community feeling like a dispossessed minority. This feeling was exacerbated by the emergence of radical dispensational views at Biola, which encouraged sectarian habits in a small coterie of Biola fundamentalists. Although these ideas were officially denied by Biola leaders, they nevertheless contributed to the emergence of a dissenting and radical fundamentalist voice within the Biola community that later became an important source of anti-MacInnis agitation. Hence, if there was anything about Los Angeles religious life that most influenced the shape and character of the MacInnis controversy, it was

---

employees, and other vocational activities, in *Minutes of the General Assembly of the Presbyterian Church in the United States of America,* 1918–1925.

[9] Frankiel, *California's Spiritual Frontiers,* 76–78.

[10] Ibid., 79–83.

[11] Singleton, *Religion in the City of Angels,* 155.

the ease with which a new and often radical idea could take root and grow, and eventually blossom into a fully packaged religious alternative for Anglo-Protestants. In this dynamic religious context, there lay the seeds of local anti-MacInnis opposition.

Emerging Fundamentalist Sectarianism at Biola

By the time John MacInnis arrived in Los Angeles in 1922, there had already been a decade of movement among Biola conservatives away from a strong denominational identity toward militant and sectarian fundamentalist ideology. When MacInnis self-consciously tried to reverse these trends, he quickly discovered that there was a network of fundamentalists unwilling to let the school reverse its course in midstream. The origin of these attitudes lay with the leaders who started the school, and their reactions to social and religious transformation between 1900 and 1930.

In spite of official statements to the contrary, Biola had for some time been nominally identified with the Presbyterian Church because of its many close associations with the Presbytery of Los Angeles. In 1954, however, an angry fundamentalist preacher, J. Vernon McGee, preached a sermon entitled "Why I Left the Presbyterian Church." McGee, who was pastor of the Church of the Open Door, an independent congregation that met in the auditorium of the Bible Institute of Los Angeles, was facing expulsion from the presbytery partly because of his affiliation with Biola. This, he griped, was a reversal of the presbytery's longstanding relationship with Biola.

> The founders of the Bible Institute of Los Angeles and the Church of the Open Door were largely Presbyterian. . . . There has been no question about Presbyterian ministers serving at the Bible Institute of Los Angeles until the edict of May 11, 1954. . . . This is a radical departure from the past policy of the Presbytery. When was it that the standards of the Bible Institute became contrary to the Presbytery of Los Angeles?[12]

Perhaps McGee's question presumed too much—that a "when" could be identified. Actually the actions of the Los Angeles Presbytery in 1954 went back to well planted roots of hostility between local ministers and Biola. But if not completely sincere, his question nevertheless focused pointedly on the fact that the former harmony between Biola and the Los Angeles Presbytery had dissipated. Whence came this state of affairs?

---

[12] J. Vernon McGee, "Why I Left the Presbyterian Church," Pamphlet, n.d., Biola University Archives, La Mirada, CA.

McGee was quite right that Biola was founded primarily by members of the Presbyterian Church: among these were T. C. Horton, J. H. Sammis, A. B. Prichard, Robert Hadden, John Hunter, Reuben Torrey, and Lyman Stewart. For Horton and Torrey, at least, it appears that denominational affiliation still had value, for both of them became members of the Los Angeles Presbytery when they moved to Los Angeles. Moreover, when he founded Biola, Horton sought the support of the Church Federation of Los Angeles, and the institute maintained its Federation membership at least through 1917.[13] In addition, statistical reports bear out the fact that students of the institute worked and attended several of the local mainline denominational churches, and some of the denominations utilized Biola's facilities.[14]

In spite of these appearances, however, Biola's leaders were not loyal denominational stalwarts, nor did they hold significant positions within their denominations: to the contrary, they showed little interest in denominational concerns. A perusal of the early principal leaders of Biola provides evidence of their weak denominational loyalties. Lyman Stewart, for example, was an active Presbyterian layman who contributed to Presbyterian causes. Around 1910, however, he became dissatisfied with the direction of the Presbyterian Church and began to withdraw his money from denominational projects.[15] A more pertinent example, however, of the sect-like mentality of Biola leaders is seen in the career of T. C. Horton.

Horton's career exemplified the pattern of many leaders who entered the organized fundamentalist movement of the 1920s. Like the famed D. L. Moody, he left a promising career in business to enter YMCA work sometime in the early 1880s. Through this avenue he became associated with the well known Presbyterian minister, A. T. Pierson. Although he lacked a ministerial education, he apparently was ordained and installed as an assistant pastor in Pierson's Philadelphia church, where he served for three years.[16] But Horton preferred YMCA work, and although he sustained his Presbyterian affiliation through the 1890s, he engaged primarily in independent ministry in St. Paul, Minnesota, both as a YMCA secretary and an evangelist. While in St. Paul, he

---

[13] Henry, "Black Oil and Souls to Save," 16; Board Minutes, 26 October 1917.

[14] Faculty Minutes, 16 April 1924, 5 November 1924, and 12 November 1924; also see the student statistics of 1924 in *The King's Business,* September 1924, 551, 588–89; for local denominational meetings held at Biola see Executive Minutes, 24 November 1925, 24 August 1926, and Board Minutes, 17 May 1927.

[15] Sandeen, *Roots,* 193.

[16] *Minutes of the General Assembly of the Presbyterian Church in the United States of America,* 1884–1887.

showed marked entrepreneurial ability by starting a Bible school and gospel tabernacle, although it seems these efforts were not under any Presbyterian aegis. Sometime around 1900 Horton moved to Dallas, Texas, where he again took up independent work, first with Scofield's congregation and later at the YMCA. Hence, by the time he arrived in Los Angeles to begin ministry at the Immanuel Presbyterian Church, he left behind a long history of independent religious work.[17] Like many conservative evangelicals then, he did not hold his Presbyterian identity with any strong affection. Rather, he preferred the interdenominational environment of 19th century evangelicalism: the YMCA, Bible conferences, Bible schools, and "tabernacle" churches. Interestingly, an indication that Horton's Presbyterian identity was increasingly tenuous came in 1928, when Horton, at the age of eighty, was baptized by immersion by W. B. Riley.[18]

Another Biola leader who displayed ambivalent attitudes toward the mainline Protestant establishment was Reuben Torrey. Having a proud New England heritage, Torrey quite appropriately began his ministerial career in the Congregational Church. His increasing dissatisfaction with the theological direction of that denomination, however, led him to become a member of the Presbyterian Church in 1908, a step that was also taken by other evangelical Congregationalists like Lewis Sperry Chafer and C. I. Scofield.[19] When Torrey went to Biola in 1911, he also transferred his ministerial membership to the Los Angeles Presbytery.[20] But, as Staggers has clearly documented, Torrey's ennui with denominational matters continued. Instead of involvement in the presbytery, therefore, Torrey continued to give his time to Bible conferences, Bible schools, and itinerant evangelism.[21]

But if Torrey was lackadaisical about his denominational commitment, he, nevertheless, did not abandon his denominational affiliation as did other evangelicals. To the contrary, he actually worried about sectarian tendencies that he saw developing at Biola. Of course, Bible schools were never, strictly speaking, mainstream institutions, and from the start they were haunted by the spectre of sectarianism. Even a re-

---

[17] For this biographical information on Horton see Henry, "Black Oil and Souls to Save," 16, and Williams and Miller, *Chartered for His Glory*, 17–19.

[18] J. Frank Norris to T. C. Horton, 19 January 1929, Folder 925, J. Franklyn Norris Papers, Southern Baptist Historical Library and Archives, Nashville, TN.

[19] Torrey joined MacInnis' Montrose Presbyterian Church in 1908; see Torrey to Keith Brooks, 22 May 1928, MacInnis Papers; for Chafer and Scofield see Hannah, "The Origins of the Evangelical Theological College," 121.

[20] *Minutes of the General Assembly of the Presbyterian Church in the United States of America,* 1914, 482.

[21] Staggers, "Reuben A. Torrey," 196.

spected Bible teacher like G. Campbell Morgan, a former associate of
D. L. Moody, could be found backstepping from "the vagaries of some
of those who associate with the [Moody] Institute," and in Los Angeles,
it seemed, such vagaries were plentiful.[22] But what troubled Torrey most
was a theological "vagary" that encouraged the growth of strong sectarian attitudes.

In 1914 Torrey complained about a "company of people" at Biola
who were, as he described it, "largely out with the churches."[23] The
"company" to which Torrey referred were friends and supporters of
Robert Hadden, a one time teacher at Biola, who had been dismissed for
teaching an extreme view of dispensationalism called Bullingerism,
which posited that Israel was really the Bride of Christ rather than the
church, and that only the so-called prison epistles of Paul belonged to
the church. Like his colleagues at Biola, Hadden's career was shaped in
the crucible of interdenominational evangelicalism; his employment at
Biola came through his earlier association with Horton at the Northwestern Bible Training School of St. Paul, Minnesota.[24] Like Horton, he
also had a long history of ministry with the YMCA, rescue missions,
and Bible schools. Although he seems to have had only a certificate
from Moody Bible Institute, he was able to enter the Congregational
ministry in Ohio. When he came to Los Angeles, he entered the presbytery as an evangelist.[25]

After Hadden was dismissed from Biola he returned to rescue mission work and began teaching independent Bible classes throughout Los
Angeles. Through this activity he gained a local following, a thing that
worried Torrey, when he observed that many people attended Hadden's
classes rather than a local church.[26] In spite of rumors that he intended to

---

[22] G. Cambell Morgan to William Rainey Harper, 27 October 1902, Moody
Bible Institute Archives.

[23] Reuben Torrey to James Gray, 14 April 1914, Moody Bible Institute
Archives.

[24] This school should not be confused with Riley's Northwestern Schools. In
a 1928 article, W. B. Riley claimed that he had a right to involve himself in
Biola affairs because Horton and Hadden were once professors at "the Northwestern." ("Breaking the Bible School Defense Line," *The Christian Fundamentalist,* April 1928, 6). But this statement was misleading, because Horton
had left the Twin Cities area by 1900, at least two years before Riley started his
Northwestern Schools. Hadden and Horton had been teachers at another school
also called Northwestern Bible School, but it closed in 1899.

[25] Henry, Biola Manuscript, 62–63; *Minutes of the General Assembly of the
Presbyterian Church in the United States of America,* 1913, 483.

[26] Torrey to Gray, 14 April 1914, Moody Bible Institute Archives. Two other
Biola teachers also left over this issue, J. R. Pratt, a Presbyterian, and Leon
Tucker, a Baptist.

start another institute, Hadden maintained cordial but restive relations with the Biola community in their common effort to promote premillennialism and fundamentalism, but he was disinclined to accept the institute's role as a support agency for mainline Protestant denominationalism.

The emergence of radical dispensationalism at Biola created a climate in which eddies of radical thought swirled in the mainstream of institutional centrism. Just as James Gray tried to dampen fundamentalist extremists and preserve a conservative center, so too, Torrey resisted the radical tendencies of dispensationalism, which seemed to threaten Biola's institutional integrity. Lacking any denominational authority, independent organizations like Biola depended on personal authority to hold together the disparate aspects of the community that could spin outside of the institutional mainstream. But such tendencies were not easily controlled, and Hadden's influence in premillennial circles and later in the fundamentalist movement continued to grow, making it more likely—years later—for a significant anti-MacInnis faction to develop in the Biola community.[27]

The Decline of Cooperative Church Relationships

Although Biola began with the tacit support of mainline denominations in Los Angeles, this initial goodwill gradually began to erode after 1915. For the most part, Biola's leaders maintained their denominational memberships, as did most fundamentalists through the 1920s, but with the development of an organized fundamentalist movement after World War I, many of these denominational fundamentalists took a militant stand against the theological and institutional changes taking place in the mainline churches. This fact led to further erosion of Biola's goodwill with Los Angeles churches and directly led to the reforming measures of the MacInnis administration.

Lyman Stewart had set the tenor for Biola's role in the community by insisting that Biola officials refrain from public criticism of Los Angeles area churches. But with headstrong and opinionated leaders, cordial relations did not come easily. Hadden's radical teaching had early on, according to Horton, antagonized many Los Angeles clergy, but Horton himself had acquired some ill-will from Presbyterian clergy as when, for example, it became known that he refused to ask God's blessing for a Biola student who wanted to attend the Presbyterian seminary at San

---

[27] For Gray's efforts to stifle radicalism see Brereton, *Training God's Army,* 141–42; for Torrey's similar efforts see the Torrey/Hadden/Gray correspondence in the Torrey correspondence file, Moody Bible Institute Archives.

Anselmo.[28] In a similar vein, mutual feelings of goodwill were not encouraged by Torrey's brash and outspoken manner, which bothered
many clergy. But these faults might have been overlooked, had it not
been for his plan to start a church in the auditorium of the Bible institute. This plan was anything but good news for downtown Los Angeles
ministers, who saw the new church as competition.

The plan to begin an independent church at Biola was probably based
on the model of Moody Bible Institute, which also had a successful
church on its premises. Following this model, Torrey had stipulated
prior to his coming that he wanted a similar independent church to meet
at Biola. Hence, when the institute was constructed, it included a mam-
moth auditorium capable of seating three thousand.[29] It seems, however,
that controversy erupted when Leander Munhall openly proposed in
1915, probably at the behest of Torrey, that a church be organized to
meet in the institute auditorium. According to one widely circulated report, Torrey had promised one Los Angeles minister that no church
would be organized at Biola, but this was probably untrue, as Torrey
had intended to start such a church before coming to Biola.[30] Conflict
over the proposed church soon followed, and meetings were called between Biola officials and local Baptist and Presbyterian clergy to diffuse
the tension. Although Biola finally received a tacit approval to organize
the church, bitter feelings lingered, so much so, that nine years later
Horton was still defending the institute's decision, and as late as 1927
charges that Torrey had broken a promise were still dogging school officials.[31] Interestingly, in spite of the ill-defined ecclesiastical relationship between the Church of the Open Door, as it was called, and the Los
Angeles Presbytery, its ministers continued to obtain membership in the
presbytery, including MacInnis, who pastored the church for approximately four months beginning October 2, 1925.[32]

---

[28] Cleland B. McAfee to MacInnis, 12 December 1922, MacInnis Papers.

[29] Cocoris, *70 Years on Hope Street,* 16, 21; Brereton, *Training God's Army,*
150.

[30] Staggers, "Reuben A. Torrey," 213–14.

[31] Staggers cites Horton's 1924 pamphlet, "To the Members of the Church of
the Open Door," as his source for this controversy, but this pamphlet was not
found in the Biola archives. For the lingering effects of Torrey's so-called
promise see Mrs. Lyman Stewart to J. H. LeGrand, 14 December 1927, MacInnis Papers.

[32] Biola Board Minutes, 2 October 1925. MacInnis submitted a resignation
as the church's pastor on 10 February 1926; see E. Lutz to MacInnis, 11 February 1926. Several letters written the next day indicate that a few in the church
objected to his pastorate; see e.g., Mrs. E. E. Chenault to MacInnis, 11 February 1926. In spite of this, he continued to preach at the church at least through
June; see Andrew Billings to MacInnis, 9 June 1926, MacInnis Papers.

Biola's delicate détente with local mainline churches rapidly began to disintegrate when premillennialism came under attack during the world war, and this situation continued to worsen as it became evident that Biola would also become the most visible representative of organized fundamentalism in Los Angeles. Seeing these changes, a local Methodist minister in Los Angeles, Dr. Charles Selecman, publicly attacked the institute claiming that at first the churches had been willing to support it, but in 1919, "not one of the regular churches supported it."

I am frank to say that I cannot work with the Bible Institute. Their spirit is censorious and narrow, their methods are unethical, their theology is dismal and disjointed, literal and almost obsolete, their educational standards superficial and their whole ecclesiastical relationship is so uncertain and anomalous that their presence in the community is a constant embarrassment to the work of the regular churches.[33]

Although Selecman's theological views motivated his harsh comments, and though he overstated the lack of support Biola received from the regular churches, nevertheless, his perception was shared by many Los Angeles area clergy. A nationally known Baptist pastor, the moderately conservative J. Whitcomb Brougher, grumbled in 1924 that he had received no help from Biola students in twelve years. Still another local Congregationalist minister, John Gardner, complained of a spirit of suspicion in Southern California, that caused Biola leaders to ignore him, in spite of the fact that he had enjoyed a close relationship to James Gray and the Moody Bible Institute.[34] In a point of unintended irony, even T. C. Horton noted the changed religious climate of post-war Southern California. When a local minister was invited to attend a Bible conference where A. C. Dixon was scheduled to speak, Horton reported that the pastor said: "If it is the Dr. Dixon of London I am agreeable, but if it is Dr. Dixon of the Bible Institute I will have nothing to do with it."[35] Horton then asked sarcastically how they differed. But this question overlooked an important point, because at least one Los Angeles pastor did see a difference. When Dixon left America in 1911 to occupy Spurgeon's old pulpit in London, the religious world was troubled, but not yet quagmired in controversy over fundamentalism and modernism. By 1919, however, when Dixon returned to the States, premillennialism was being attacked, fundamentalists were raising their battle cries, and a

---

[33] "Scores Bible Institute," Los Angeles *Times*, 17 November 1919, Part II, p. 6.

[34] For Brougher see Faculty Minutes, 5 November 1924; for Gardner see John Gardner to MacInnis, 13 May 1926, MacInnis Papers.

[35] "Bible Institute Happenings," *The King's Business*, January, 1920, 31.

crisis mentality infused the American psyche. Under these circumstances, it is, perhaps, no surprise that the A. C. Dixon of London could appear quite different than the A. C. Dixon of Los Angeles.

The assault on premillennialism begun by Shailer Mathews and Shirley Jackson Case of the University of Chicago inflamed tensions that had already been smoldering for some time. Biola conservatives were particularly stung by the charge that premillennialists were unpatriotic, a claim that gained real teeth when Torrey publicly denounced Woodrow Wilson's efforts to establish the League of Nations in 1919.[36] Torrey later denied the charges that he had called Wilson a traitor, but his bombastic and ill-advised language galvanized local opposition, and even attracted national attention when complaints were filed with the United States District Attorney for possible prosecution under the Espionage Act, which prohibited public speech that would bring scorn or contempt on the United States.[37] Although he was never prosecuted, he was pilloried by his ministerial colleagues. Charles Selecman, for example, seized the opportunity to excoriate Torrey for his un-American statements, which in Selecman's view were seditious and linked to premillennial pessimism. In the Los Angeles Minister's Association, a resolution was passed deploring his statements, because they encouraged anarchy, disloyalty, and violence.[38] In all the disturbance, however, Torrey remained resolute, claiming that almost all the members of the Church of the Open Door supported his views.[39]

The rise of an organized fundamentalist movement, which crystallized around premillennial conservatives at Biola, exacerbated tensions between the mainline clergy and Biola. In Los Angeles, the institute quickly became the local rallying center for the new World's Christian Fundamentals Association, which alienated clergy by its militancy. Many bellicose editorials appeared in *The King's Business,* some of which were so nasty that they even offended the conservative W. H. Griffith Thomas.[40] Moreover, the continuing presence of extreme fundamentalists hovering in Biola's shadow tarnished the school's image,

---

[36] "Dean's Slap at President is Resented by Bible Institute Auditors," Los Angeles *Times,* 10 November 1919, Part II, p. 1, For the 1918 premillennial controversy see Weber, *Living in the Shadow of the Second Coming,* 118–19.

[37] "No Criticisms from Deacons," Los Angeles *Times,* 11 November 1919, Part II, p. 1; and "Dixon Attacks Conduct of Our Allies' Armies," 12 November 1919, Part II, p. 7.

[38] "Torrey Speech Deplored," Los Angeles *Times,* 18 November 1919, Part II, p. 1.

[39] Torrey to James Gray, 13 November 1919, Moody Bible Institute Archives.

[40] W. H. Griffith Thomas to MacInnis, 16 September 1922, MacInnis Papers.

even though not everyone associated with Biola liked the new warlike attitudes encouraged by the national fundamentalist movement.

Although not officially connected to Biola, Robert Hadden was one who continued to hover in Biola's shadow. As the fundamentalist movement took off, Hadden responded by forming the Christian Fundamentals League, which distributed leaflets and sponsored independent Bible classes throughout the city.[41] Another leader who attracted considerable opposition from mainline clergy as well as Biola itself was French Oliver, a member of the Los Angeles Presbytery. As early as 1915 Oliver was complaining of mainline clergy that were trying to block his evangelistic campaigns. In 1917, he nearly split the Vancouver Ministerial Association with his denunciation of liberal ministers, whom he called "ecclesiastical buzzards," revealing why he was not welcome in many cities.[42] Not surprisingly, Oliver later became one of MacInnis' most vociferous critics, and during the height of the MacInnis controversy he quit the Presbyterian church to start an independent fundamentalist church.[43]

Although it is impossible to clearly identify how many churches were alienated by Biola's fundamentalist image, it is at least clear that many local clergy came to believe that Biola's teaching encouraged a sectarian spirit. To one MacInnis supporter, it seemed that the majority of churches in Southern California were not friendly toward the institute.[44] Regardless of whether or not most clergy believed Biola fostered a sectarian mentality, the power of a single incident could still profoundly affect popular opinion and prejudice. A schism at the Placentia Presbyterian Church, for instance, encouraged by the recent Biola graduate, Charles Fuller, caused tensions between Presbyterians and Biola which were not easily forgotten.[45]

---

[41] Edmondson, "Fundamentalist Sects of Los Angeles," 243–59.

[42] For clerical resistance to Oliver see, Oliver to Billy Sunday, 22 December 1915, Billy Sunday Collection 61, Box 1, Folder 24, Billy Graham Archives, Wheaton IL. For the Vancouver campaign see Robert K. Burkinshaw, "Conservative Evangelicalism in the Twentieth-Century 'West': British Columbia and the United States," in *Amazing Grace: Evangelicalism in Australia, Britain, Canada, and the United States* (Grand Rapids: Baker Books, 1993), 323–24.

[43] "The First Fundamentalist Church of Los Angeles," *Christian Fundamentalist,* November 1928, 26.

[44] Ford L. Canfield to MacInnis, n.d., MacInnis Papers.

[45] Fuller, *Give the Winds a Mighty Voice,* 53.

MacInnis and the Restitution of Goodwill
Between Los Angeles Churches and Biola

When MacInnis agreed to teach at Biola, he did so believing that the Bible school movement in America had a valuable and useful service to offer the work of the church. In his idealism, which hearkened to the Moody era, MacInnis believed that the Bible school should be a servant of the church by offering lay Christian education and missionary training. In this concept, the Bible school was, in effect, a training arm of the Protestant establishment. A few months after his arrival, and sensing the divisive drift at Biola, MacInnis expressed his desire to preserve this cooperative ideal. "It would break my heart," he exclaimed, "if I thought I were going to be put outside of the vital interests of the Presbyterian Church because I came to the Bible Institute."[46] Four years later he was still emphasizing this ideal: "My own great desire in connection with all our Institute work . . . is to line it up in a constructive way with the Evangelical church."[47] Although his statements reflected those of an earlier day, such as Biola's own expressed goal to "be a real blessing to every evangelical church," MacInnis found himself torn between his ideals and the reality that Biola was, in fact, perceived by many clergy as being outside the vital interests of the Protestant establishment. Hence, when elected dean, he determined to reverse the corrosive effects of fundamentalist militancy, and although he achieved some minor successes, his efforts failed to mitigate intransigent fundamentalist attitudes.

To avoid any misinterpretation of his intentions, MacInnis published a "declaration" of his goals in June 1925, in which he strongly declared that he conceived of the Bible institute as part of the church and not an independent organization in competition with the Church.[48] Having signaled his intention to restore harmony with the churches, MacInnis reported in October that his efforts were already bearing fruit.

> The feeling of the churches towards the Institute has very materially changed and this change is indicated in the fact that whereas we used to find places for our students to teach in Sunday Schools, etc., this year we have more than twice as many applications as we can fill. There is a long waiting list. This is along the line that I have had in mind and I did not

---

[46] MacInnis to Cleland B. McAfee, 19 January 1923, MacInnis Papers.

[47] MacInnis to Robert Speer, 3 June 1927, MacInnis Papers.

[48] MacInnis, "A Declaration of Understanding, Policy, and Motives," 242–43.

dare to hope that we could get as manifest a co-operation from the churches in such a short time.[49]

Perhaps his letter was colored by excessive optimism, but placements give solid evidence of increased cooperation. His optimism was bolstered by a vote of confidence from the Los Angeles Presbytery. Commenting on that vote, MacInnis wrote to a friend: "As you may know this is a great change in the attitude of the Presbytery and one man said that he never expected to live to see the day when such a thing should take place."[50] Similar feelings were expressed by a Baptist minister, who thanked MacInnis for his talk to a gathering of Baptist clergy: "I do not need to go into the matter of our former feeling toward the B. I. So far as I am concerned that is ancient history; and we all rejoice in a new day."[51]

Not all comments were so favorable. Lewis Thurber Guild, the District Superintendent of Los Angeles of the Methodist Church, hoped that institute patrons would now avoid making trouble in the churches, but concluded that he still could not recommend the school.[52] Yet denominational reticence on one flank was matched by fundamentalist opposition on the other. Gerald B. Winrod, that feisty evolution fighter, warned his friend of this dilemma: "If you carry it too far you will cut off that great amount of support from people who believe that denominationalism is in apostasy." To this he logically concluded, "Such a program is not consistent with the work of Bible Institutes in general."[53] Winrod's analysis was exactly correct. An instance of this reality occurred when MacInnis agreed to talk at the Placentia Presbyterian Church, which was still smarting from the Fuller led schism a few years earlier. Now a board member of Biola, Fuller urged MacInnis to cancel his engagement at the Placentia Presbyterian Church, in order to avoid giving offence to Fuller's independent Calvary Church.[54] Here was his predicament in a nutshell; for MacInnis to win denominational cooperation, he had to risk alienating a part of Biola's independent fundamentalist constituency. But this could be a risky business, for unless the school could raise support elsewhere, it stood to lose its existing base of support.

---

[49] MacInnis to W. W. Plumb, 7 October 1925, MacInnis Papers.

[50] MacInnis to W. M. Hayes, n.d. , MacInnis Papers.

[51] Ernest E. Ford to MacInnis, 13 January 1926, MacInnis Papers.

[52] Lewis Thurber Guild to MacInnis, 2 May 1925, MacInnis Papers.

[53] Gerald Winrod to MacInnis, 21 November 1928, MacInnis Papers.

[54] Charles Fuller to MacInnis, 15 February 1928, MacInnis Papers.

The Emergence of Local Opposition to MacInnis

No doubt it came as a surprise to many board members that when he accepted the position of dean on April 6, 1925, MacInnis became the instant focal point of controversy. To their chagrin, his statements published in the Los Angeles *Times* touched off a firestorm of criticism from Los Angeles area fundamentalists. Wanting to know his position on issues of the day, a *Times,* reporter asked MacInnis about his relation to the fundamentalist movement, and, in particular, his views on the evolution controversy. His answers were not what local fundamentalists wanted to hear. Instead of his endorsement of anti-evolution political campaigns and hearty agreement with the efforts of militant fundamentalists, MacInnis gave reserved and qualified responses, which failed to satisfy some Biola fundamentalists. After this, in spite of his efforts to explain his views, he found himself mired in misunderstanding. In order to alleviate further criticism, MacInnis penned a statement explaining his views, which he read to the Church of the Open Door and which was later published as a tract. The *Times* article and his written response became the first volley in a conflict between moderate and radical fundamentalists. The main issues in this early skirmish were his attitudes about fundamentalism, anti-evolutionism, and premillennial dispensationalism.

MacInnis and the World's Christian Fundamentals Association

When MacInnis stated that he was not allied with the fundamentalists or the modernists, but that he was a "conservative thinker,"[55] he was hoping to sidestep the theological controversy then upsetting the mainline churches. But in the heat of controversy, subtle distinctions were easily lost. To clarify his position, therefore, MacInnis said:

> I am a fundamentalist in the sense that I believe with all my heart, without apology or reservation, the foundation truths of the Christian religion. . . .
> I am not a fundamentalist in the sense of belonging to the recently organized party calling itself by that name.[56]

The party that he referred to was the World's Christian Fundamentals Association (WCFA), which had been organized six years earlier. The idea of an association of like-minded conservatives had been contemplated for some time before steps were taken to organize the WCFA in

---

[55] Los Angeles *Times,* April 7, 1925, Part II, p. 1.
[56] MacInnis Statement, Typed Document [1925], MacInnis Papers.

1919. W. B. Riley, for example, had hoped to create a similar organization as early as 1909, though his initial attempts foundered.[57] Writing in 1918, Torrey stated that several attempts to organize conservatives had earlier been made, but because "each one wanted to be the leader in the matter" their efforts failed.[58] A revival of interest in prophetic themes stimulated by the world war, however, created an auspicious opportunity to gather evangelicals into an organized coalition.

From the beginning, the WCFA experienced difficulties. One issue that troubled the organization was its failure to define a specific constituency. On this point, Torrey felt particularly disgruntled. Writing to James Gray before the WCFA was formed, Torrey anticipated this problem.

> If such a gathering as that could be called together I would be glad to be in it, but I do not think the Bible Institutes collectively are the organizations around which that should center.
>
> If . . . by the 'we' you mean we orthodox men throughout the country, I agree with you, but if you mean simply the Institutes, I do not. If you could gather together a company of the leading men of the orthodox type, not only in the Institutes, but in the seminaries and in the ministry and in placed [sic] of other leadership, men like John Timothy Stone, Mark Matthews, Robertson and Mullens [sic] of Louisville, and perhaps others there, Charles Erdman and perhaps others at Princeton, a real representative company of those who are agreed on the fundamentals, I would be glad to attend and do what I could to make the thing a success.[59]

Torrey's comments illustrate nicely the problem conservatives faced: how could the organization have broad support if it were comprised only of Bible school and Bible conference constituents and excluded denominational conservatives, who were not part of these institutions? Gray replied that he agreed, but pointed out pragmatically that there was none other to take the lead.[60] Torrey's viewpoint was not isolated, however, for other leaders saw essentially the same difficulty. Rowland Bingham, founder of the evangelical Sudan Interior Mission, stated the same objection: "We believe that a wider selection will be necessary be-

---

[57] Trollinger, *God's Empire,* 34; Szasz, "Three Fundamentalist Leaders," 98.
[58] Torrey to James Gray, 11 December 1918, Moody Bible Institute Archives.
[59] Ibid.
[60] James Gray to Reuben Torrey, 2 January 1919, Moody Bible Institute Archives.

fore we can regard them [WCFA] as thoroughly representative of all those who are in the evangelical church."[61]

MacInnis shared these objections. Although he was known to many of the founders of the WCFA, he was not a part of its inception. After the initial 1919 conference, however, he was asked to assist in sponsoring an extension program of the WCFA in Syracuse, New York. This he rejected, because in his view the WCFA was "far from adequately representing the Christian Church in North America." MacInnis continued:

> I have no sympathy whatever with the tendency among that particular coterie to divide up the church on such a narrow basis as they are operating upon. They seem to be characterized by a very narrow interpretation and, therefore, in my judgement non-Christian spirit that is unworthy of men who would cause a split in the church for the sake of sound doctrine. . . . It would seem to me that these men represent certain Institutions that they are seeking to support and are willing to gain sympathy for them at the expense of some of the great interests of the church of Jesus Christ.[62]

MacInnis could hardly have expressed his views more frankly. Like Torrey, he believed that the WCFA had little in common with the evangelical coalition of an earlier day, which better represented the mainline churches. But in addition, MacInnis accused the association of being divisive, pursuing the interests of their "institutions" at the expense of the church. Perceptions of divisiveness and sectarianism troubled the WCFA from the beginning, and this probably alienated some conservative clergy who might otherwise have shared its goals. James Gray, for example, who took early initiative to bring Torrey into the association, found himself backstepping only five years later, when Torrey invited him to address the 1925 convention: replied Gray, "I do not feel free to accept the invitation."

> My reason is that the [Moody] Institute's supposed leadership in the Fundamentals Association has brought us much trouble and loss in the last two or three years. . . . we are charged with leading an organized movement to disrupt the churches, all our denials of which are unavailing in the face of what appears to be circumstantial evidence to the contrary.[63]

---

[61] Quoted in McKenzie, "Thought of Rowland Bingham," 173.

[62] MacInnis to Robert Cameron, 3 June 1919, MacInnis Papers.

[63] Gray to Reuben Torrey, 26 December 1924, Moody Bible Institute Archives.

Charges of divisiveness stemmed in part from the militant rhetoric of WCFA convention speeches, which attacked the mainline denominations and threatened fundamentalist separation. At the very first convention in 1919, for example, speakers resolved to "find for ourselves a new fellowship," if an ecumenical plan of church federation were approved by mainline churches.[64] A bellicose J. Frank Norris said in the late 1920s, that "independent churches were springing up on every hand." Although there is no definitive statistical study of this movement toward independent churches, there is no doubt that WCFA rhetoric aided the cause, when its prominent leaders suggested that association members might leave their denominations to form hundreds of "independent fundamentalist tabernacles."[65]

In spite of assurances from Torrey and the Canadian fundamentalist Sydney Smith, that they were trying to get the WCFA on "saner ground," the stance of the association had estranged many conservative evangelicals, and it had failed to achieve the broad evangelical representation that Torrey had hoped for in 1918.[66] Writing in 1924, Graham Scroggie acknowledged that a "vast majority of Fundamentalists" were not even members of organizations like the WCFA.[67] Just as important were those evangelical leaders who came to reject or distance themselves from the association.

By 1925, when MacInnis was explaining that he did not belong to the WCFA, many other evangelicals had come to the same position. G. Campbell Morgan, James Gray, F. B. Meyer, and J. C. Massee, had all participated in the regional meetings of the WCFA in 1919, but by 1925 these leaders had taken steps to leave the movement or lessen their association with it.[68] Moreover, ill-conceived planning and perceptions of

---

[64] *God Hath Spoken,* 15.

[65] For the Norris quotation see "An Independent Fundamentalist Church for Dallas," *The Fundamentalist,* 1 June 1928, 1; for the Riley citation see Trollinger, *God's Empire,* 43.

[66] For the "saner ground" quotation see Torrey to James Gray, 8 January 1925, Moody Bible Institute Archives.

[67] Graham Scroggie, "Fundamentalism," *Evangelical Christian and Missionary Witness,* November 1924, 446.

[68] For their participation in the WCFA see Cole, *History of Fundamentalism,* 235; for their growing distance from the movement see the following: on Morgan see Sandeen, *Roots,* 268; for Gray see John David Hannah, "James Martin Gray, 1851–1935" (Th.D. diss., Dallas Theological Seminary, 1974), 178; for Meyer see Ian Randall, "A Christian Cosmopolitan: F. B. Meyer in Britain," in *Amazing Grace: Evangelicalism in Australia, Britain, Canada, and the United States,* ed. George A. Rawlyk and Mark A. Noll (Grand Rapids: Baker Books, 1993), 181; for Massee see Russell, *Voices of American Fundamentalism,* 125–28.

unworthy motives alienated other conservatives, who might have strongly supported the movement. Bingham, for example, suspected Riley of "human ambition," in his attempts to control the movement, and A. C. Gaebelein felt excluded by the militant brethren. In 1923, Gaebelein told Lewis Sperry Chafer, a founder of the WCFA, that in his opinion, "the days of the Fundamentalist movement are numbered." Just two years later he dropped his membership. Likewise, by 1925 Chafer was also trying to remove himself from the unseemly reputation of the WCFA, but his claim in 1930, that he had never been in sympathy with the fundamentalist movement, appears disingenuous given his prominent role in its formation.[69]

MacInnis was not an exception, therefore, when he qualified his use of the term fundamentalist. The Moody Bible Institute had stated virtually the same qualification a year earlier.

> We are not Fundamentalists in the sense that we have joined that association or become a part of that movement as a movement. We shrink from "movements," and as we have said before, "evangelism" is all the name we want.[70]

Though the term had only been recently coined in 1920 by Curtis Lee Laws, editor of the Baptist periodical, the *Watchman-Examiner,* by 1925 Laws was nonplussed that the term had become associated with radicals in the Baptist Bible Union and with anti-evolution political campaigns, rather than with his own moderate theological stance.[71] Presbyterian conservatives did not very much like the term either. J. Gresham Machen and Clarence Macartney were loathe to use it, although they were willing to endorse it in a qualified sense for the sake of battling a common enemy. A more moderate Charles Erdman was willing to say in 1925 that he was a "fundamentalist in his beliefs," if by that term one meant "old-fashioned orthodoxy and Christian spirit."[72]

---

[69] On Bingham see McKenzie, "Thought of Rowland Bingham," 173, for Gaebelein on the WCFA see David A. Rausch, *Arno C. Gaebelein, 1861–1945. Irenic Fundamentalist and Scholar: Including Conversations with Dr. Frank E. Gaebelein* (Lewiston, New York: Mellen Press, 1983), 264–65; for Gaebelein's exclusion see Szasz, "Three Fundamentalist Leaders," 138–39; for the Gaebelein/Chafer correspondence on this subject see Hannah, "Origins of the Evangelical Theological College," 153, 212–14.

[70] "The *Christian Century* Sustains Professor J. Gresham Machen," *Moody Bible Institute Monthly,* April 1924, 402.

[71] Norman Maring, "Conservative But Progressive," in *What God Hath Wrought,* ed. Gilbert L. Guffin (Chicago: Judson Press, 1960), 25.

[72] For Machen see Darryl G. Hart, *Defending the Faith: J. Gresham Machen and the Crisis of Conservative Protestantism in Modern America* (Baltimore:

About four years later, in spite of his differences with the organized movement, G. Campbell Morgan was still willing to call himself a fundamentalist, though he added, "of quite a different school."[73] It certainly was not unusual then, that MacInnis would have qualified his use of the word. But it seems that in Los Angeles, where militant enthusiasm ran particularly high, to hedge on its use became a sign of weakness and compromise. One critic wrote that to identify himself as a "conservative thinker" was deliberately vague, and regardless of whether or not he was a member of the WCFA, in his thought he was either a fundamentalist or a modernist, and therefore, his reserve was simply a sign that he was modernist.[74] Such attitudes were not unusual and demonstrate the particularly strident character of some Los Angeles fundamentalists, who now began to oppose MacInnis and his policies.

MacInnis and Fundamentalist Attitudes Toward Evolution

MacInnis made his comments to the *Times* during a period of intense public interest in evolution. In May 1925 fundamentalist editors were much exercised over what they considered to be E. Y. Mullins' compromising views on evolution.[75] Mullins, the president of Southern Baptist Seminary, had left the door open for a theistic interpretation of evolution, which in the opinions of most fundamentalists was not acceptable. But the most famous event was the Scopes Trial, which followed shortly thereafter, when a Tennessee biology teacher decided to challenge the state's anti-evolution law. Although Scopes lost the court battle the enduring images of fundamentalist ignorance which were generated by the trial, and the death of William Jennings Bryan, caused the anti-evolution movement to become fragmented and ineffective. With so much foment over evolution, it is not difficult to see why MacInnis' views on the subject were so closely watched by wary fire-breathing fundamentalists. Like his statements on the fundamentalist movement,

---

Johns Hopkins University Press, 1994), 63; on Macartney see his autobiography entitled *The Making of a Minister* (Great Neck, NY: Channel Press, 1961), 183–85; for Erdman's quotation see the *Presbyterian Banner*, 7 May 1925, 5, cited by Ki Hong Kim, "Presbyterian Conflict in the Early Twentieth Century: Ecclesiology in the Princeton Tradition and the Emergence of Presbyterian Fundamentalism" (Ph.D. diss., Drew University, 1983), 90.

[73] "Dr. Cambell Morgan and the Los Angeles Bible Institute," *British Weekly*, 5 July 1928, 295.

[74] Arthur J. Fry to MacInnis, 10 April 1925, MacInnis Papers.

[75] See, e.g. T. T. Shields, "Southern Baptists at the Cross Roads," *Gospel Witness*, 21 May 1925, 12–21; on this controversy see William E. Ellis, "Edgar Young Mullins and the Crisis of Moderate Southern Baptist Leadership," *Foundations* 19 (1976): 177.

MacInnis tried to articulate a moderate position on the question of evolution. Regarding the creation of the world, he affirmed that theologians and scientists could easily agree that God made the world, but that no one could be certain as to how it was made, nor the length of time involved.[76] This position was quite similar to the ideas of other moderate evangelicals, like E. Y. Mullins, who was at the same time trying to defend a middle position that would accommodate some aspects of evolutionary science, without giving up a belief in divine creation. But also like Mullins, MacInnis found himself embroiled in controversy with fundamentalists who felt no need to accommodate theories of evolution.

Los Angeles was a particularly fertile ground for a controversy of this sort, for it was home to more than one anti-evolution organization, the most influential of which was probably Harry Rimmer's Research Science Bureau. Rimmer was a member of the Los Angeles Presbytery, although like Hadden, Horton, and Oliver, he appears to have valued his Presbyterian identity more for the social standing that it conferred than for any particular regard for its traditions.[77] Rimmer does not seem to have involved himself in controversy over MacInnis' views on evolution, perhaps because he did not wish to injure his relations with the institute, but his strict no-compromising anti-evolution beliefs, which even disallowed Riley's embrace of a day-age interpretation of Genesis, no doubt encouraged many fundamentalists in Los Angeles to adopt similar hard-line views. Ironically, however, Rimmer's unbending literalism had not been the dominant position of most evangelicals prior to the 1920s.

By the end of the 19th century many evangelicals had reconciled their theology of creation with the theory of evolution, often by arguing that God's act of creation occurred through a process of gradual development over eons, rather than occurring in brief moments of time.[78] In the early 20th century, however, a "great divide" was beginning to form, as one historian of science put it, between some evangelicals who completely rejected any evolutionary concepts, and those who tried to preserve a reasonable synthesis of creation and evolution. That divide has been illustrated in the divergent attitudes of contributors to the *Fundamentals:* essays by James Orr and George Frederick Wright argued for qualified acceptance of biological evolution, maintaining a distinction between evolution as a scientific explanation of biological change, and

---

[76] Los Angeles *Times,* April 7, 1925. Part II, p. 1.

[77] Ronald Numbers, *The Creationists* (New York: Alfred A. Knopf, Inc., 1992), 64.

[78] David N. Livingstone, *Darwin's Forgotten Defenders: The Encounter Between Evangelical Theology and Evolutionary Thought* (Grand Rapids: Eerdmans, 1987), 65–77, 85–99; Numbers, *The Creationists,* 17.

"evolutionism" as a philosophical and materialistic explanation of human origins. Two other essays, however, put forward an "untempered and frank" attack on evolution, avoiding more judicious compromises for an out-and-out rejection of it as contrary to "the plain reading of scripture."[79]

In the 1920s, this breadth of evangelical opinion became considerably less tolerable, even unacceptable to most fundamentalists, but particularly so for those who strongly defended the anti-evolution crusade. In Los Angeles, editors of *The King's Business* seem to have forgotten that they were going to carry on the testimony of the *Fundamentals,* and instead, filled the magazine with anti-evolution diatribes, such as the influential articles of S. J. Bole, that characterized evolution as one side of "Satan's Triangle."[80] A similar process of narrowing occurred in Rowland Bingham's magazine: in 1912 he published an article by W. H. Griffith Thomas, a Canadian evangelical with conservative dispensational views, which asserted that a modified form of evolution could be reconciled with Christianity. After 1922, however, when fundamentalists made evolution their principal enemy, Bingham no longer had room for such mediating positions in his magazine.[81] In general, most fundamentalists held the blithe opinion of Billy Sunday, that one simply could not accept evolution and also be a Christian.[82] This intolerance toward divergent interpretations provides an apposite example of Timothy Smith's point that fundamentalism represented an ideologically truncated version of a more intellectually broad evangelical tradition.[83]

Although conservatives had fulminated for some time over the threat of evolution, and J. Frank Norris began his opposition to Baylor University as early as 1919, the attempt to eradicate evolution from the public schools did not take center stage until William Jennings Bryan chose to make it the focus of his energetic opposition in mid 1921.[84] With so im-

---

[79] David N. Livingstone, "B. B. Warfield, the Theory of Evolution and Early Fundamentalism," *Evangelical Quarterly* 58 (January 1986): 69–78; but note Wright's ambivalence on the issue documented in Numbers, *The Creationists,* 32–36.

[80] See his series of articles entitled "Satan's Triangle: Evolution, Philosophy, Criticism," *The King's Business,* May–December, 1925.

[81] McKenzie, "Thought of Rowland Bingham," 153–55.

[82] William A. Sunday to William Jennings Bryan, 4 July 1925, quoted in Willard B. Gatewood, ed., *Controversy in the Twenties: Fundamentalism, Modernism, and Evolution* (Nashville, TN: Vanderbilt University Press, 1969), 342.

[83] Timothy L. Smith, "The Evangelical Kaleidoscope and the Call to Christian Unity," *Christian Scholar's Review* 15 (1986): 133.

[84] On precursors of the fundamentalist crusade in the South see Numbers, *The Creationists,* 46; for Bryan's entry into anti-evolutionism see Lawrence W.

portant a spokesman at the helm, fundamentalists downplayed their earlier emphasis on modernism, and began to stress instead the perils of evolution. Bryan's involvement, and recent fundamentalist defeats in the Northern Baptist Convention, created an opportune moment for a shift to anti-evolutionism at the WCFA meeting held in Los Angeles in 1922. The new theme was so dominant that Riley virtually apologized for the lack of attention paid to prophetic subjects.[85]

But not everyone who was called a fundamentalist liked the new note or thought that evolution posed the threat that Riley and others claimed, and after the Scopes debacle many more became alienated from the movement.[86] Some conservatives, especially those who were influenced by holiness views, were repelled by fundamentalist methods, which to them seemed worldly.[87] Others objected to the crusade for practical reasons, seeing in it a distraction from soul-winning.[88] Or less commonly, some fundamentalists did not think that evolution was a great problem for Christian faith, and so found a way to harmonize their beliefs with Darwinism. It must be conceded, however, that among Bible school leaders, there were very few who publicly disapproved of organized fundamentalist anti-evolutionism.

Although there were many conservatives who opposed fundamentalist anti-evolutionism, including E. Y. Mullins, J. C. Massee, Curtis Lee Laws, L. R. Scarborough, J. Whitcomb Brougher, Charles Erdman, and J. Gresham Machen, these leaders represented a conservative to moderate view in the mainline Protestant churches. But constructing a similar list for Bible school leaders is more difficult. Although he spent most of his career behind the pulpit, one might think of A. C. Dixon, who resigned from the Baptist Bible Union in part because of differences over

---

Levine, *Defender of the Faith: William Jennings Bryan: The Last Decade, 1915–1925* (New York: Oxford University Press, 1965), 264; for his growing influence in the fundamentalist movement see Numbers, *The Creationists*, 42, and the notice, "Bryan Blasts Evolution," *The King's Business,* July 1921, 638.

[85] Szasz, *Divided Mind,* 107; Trollinger, *God's Empire,* 48, 56.

[86] Szasz, *Divided Mind,* 131–32.

[87] See just this point by Fred Waehlte, editor of a fundamentalist periodical from Mulino, Oregon, entitled *The Faith*. There is a page from this magazine preserved in the MacInnis Papers, ca. 1928, in which the editor enjoins "worldly and carnal methods" of fundamentalists to enforce "the fundamentals by legislation."

[88] Interestingly, this was a position that Howard Kelly took, even though Kelly's reputation as a Johns Hopkins professor was evoked as an anti-evolution authority; see Howard Kelly to Biola Book Room, 23 September 1927, and MacInnis to Kelly, 17 October 1927, MacInnis Papers.

evolution.[89] Another leader with a limited Bible school background, who disliked the anti-evolution focus of the WCFA, was G. Campbell Morgan.[90] Perhaps a better example is Reuben Torrey, who under the tutelage of James Dwight Dana at Yale adopted a moderate position. But, oddly enough, Torrey's views seemed so out of place in the 1920s that when he suggested that a Christian could be an evolutionist and also be "sound in the scriptures," James Gray found it necessary to upbraid his old colleague.[91] Ironically, each of these leaders was, at one time or another, associated with the Bible Institute of Los Angeles. With so few Bible school leaders holding a moderate position on evolution, it is not difficult to see why MacInnis was so easily misunderstood and rejected by local radical fundamentalists.

MacInnis tried to clear up misunderstanding about his position. First, he denied that he was an evolutionist, because he believed that "God created all things." But, to the chagrin of some hard-line militants, he added: "God's purpose was the final explanation of all the development and the progress in nature, history and human experience." Second, he asserted that he opposed "empty disputations about scientific and theological theories."[92] It is evident from his carefully worded statement that he intended to follow a *via media* which would avoid contentious issues about how God created the world, and how Genesis should be understood as an explanation of creation. But to some in the Biola community, his explanation seemed weakly latitudinarian.

Letters of criticism, like that of Arthur Fry's, stated the matter bluntly: "If 'conservative thinkers' think Christians can believe that the Creator may have made man as a monkey instead of in the image of God," he wrote, "then it is hard to think of such thinkers as being conservative."[93] Fry went on to object to the vague manner in which Mac-Innis described his beliefs, hedging and failing to define precisely what he did think about evolution. Fry's note illustrates the fact that many fundamentalists were unaware of the diversity of evangelical interpretation on the subject of evolution, and also shows that many were ignorant of the similar views held by Torrey, Dixon, and Morgan.

---

[89] Brenda Meehan, "A. C. Dixon: An Early Fundamentalist," *Foundations* 10 (January–March 1967): 60; but for a different understanding of Dixon's split with the Baptist Bible Union see Beale, *In Pursuit of Purity*, 225, 229.

[90] Sandeen, *Roots*, 268.

[91] Numbers, *The Creationists*, 39; Staggers, "Reuben A. Torrey," 279.

[92] MacInnis Statement, [1925], MacInnis Papers.

[93] Arthur Fry to MacInnis, 10 April 1925, and 17 April 1925, MacInnis Papers. For other similar anti-evolution criticisms see Ben S. Candee to MacInnis, 26 February 1925; J. Paul Hatch to T. C. Horton, 5 May 1925, and MacInnis to Hatch, 15 May 1925.

MacInnis and Premillennial Dispensationalism

Although premillennialism was not made an issue by the *Times* article, doubts about MacInnis' views on premillennialism formed a major component of local anti-MacInnis opposition. Concerns about his premillennialism began much earlier than 1925, and probably soon after he arrived at Biola in 1922. James Gray, for example, was bemused at Torrey's choice of MacInnis, noting that MacInnis had written an introduction to a book that accused Torrey and himself of "absurd" statements and "dangerous" methods of interpretation in regard to the Lord's coming.[94] But Torrey was not concerned about this little incident, which he sloughed off as an "unwise thing." It seems as long as the institute remained under the firm leadership of Stewart and Torrey, dissent was effectively suppressed. By the end of 1924, however, with both Stewart and Torrey gone, some Biolans began to criticize MacInnis' premillennial ideas. One student wrote a critical letter asking Horton for clarification.

> Is there a change in the attitude of the B. I. in regard to the second coming of Christ? Until I came here, I had been of the opinion that the B. I. expected the return of the Lord at any moment. Now I often find myself at a loss to know what to say when trying to testify for the Lord.
>
> After I arrived last fall, and before school began, I learned that many B. I. students did not agree with me . . . soon I was told that some of them didn't believe in dispensations.
>
> I had not been in school long until I began to see the reason for all this. Many questions were raised and viewed from various angles in the classes in Philosophy and Church History. Often the views expressed were at variance to what I thought the B. I. stood for, and also seemed to conflict with what is preached by such men as Dr. Oliver, Dr. Dean, Dr. Munhall and yourself.
>
> It was not uncommon last winter to hear the remark among the students: "If Dr. MacInnis is right, every Scofield Bible should be burned." Many of the students have decided that the Scriptures cannot be harmonized. Others have decided that everything addressed to Israel is for "Spiritual Israel—the church."[95]

---

[94] Gray to Torrey, 4 August 1922, and Torrey to Gray, 22 August 1922, Moody Bible Institute Archives. The book in question was Robert Cameron's *Scriptural Truth About the Lord's Return* (New York: Fleming H. Revell Company, 1922).

[95] J. Shelby Bullock to T. C. Horton, 2 September 1924, MacInnis Papers.

Another student wrote a similar letter asking that Horton respond to his questionnaire signed by several students, which was entitled, "Has Biola Lost the Blessed Hope?"[96] Such critical questioning indicates the importance that premillennialism had to fundamentalists at Biola.

Figure 8: Premillennial Illustration

Fundamentalists made premillennialism a key litmus test of fundamentalist orthodoxy, as this illustration suggests.
(Source: *The King's Business,* July 1925, p. 293)

---

[96] J. E. McKee to T. C. Horton, 16 March 1925, MacInnis Papers.

Although fundamentalists frequently denied that premillennialism was an essential Christian belief, in practice, the doctrine that Christ would return before his thousand year reign on earth was guarded with no less a zeal than any of the so-called "fundamental" doctrines of Christianity. This zeal was, in many cases, motivated by the assumption that premillennialism was the only adequate bulwark against theological infidelity. In 1886, for example, it was said that premillennialism would form a breakwater against an advancing tide of "jelly-fish theories evolved out of man's erratic consciousness, pride, and self-will."[97] This idea was often repeated by fundamentalists zealous to stop the onslaught of liberalism, evolutionism, and skepticism. Riley, for example, claimed that the loss of premillennialism was the first step toward unbelief.[98] J. Frank Norris boldly declared war on the enemy, and identified the issue as the second coming. The bold statements of Norris and other fundamentalists led one historian to conclude that in the early 1920s, premillennialism became a definitive test of the fundamentalist faithful.[99]

But why, if MacInnis was a premillennialist as he unequivocally stated, was he charged with denying the blessed hope? The answer to this question goes to the historic roots of premillennialism in America and the development of dispensationalism in the last quarter of the 19th century. As premillennial evangelicals gathered together in prophetic conferences in the last quarter of the 19th century, they began to more closely define certain ideas, which had developed in the works of John Nelson Darby.[100] Some premillennialists took a path of interpretation that eventually became popular in the Scofield Bible, which taught certain distinctives such as the notion that the Bible revealed a separate plan of redemption for Israel and the church, and that the return of Christ was imminent, which meant that he could come at any moment. Other premillennialists, however, defended the notion that Christ would come before the millennium to reign over nations of the earth, but they denied that he was coming at any moment, arguing instead that Christ would come after certain conditions in world history had been fulfilled, such as a time of tribulation in the world and worldwide proclamation of the gospel. MacInnis followed the latter interpretation, which by the 1920s had become very rare among Bible school fundamentalists.

A significant split between these two forms of premillennialism came in 1901, when former leaders of the Niagara Bible Conference took

---

[97] Quoted in Kraus, *Dispensationalism in America*, 98.

[98] Riley, "Breaking the Bible School Defense Line," 5.

[99] Szasz, *Divided Mind*, 87.

[100] For a reassessment of Darby's contribution to Scofield dispensationalism see Larry V. Crutchfield, *The Origins of Dispensationalism: The Darby Factor* (Lanham, MD: University Press of America, 1992), 10–16.

sides over a book by Robert Cameron, attacking the "any moment theory" of the return of Christ.[101] Cameron, a Canadian Baptist, had rejected several years earlier the idea that Christ's coming would precede the tribulation as a secret rapture of the church. He and the veteran Niagara leader, William Erdman, became the most outspoken critics of the dispensational school led by Cyrus Scofield and Arno C. Gaebelein. Although premillennialists continued to cooperate in many evangelical endeavors, this schism fractured the former unity of the Niagara Bible Conference, which subsequently collapsed, and led to a continuing state of discord in the ranks of premillennialists.

Between 1902 and 1918, this issue simmered and boiled occasionally but mostly remained lukewarm. Yet the occasional disagreements between these parties are less interesting than the fact that eventually the Gaebelein-Scofield school emerged as the more dominant premillennial interpretation.[102] In Sandeen's view, Cameron's side lost control of the premillennial movement, because several strategic allies from the Niagara Conference days passed on, and there were few new recruits to defend Cameron's position. But one new recruit that Sandeen overlooked was John MacInnis.

It is not exactly known when MacInnis first accepted premillennialism, or for that matter, when he became allied with the post-tribulation camp: it is probable, however, that he first embraced a post-tribulation position after he came to Montrose and started the Montrose Bible Conference with Torrey. Although Torrey was personally inclined to the pre-tribulation view, he was not doctrinaire about it, and so he continued to maintain his friendships with leaders of both parties, one of whom was William J. Erdman. Erdman was at that time living not far from Montrose, in Germantown, Pennsylvania. When the Montrose conference began in 1908, Erdman was invited to speak, and it was through this connection, most likely, that the younger MacInnis entered the post-tribulation camp. It seems that Erdman had found a loyal confidant in MacInnis, for much later he shared with him the painful experience of the 1901 schism, noting sadly that fellowship with leaders of the pre-tribulation party "was withdrawn from me long ago."[103]

The leaders that he referred to, of course, included Scofield, Gaebelein, Gray, Pettinghill, and others, all prominent spokesman for the doctrine of the imminent return of Christ. In yet another letter, Erdman sounded even more despondent: writing in response to an article that MacInnis had published on this very topic, he decried the present state of affairs. "See how hopeless the undertaking is with brethren who

---

[101] Kraus, *Dispensationalism in America*, 99–104; Sandeen, *Roots*, 208–12.
[102] Weber, *Living in the Shadow*, 240.
[103] William J. Erdman to MacInnis, n.d., MacInnis Papers.

have 'institutes,' 'schools,' 'magazines,' and 'Scofield Bibles,' et al. They die hard or never will."[104] Really, what Erdman was acknowledging, in effect, was the eclipse of a post-tribulation viewpoint both in the popular evangelical press and in the premillennial Bible institutes. Forged in the crucible of 19th century premillennialism, Bible schools had now become a major institutional voice for pre-tribulational dispensationalism.

The world war brought about a resurgence in prophetic interpretation, and with it renewed discussion about the "any moment" theory. There were few, however, willing to counterpose the prevailing interpretation, which by this time indelibly bore the name of Scofield. By an odd twist of serendipity, however, MacInnis was called on to take Scofield's place at a major prophetic conference. The irony could not have been greater! Erdman wrote gleefully, "Your taking Dr. Scofield's place has to me a humorous poetic retribution."[105]

The event was the well-attended Philadelphia Prophetic Conference of 1918, which, by another humorous coincidence, became the very next year a conference of the newly formed World's Christian Fundamentals Association. As originally planned, Scofield was to give two speeches at the conference on a topic of prophetic interpretation. But three days before the conference was to open, Scofield wired a telegram advising the conference organizers that he was ill and could not attend. In a last minute decision, therefore, conference leaders asked MacInnis to take Scofield's place.[106] Why the committee chose him is unknown, but that he now shared a podium with such pre-tribulation advocates as W. B. Riley, William Pettinghill, Charles Trumbull, P. W. Philpott, James Gray, B. B. Sutcliffe, Courtland Myers, and L. W. Munhall, was striking. It now appeared to Erdman, as he later wrote, that "the burden of scriptural testimony concerning the second coming is squarely on your shoulders."[107]

Actually, MacInnis never raised the contested issue, even though in a question and answer session Riley glossed over a slight discrepancy that one puzzled attender noticed between MacInnis and other conference leaders.[108] Instead, he discussed a favorite theme, the relation of history

---

[104] Ibid.

[105] Erdman to MacInnis, 16 September 1918, MacInnis Papers.

[106] *Light on Prophecy: Proceedings and Addresses at the Philadelphia Prophetic Conference, May 28–30, 1918* (New York: The Christian Herald Bible House, 1918), 32–35.

[107] Erdman to MacInnis, 16 September 1918, MacInnis Papers. Note that Sandeen incorrectly stated that there were no Presbyterians at the conference, perhaps because MacInnis had not been on the original invitation list (*Roots*, 239).

[108] *Light on Prophecy*, 344.

to premillennial prophetic interpretation, in which he argued that premillennialism was not inherently pessimistic. It is a noteworthy co-incidence that many of his ideas, which later appeared in *Peter the Fisherman Philosopher*, were expressed at this conference. Strangely, there remains no record of any objections to his speeches. But more consequential than his speeches was his opportunity to hobnob with leaders of the dispensational premillennial viewpoint, who would soon be closely identified with militant fundamentalism. It is reasonable to assume, in the absence of any evidence to the contrary, that his participation in this conference helped to enhance his status and name recognition in the emerging fundamentalist movement.

The story of post-tribulation premillennialism after 1918 is virtually a book with no pages. Across the horizon of the "lost generation" there was no one to carry on the discussion. Cameron's periodical, *Watchword and Truth*, which had been the main vehicle for his interpretation, ceased publication in 1921. Cameron published a book on the subject in 1922, for which MacInnis wrote an introduction, and Charles Erdman also tried to revive the issue that year, prompting Cameron to conclude wrongly that the post-tribulation view was finally gaining ground.[109] But probably the most noteworthy attempt to challenge the status quo of dispensationalism was made by Philip Mauro.

Mauro, a patent lawyer turned religious writer, had achieved some renown in popular conservative evangelical circles due to the publication of his religious conversion story in the *Fundamentals*. Sometime around 1918, however, he started becoming an irritant to dispensationalists, because of his growing breach with the Scofield school of interpretation. The incident that caused the most controversy, however, was the publication of his attack on dispensationalism in 1928, at the height of the MacInnis controversy. Mauro was accused of modernism by some radical fundamentalists inclined to see a modernist in any departure from Scofield's notes, while Mauro returned the favor, denouncing dispensationalism as a "subtle form of modernism."[110] His contrarian ideas may have encouraged WCFA leaders to cancel his scheduled ap-

---

[109] Robert Cameron to MacInnis, 24 September 1925, MacInnis Papers. Erdman's book was entitled, *The Return of Christ* (New York: George H. Doran Co., 1922).

[110] Philip Mauro, *The Gospel of the Kingdom: With an Examination of Modern Dispensationalism* (Boston: Hamilton Brothers, 1928). For accusations of modernism see Gordon P. Gardiner, *Champion of the Kingdom: The Story of Philip Mauro* (New York: Bread of Life, 1961), 69, and Ribuffo, *Old Christian Right*, 86. For criticisms of Mauro's book see Charles Trumbull, "Mauro's Strange New Book," *Sunday School Times,* 2 March 1929, 135–36; Grant Stroh, "Philip Mauro on 'The Gospel of the Kingdom,'" *Moody Bible Institute Monthly,* March 1929, 335–36.

pearance at the 1928 annual meeting, though this was vehemently denied. Nevertheless, editorial opinion at *The King's Business* suggested that Mauro's exclusion was a signal that fundamentalism was being redefined to exclude anyone who did not follow Scofield's biblical interpretations.[111]

Although MacInnis never carried the baton of leadership that Erdman had hoped, he made a few small contributions to the discussion. Aside from the introduction that he wrote for Cameron's book, he also contributed a few articles to the *Evangelical Christian,* which challenged some assumptions of a dispensational interpretation.[112] This magazine advocated a post-tribulation viewpoint, as did many premillennial fundamentalists in Toronto, contrary to the pattern of fundamentalists in the United States.[113] Finally, as the debate over Mauro's book was stirring up old controversies, William P. White of the Biblical Seminary in New York approved a contribution from MacInnis on the issue, which was published in the *Biblical Review* in 1930.[114]

Aside from Torrey, there were probably few at Biola who knew of his differing millennial position, but if it had not been for Torrey's friendship, his views probably would have kept him from coming to Biola. Not surprisingly, Torrey did consider the issue briefly, but then he assured MacInnis that the issue would not be a problem: the only point of difference, he observed, was that MacInnis believed the church would go through the tribulation—but the Biola statement of faith did not require a belief in the pre-tribulation coming of Christ.

Torrey, of course, seriously underestimated how Biola fundamentalists would react to the different millennial views of MacInnis. Moreover, with the continuing influence of radical dispensationalists in Los Angeles, for instance, Robert Hadden, who was now the president of the Premillennial Association of Southern California, MacInnis' ideas about Israel and the church, the Scofield Bible, Old Testament prophecies, and the blessed hope, may have seemed too unusual, and even radical.[115] Hence, in spite of his strong assertions that he too was a premillennial-

---

[111] "Is Fundamentalism Being Redefined?" *The King's Business,* September 1928, 517–18.

[112] "Reality—In the Church," August 1919, 233–35;. "The Prophetic Message and Challenge of Our Day," September 1919, 261–64; "Theological Challenge of the Prophetic Message," October 1919, 296–98.

[113] Stackhouse, *Canadian Evangelicalism,* 62–63; McKenzie, "Rowland Bingham," 272, 312–13; Sawatsky, "Looking for that Blessed Hope," 287.

[114] John M. MacInnis, "Israel—The Fulfillment of the Promise," *Biblical Review* 15 (January 1930), 59–78. For the initial inquiry see R. M. Kurtz to MacInnis, 7 February 1929, MacInnis Papers.

[115] For Hadden's presidency of the Southern California Premillennial Association see his *Christian Fundamentals Magazine,* January 1928, 14.

ist, many were not satisfied. Exasperated, he sniped at an antagonist: "I would like to ask if it has come to pass that the brethren on this Coast are going to judge me as to my faithfulness and orthodoxy on my atti- tude to the Scofield or someone else's interpretation."[116] That most of his critics on this issue came from the Pacific Coast appears to support the notion that dispensationalism, especially in its more radical forms, was sufficiently ensconced in the region to suppress any viable alterna- tive millennial views in the Biola community. When opposition to Mac- Innis became national in 1928, however, objections to his non-dispen- sational views were not as prevalent as they had been in Los Angeles, suggesting that this issue could not sustain an adequate anti-MacInnis argument on a national level.

The premillennial issue did not wane at Biola during the MacInnis years as did the matter of evolution. It rather gained momentum, be- cause it was a dearly loved subject of fundamentalists, and because cer- tain of his actions as dean reinforced worries that Biola had dropped this hallowed line of defense. The first action which deeply troubled local fundamentalists was the board's decision to cancel the Scofield Radio Bible Class.[117] Although it is not known why the radio program was can- celled, to many Biolans it signaled the dean's anti-dispensational bias. A second issue was T. C. Horton's attempt to change Biola's doctrinal position. When Torrey first drafted the institute's statement of doctrine, neither premillennial nor dispensational beliefs were required. In 1926, however, T. C. Horton began to clamor for a change in Biola's doctrinal statement, requiring some form of subscription to premillennialism.[118] While the details of this internal debate are almost unknown, it may reasonably be inferred that Horton's efforts were inspired by anti- MacInnis sentiments, for Horton himself denied that MacInnis was a premillennialist.[119] In the end, his efforts to change the statement failed.

This issue, perhaps more than others, was replete with contradictions and ironies. Why, for example, did Torrey accommodate an alternative view of the second coming, but Horton could not even accept that Mac- Innis was a bonafide premillennialist? For MacInnis, who once claimed that the president of Auburn Seminary, George Stewart, had accused him of "filling central New York with premillennialism," such attitudes were incomprehensible.[120] There were several reasons. First, although

---

[116] MacInnis to B. B. Sutcliffe, 11 May 1927, MacInnis Papers.

[117] Board Minutes, 5 July 1926.

[118] Biola Society Minutes, 25 February 1926; Board Minutes, 5 November 1926.

[119] MacInnis to T. C. Horton, 20 December 1927, and T. C. Horton to MacInnis, 28 December 1927, MacInnis Papers.

[120] For Stewart's putative statement see Transcript of Minutes of Special

Torrey was inclined to Scofield's views, he avoided partisan bickering on the issue and continued to espouse a broad acceptance of all millennial interpretations within the frame of a conservative evangelical theology. Horton, however, never enjoyed Torrey's cosmopolitan advantages, and having been deeply influenced by Scofield himself, he could not easily accommodate another interpretation. Ironically, Horton's position was more consistent than Torrey's, because if dispensational ideas were not merely "theories," as MacInnis often said, but were truly "Bible doctrines," it would be impossible on this basis to tolerate alternative positions. A second reason for Horton's difficulties appears to be some continuing terminological ambiguity. In the latter decades of the 19th century, dispensationalism was still being formulated, and so most premillennialists had not yet made precise distinctions between "historicist" and "dispensational" positions. But by 1900 the differences between the two schools were becoming increasingly evident. Nevertheless, many premillennialists of the Cameron school continued to think of themselves as dispensational, and the word continued to be used freely by both sides.[121] This usage may have confused some premillennialists, who like Horton, assumed that all premillennialists were dispensational. A similar kind of confusion attended the great codifier of dispensationalism, Lewis S. Chafer, who as late as 1936 was still asserting the idea that all premillennialists were dispensationalists contrary to J. Oliver Buswell, who said he was premillennial but not dispensational.[122] With this point of view, when it became clear that MacInnis did not "think very highly" of dispensationalism, as Mrs. L. Stewart said in 1925, it was easily concluded that he also spurned premillennialism.[123] This perception was also reinforced by his avoidance of dispensational terms that functioned as boundary descriptors between the two schools of thought. Hence, when student's complained of not hearing about "dispensations," or of "rightly dividing the word of truth," or worse, were told by so great a teacher as G. Campbell Morgan, that so-called "signs of the times" do not indicate that the end of the age is close, it left some students with a feeling that there was "something wrong with Dr. MacInnis" and his administration.[124]

Board of Directors Meeting with Marion Reynolds, 17 January 1928, MacInnis Papers (hereafter Reynolds Transcript).

[121] Kraus, *Dispensationalism in America*, 106.

[122] Hannah, "Origins of the Evangelical Theological College," 358–59.

[123] Mrs. Lyman Stewart to MacInnis, 22 July 1925, MacInnis Papers.

[124] Roy H. Fuller, Handwritten Diary, entries dated 9 February and 12 February, 1928, in this writer's possession (hereafter called Fuller Diary).

From Local Opposition to National Controversy

While concerns over premillennialism devolved mostly on Biola patrons and students, hints of concerns about the direction of Biola were beginning to surface beyond the Pacific Coast. G. Campbell Morgan's decision to join Biola in 1927, for instance, brought a figure of international reputation to the staff, who could help or hinder the school's image depending on who considered it. For most evangelicals, particularly those denominational moderates that John MacInnis hoped to attract, Morgan's association with the institute was highly esteemed. But to many fundamentalists, it was a sign that the school would continue its independent course apart from the militant agenda of organized fundamentalism. Reuben Torrey, for example, upon hearing of Morgan's new association with the institute, wrote to Mrs. Stewart expressing his worries in a way that showed how easily one could pass from local issues over the Bible Women to fears that Biola was becoming another victim in a national pattern of theological decay. "What I wish to write you about primarily," he said, "is the work of the Bible Women in Los Angeles." But, a paragraph later, Torrey was more worried about Morgan's involvement at Biola. "If he is permitted to be a regular teacher," he continued, then "it will be the entering wedge for the Institute to go the same way that other institutions have gone."[125] In his mind, Biola's problems were fast moving beyond the sphere of local concerns like the Bible Women, to problems with Biola's growing divergence from the fundamentalist movement in America.

---

[125] Reuben Torrey to Mrs. Lyman Stuart [sic], 4 May 1927, MacInnis Papers.

CHAPTER 6

A Fractured Front:
The MacInnis Controversy, 1927–1929

Until 1927 criticism of MacInnis came mostly from those who were at one time or another associated with Biola, and such criticism probably would have remained within the extended Biola community had it not been for two changes, which gave MacInnis an opportunity to reach a wider audience with his vision of a reformed fundamentalism. The first change came suddenly at the new year, when MacInnis became editor-in-chief of Biola's magazine, *The King's Business*. The second change came at the end of that year as MacInnis broke into print with a new book provocatively entitled, *Peter the Fisherman Philosopher: A Study in Higher Fundamentalism*. With these two ventures in publishing, MacInnis obtained an unanticipated opportunity to articulate his reformist vision for American fundamentalism on a national level.

The New Policy and the Problem of Militancy

Worries that MacInnis was a "modernist" began to surface as early as 1925, and these became sufficiently widespread the next year to cause the Biola Student Association to pass a resolution of confidence in MacInnis, that denied reports being spread "in some circles" that MacInnis held a modernist viewpoint.[1] Like ripples on a pond, rumors of his modernism spread in ever widening circles. Through the efforts of French Oliver, for example, the word was widely spread that the institute was losing its fundamentalist verve. His reports led fundamentalists from Hawaii to Canada to conclude that MacInnis had slipped into modernism.[2] Though there is no way to estimate the extent of rumor spreading

---

[1] Biola Student Association, Resolution of Confidence in Dean MacInnis, TD, 11 June 1926, MacInnis Papers.

[2] For Oliver's influence in Hawaii see Mrs. Cecil C. Martin to MacInnis, 15 June 1926; for Oliver's influence in Canada on a one-time president of the WCFA see Sydney T. Smith to MacInnis, 18 November 1926, MacInnis Papers.

that came from local fundamentalists like Oliver, there is no doubt that by the end of 1926, many fundamentalists around the country were privately expressing their doubts about Biola and its dean. But still, no significant fundamentalist editor had seen fit to publish any of these reports or discussions, nor even express a lack of confidence in the man who headed one of the nation's largest Bible schools.

But any reluctance to criticize a fellow fundamentalist leader rapidly evaporated after MacInnis began publishing his views in *The King's Business*. Through the pages of this fundamentalist magazine, which had once received the fundamentalist imprimatur of Riley himself,[3] MacInnis found a forum for his views that could reach an international audience. Although its circulation was modest when compared to some popular American magazines, inside the smaller world of evangelical publishing, *The King's Business* was a significant voice of fundamentalism. Its approximate circulation of 28,000, for instance, exceeded the circulation of Moody's magazine, which in 1928 was only about 21,000, but was less than the influential *Christian Century* at 35,000. For the sake of comparison, the following chart gives the reported circulation figures of some denominational and independent evangelical magazines.

TABLE ONE
Circulation Data for Eleven Religious Magazines in 1928*

Evangelical Christian	Fundamentalist	5,700 (Reported)
Presbyterian Banner	Denominational Liberal	9,003 (Reported)
Bob Shuler's Magazine	Fundamentalist	11,000 (Reported)
Presbyterian Advance	Denominational Moderate	15,664 (Reported)
Western Recorder	Fundamentalist	20,332 (Reported)
Moody Monthly	Fundamentalist	21,300 (Reported)
Watchman-Examiner	Fundamentalist	22,577 (Estimated)
King's Business	Fundamentalist	28,000 (Reported)
Christian Century	Denominational Liberal	35,000 (Estimated)
Presbyterian Magazine	Denominational Centrist	40,000 (Estimated)
Searchlight	Fundamentalist	48,850 (Reported)
Sunday School Times	Fundamentalist	93,400 (Reported)

*Circulation defined as average paid subscriptions. Source: N. W. Ayer & Sons, *American Newspaper Annual and Directory* (Philadelphia: N. W. Ayer & Son, 1928).

---

[3] W. B. Riley, "The Christian Fundamentals Movement," in *Scriptural Inspiration versus Scientific Imagination,* 11.

Although there is little hard data regarding the readership and geographical distribution of *The King's Business,* it is reasonable to assume that it reached a wider audience than merely the clientele of the Bible institute. Just as the Moody magazine tried to appeal to a broad fundamentalist readership, so too did *The King's Business,* with a variety of articles on religious subjects as well as special features for children and for religious workers. Its strongest base of readership was probably along the Pacific Coast, but as a representative of the fundamentalist movement it was read by fundamentalist leaders around the United States as well as Canada, Britain and New Zealand. Consequently, when MacInnis became editor of *The King's Business* on January 1, 1927, his views on various fundamentalist issues suddenly became subject to scrutiny. Moreover, a new format and editorial policy was certain to attract the notice of more than one fundamentalist leader.

An initial provocation came over the new editorial policy which was announced, quite boldly, in the first issue under his control. The new policy, which was intended to supplant the militant and bellicose editorial practices of T. C. Horton,[4] called for an end to the tactics of personal denunciation. The new policy involved three things, which Riley regarded as a direct challenge to the fundamentalist program. First, MacInnis called for "bright, up-to-date, constructive, orthodox literature," that would give an attractive and credible image to evangelicalism.[5] His plea for a new literature was not motivated by a shortage of fundamentalist books and periodicals—instead, MacInnis felt a profound dissatisfaction with the inane and repetitive quality of many books and magazines then pouring from the fundamentalist press. The need of the moment was to produce a conservative literature that entered the twentieth century conversation on religious belief with wit, reason and critical acumen. Second, the new policy called for an end to denunciation of opponents and, in its place, called for a balanced and objective dialogue. Ridicule of modernists had long been a popular practice of fundamentalist editors, but MacInnis felt this detracted from serious discussion. Therefore, the conversation must not "indulge in personalities" but deal with principles, and fairness should be the editor's constant concern. Third, the new policy would emphasize the "power of Christianity in practical daily living." Though not explicitly stated, this last point hinted at his desire to move away from ideological debate and focus on the Christian life instead.

---

[4] For Horton's militant editorials see, e.g., "From Barracks to Battlefield," *The King's Business,* February 1926, 60, and "The Church Thrives on Militancy," January 1925, 15.

[5] John MacInnis, "The Editor's Statement," *The King's Business,* January 1927, 4.

MacInnis' new policy came at a time when militancy had fallen out of favor in the mainline denominations.[6] After 1925, virtually everywhere one looked Protestant leaders were calling for an end to fighting, especially after the Scopes debacle added new and very unwelcome connotations to the word fundamentalist. Typical of this attitude was J. C. Massee, who called for a six month cessation of controversy in the Northern Baptist Convention. Militant fundamentalists met his suggestion with attacks on his orthodoxy, prompting Massee to defend his proposal with alacrity: "I do not believe in the wisdom or the righteousness of denunciation, misinterpretation, the impugning of motives and the wide-spread directing of suspicion toward men who declare their conservatism and their faithful adherence to the Word and to the Christ of God."[7] Riley, of course, disclaimed Massee's subtle criticisms of the Baptist Bible Union, but he nevertheless still argued that controversy had a salutary effect on evangelism.[8] Similarly among the Northern Presbyterians, Charles Erdman managed to diffuse the militant party in the 1925 General Assembly with a strategic organizational maneuver. The next year, the tide of popular opinion rose against the militant party. From Stewart Cole's perspective, the pleadings of the fundamentalist minister Mark Matthews for peace and unity revealed the enervation of the militant party in the Presbyterian Church.[9]

Although James Gray had said in 1918 that the prevailing mood of the nascent fundamentalist movement was to stop "acting on the defensive," and a year later Curtis Lee Laws made militancy practically a *sine qua non* of the fundamentalist movement, when he said that fundamentalists were ready to do "battle royal" for the fundamentals, by 1922 a few in the movement were already backing away from its pugnacious character. Leander Keyser, editor of the *Bible Champion,* for example, was willing to admit that militancy could become "a heresy of the orthodox," and by 1925 fundamentalist writers A. C. Gaebelein, Keith Brooks, and Melvin G. Kyle had also expressed similar points of view.[10] Indeed, Gaebelein seems to have left the WCFA precisely because of

---

[6] Marsden, *Fundamentalism and American Culture,* 182–84.

[7] "Letter from Rev. J. C. Massee, D.D.," *Moody Bible Institute Monthly,* August 1926, 558. On Massee's truce and fundamentalist reactions see Russell, *Voices,* 128–29.

[8] "Dr. Riley Replies to Dr. Massee," *Moody Bible Institute Monthly,* October 1926, 54–55.

[9] Cole, *History of Fundamentalism,* 115.

[10] For the anti-militant positions of these writers see Robert E. Wenger, "Social Thought in American Fundamentalism, 1918–1933" (Ph.D. diss., University of Nebraska, 1973), 45, n. 78.

his opposition to militant personal attacks, which in his view were neither spiritual nor constructive.[11]

Figure 9: Apostasy Cartoon

This cartoon appearing in *The King's Business* accuses the mainline churches of
apostasy. (Source: *The King's Business,* March 1926, p. 119.)

But militancy could not be easily dismissed from independent groups
like the WCFA or Gerald Winrod's "Defenders of the Faith," because it
served to identify the hard core support of their organizations and rallied
the troops to get out and support the fight against the modern infidel.
Riley understood the problem perhaps better than most: a policy of
"constructive engagement" would threaten the very basis of the organization by dulling its intensity and eroding its base of support. Thus, it is

---

[11] Hannah, "Origins of the Evangelical Theological College," 153.

no surprise, as Trollinger commented, that fundamentalists saved their most bitter attacks for fellow conservatives who failed to demonstrate the requisite militancy.[12]

A rift over the issue of militancy began to open between MacInnis and Riley toward the end of 1926, when MacInnis wrote an article titled "Blessed are the Peace Makers."[13] Feeling disgruntled at what he perceived to be soft peddling, Riley published a responsive article emphasizing the importance of militancy: it is unfortunate, he unctuously crowed, to see "certain of our Bible training school leaders capitulating to this slogan of modernism."[14] Seeing in his statement an underhanded criticism of MacInnis, Charles Hurlburt, Biola's associate dean, penned a strong rejoinder. Why, he asked, had Riley implied that MacInnis was capitulating to modernism? Never timid, Riley fired back that if MacInnis was willing to state publicly that "he believes in fighting for the faith," then he would publish a retraction.[15]

This unpleasant *tete-a-tete* between two Bible school leaders was not unlike the differences between Riley and Massee. Like Massee, MacInnis did not see the need for shrill militant rhetoric, nor did he believe like Riley that controversy had a salutary effect. Better to cooperate with those who differ, he thought, and get on with the business of evangelism, than to be bogged in controversy. But this exchange had an added significance, for it also showed Riley's proprietorial interests in the affairs of other Bible schools in America. Riley had little or no influence over Massee: both were voices in the arena of denominational politics. But within the arena of Bible schools, Riley was able to gain an informal authority based on his role as a respected fundamentalist leader and by appealing to a similar constituency. As fundamentalism began to decline in the mainline denominations, Riley's role as a keeper of the Bible school defense line, as he called it, became ever more important.[16]

In spite of Riley's criticism, MacInnis reported after only three months that his new policy was a success. "We are receiving hundreds of letters that are almost extravagant in their praise," he told Mrs. Stewart, noting that such praise often came from "solid fundamentalist" sources.[17] Perhaps if methods and style had been the only issues, Riley

---

[12] Trollinger, *God's Empire,* 165, n. 6.

[13] John MacInnis, "Blessed Are the Peacemakers," *The King's Business,* September 1926, 503ff.

[14] W. B. Riley, "Shall We Have Peace?" *The Christian Fundamentals in School and Church,* October–December 1926, 7.

[15] W. B. Riley to Charles Hurlburt, 29 November 1926, MacInnis Papers.

[16] "Breaking the Bible School Defense Line," *Christian Fundamentalist,* April 1928, 5–9.

[17] MacInnis to Mrs. Lyman Stewart, 30 March 1927, MacInnis Papers; see also the following notices: "Our Subscribers Are Pleased," *The King's Busi-*

would have been able to overlook a wayward brother in the fundamentalist family. But Riley intuitively realized that the new policy was more than style and methods: it was a basic attitude that ran counter to the underlying defensive mood of fundamentalism. Even so, there was not yet sufficient reason for a public breach with MacInnis, and so in a brief meeting sometime in early 1927 they resolved their differences: Riley agreed that his published statement had given a misleading impression of MacInnis, and for his part, MacInnis admitted Riley's point, that the times required an "outspoken frankness," which probably came as close to a "battle cry" as MacInnis ever uttered.[18] Their harmony, however, was to last only a short while, for a new controversy would soon undermine the last confidence of fundamentalists in the orthodoxy of MacInnis and the wisdom of the Biola Board of Directors.

E. Stanley Jones and Biola's Loss of Credibility

In 1925, a Methodist missionary named E. Stanley Jones published a book called *The Christ of the Indian Road* (hereafter *CIR*). It quickly became a best-seller, going through twenty-one printings in less than two years and eventually selling more than six hundred thousand copies.[19] In the mainline churches, *CIR* was mostly well received. A typical panegyrical review by the moderate Southern Baptist, William O. Carver, appeared in the January 1926 issue of *Review and Expositor*. "Modest but thrilling," he exclaimed: "A study of this book will help in getting down to essential elements in Christianity."[20] But not all comment was so favorable. In October, Caspar Hodge of Princeton Seminary reviewed the book and concluded that it was a "subtile [sic] attack upon Christian doctrine."[21] Strangely, however, in the fundamentalist press Jones' book was ignored.

The reason for this silence is not clear. The editors of the *Moody Bible Institute Monthly,* for example, noted that they received the book in January 1926, but they waited for more than a year to review it.[22]

---

ness, March 1927, 417; "This Is No Mean Compliment!" July 1927, 417.

[18] See "President of Christian Fundamentals Association Strongly Endorses Bible Institute of Los Angeles," *The King's Business,* March 1927, 132.

[19] For the number of printings in its first year see Charles Trumbull, "Notes On Open Letters," *Sunday School Times* 25 June 1927, 386; for its sales see Daniel G. Reid, et al., *Dictionary of Christianity in America,* s.v. "E. Stanley Jones," by J. E. Stanley.

[20] W. O. Carver, review of *The Christ of the Indian Road,* by E. Stanley Jones, in *Review and Expositor* 23 (January 1926): 120.

[21] Caspar W. Hodge, review of *The Christ of the Indian Road,* by E. Stanley Jones, in *Princeton Theological Review* 24 (October 1926): 678.

[22] See the section "Books Received," in *Moody Bible Institute Monthly,*

Likewise, a delay also happened at other fundamentalist papers, like the *Sunday School Times* and *Our Hope*.[23] At the Bible Institute of Los Angeles, however, Jones' book received favorable advertising in *The King's Business* as early as April 1926. "It is one of the rarely vital books," they extolled, "one which grips and holds and will not let go."[24] Subsequent issues continued to praise the book, while other fundamentalist editors continued to ignore it.[25]

It was not until the book began to raise questions for fundamentalists, that it finally received any attention. After more than a year of circulation, a favorable review of the work appeared in Leander Keyser's *Bible Champion*. Interestingly, Keyser, whom Riley considered "the keenest book reviewer on the American continent," commended Jones' book, arguing that if "taken as a whole, the book seems to us to be so orthodox that the Modernists . . . will find no comfort in it."[26] But just before this review went to press, Keyser noticed some alarming criticisms of *CIR* in a conservative British magazine, the *Bible League Quarterly*. In spite of British reticence over Jones, Keyser chose to go ahead with his article anyway, with the caution that the book should be read carefully as a whole.

Keyser had the misfortune of publishing his opinion before the rest of his fundamentalist peers had delivered on the topic. By August of that year, the tide of fundamentalist opinion had turned against Jones, notwithstanding the earlier pronouncements of Keyser. Thus, in an effort to save face, Keyser put forward another opinion, less positive than the first. "Some outstanding conservative scholars commend it," he noted. But, he admitted, Jones "makes some statements that have a modernistic slant."[27] Hence, approximately five months after his initial review, Keyser was beginning to back away from his earlier endorsement of Jones. His final capitulation to a virtual tidal wave of fundamentalist

---

January 1926, 251; for their eventual review see Harry Safford, "The Christ of the Indian Road," *Moody Bible Institute Monthly,* June 1927, 479f.

[23] Arno C. Gaebelein, "The Christ of the Indian Road," *Our Hope,* July 1927, 35–39; Charles G. Trumbull, "The Christ of India, or of the Bible?" *Sunday School Times,* 2 July 1927, 397–98.

[24] *The King's Business,* April 1926, 240.

[25] See the advertisements in *The King's Business:* August 1926, 495; October 1926, 599; November 1926, 680; December 1926, 780; May 1927, 331; July 1927, 468.

[26] Leander Keyser, review of *The Christ of the Indian Road,* by E. Stanley Jones, in the *Bible Champion,* March 1927, 182–83. For Riley's estimate of Keyser see "Breaking the Bible School Defense Line," *Christian Fundamentalist,* April 1928, 5.

[27] Leander Keyser, "Notes and Comments," *Bible Champion,* August 1927, 405.

opposition to Jones, however, did not come until a year later, when he published a lengthy article by an Indian convert attacking Jones.[28] But by this time, fundamentalist passions had moved on to other matters.

Keyser's movement from a position of relative openness toward Jones in early 1927 to a condemnation of Jones in late 1928 shows that in the first stage of this controversy opinion was still fluid. Indeed, as pointed out, Biola was also endorsing the book at this time without criticism from other editors. But this early fluidity evaporated when three influential editors, James Gray, Arno Gaebelein, and most importantly, Charles Trumbull, published full page attacks against Jones' book in June and July 1927. After this, fundamentalist opinion turned solidly against Jones.

It is not known exactly why these magazines all launched their attack simultaneously. Perhaps it was no more than the need to define a consensus on a popular book. But that it was partly on account of Biola's open support of Jones' book cannot be doubted, because Trumbull noted the endorsements of "a well known Bible Institute."[29] Indeed, just prior to this united crusade against Jones' book MacInnis published a new advertisement, which declared boldly that Jones' book was "the greatest missionary book we have seen in recent years."[30] The new advertising may well have motivated Trumbull to take his criticisms of Jones public. Whatever his reasons, the result was now a line drawn between MacInnis and his staff, and the most powerful leaders of the fundamentalist movement.

In April 1927 MacInnis published a defense of Jones' book, in which it was asserted that Jones should not be called a modernist just because he did not use "certain stereotyped expressions," or failed to say all that needs to be said.[31] This defense, which was to have later important consequences for his own writing, challenged the implied rules of discourse in the fundamentalist community.[32] The criticisms of Jones indicate that fundamentalists assumed at least two rules of discourse: first, that a true fundamentalist would always state in an approved way the beliefs which would identify him as a member of the fundamentalist community; second, a true fundamentalist would make certain not to omit or ignore the hallmarks of fundamentalist belief. A point which bothered fundamen-

---

[28] S. P. Bannerji, "The Christ of the Indian Road," *Bible Champion,* September 1928, 518–20.

[29] Trumbull, "The Christ of India, or of the Bible?" 397.

[30] *The King's Business,* May 1927, 331.

[31] "The Christ of the Indian Road: A Discussion of E. Stanley Jones' Book," *The King's Business,* April 1927, 252–53.

[32] For an application of "rules of discourse" to Protestant fundamentalism see Kathleen C. Boone, *The Bible Tells Them So: The Discourse of Protestant Fundamentalism* (Albany: State University of New York, 1989).

talists, for instance, was that Jones emphasized the production of Christlike character as a motive for evangelism rather than the need for repentance and salvation.[33] That Christlike character was a worthy goal none denied, but its affinity to liberalism and his concomitant neglect of "salvation language" persuaded many that Jones was no fundamentalist, and very likely a modernist.

The problem of language and meaning became a central theme in the Fundamentalist Modernist Controversy. Fundamentalists often criticized the liberal practice of giving traditional religious language new meanings.[34] This practice also contributed to feelings of confusion, suspicion, and mistrust, for it was not always clear just what a writer intended; to guard against possible confusion, fundamentalists stridently emphasized a few doctrines that would clearly identify fundamentalist belief, such as the virgin birth of Jesus, or his substitutionary atonement. But some clergy, both liberals and conservatives, objected to the use of these doctrines as "shibboleths," that is, as hollow tests of orthodoxy.[35] J. C. Massee, for example, exclaimed somewhat defiantly that no human being had the right to select his vocabulary of faith.[36]

Similarly, MacInnis asserted that the fundamentalist attacks on Jones conflicted with his editorial policy of fairness. Jones should not be judged by what he did not say, asserted editors at *The King's Business*, nor should he be judged because he did not use "certain stereotyped expressions." Thus, they continued to exonerate Jones, in spite of overwhelming anti-Jones sentiment. "Time may prove that we erred," stated Keith Brooks, managing editor of *The King's Business*, "but God knows our desire is to be fair and Christian, and we reaffirm our editorial policy as stated at the beginning of the year."[37]

Many readers worried, however, that a policy of fairness might easily lead them into the path of modernism. Until early 1927, this had not been a major concern. But after the tide turned against Jones, MacInnis and Brooks were suddenly left without adequate support. The interpretation of CIR now became a contest of authority in the fundamentalist community. Who would define the acceptable limits of fundamentalist

---

[33] E. Stanley Jones, *The Christ of the Indian Road* (New York: Abingdon, 1925), 42; for a criticism of this point see Trumbull, "The Christ of India or of the Bible?" 397.

[34] For examples see the following editorials in *The King's Business:* "Evangelical Infidelity," April 1923, 434; "A Free Thinker on the Fundamentalists," August 1923, 823–24; "Indefinite Definitions," February 1923, 205.

[35] For this point see Norman Maring, "Baptists and Changing Views of the Bible, 1865–1918, Part II," *Foundations*, 1 (October 1958): 53.

[36] Russell, *Voices of American Fundamentalism*, 130.

[37] Keith Brooks, "Tempest in a Teapot," *The King's Business*, September 1927, 546.

belief? Who would become a trustworthy religious guide? Each side gathered its expert witnesses and its credentials to speak for the community. Toward the end of 1927, *The King's Business* published a five-page spread listing some authorities who defended Jones.[38] Most prominent among these were Leander W. Munhall, that grand old Methodist fundamentalist, Gerald Winrod, a friend and associate of W. B. Riley, and not surprisingly, Leander Keyser. But Charles Trumbull, who took the debate to its greatest extent, reacted with his list of authorities, including James Gray, Robert McQuilkin, and many ministers and missionaries.[39]

There was no precise end to this contest of authorities. Rather, at the end of 1927 there was not much else to be said about Jones. The discussion waned, and no more articles appeared. But beneath the silence, there was a new awareness that the unity of the fundamentalist front had been severely fractured.

Jones published another book in January 1928 entitled *Christ at the Round Table*. Many conservatives hoped that Jones would come out in favor of the fundamentalist position and dissipate the clouds of suspicion. To their chagrin, however, Jones took no sides in the debate. Rather, in his discussion of the round table conferences which he sponsored throughout India, he took some positions that disappointed his fundamentalist defenders. One position, for example, was his argument for a "vital infallibility" rather than a "verbal infallibility." Jones also argued that a substitutionary view of the atonement was not a fundamental of Christian belief.[40] In view of these statements, his defenders at Biola were backed into a corner. How far could they go without abandoning their fundamentalist identity? Clearly, for Keith Brooks, the line had been crossed—Jones was outside of the camp. In May 1928, Brooks took full responsibility for the defense of Jones in *The King's Business* and wrote a painful retraction of his previous endorsement: I must take my stand against him, he lamented. "I gave him the benefit of every doubt. I am now deeply disappointed and humiliated."[41]

Though Brooks bravely recanted, the silence of his boss, the editor-in-chief, must have been deafening. No words were forthcoming from

---

[38] "In the Interests of Fair Play," *The King's Business*, November 1927, 708–12.

[39] See these articles in the *Sunday School Times:* "The Christ of the Indian Road," 25 June 1927; "Moody Institute and Stanley Jones," 16 July 1927; "Readers' Views of 'The Christ of the Indian Road,'" 20 August 1927, 494; "India Missionaries' Views of Stanley Jones' Book," 3 September 1927, 518f.

[40] E. Stanley Jones, *Christ at the Round Table* (New York: Abingdon, 1928), 157.

[41] Keith Brooks, "Wither Is Dr. Jones Now Headed?" *The King's Business*, May 1927, 300.

MacInnis himself. The other leading fundamentalist magazines came forward with an avalanche of renewed criticism of Jones' newest book, but *The King's Business* had nothing else to say about the topic. Though MacInnis casually described the controversy over Jones as a "tilt with the Times," in fact, it caused severe damage to his own credibility in the Biola community. First, it cost hundreds of subscriptions to *The King's Business*.[42] But more importantly, it cost him a great deal of public confidence and encouraged those who opposed him. The editor of the *Searchlight*, for example, expressed wonderment that MacInnis and his staff were so easily duped.[43] Judgements such as these damaged his public confidence. The controversy also led to a widespread perception that religious authority lay not with leaders at Biola, but with Riley, Trumbull and Gray. One fundamentalist, W. A. Hillis, an employee of Biola, stated this point explicitly: "it did not matter," he asserted, "whether or not they were right in their contentions against Jones, but it was the fact that these men [Trumbull, et al.] were against him which made it dangerous for us to handle the book or speak favorably of it."[44]

A Revival of the Moody Spirit

To many fundamentalists, 1927 seemed to be a year of utter tumult in the life of Biola. Several personnel problems, leading to the resignations of a number of "old stand-bys," such as Julius Haavind, Besse McAnlis, W. R. Hale, and A. A. Maxwell, led Torrey to muse that he "trembled for the Institute."[45] Other matters also sullied the view. MacInnis was dismayed, for example, to discover that some at the Moody Institute were withholding fellowship from his administration over an incident that had occurred a few years earlier. It seems that a cantankerous T. C. Horton had subjected William P. White of the Moody Institute to some ill-treatment, probably because White had criticized Horton in the controversy over Aimee Semple McPherson. But now MacInnis was being held responsible for the unhappy incident. Reluctantly, he sent an apology but refused to accept any blame.[46]

In spite of these problems, MacInnis was optimisitic about the future of Biola.[47] His confidence reflected, in part, his optimism about the

---

[42] MacInnis to William MacInnes, 29 October 1927, MacInnis Papers.

[43] "Under the Searchlight," a page cut from *The Searchlight*, edited by James P. Welliver [June 1927], MacInnis Papers.

[44] Quoted in Keith Brooks to W. A. Hillis, 19 July 1927, MacInnis Papers.

[45] Torrey to James Gray, 22 February 1927, Moody Bible Institute Archives.

[46] Biola Board Minutes, 2 December 1927; MacInnis to President and Directors of the Moody Bible Institute, 5 January 1928, MacInnis Papers.

[47] MacInnis to Mrs. Lyman Stewart, 24 June 1927, MacInnis Papers.

teachers leading the institute. From the start of his administration, MacInnis worked to gather a group of teachers who were not part of organized fundamentalist groups like the WCFA and the Baptist Bible Union. Rather, he tried to build a staff that was broadly evangelical, conservative but tolerant, and committed to cooperation with the mainline Protestant churches. To recreate this ethos, MacInnis surrounded himself with individuals who hearkened to the Moody era of evangelical piety: these included Charles Hurlburt, his superintendent; Ralph Atkinson, associate dean and evangelism instructor; John McNeill, who served as pastor of the Church of the Open Door, and instructor in homiletics; G. Campbell Morgan, the acclaimed British Bible teacher; and finally, J. Stuart Holden, director of the British Keswick Convention. Although Holden did not work at Biola, his friendship with MacInnis was an important element in the revival of a Moody-like esprit.

One Biola leader, who became a staunch ally of MacInnis, was Charles Hurlburt. Hurlburt was the oldest of MacInnis' new colleagues and a veteran leader in the Bible school and faith missions movement. While serving at the Philadelphia Bible School in 1896, he was elected as the first general director of the recently formed Africa Inland Mission. This post was held for twenty-five years.[48] Hurlburt was also no stranger to Biola. He had long known T. C. Horton, because in 1911 he had accompanied Horton to Estes Park, Colorado, where Horton first asked Torrey to consider becoming Biola's dean.[49] Hence, when he came to Biola in August 1926 to replace Horton as superintendent, he did so with Horton's approval. Quite ironically, however, Hurlburt turned out to be something of a Thomas Becket, when he turned against Horton and defended MacInnis.

Horton had hoped that Hurlburt would not only replace him as Biola's superintendent but also take over *The King's Business,* which he did not want to fall under the control of MacInnis.[50] But to Horton's displeasure, Hurlburt recommended that MacInnis take over the magazine. Thus, the board voted over the objections of Horton's key ally, A. A. Maxwell, to make MacInnis the editor-in-chief.[51] This gave MacInnis sweeping powers that no other leader at Biola had ever enjoyed.

As this incident indicates, Hurlburt proved to be a loyal supporter of MacInnis throughout his brief tenure. Although Torrey bitterly complained about Hurlburt, telling James Gray that he was causing trouble

---

[48] Daniel Reid et al., *Dictionary of Christianity in America,* s.v. "Africa Inland Mission," by J. Gration; also see Keith Brooks, "The Africa Inland Mission," *The King's Business,* December 1927, 781.

[49] Torrey to Keith Brooks, 22 May 1928, Moody Bible Institute Archives.

[50] Biola Board Minutes, 2 July 1926.

[51] Biola Board Minutes, 3 September 1926.

for Biola, the record reveals that Hurlburt was very active in following and implementing MacInnis' organizational and ideological goals. On the organizational side he became the front man in the efforts to streamline programs that appeared to conflict with denominational mission projects, and this role led to his conflict with institute employees and especially Mrs. Stewart, who resisted efforts to place the Bible Women under his supervision. On the ideological side he also defended MacInnis, arguing against Horton's efforts to make premillennialism a part of the Biola Statement of Faith.[52] Although it is not really known why he resigned at the end of 1927, he remained steadfastly loyal to MacInnis.[53]

Another Biola leader who came of age in the Moody era and became a strong defender of MacInnis was the associate dean, Ralph Atkinson. He had taught evangelism and homiletics at Biola at least since 1918, and though he was one of the links to the Torrey administration, he became a helpful ally in MacInnis' hope to reform fundamentalism. Atkinson had enjoyed a personal friendship with Dwight L. Moody, and hence, like MacInnis, he remembered well the theological largess of his evangelistic mentor. During Moody's 1893 evangelistic campaign at the Chicago World's Fair, Atkinson became a central evangelist, leading a tent meeting virtually every night through the duration of the fair.[54] His long contacts with Moody Bible Institute made him an ideal ambassador to win support for MacInnis, but when he traveled to Chicago in 1927 he found that anti-MacInnis attitudes were deeply entrenched.[55] Like Hurlburt, Atkinson continued to support MacInnis, and when it became clear that fundamentalists would not be assuaged, he resigned from Biola.[56]

---

[52] For the Torrey complaints see Torrey to Gray, 22 February 1927, Moody Bible Institute Archives; for his organizational support of MacInnis see Biola Board Minutes, 17 May 1927 and 3 June 1927; also see the Biola Executive Board Minutes, 11 October 1927; also see MacInnis to Mrs. Lyman Stewart, 21 December 1926 and 24 June 1927, MacInnis Papers; for his position on the premillennial dispute see Biola Board Minutes, 5 November 1926.

[53] A cryptic reference to Hurlburt's "break down" may suggest that he left due to job stress; see MacInnis to Mrs. Lyman Stewart, 24 May 1927, MacInnis Papers; but in 1928 he organized a new faith mission; see "Unevangelized Africa Mission," *Defender*, October 1928, 1; for his support of MacInnis see his statement in Biola Board Minutes, 6 January 1928; and "Dr. Hurlburt and the Institute," *The King's Business*, April 1928, 248.

[54] Hartzler, *Moody in Chicago*, 45, 56, 59.

[55] Ralph Atkinson to MacInnis, 2 June 1927, MacInnis Papers.

[56] See "Open Letter from Ralph Atkinson," 16 January [1928], MacInnis Papers; also see his article, "Knowing Christ in Soul Winning," which defends MacInnis from charges of curtailing evangelism: *The King's Business*, April 1928, 213.

Another ex-Moody associate, whom MacInnis invited to the Church of the Open Door and the Biola teaching staff, was John McNeill. A burly, thick bearded Scottish evangelist, who was well known in England for his oratory, he first came to the attention of American evangelicals at Moody's campaign at the Chicago World's Fair. After this, McNeill went on to accept pastorates in Denver, New York City, and Philadelphia.[57] In 1926, while MacInnis was the temporary pastor of the Church of the Open Door, he recommended that the church call McNeill as their minister. In November 1926, McNeill visited the church, and after holding a series of revivals he accepted their call. This was good news for MacInnis, who then added McNeill to his Biola staff.[58]

Unfortunately, McNeill was an ill-suited fit for the contentious church. Only three months after his arrival in Los Angeles, MacInnis had to clear up rumors that the new faculty member was a Canadian Baptist minister by the name of John MacNeill, who at this time was gaining unsolicited notoriety for his opposition to T. T. Shields.[59] Although this was only a minor problem, it signaled a rough road ahead. The actual crisis came in early 1928, when he accepted an invitation to preach at the Pasadena Presbyterian Church, whose pastor was well known for his theological liberalism. Some in the church felt that he should have obtained their approval before accepting the invitation. But for the independent minded Scottish preacher, his church board did not have a right to choose where he could preach. "I preached fundamentalism," he said: "I have no sympathy for modernism." But this justification did little to soothe his ruffled church board members, a few of whom tried vigorously to oust him. Although he seems to have had the support of his congregation, he endured the criticism only a brief while longer: he resigned October 1928, citing the ill-health of his wife.[60] Ironically, this dispute was perhaps fitting for McNeill, the "Scottish Moody," for the great Moody himself had also been the victim of similar criticisms when he had shared a platform with "liberals" like Wil-

---

[57] "John McNeill," Typed Biographical Memoir, n.d., Biola University Archives.

[58] For MacInnis' initial invitation to McNeill to become pastor of the church see MacInnis to John McNeill, 20 May 1926, MacInnis Papers.

[59] "Who Is John McNeill?" *The King's Business,* March 1927, 150. John MacNeill was the minister of the Walmer Road Baptist Church of Toronto. It is probable that some fundamentalists had wrongly assumed through their reading of the *Gospel Witness* that McNeill of Biola was also the John MacNeill of Toronto, who at that time was opposing T. T. Shields.

[60] John McNeill to the Church of the Open Door, 11 April 1928, MacInnis Papers; also see the notice of the controversy in *The Defender,* June 1928, 2.; for a discussion of this controversy see Cocoris, *70 Years on Hope Street,* 35–42.

liam Rainey Harper, Henry Drummond, and George Adam Smith.[61] It is unknown to what extent McNeill participated in the MacInnis controversy, but his presence at the institute was at least another sign of the Moody-like ethos that MacInnis hoped to resurrect at Biola.

Probably the most obvious symbol of MacInnis' rejection of a militant fundamentalism and his advocacy of a broader evangelicalism is seen in his relationship with G. Campbell Morgan. Early in 1927, MacInnis invited the well-known Bible teacher to join the Biola faculty.[62] How he knew Morgan is not known, but that he was able to get the renowned preacher indicates that they enjoyed a close and trusting relationship, for Morgan was never lacking in opportunity.[63] Morgan, like his friend John McNeill, first became popular in America through the influence of Dwight L. Moody, who invited him to the Northfield Bible Conferences in the late 1890s. Morgan enjoyed a very close relationship with Moody, and after Moody died he left his London church to take over Northfield's extension Bible conferences. Hence, for three years he traveled extensively preaching and teaching on behalf of Northfield.[64]

After leaving Northfield in 1904, Morgan returned to parish ministry, pastoring several churches in England and the United States. His travels and publications gained for him an international audience. In 1920 he founded a Bible training academy in connection with the Winona Lake Bible Conference, which he led until 1923.[65] These favorable circumstances, however, did not save him from criticism, particularly as his own religious tendencies began to diverge from the fundamentalist movement in America sometime during the early 1920s. Riley, for example, asserted that he had once criticized Morgan for speaking on a platform with "three of America's most destructive critics," and a feisty A. H. Carter, British fundamentalist extraordinaire, said in 1928 that he had been dissatisfied with Morgan "for many years."[66] Yet criticisms of Morgan did not become pronounced until he was associated with MacInnis at Biola.

---

[61] Findlay, *Dwight L. Moody*, 411–12.

[62] Biola Board Minutes, 24 January 1927.

[63] Extant correspondence between MacInnis and Morgan implies that they were friends as early as 1904; see Morgan to MacInnis, 1 December 1904, MacInnis Papers.

[64] Harries, *G. Campbell Morgan: The Man and His Ministry*, 61–74.

[65] Vincent Gaddis and John A. Huffman, *The Winona Lake Story* (Winona Lake, IN: Winona Lake Assembly, 1960), 65.

[66] W. B. Riley, "Dr. Campbell Morgan and the Los Angeles Bible Institute," *The Christian Fundamentalist*, August 1928, 14; A. H. Carter, "Studies in 'Higher' Fundamentalism," *The Bible Witness*, April 1928, 4.

Figure 10: Photograph of G. Campbell Morgan

G. Campbell Morgan was a close friend and ally of MacInnis,
but his international fame was insufficient to quell fundamentalist criticisms of
himself and MacInnis.

The decision to bring Morgan to Biola as a regular teacher was not
well received by some Biola fundamentalists. Torrey, for example, was
especially disturbed by the decision, claiming that Morgan could not
sign the Statement of Faith.[67] But more distressing than this was
Morgan's smoking. How could the school hire a smoker if students

---

[67] Torrey to Mrs. Stewart, 4 May 1927, MacInnis Papers. Torrey apparently
had concerns that Morgan did not believe in an eternal punishment of the
wicked; see G. E. Hiller to Editor, *The King's Business,* 8 March 1927, and
MacInnis to Hiller, 14 March 1927.

were not allowed to smoke?[68] Torrey's objection was pointed. Although Morgan had come out of a Congregationalist evangelical tradition that tolerated moderate use of alcohol and tobacco, this was not typical of Bible school fundamentalists. Rather, suffused with a deep sense of piety and consecration, fundamentalists objected to smoking, even if it was only abstemiously indulged. This attitude appeared to be particularly strong in the West, for Robert Dick Wilson, a professor at Princeton Seminary and himself a smoker, used to advise graduating students not to smoke west of the Mississippi.[69]

This issue was full of contradictions. On the one hand, fundamentalists revered the famous Baptist preacher, Charles Spurgeon. But when MacInnis pointed out that Spurgeon was a smoker, one fundamentalist concluded that if Spurgeon were living today he would not have smoked![70] But on the other hand, MacInnis was surprisingly naive, knowing that such behavior was sure to offend many in the Biola community. Did he assume that fundamentalists would wink at Morgan's peccadillos? If so, he grossly misunderstood how an apparently innocent use of tobacco could be connected in the fundamentalist mind with modern social evils, the decline of Christian civilization, and even theological modernism.[71]

In addition to the regular faculty members who set the moderate tone of the MacInnis administration, MacInnis also tried to bring into Biola's orbit guest teachers and speakers, who shared his non-militant evangelical values. Two measures of the changing commitments of the MacInnis administration are seen in the list of contributors to *The King's Business,* and the individuals who were given prominent attention by MacInnis and his staff.

When militant fundamentalist T. C. Horton was editing Biola's monthly magazine, a list of contributing editors was proudly displayed in every issue. The list was a who's who of fundamentalist leaders: William Jennings Bryan, Clarence Macartney, J. Frank Norris, Leander Keyser, L. W. Munhall, Mark A. Matthews, W. B. Riley, W. B. Hinson, A. C. Dixon, and I. M. Haldeman, to name just a few. But when MacInnis began editing the magazine, he dropped this list of contributing editors. The very first issue featured, not surprisingly, G. Campbell Morgan

---

[68] Torrey to Mrs. Stewart, 4 May 1927. For Torrey's extreme worry over smoking see Ralph Atkinson to MacInnis, 2 June 1927, MacInnis Papers.

[69] Sam Sutherland, Interview by Author, 28 May 1993, Chicago Illinois.

[70] F. N. Sperry to *The King's Business,* 27 February 1927, MacInnis Papers.

[71] For these implications see MacInnis to D. L. Foster, 19 November 1927; William Kendall to MacInnis, 12 March 1928; "Notes on Unofficial Meeting of Biola Graduates in Trinity Congregational Church," 15 March 1928; and Torrey to Mrs. Stewart, 4 May 1927, MacInnis Papers.

on its cover page. The contrast was obvious. Over the next two years MacInnis and his managing editor, Keith Brooks, gave preeminent place in the magazine to writers not connected to organized fundamentalism. The contributors to the magazine under MacInnis were less well known than before; often they were denominational ministers. A few, like David Burrell, Delavan Pierson, J. Stuart Holden, and Joseph Parker were not devoid of wide name recognition, but none was likely to be widely known in fundamentalist circles. Although the changes in the magazine indicate that MacInnis wanted it to reflect his vision of a moderate evangelicalism, they may not have made good business sense, because the magazine would no longer provide the kind of information that a typical fundamentalist wanted. This problem surfaced, for example, when Keith Brooks failed to announce the dates of an upcoming WCFA conference, much to Riley's discontent.[72]

A second measure of change is evident in the invited speakers of the institute. Prior to MacInnis' administration, Biola became a frequent stop of fundamentalist ministers too numerous to mention. But during the MacInnis years efforts were made to include speakers who had no official links to the fundamentalist movement. Of the special lecturers listed for 1927, only one or two had any undisputed fundamentalist credentials: the rest were outside the pale of the organized movement: Charles R. Erdman and W. I. Wishart, for example, were each moderators of their Presbyterian denominations; Robert Wilder was a director of the Student Volunteer Movement; L. R. Scarborough was a moderate Southern Baptist, president of the Southwestern Theological Seminary.[73] Perhaps just as telling, however, were the "minor mix-ups" that created ill feelings between Biola and invited guests. A visit from W. B. Riley in earlier years would have been a special occasion, but in 1926 his proposed visit took second billing to John McNeill. Three months later the board found itself in an embarrassing position of having to revoke a "mistaken invitation" sent to J. Frank Norris. Though the reason for this mistake is not known, it is likely that Norris was not very welcome at the institute, not only because he was supporting T. C. Horton's anti-MacInnis activity, but also because he had just recently gained notoriety for killing a man in his church study.[74]

---

[72] "A Word to Literary Contributors," *The King's Business,* July 1927, 419.

[73] *Biola Bulletin,* July 1927, 7.

[74] For the Riley incident see Biola Board Minutes, 16 November 1926; for Norris see Biola Board Minutes, 4 February 1927. For Norris' backing of Horton see Norris to T. C. Horton, 8 December 1928, Folder 924, Norris Papers. For the killing see Charles H. Lippy, ed., *Twentieth Century Shapers of American Popular Religion* (New York: Greenwood Press, 1989), s.v. "John Franklyn Norris," by Mark G. Toulouse.

If guests of the institute held an important clue for the new reality of Biola, one invited speaker became its best representative. In February 1927 *The King's Business* gave front page billing to J. Stuart Holden, who would be visiting the institute for one week. Holden became an important theological soul-mate in MacInnis' efforts to reform fundamentalism. He was an English evangelical and the director of the renowned Keswick Convention. During his visit, Holden invited MacInnis to speak at the 1927 Keswick Convention: this invitation MacInnis considered a great honor, because from his early days of ministry he had followed the Keswick teachings on the higher life, especially in its emphasis on the experience of the indwelling Spirit. Keswick teachings formed an important part of MacInnis' rejection of militant fundamentalism.

The cardinal doctrine of Keswick was its emphasis on the "higher life," a spiritual state characterized by freedom from the power of sin. Unlike the traditional reformed doctrine of sanctification, Keswick leaders taught that a Christian could obtain freedom from the power of sin by simple surrender of the will to God. Although it began in the 19th century and was spread in the United States partially through speakers at the Northfield Bible Conference, a Keswick doctrine of sanctification always held an ambivalent position in the evangelical psyche.[75]

Following its introduction into the United States in the last quarter of the 19th century, Keswick holiness teachings alarmed several conservatives, because they worried that it was a recrudescence of perfectionism within the evangelical camp. Concerned that the great Moody himself had imbibed this new teaching during his travels to England, some evangelicals confronted the unlettered evangelist, asking if he had embraced the perfectionist doctrine of total eradication of sin. This questioning of Moody reassured "the old guard" (as Moody called them) that Keswick teaching was not a perfectionist heresy. After this, Northfield became a major launching pad for Keswick speakers to reach American audiences: G. Campbell Morgan, F. B. Meyer, Andrew Murray, and other Keswick luminaries established deep roots in the soil of American evangelicalism through a platform at Northfield.[76]

Not until 1913, however, did an American Keswick movement begin in earnest. In that year, several leaders organized an American counter-

---

[75] David Bundy, "Keswick and the Experience of Evangelical Piety," in *Modern Christian Revivals,* ed. Edith Blumhofer and Randall Balmer (Urbana: University of Illinois Press, 1993), 131–33.

[76] Shelley, "Sources of Fundamentalism," 72–73. For the tensions of Wesleyan views with evangelicalism see Paul M. Bassett, "The Theological Identity of the North American Holiness Movement: Its Understanding of the Nature and Role of the Bible," *The Variety of American Evangelicalism,* ed. Donald W. Dayton and Robert K. Johnston (InterVarsity Press, 1991), 72–76.

part to the annual British convention. Important for this movement were
Robert C. McQuilkin and Charles G. Trumbull. McQuilkin later became
the president of Columbia Bible College, while Trumbull, a Presbyterian layman, gave Keswick its widest voice through the pages of the
Sunday School Times. In the 1920s Trumbull's message of the "conse-
crated life" reached more than one hundred thousand subscribers. In
spite of these impressive gains, however, Keswick ideas continued to be
suspect in some evangelical quarters. Conservatives at Princeton Seminary, for example, opposed a Keswick view of sanctification.[77] Within
the fundamentalist movement, Keswick teachings continued to exert an
ambivalent influence, perhaps best seen in the moderate position of
Keswick advocate Charles Erdman. Although Erdman stood on the
same side of the theological aisle as his rival, J. Gresham Machen, they
were miles apart in their attitudes. Erdman emphasized the spiritual life
and depreciated the importance of right doctrine. Reflecting the view of
most Keswick leaders, he opined: "A man may recite an orthodox creed
and believe it, and yet be self-deceived as to his relation to Christ."[78]
This lack of emphasis on doctrine set Erdman in opposition to fundamentalists who made doctrinal conformity the highest goal. Moreover,
the Keswick stress on spirituality tended to mitigate tendencies toward
militancy. F. B. Meyer, for example, still alive in 1926, did not join the
American fundamentalist movement in any significant way, and in an
interview for the Moody Bible Institute he expressly distanced himself
from the militant wing of fundamentalism: "I have kept out of debate on
the matter," he said. "I have found the positive preaching of truth to be
my aim and end."[79] Like Erdman and Meyer, many conservatives could
not reconcile their emphasis on the higher Christian life with the vituperative militancy of organized fundamentalism.

Fundamentalist ambivalence about Keswick turned into suspicion and
doubt during the 1920s, as British conservatives began to question
Keswick's commitment to traditional Christian orthodoxy.[80] A key figure in this debate was J. Stuart Holden, who was suspected of doctrinal

---

[77] Bundy, "Keswick and Evangelical Piety," 133; Beale, *In Pursuit of Purity,*
139.

[78] Quoted in Longfield, *The Presbyterian Controversy,* 141.

[79] Quoted in William Runyan, "An Interview with F. B. Meyer, of London,"
Moody Bible Institute Monthly, November 1926, 114. Cf. David W. Bebbington, "Martyrs for the Truth: Fundamentalists in Britain," in *Martyrs and Martyrologies,* ed. Diana Wood, Studies in Church History 30 (Oxford: Blackwell,
1993), 426, 447.

[80] David W. Bebbington, "Baptists and Fundamentalism in Inter-War Britain," in *Protestant Evangelicalism: Britain, Ireland, Germany and America,* ed.
Keith Robbins, Studies in Church History, Subsidia, vol. 7 (Oxford: Blackwell,
1990), 315–16.

laxity, if not heresy. At the very moment that Holden was visiting Biola in January 1927, A. H. Carter was accusing him of being a modernist in his periodical, the *Bible Witness.*[81] Carter was an organizer of the London Bible League and a truly rare militant British fundamentalist.[82] The accusations caught American fundamentalists by surprise and caused no small stir, because Holden was a popular speaker at such venerable fundamentalist institutions as Moody Bible Institute. As a guardian of the faith, therefore, James Gray interviewed Holden extensively, seeking his assurances that he had not fallen into the beguiling clutch of the enemy. Feeling reassured by his answers, Gray continued to defend Holden's orthodoxy, in spite of Torrey's continuing doubts.[83] Rumors are seldom easy to quell, however, and so Keswick's reputation continued to suffer within the fundamentalist movement.[84]

Holden's unpleasant experiences left him with a bitter impression of fundamentalism. Writing to MacInnis in mid-1928, just as MacInnis himself was under intense criticism, Holden noted his rejection of fundamentalism:

> I never want to have anything to do with so-called "Fundamentalists." Their theology is barren, and their religion (if it can be so called) is as unlike the New Testament as can be imagined.
>
> I do not believe that the [Keswick] Council is going to suffer in any degree. If it loses the camp followers of "Fundamentalism" we shall be richer, for such a pruning of Keswick ranks has been long overdue. . . . Perhaps the time has come for those of us who refuse to live in blinkers and to utter the silly Shibboleths of the Fundamentalists openly to declare ourselves as having no connection with men, who, in the name of fidelity to the Bible, deny its spirit and purpose.[85]

Though Holden was never actually a part of the Biola teaching staff, he came to hold with MacInnis the opinion that fundamentalism was flawed. It had betrayed its roots: instead of the generous spirit of its great hero, Dwight L. Moody, it had taken on a narrow intolerant attitude. It had revealed in its obsession with doctrinal purity and its lack of

---

[81] *Bible Witness Supplement,* January 1927, MacInnis Papers.

[82] Bebbington, "Baptists and Fundamentalism in Inter-War Britain," 305.

[83] For Torrey's doubts see Torrey to Gray, 22 March 1927, Moody Bible Institute Archives; for other fundamentalist doubts see the section "Notes and Comments," *The Bible Champion,* April 1927, 196; for Gray's confidence in Holden and Keswick see the editorial "No Modernism at Keswick," *Moody Bible Institute Monthly,* May 1929, 424.

[84] W. B. Riley, "A Solid Front for Fundamentalists," *Christian Fundamentalist,* September 1928, 7, 17–18.

[85] J. Stuart Holden to MacInnis, 15 May 1928, MacInnis Papers.

grace, that the spirit of Moody no longer dwelt in its barren house. Thus, Holden came to the same position as MacInnis and Morgan, namely, that if fundamentalism were not reformed, it would eventually be cut off from the greater world of Christian fellowship. But at the time Holden wrote these words, MacInnis had not yet abandoned his dream of reforming fundamentalism at Biola, or to use his term, to make Biola a true representative of "higher fundamentalism."

Peter the Fisherman Philosopher

MacInnis' concept of a "higher fundamentalism" was finally born after a decade of intellectual gestation on October 11, 1927, when the Biola board of directors agreed to print two-thousand copies of his book, called *Peter the Fisherman Philosopher: A Study in Higher Fundamentalism* (hereafter called *PFP*). By December the book was printed and ready to sell.[86] It was a small unpretentious volume, slightly more than two hundred pages. For MacInnis, however, it was an exciting moment, because it represented several years of musing on the intellectual problems of life from a Christian and philosophical perspective. Little did he realize that his readers would view his work in an entirely different vein. In their perspective *PFP* was no simple philosophical meditation, but a frontal assault on fundamentalism itself.

MacInnis had not written *PFP* recently, nor had he written it in haste. Rather, he had begun the book almost a decade earlier.

> The following studies had their origin in a philosophical seminar in which men representing some of the leading universities of the East, as well as some of the universities of Europe, discussed two questions: First, why the collapse of civilization represented by the World War: Second, what is necessary to the building up of an effective and abiding society?[87]

MacInnis had attended this seminar at Syracuse University shortly after the First World War. There, as he listened to the philosophers discussing the ills of modern society, he thought of writing a book that would present answers to the fundamental questions of modern life, based on a study of the Apostle Peter.

With this ambitious goal, MacInnis hoped to demonstrate that Peter's insights included "a most comprehensive view of God and our world and can stand the test of the most searching thinking of our day." In

---

[86] Biola Board Minutes, 11 October 1927; *The King's Business,* December 1927, 833.

[87] John M. MacInnis, *Peter the Fisherman Philosopher* (Los Angeles: Biola Book Room, 1927), Preface.

other words, by comparing Peter's "insights" to modern thinkers, Mac-Innis believed he could demonstrate the coherence and contemporary relevance of Christian beliefs. Beginning with Peter's experience of Christ, he showed step-by-step how the simple fisherman had understood the great philosophical problems of human existence: the origin and meaning of the world, the problems of personal and social evils, the need for a community of believers, and the purpose and goal of history. Ambitious though it was, he thought that a simple introduction to these questions from an evangelical perspective would help Christians find a way through the maze of modern thought.

If *PFP* was initially written shortly after the war, the manuscript was not afterward shelved and forgotten. In 1922 MacInnis presented some of it as a series of lectures to students and teachers at Moody Bible Institute, and later that year at the Bible Institute of Los Angeles. When the book began to suffer intense criticism in 1928, MacInnis remembered these lectures. Why, he asked, did no one object to the material six years ago? To make his point even sharper, MacInnis also claimed that after the lectures he was offered a position with the Moody Institute as well as Biola: this implied that Gray and Torrey had approved the lectures.[88] This latter claim intensely rankled Gray and Torrey, and they strongly denied that they offered him a position based on hearing his 1922 lectures. But, to pour oil on the fire, MacInnis produced a letter written by Gray's then assistant dean, Lew Wade Gosnell, that highly commended his Moody lectures.

Just before you left the Institute I was telling you about the impression made by your lectures on our Faculty and student body.

First of all, our Faculty were greatly interested in your messages. I have never seen so many of them attend almost continuously such an extended course of lectures: indeed, it is not easy for them to get away from their offices and their presence was an evidence of real appreciation. All of them discerned your proficiency in the field of philosophy and your fidelity to a conservative view of the Scriptures, which has evidently been strengthened rather than weakened by your delvings into philosophy. . . .

I think your addresses are calculated to strengthen faith in that they demonstrate the agreement between scriptural teaching and the best philosophical and scientific thought of the day. . . .

I am writing you . . . unofficially, but I have heard enough to believe that I pretty well reflect the mind of most of our workers and students in what I have said.[89]

---

[88] John MacInnis to Members of the Los Angeles Premillenial Association, 25 January 1928, MacInnis Papers.

[89] Lew Wade Gosnell to MacInnis, 1 August 1922, MacInnis Papers.

Gosnell's encomiastic letter created quite some consternation for James Gray and Reuben Torrey, who were now placed in the embarrassing situation of having to explain why they chose MacInnis in the first place. Some letters were hurriedly exchanged between Gray and Torrey trying to nail down the exact dates and details of the lectures, but both of them denied having heard his lectures, or at least most of them.[90] Though MacInnis continued to assert that the lectures had been favorably received, he was finally forced to admit that they had nothing to do with his job offers at Moody or Biola.[91] But more important than the details of this acrimonious discussion is the apparent fact that in 1922 the material which MacInnis claimed was the substance of *PFP* had not raised a single protest either at Moody or Biola. How could this be?

There are likely two reasons for this curious circumstance. First, when he gave his lectures in 1922, MacInnis was not under a cloud of suspicion or animus. His lectures, therefore, were probably heard with less scrutiny and greater charity. Moreover, in 1922 fundamentalists were still sowing their oats and feeling ebullient about their prospects of routing the liberal foe. By 1928, however, optimism had vanished.[92] In the wake of crippling losses in the denominations and in the anti-evolution campaign, fundamentalists were more likely to turn a critical eye inward on themselves. This too would help to explain why MacInnis engendered such intense criticism in 1928, but not in 1922. Second, it is very likely that the lectures which MacInnis delivered in 1922 were not identical to *PFP* and were not yet understood as a "higher" alternative to fundamentalism. This point is suggested by the title which he gave his lecture series: "Christian Religion in the Light of Philosophy, Science, and Criticism."[93]

Beginnings of the Controversy

The first major assault on *PFP* came from an employee of Biola named Marion Reynolds. Reynolds had been associated with Biola for a long while, first as a student and later as Biola's evangelist to workers in the "car barns" and factories of Los Angeles. His life was almost stereotypical of the militant fundamentalist: fervently religious, rigidly conserva-

---

[90] See the extensive Gray/Torrey correspondence: 26 May 1928, 29 May 1928, and 31 May 1928, Moody Bible Institute Archives; also see the extensive MacInnis/Torrey correspondence, 20 January 1928, 8 May 1928, and 18 May 1928, MacInnis Papers.

[91] MacInnis to Torrey, 25 June 1928, Moody Bible Institute Archives.

[92] For Riley's 1922 optimism see "The Christian Fundamentals Movement," 7–23; for his feelings of defeat in 1928 see "Fundamentalism at the Crossroads," *The Christian Fundamentalist,* October 1928, 8.

[93] Reynolds Transcript, 17 January 1928, 8, MacInnis Papers.

tive, suspicious of things intellectual, anti-denominational, and prone to conflict. An alumnus of Biola remembered Reynolds' graduation in 1917.

> I recall attending the alumni dinner the year that Marion Reynolds graduated, and there were two speakers from his class, Miss Katherine Bomberger of Philadelphia, and Marion. Miss Bomberger spoke beautifully and spiritually, and Marion followed with great fervor and with complete abandon in the use of the King's English. Then Dr. Torrey spoke and went at length to say that in spite of all his blunders in speech that God would probably use Marion as much or more than the educated young woman who had spoken so beautifully.[94]

In addition to his employment at Biola, Reynolds was also a pastor of the San Gabriel Union Church, an independent fundamentalist church in the San Gabriel Valley of Los Angeles County.[95] After his termination from Biola in January 1928, Reynolds became a magnate for fundamentalist enterprises throughout Southern California, through his new-formed organization called the Fundamental Evangelistic Association. This militant group, which later became affiliated with the Independent Fundamental Churches of America (IFCA), proved to be so divisive that a permanent schism occurred between Reynolds and the IFCA in the 1940s.[96]

In spite of Reynold's lack of education and refinement, he now sensed with the publication of *PFP* that it was time to openly criticize MacInnis. On January 6 the Biola board met to discuss persistent rumors and criticism, and that evening they voted to ask Horton and Reynolds to cease their campaign of opposition: "We earnestly protest against this opposition," they declared.[97] But the opposition continued. On January 16 an announcement was made in the Southern California Premillenial Association that Reynolds had written a critique of *PFP*. Swift action followed. In a hastily called meeting, the board gave Reynolds an opportunity to explain his actions. He was then terminated on grounds of insubordination.

The news of Reynolds' dismissal went like a shock wave through the Biola community, for Reynolds had extensive contacts with Biola

---

[94] David J. Donnan to J. H. Hunter, n.d., MacInnis Papers. For his graduation date see the *Biolan* (1927), 52.

[95] "San Gabriel Union Church 75th Anniversary, 1919–1994," Printed Brochure, n.d., n.p., in this author's possession. Reynolds pastored this church from 1920 to 1930.

[96] On Marion Reynolds see James O. Henry, *For Such a Time as This: A History of the Independent Fundamental Churches of America* (Westchester, IL: 1983), 36, 98–104.

[97] Biola Board Minutes, 6 January 1928.

friends and alumni. Many letters sent to MacInnis and the board decried
the treatment of Reynolds, and in order to quell new rumors and divisions, MacInnis called a student assembly to explain his side of the
story.[98] Reynolds continued to stir up opposition, taking his case to the
Alumni Association in a February 3 meeting, where he argued along
with V. V. Morgan that a committee ought to be appointed to investigate whether or not he was "disloyal to the dean." By February 6, the
situation had become so tenuous that a vote of confidence in MacInnis
was arranged for faculty and students, which resulted in an almost
unanimous show of support with the exception of six students who
stood up in opposition to MacInnis when the negative vote was called.[99]
Fallout over the Reynold's resignation continued, however, as yet another Biola employee, W. A. Hillis, also resigned. Unfortunately, Hillis
had widespread contacts with patrons who had purchased Biola annuities. With these contacts, he began to encourage investors to liquidate
their annuities, which, of course, could have threatened the school's financial security. Biola thus responded with a threat of legal action
against Hillis.[100]

Reynolds was perhaps the most important local opponent of
MacInnis, because he became a major source of information for fundamentalist leaders across the country. His sixty-two-page criticism of
PFP, for example, was sent to editors of fundamentalist periodicals such
as Leander Keyser. Notes about his evangelistic activities suddenly appeared in Moody's magazine, and Riley noted that Reynolds' criticisms
had received wide publicity.[101] Hence, many of his objections to *PFP*
were widely repeated.

---

[98] For examples of protests of the Reynolds firing see A. W. Hybey to Mac-
Innis, 23 January 1928; Mrs. J. T. Hackett to MacInnis, 10 February 1928; Hal
Reed to MacInnis, 16 March 1928, MacInnis Papers; for MacInnis' address see
"Address Given by Dr. John M. MacInnis at an Assembly of the Faculty and
Student Body," TMs, 20 January 1928.

[99] For Reynolds' actions in the alumni association see entry dated, 3 February 1928, Fuller Diary; for the vote of confidence see entry dated 6 February
1928; also see Riley's criticism of this vote in "Biola Boiling," *Christian Fundamentalist,* May 1928, 8.

[100] For Hillis' solicitation of Biola annuitants see W. A. Hillis to Miss
Robertson, 9 March 1928; for Biola's threatened lawsuit see Nathan Newby to
Hillis, 14 March 1928, MacInnis Papers.

[101] For wide distribution of his manuscript note "Additional Book Notices,"
Bible Champion, June 1928, 299; on his notice at Moody see the *Moody Bible
Institute Monthly,* November 1928, 136–37, and December 1928, 208; Riley's
comment is in "Biola Boiling," *Christian Fundamentalist,* May 1928, 7.

Figure 11: Science and Philosophy Cartoon

This editorial cartoon illustrates some fundamentalist attitudes toward science and philosophy. (Source: *The King's Business*, January 1926, cover.)

Reynolds argued that the basic theme of the book, namely, to consider "the Christian view of God and the world," was itself flawed. There are many Christian views he asserted, but there is only one scriptural view.[102] It is no coincidence that Reynold's began on a note dear to Bible students: that there was a distinct difference between the teachings of the Bible and the multiple expressions of Christianity in history permeated fundamentalist thinking. A "back to the Bible" primitivism was

---

[102] Reynolds Manuscript, n.d., p. 7, MacInnis Papers.

so pervasive in Bible school rhetoric that most veterans of the movement would have easily sensed a slight distinction between the "Christian view" of MacInnis and the "biblical view" of Reynolds. A. C. Gaebelein, for example, allowed exactly this point: "What is the Christian view of anything?" his reviewer asked rhetorically: "We wish that the author had intended to discuss the 'Scriptural' doctrine of God and of the world."[103] Though his objection had little more than rhetorical effect, it certainly played on fundamentalist fears that Bible study had taken a back seat to philosophy and history.

Reynolds went on to attack many other aspects of *PFP:* its language, its putative rejection of doctrines like biblical inerrancy, the deity of Christ, and divine revelation. He objected to the frequent quotations from philosophers and godless atheists, which in his view inferred that the Bible was inferior to modern thought. He charged that MacInnis had made Peter into a modernist philosopher, because he made Peter's knowledge based on experience rather than divine revelation. In addition, MacInnis had denigrated the Bible in his attempts to make it relevant to modern thinking, because this implied that it was unscientific and unscholarly. Finally, in his bugle call on the last page, Reynolds declared, "Let us be done with tobacco smokers!"

The attacks of Reynolds and the unhappy turmoil in the school quickly attracted the attention of national leaders. W. B. Riley was one of the first to excoriate *PFP:* "In a lifetime I have never suffered so sore a disappointment," he wrote.[104] In two lengthy letters Riley denounced *PFP,* charging MacInnis with teaching evolution and rejecting principal doctrines of fundamentalism, including verbal inspiration, conversion, the second coming of Christ, and the substitutionary atonement. Riley, who had once recommended MacInnis for Biola's deanship, now bitterly called for his resignation.[105]

Other leaders also took up their cudgels against MacInnis. Torrey, in a bitter mood, deplored "the stabs" that MacInnis had taken at the doctrine of the atonement. "Oh, Mack," he wrote, "get on your face before God. Ask him to show you your duty. Repent, retract the book, and make your retractions as public as the book. I am amazed, bewildered, brokenhearted." Later, a grieving Torrey wrote privately to James Gray

---

[103] Arthur Forest Wells, review of *Peter the Fisherman Philosopher,* in *Our Hope,* May 1928, 684.

[104] W. B. Riley to H. G. Dean, 19 January 1928, MacInnis Papers.

[105] W. B. Riley to J. M. Irvine, 30 January 1928, and Riley to MacInnis, 31 January 1928, MacInnis Papers.

that *PFP* was "one of the most vicious, pernicious attacks on the substitutionary atonement I have seen."[106]

Apparently, MacInnis felt that the tide had finally turned against him, because on February 6 he tendered his resignation. The Biola board was not prepared to give up, however, so with the exception of one vote they refused to accept it.[107] Apparently, Riley and other magazine editors were waiting to see if MacInnis would resign before they opened their magazines to criticism of *PFP*.[108] But now that the board, indeed, the entire school, had declared its faith in MacInnis, several prominent leaders felt that an open assault on *PFP* was needed. Thus, between January and June at least eleven fundamentalist magazines published criticisms of *PFP*, and several of these continued to run additional articles for the remainder of the year.

Opinions about *PFP* were a mixed lot. In general, magazines that were positively oriented toward the Protestant denominations gave *PFP* a positive review, but these were admittedly few. By far most of the reviews occurred in independent fundamentalist magazines, either self-supporting such as *Our Hope*, or aligned with a Bible school, or in the case of one widely read paper, the *Gospel Message*, a faith mission agency. Not surprisingly, all of these had negative opinions with the exceptions of A. P. Fitt's *Record of Christian Work*, which was a voice of the Northfield Schools, and Bob Shuler's little magazine, which was fundamentalist but more concerned about local politics. Although every article can not be discussed, the perspective of some magazines can be tabulated as shown in Table Two below.

It is also important to note who ignored the book and the controversy surrounding it. For members of the Nazarene Church, no reference to the book appeared in the *Herald of Holiness;* neither was it mentioned in Aimee Semple McPherson's *Bridal Call.* For conservatives in the Methodist church, the MacInnis controversy was absent from the pages of the *Essentialist,* the official organ of the Methodist League of Faith and Life, as well as the official Methodist Church publication, the *California Christian Advocate.* Moreover, a survey of Robert Hadden's *Christian Fundamentals Magazine* reveals no sign of the controversy. This is perhaps not surprising, however, because his own proximity to Biola and his position as a potential competitor probably made it awkward, if not precarious, to engage in public criticisms.

---

[106] Reuben Torrey to MacInnis, 2 February 1928, MacInnis Papers, and Torrey to Gray, 14 February 1928, Moody Bible Institute Archives.

[107] Biola Board Minutes, 6 February 1928.

[108] Riley to H. G. Dean, 19 January 1928, MacInnis Papers, and Torrey to Gray, 14 February 1928, Moody Bible Institute Archives.

TABLE TWO
Attitudes of Magazines that Discussed
Peter the Fisherman Philosopher

Periodical	Religious Viewpoint	Attitude
Bible Champion	Fundamentalist	Negative
Bible Witness	Fundamentalist-England	Negative
Biblical Recorder	Fundamentalist-New Zealand	Positive
Bibliotheca Sacra	Moderate Evangelical	Negative
Bob Shuler's Magazine	Fundamentalist	Positive
Christian	Moderate Evangelical-England	Positive
Christian Fundamentalist	Fundamentalist	Negative
Defender	Fundamentalist	Positive
Eastern Methodist	Fundamentalist	Positive
Evangelical Christian	Fundamentalist-Canada	Negative
Fundamentalist	Fundamentalist	Negative
Gospel Message	Fundamentalist	Negative
Gospel Witness	Fundamentalist-Canada	Negative
Grace and Truth	Fundamentalist	Negative
Moody Bible Institute Monthly	Fundamentalist	Negative
Our Hope	Fundamentalist	Negative
Presbyterian Advance	Presbyterian-Progressive	Positive
Presbyterian Banner	Presbyterian-Progressive	Positive
Presbyterian Magazine	Presbyterian-Centrist	Neutral
Princeton Theological Review	Presbyterian-Conservative	Positive
Record of Christian Work	Moderate Evangelical	Positive
Serving-and-Waiting	Fundamentalist	Negative
Southern Baptist Trumpet	Fundamentalist	Negative
Sunday School Times	Fundamentalist	Negative
Watchman-Examiner	Moderate Evangelical	Neutral

Any survey of fundamentalist opinion, however, would miss the mark if it failed to account for the numerous unpublished materials that circulated throughout the informal network of radical fundamentalists. Pamphlets and unsigned mimeographed letters were widely circulated, and sometimes these materials became important communication links between leaders like Riley and the grassroots.[109] One particularly effective form of communication was the church newsletter. One such newsletter was called the Trinity Herald. It was written by Franklin Huling, a Baptist minister in Salt Lake City, who was also a graduate of Biola and an old friend of Marion Reynolds. Huling mailed his newsletter to more than twelve hundred people each month, and through this medium he successfully spread feelings of anti-MacInnis discontent. But other pastors used sermons and church bulletins to defend MacInnis, such as Harold E. Barton, who warned his Baptist congregation that the accusations of modernism against MacInnis were nothing but the "Devil's lies."[110] Although the extent of this informal communication cannot be exactly measured, there is no doubt that it was extensive and influential in shaping popular attitudes toward MacInnis.

Responses to the Growing Crisis

The controversy, which had grown to alarming proportions by March, developed into a contest of authority, like the earlier struggle over E. Stanley Jones. To forestall further criticism, Biola formed a ministerial committee to review the book. This group consisted of local pastors all well known in the fundamentalist community of Los Angeles. They produced a positive review of *PFP*, which was printed and distributed as a tract along with a supportive letter from Mrs. Lyman Stewart, who had not been on the committee.[111]

The conclusions of this committee, however, were widely discounted by fundamentalists. From the start, some suspected that it was biased. For example, Charles Trumbull agreed to withhold his published criticisms until the committee gave its report. But this was mostly for appearances sake, for James Gray mentioned Trumbull's doubts about the committee well before it had finished its review.[112]

---

[109] For examples of these links see Gerald Winrod, "The Muckraker" *Defender,* March 1928, 10; and W. B. Riley, "Biola Boiling," 7, 9.

[110] February, March, and April 1928 issues of the "Trinity Herald" are preserved in the MacInnis Papers. For Barton's quotation see his church bulletin called the "First Church Advocate," First Baptist Church of San Jose, 17 June 1928, MacInnis Papers.

[111] Copies of this tract, "What Those Who Know Say About the Bible Institute of Los Angeles," are preserved in the MacInnis Papers.

[112] James Gray to Torrey, 24 February 1928, Moody Bible Institute Archives. Also note Riley's doubts in Riley to Alexander MacKeigan, 21 March 1928, MacInnis Papers.

TABLE THREE
Members of the Ministerial Review Committee

Stewart MacLennan, Chairman	Presbyterian USA
William E. McCulloch	United Presbyterian
Lincoln A. Ferris	Methodist Episcopal
Walter E. Edmonds	Presbyterian USA
Robert. P. Shuler	Southern Methodist
Gustav Briegleb	Presbyterian USA
Frederic Farr	American Baptist
Fred E. Hagln	Affiliation unknown
Louis Bauman	United Brethren

The committee consisted of denominational conservatives well known in local circles, but not especially well known elsewhere. In the national eye, therefore, the committee would not have carried much weight. But the goal, no doubt, was to win support for Biola among their local constituents and to counteract the aggressive efforts of local agitators. Yet even here, credibility doubts marred the committee's status. One fundamentalist noted that it was not a committee appointed by the local premillennial association.[113] A few of the men on the committee had their own credibility problems. Frederic Farr, for example, though active in the WCFA, was later ostracized by Biola leaders because of his putative sympathy with McPhersonism.[114] Although "fighting Bob Shuler" was a particularly visible leader, his efforts at civic reform were better known than his zeal for heresy hunting. Indeed, on things theological such as premillennialism, Shuler differed markedly from his Biola friends.[115] Even the respected fundamentalist, Louis Bauman, found himself assailed by charges of heresy while he was trying to exonerate MacInnis.[116]

Not only did the problem of credibility and bias make the committee's report ineffective, it also failed to give the crystal clear affirmations that the critics expected. Nowhere was MacInnis identified as a

---

[113] "Notes on Unofficial Meeting of Biola Graduates in Trinity Congregational Church," 15 March 1928," Typed Document, MacInnis Papers.

[114] Biola Board Minutes, 2 December 1927.

[115] Mark Sumner Still, "'Fighting Bob' Shuler: Fundamentalist and Reformer" (Ph.D. diss., Claremont Graduate School, 1988), 470–71, and n. 27, where Still states that Shuler did not work closely with Biola until the 1930s.

[116] For heresy charges see his Church Bulletin, First Brethren Church of Long Beach, 24 March 1928, MacInnis Papers.

fundamentalist. Yes, he was a "thorough Christian gentleman, sound in the faith," but this could be said of any upstanding citizen. Concluding that he was a man of integrity did little to reassure his critics, for affirmations of his integrity had nothing to do with his orthodoxy. Indeed, one could well be an honest modernist! Bauman gave his own report, which affirmed in a more direct way that MacInnis had not denied any fundamental doctrines in *PFP*. But his opinion that MacInnis was simply misunderstood failed to convince anti-MacInnis radicals. Finally, Mrs. Stewart's plea for a spirit of peace and non-judgment fell on deaf ears. Torrey's response was typical: the report, he wrote, "is more an apology than endorsement."[117]

Hardly before the minister's report was finished, another challenge to Biola appeared. Marion Reynolds and several other former Biola employees, students, and alumni, organized a meeting to discuss what should be done to restore Biola to the fundamentalist movement. Notes taken at this unofficial meeting reveal that opinions were expressed both for and against MacInnis. Once again lists of authorities were lined up against each other: Torrey, Gray, Keyser, and Riley were quoted as anti-MacInnis authorities, as well as Harry Ironside, later minister of the Moody Memorial Church in Chicago, William P. White of the Moody Bible Institute, and I. R. Dean, an itinerant evangelist.[118] Only a few MacInnis defenders were present and their list of authorities was noticeably shorter and less impressive—the minister's committee and Gerald Winrod. This meeting failed to bring the sides closer together. Rather, it led to a new opposition party consciousness in those resolved to oust MacInnis.

Biola's alumni association, which supported MacInnis, responded with another pamphlet in mid-June. During the summer months, the controversy appears to have slowed, and at least one leader, Gerald Winrod, thought that Biola would come through it unscathed.[119] But while local efforts simmered, a few national papers continued to ply pressure against Biola, particularly in the diatribes of W. B. Riley and

---

[117] For these misgivings see Franklin Huling, *Trinity Herald Supplement*, April 1928; "Fellow Graduate Letter," 31 March 1928, MacInnis Papers; for Torrey's quotation see Torrey to Gray, 24 April 1928, Moody Bible Institute Archives.

[118] For the call of this meeting see "Open Letter to B. I. Graduates," 1 March 1928; for what occurred in the meeting see "Notes on Unofficial Meeting of Biola Graduates in Trinity Congregational Church," 15 March 1928; for refusal of the official Biola Alumni Association to aid anti-MacInnis groups see I. J. Hazelton to W. Stace Goulding, 13 March 1928, MacInnis Papers.

[119] "Open Letter of the Alumni Association," 13 June 1928, MacInnis Papers; for Winrod's optimism see "The Storm is Passing," *The Defender*, July 1928, 1.

Charles Trumbull, who did more than anyone to keep the controversy before the public, much to Biola's chagrin.

Divisions in the Fundamentalist Camp

By May 1928 personal acrimony had reached intense proportions, and the question now lay open, what would become of Biola? Riley was adamant that Biola should not be lost to modernism. Thus, more than anyone else, he perpetuated the tirade of criticism against *PFP* and the board that refused to terminate MacInnis. Rhetorical embellishments flowed from his pen. About T. C. Horton, for example, Riley wrote sanctimoniously that he "prayed Biola into existence," giving the impression that Horton's prayers were now being subverted. By claiming that MacInnis adopted his policies in the interests of popularity, Riley could appeal to a "remnant psychology" of fundamentalism. Equally effective were insinuations that MacInnis and his staff, in an image reminiscent of Tammany Hall, were exploiting the work of others by drawing high salaries that they did not deserve.[120]

Few, however, reacted with such snide invective. Rather, both critics and defenders of MacInnis displayed a variety of attitudes and opinions that are not easily classified. On the opposition side, William Pettinghill saw *PFP* as a work to be wary of, Riley preferred to label it modernist, but Trumbull was unwilling to call it modernist, saying instead that it was unscriptural.[121] Other shades of opinion were seen in James Gray's approach, who stayed out of the fray in the public arena, but worked privately to encourage opposition to MacInnis. Torrey, who was probably closer to MacInnis than any other of his critics, blamed the book for his illness and begged MacInnis to resign, but when asked to write a critical review he refused, limiting his public stand to a terse: "I will not endorse the book." Even more tenuous was the position of A. C. Gaebelein, who opened his magazine to criticism of *PFP*, but in personal correspondence with Mrs. Milton Stewart (a staunch supporter of MacInnis), claimed that he had no sympathy with attacks on MacInnis.[122] Others were puzzled by the whole row: Lewis Sperry Chafer, for example, praised Charles Trumbull for his forthright editorials, that ex-

---

[120] "Biola Boiling," *Christian Fundamentalist,* May 1928, 7–8.

[121] William L. Pettinghill, "Dean MacInnis' Book," *Serving-and-Waiting,* June 1928, 40; Riley, "The MacInnis Book Again," 15–17; Trumbull, "The Bible Institute of Los Angeles," 562.

[122] For Gray's involvement see "Notes on Unofficial Meeting of Biola Graduates in Trinity Congregational Church." For Torrey see Torrey to MacInnis, 10 March 1928; for Gaebelein see A. C. Gaebelein to Mrs. Milton Stewart, 20 April 1928, MacInnis Papers.

uded a "spirit of Christian love," but he did not offer his concurrence with Trumbull's views and even allowed that MacInnis "did not intend" to be in error.[123] Harry Ironside wrote asking if MacInnis had become a "semi-Modernist." When MacInnis mailed back his profession of orthodoxy, Ironside was gratified. Nevertheless, anti-MacInnis groups claimed Ironside for their side.[124] Reticence on the part of some well seasoned fundamentalists to attack MacInnis may have been motivated by a perception, as Robert Shuler exclaimed, that there was a "lot of meanness" in the whole affair.[125]

MacInnis' defenders displayed a wider theological diversity than those who attacked him. There were a few self-avowed fundamentalist dissenters, like Gerald Winrod, who took up the gauntlet for MacInnis. On the other side of the spectrum, some Presbyterian liberals such as James Snowden admired MacInnis' work. His strongest support, however, came from that vast middle ground of moderate mainline clergy, who shared his beliefs and harbored an instinctive distaste for theological controversy.

Bible School and Independent Fundamentalist Support

Although it was probably a small number, MacInnis did acquire a few cobelligerents from other Bible school leaders. Some may have sympathized with his situation merely because they disliked the uncharitable spirit of the controversy, and others may have sided with MacInnis because of jealousies or rivalries within the fundamentalist movement. Lew Gosnell, the man who wrote the 1922 letter commending MacInnis' lectures, appears to have sided with MacInnis in the controversy over *PFP,* but his views were influenced by personal bitterness toward James Gray.[126] Nevertheless, MacInnis welcomed his support, knowing that as a dean of the Bible Institute of Pennsylvania he could be a badly needed ally. Yet another Bible school leader, H. S. Miller of the National Bible Institute in New York, wrote to Keith Brooks affirming that he and his president, Don Shelton, sympathized with MacInnis and Campbell Morgan. "How the Devil likes to bring trouble," he averred, "to those who are hewing to the old line." Interestingly, Miller blamed the Plymouth Brethren and Scofield dispensationalists for the contro-

---

[123] Lewis Sperry Chafer to Charles Trumbull, 26 September 1928, Lewis Sperry Chafer Papers, Dallas Theological Seminary Archives, Dallas, Texas.

[124] Harry Ironside to MacInnis, 16 February 1928 and 16 March 1928, MacInnis Papers.

[125] Robert P. Shuler to W. B. Riley, 13 March 1928, MacInnis Papers.

[126] Lev Wade Gosnell to MacInnis, 19 March 1928, and MacInnis to Gosnell, 26 March 1928, MacInnis Papers.

versy, which suggests that some Bible school leaders might have supported MacInnis based on their common commitment to "historical" premillennialism.[127] On the other hand, W. J. Scott of the Vancouver Bible School, who appeared to hold to dispensational views, also supported MacInnis. His support may have reflected the moderate tone of VBS leader Walter Ellis, who was very similar to MacInnis, a non-militant Presbyterian conservative, premillennial but not dispensational, and strongly influenced by Keswick ideas.[128] It is likely that MacInnis also enjoyed much support at the Toronto Bible Training School for similar reasons, although no record of this remains. One other Bible school leader who strongly defended MacInnis was William Evans. Though Evans had retired from Biola in 1918, his standing with Biola fundamentalists led Marion Reynolds to ask him what he thought of *PFP*. Evans responded that he trusted MacInnis and cautioned Reynolds not to criticize him.[129] Although the picture of Bible school dissent in the MacInnis controversy remains incomplete, it is clear that Riley's image of a uniform "Bible school defense line" against MacInnis was overdrawn.

Yet not to be ignored in this picture were Bible school fundamentalists at Biola itself, whose views of the crisis were disdainfully neglected by other leaders, because it was widely assumed that they had been deluded by their personal loyalty to MacInnis. One leader, who at this time was just starting his fundamentalist career, was Alva McClain. McClain eventually went on to found the fundamentalist Grace Theological Seminary in 1937. But in 1928 he was teaching at Biola and trying to find a middle ground in the crisis over *PFP*. McClain believed that criticisms of MacInnis were unwarranted, and to redress the imbalance he wrote a review of *PFP*, which objectively discussed his areas of agreement and disagreement.[130] This essay he submitted to the *Sunday School Times*, but Trumbull declined to publish it, probably because he considered it too positive.[131]

---

[127] H. S. Miller to Keith Brooks, 12 December 1928, MacInnis Papers.

[128] On Scott's support see W. J. Scott to MacInnis, 20 April 1928, MacInnis Papers; for his probable dispensationalism see Bob Burkinshaw to Daniel Draney, 26 June 1995, in this writer's possession; for Ellis see Robert Burkinshaw, *Pilgrims in Lotusland: Conservative Protestantism in British Columbia, 1917–1981* (Montreal & Kingston: McGill-Queen's University Press, 1995), 58–66.

[129] Marion Reynolds to William Evans, 27 January 1928, MacInnis Papers.

[130] Alva J. McClain, "Peter the Fisherman Philosopher," Unpublished Review of *Peter the Fisherman Philosopher,* Typed Document, n.d., MacInnis Papers.

[131] For Trumbull's refusal to publish the review see Gray to Torrey, 24 February 1928 and Torrey to Gray, 28 February 1928, Moody Bible Institute Archives.

Another Bible school leader and outspoken defender of MacInnis was Keith Brooks. Brooks started his Bible institute career at the Practical Bible Institute in Binghamton, New York. There he made the acquaintance of R. A. Torrey, and through this connection he eventually came to Biola in 1917.[132] Shortly thereafter, Brooks' credentials as a solid fundamentalist became well established by the publication and distribution of his pamphlet entitled "The Spirit of Truth and the Spirit of Error." This leaflet became a catalyst for the development of Robert Hadden's Christian Fundamentals League, which was, as previously noted, hostile toward MacInnis.[133] Given this background, it is not clear why he was attracted to the moderate tone of the MacInnis agenda, although he did raise doubts about militancy a year before MacInnis became dean.[134]

One other MacInnis defender was William E. Blackstone. Blackstone is most often remembered for his best-selling book *Jesus is Coming,* but he was also a founding member of the Bible Institute of Los Angeles and the school's first dean. Unfortunately, there is nothing known about his role in the crisis except that he sided with MacInnis. This fact is not surprising, however, for Blackstone was a trustee of the Milton Stewart Evangelistic Fund. As trustee, Blackstone worked closely with Mrs. Milton Stewart, who was a close friend of MacInnis, and like him, a Canadian. Her relationship with MacInnis would have made it difficult for Blackstone to oppose MacInnis, even if he had felt so inclined, but there is no reason to suspect that his support was in any way half-hearted or insincere.[135]

In addition to the meager support that MacInnis received from fellow Bible institutes, there were a few independent fundamentalist entrepreneurs who also took up the cudgels for MacInnis. The most important of these was Gerald Winrod. None campaigned harder than he to exonerate the embattled MacInnis. Yet his outspoken support of MacInnis is also the most enigmatic, because Winrod was highly placed in the WCFA

---

[132] For the Binghamton connection see Reuben A. Torrey to Brooks, 22 May 1928, Moody Bible Institute Archives; for his arrival date see Biola Board Minutes, 26 October 1917. It is likely that Brooks and MacInnis first met in Binghamton, for MacInnis was a teacher there in 1908, while a pastor in Montrose, Pennsylvania.

[133] Keith Brooks, "The Spirit of Truth and the Spirit of Error," Pamphlet, n.d., Biola University Library Archives; "What God Has Done Through One Tract," *The King's Business,* May 1928, 293; and Edmondson, "Fundamentalist Sects of Los Angeles," 244–47.

[134] Keith L. Brooks, "The Forgotten Fundamental" *Moody Bible Institute Monthly,* March 1924, 340–41.

[135] For Blackstone's position see Henry Manuscript, 84–85; for his trusteeship see "The Stewarts as Christian Stewards," 597–98.

and a militant anti-evolution fighter, qualities which seemed quite at variance to MacInnis.

Winrod's meteoric rise to leadership in the fundamentalist movement had begun only two years earlier, when in April 1926 he started a monthly magazine called *The Defender,* and later that same year he delivered a spell-binding address at the WCFA convention, receiving a standing ovation. With these achievements, Winrod quickly moved into the center of fundamentalist activities: he became a member of the WCFA executive committee, travelling extensively on its behalf in the anti-evolution campaigns.[136] His own Kansas based organization, Defenders of the Christian Faith, grew from a small 1,300 members in 1927 to a reported 60,000 seven years later, although probably these membership figures were greatly exaggerated.[137] Just as his star was rising, however, the fundamentalist controversy over E. Stanley Jones began. Winrod leapt to the defense of Jones in August 1927, arguing that Jones' book was sound on all the cardinal doctrines including "the ministry of healing," in spite of overwhelming opposition to Jones from other fundamentalist papers. It may be that this initial split with the majority of fundamentalist leaders in America primed Winrod for his even greater fight over MacInnis. Whatever his motivation, Winrod vigorously entered the battle, writing at least fifteen articles in support of MacInnis for his *Defender* magazine. Without naming a soul, he accused anti-MacInnis belligerents of muckraking, mud-slinging, and deceit, not to mention ignorance and confusion. These accusations must have aroused some protest, for he later apologetically explained that his criticisms were not intended for certain "fundamentalists in the East."[138] His trenchant defense of MacInnis, however, severely strained his relationships with many fundamentalists, and contributed to his early resignation from the WCFA in June 1928.[139]

Why did Winrod support MacInnis to the jeopardy of his own status in the fundamentalist movement? His admirers would have claimed that when he believed in something he followed his conviction, regardless of the cost, to the bitter end. While that may have been true, it is also noteworthy that his holiness religious roots set him apart from many of a fundamentalist ilk. His religion was intensely practical, learned from

---

[136] Ribuffo, *The Old Christian Right,* 81, 87: for a devotional biography see G. H. Montgomery, *Gerald Burton Winrod* (Wichita, KS: Mertmont, 1965).

[137] Ribuffo, *The Old Christian Right,* 88. Winrod claimed that 30,000 copies of his magazine were being printed in 1928: see "This Magazine," *Defender,* May 1928, 1.

[138] For his charges see "The Muckraker," *Defender,* March 1928, 10; for his later explanation see "The Bible Institute Will Triumph," June 1928, 13.

[139] *Defender,* June 1928, 2, Winrod had also expressed dissatisfaction at the anti-pentecostal stance of the WCFA; see *Defender,* August 1928, 3.

the zealous Holy Ghost healing ministry of his parents. His concern, therefore, was more often for the use of religion than for its precise doctrinal formulation. This is why he objected to the attacks on MacInnis. Winrod could not see the practical sense of splitting the fundamentalist forces over men like Jones and MacInnis, when he knew that they professed an orthodox faith. Better to strike your axe at the root of an enemy's tree than your own, he reasoned. In this he paralleled the views of other Wesleyan fundamentalists, like fighting Bob Shuler and Leander W. Munhall, none of whom were lacking in militancy when it came to facing the real enemy. "Let it be remembered," he chided, "that fundamentalists agree on only about seven to nine points of doctrine. Get out of the circle and they will fight at the drop of your hat."[140] The problem for most fundamentalists, however, was how big to draw the circle.

In spite of his extensive defense of MacInnis, Winrod had little impact on anti-MacInnis opposition. Friends of MacInnis cited his name frequently as evidence that MacInnis was no modernist, and MacInnis himself seems to have welcomed his support, so much so that Biola offered a free three month subscription to *The King's Business* for every *Defender* reader, in appreciation of his efforts.[141] But Winrod was too easily dismissed as a pariah shouting at "the custodians of truth" from a lonely writer's garret. In the end, his efforts did little to dissuade anti-MacInnis opposition.[142]

Interdenominational Moderate Evangelical Support

MacInnis also received support from a class of evangelicals who were moderate theologically, non-militant, and focused in their ministries toward an inter-denominational constituency. One such figure was A. P. Fitt, son-in-law of D. L. Moody, and heir of the Northfield Schools and Bible Conferences. Fitt wrote to encourage MacInnis, declaring that his critics were full of "folly and false zeal."[143] But Fitt's support was of little usefulness: fundamentalists had long lamented the decline of Northfield, believing that Fitt and Moody's son, Will, had departed from the

---

[140] For Winrod's holiness roots see Montgomery, *Gerald Burton Winrod*, 9–16, and Ribuffo, *Old Christian Right*, 80–81; for the quotation see "Higher Fundamentalism," *Defender*, June 1928, 15.

[141] *Defender*, February 1928, 24.

[142] For the "custodians of truth" quotation see Ribuffo, *Old Christian Right*, 89.

[143] A. P. Fitt to MacInnis, 27 November 1928, MacInnis Papers; also see [A. P. Fitt], review of *Peter the Fisherman Philosopher*, by John MacInnis, in *Record of Christian Work*, March 1928, 186.

elder Moody's conservative theology.[144] To MacInnis, however, this support was greatly prized, for Northfield embodied his vision of a moderate evangelicalism.

Another moderate evangelical leader in Canada was Rowland Bingham, who founded the Sudan Interior Mission and the Evangelical Publishers. He found himself under criticism for his stance in the controversy. Ironically, a review published in his monthly magazine, *The Evangelical Christian,* did not endorse *PFP.* "I do not consider this book coming from the Dean of a notable Bible Institute," Bingham penned, "as adding in any way to his position as an evangelical teacher."[145] In spite of this, Bingham disapproved of the vitriolic attacks on MacInnis arguing that after visiting the institute, he was confident of MacInnis' orthodoxy. His mild defense elicited a blistering response from T. T. Shields, who used the occasion to draw attention to Bingham's less than militant fundamentalism.[146] This controversy between Shields and Bingham illustrates how the MacInnis crisis could sometimes widen existing tensions between rival fundamentalists, even as far away as Toronto.

Some evangelical institutions, in spite of support for MacInnis, stayed above the fray. J. Oliver Buswell of Wheaton College, for example, appeared to support MacInnis though not with much verve. He called for a committee of fundamentalists, including Riley, Torrey, Keyser, and Trumbull, to resolve the crisis, but no such meeting was ever arranged.[147] A few other educators also followed Buswell's approach, perhaps not wanting to become too visible in their defense of MacInnis. Wilbert White of Biblical Seminary, New York, and David Breed of Western Theological Seminary, Pittsburgh, wrote letters supporting his general position and disclaiming the criticism against him, but neither of these respected evangelicals did much to speak out against his ill-treatment at the hand of fundamentalists.[148] Indeed, when MacInnis sought the aid of W. Graham Scroggie, the respected British evangelical replied that he was relieved that he would not have to review the book publicly. But his relief did not come from doubts about MacInnis, for although he felt that the book was sometimes ambiguous, he disowned that it was unorthodox.[149] His relief came, instead, from his own mediate position

---

[144] See e.g. "News from Northfield and the Moody Muddle," *The King's Business,* November 1925, 470.

[145] *Evangelical Christian,* February 1928, 68.

[146] Rowland Bingham to MacInnis, 23 August 1928, MacInnis Papers.

[147] J. Oliver Buswell to MacInnis, 10 May 1928, and MacInnis to Buswell, 29 June 1928, MacInnis Papers.

[148] Wilbert W. White to MacInnis, 12 June 1928, and David Breed to MacInnis, 22 May 1928, MacInnis Papers.

[149] W. Graham Scroggie to MacInnis, n.d., MacInnis Papers.

in British evangelicalism, which found him carefully trying to avoid fanning the flames of controversy in England. Given the negative reviews that *PFP* was receiving from British fundamentalists like A. H. Carter, who called higher fundamentalism "a new cult," Scroggie probably saw the potential for criticisms and preferred to stay out of the battle.[150]

Mainline Protestant Support

In addition to these sources of support, MacInnis received his greatest defense from denominational clergy. MacInnis received hundreds of letters from ministers across the United States, most of which decried the attacks on him and offered their encouragement. Ironically, probably few had read his book—a conclusion that is suggested by the fact that only two thousand were printed and many of these were eventually destroyed. But many who heard of the controversy believed that the attacks were unworthy of Christians.

Official denominational periodicals ignored the controversy because it had little bearing on denominational matters, and because they usually took a non-controversial editorial stance. Probably for this reason editors at the unofficial Baptist periodical, the *Watchman-Examiner*, though writing a brief nondescript review of the book, made no mention of the controversy. Their silence was surprising, however, given their obvious affinities for a moderate evangelicalism. Some fundamentalist Baptists privately supported MacInnis. J. C. Massee, for instance, commended *PFP*, and John Marvin Dean, minister of the Hinson Memorial Church of Portland, Oregon complimented him: "No man ever did more for the West," he said, "in the spiritual and Biblical sense than did you."[151] By and large, MacInnis received the support of many Baptists in Southern California, who mostly followed the moderate conservative stand of J. Whitcomb Brougher.[152]

By far his greatest support came from Presbyterians who ranged over the theological spectrum. Although the Princeton conservatives like Machen and Macartney seem not to have commented on the dispute, others from the fundamentalist side were deeply involved. Stewart MacLennan, minister of the prestigious Hollywood Presbyterian Church

---

[150] David W. Bebbington, *Evangelicalism in Modern Britain: A History from the 1730s to the 1980s* (London: Unwin Hyman, 1989), 222, 227.

[151] John Marvin Dean to MacInnis, n.d., and MacInnis to Dean, 27 August 1928, MacInnis Papers.

[152] On Brougher's moderating influence in Southern California see Leland Hine, *Baptists in Southern California* (Valley Forge, PA: Judson Press, 1966), 168.

supported MacInnis and took an active role in the controversy, chairing the ministerial committee charged with reviewing the book. His views were valuable, because he was linked to WCFA activities in Los Angeles. Another fundamentalist Presbyterian, Mark Matthews, invited Mac-Innis to preach at his huge Seattle church as a show of his support.[153] Although both of these leaders expressed their confidence in MacInnis' orthodoxy, they argued that *PFP* should be withdrawn, because it was too easily subject to misinterpretation.[154] MacLennan made an effort to reconcile Trumbull and MacInnis in July 1928, when he arranged a meeting between them to discuss their differences. In spite of his efforts to persuade Trumbull that MacInnis was a solid fundamentalist, Trumbull did not budge. Later, MacLennan wrote to Trumbull: "I am glad that you expressed yourself as you did for I feel that MacInnis is a devout and sincere Christian, and that he is a fundamentalist just as truly as any of us."[155]

On the other side of the theological spectrum, two editors of unofficial Presbyterian weeklies representing a progressive voice in the church, James Clarke of the *Presbyterian Advance,* and James Snowden of the *Presbyterian Banner,* published regular notices of the controversy and defended MacInnis from the criticisms of Riley and others. Strangely, Clarke's magazine printed a negative review of *PFP* in March 1928, written by an outside reviewer who called parts of the book "very far fetched." Disagreeing with this review and learning of the attacks against him, Clarke decided to make MacInnis and his book front page news. In a review entitled "Higher Fundamentalism," Clarke gushed with enthusiasm for a type of fundamentalism that "finds its roots in life and experience rather than in tradition and form," and he noted that any liberal could heartily subscribe to this kind of fundamentalism.[156] Riley, not slow to notice this endorsement from one who had been branded by William Jennings Bryan as "belonging to a class worse

---

[153] Mark Matthews to MacInnis, 6 June 1928, MacInnis Papers.

[154] Mark Matthews to Ralph Atkinson, 10 February 1928; Stewart MacLennan to MacInnis 19 May 1928, MacInnis Papers.

[155] For their meeting, the exact date of which is uncertain, see Charles Trumbull to MacInnis, 16 July 1928; for his quotation see Stewart MacLennan to Charles Trumbull, n.d., MacInnis Papers; for Mrs. Milton Stewart's opinion that MacLennan "straddled the fence" see Mrs. Mary W. Stewart to MacInnis, n.d., MacInnis Papers.

[156] For Clarke's explanation of the negative review and his just learning of the attacks on MacInnis see James E. Clarke to MacInnis, 26 June 1928, MacInnis Papers; for his review see "Higher Fundamentalism," *Presbyterian Advance,* 16 August 1928, 1.

than atheists,"[157] used Clarke's statement in a demagogic way, as a vindication of his own position.[158]

The MacInnis controversy probably would have gained more attention in the Presbyterian church, had it not been for the struggle then taking place over Princeton Seminary. This struggle began to assume greater proportions in 1926 when a committee of the General Assembly was formed to study the problems between the seminary's faculty and administration. The following year this committee recommended that the seminary be reorganized under a single board. Although this advisement was ostensibly put forward to obtain a better management of the school's affairs, conservatives interpreted it as a political maneuver to make the seminary inclusive of liberal interests. Thus, the committee's recommendation generated heated controversy — so much so that in 1928, a move was made to end discussion of the seminary's problems for one year. Because the Princeton controversy reached its apogee between 1928 and 1929, the MacInnis crisis had little chance of acquiring any greater attention in the Presbyterian Church.[159]

In spite of the Princeton distraction, however, one Presbyterian editor of pronounced fundamentalist convictions decided to give the MacInnis crisis attention in New Zealand. P. B. Fraser, once called the "stormy petrel of New Zealand Presbyterianism," used his magazine, the *Biblical Recorder*, to defend MacInnis. Fraser was a lonely figure in New Zealand Presbyterianism, for he had no substantial influence or following for his militant conservatism, which was highly influenced by Machen and the Princeton theology.[160] He appears to have enjoyed extensive contacts with American fundamentalists, including Reuben Torrey, who probably had met Fraser during his evangelistic travels. There is no evidence that MacInnis knew Fraser prior to 1925, because when he was appointed dean, he asked Torrey to write a notice to "a paper in New Zealand," hoping that this would give him an introduction abroad. The paper was probably the *Biblical Recorder*, because Biola had recently sent its anti-pentecostal resolution to Fraser's magazine.[161] MacInnis,

---

[157] "Modernist Hope for Better Days," *The Literary Digest*, 12 September 1925, 32.

[158] W. B. Riley, "The MacInnis Controversy," *The Christian Fundamentalist*, December 1928, 13.

[159] For accounts of the controversy see Loetscher, *The Broadening Church*, 146; Longfield, *The Presbyterian Controversy*, 162–80.

[160] Allan K. Davidson, "A Protesting Presbyterian: The Reverend P. B. Fraser and New Zealand Presbyterianism, 1892–1940," *Journal of Religious History*, 14 (December 1986), 193, 214–15.

[161] MacInnis to Torrey, 13 April 1925, MacInnis Papers; for the resolution sent to the *Biblical Recorder* see Biola Board Minutes, 5 December 1924.

however, does not appear to have had any significant contacts with Fraser until the crisis began in 1928.

Fraser learned of the crisis through several American fundamentalist periodicals, including *The King's Business* and the *Sunday School Times*. But after reading these magazines he concluded that the controversy was caused by "the Plymouth Brethren sect," apparently unaware that most of MacInnis' opponents were either Baptist or Presbyterian, and few actually belonged to the Plymouth Brethren. Fraser's opinion, however, reflected his New Zealand context, where dispensationalism had been confined largely to the Plymouth Brethren. Hence, when he stated that there was an effort "of a certain school of Fundamentalists to stampede the Bible Institutes into being mere schools of Brethrenism of a narrow type," he was seeing the controversy as an effort of dispensationalists to monopolize the Bible school movement. Strangely, he never expressed any doubts about MacInnis, even though he was opposing a Presbyterian churchman in New Zealand, John Dickie, who held similar views to MacInnis.[162] This ironic circumstance suggests that Fraser's support, like Winrod's, was anomalous. MacInnis was not militant like Fraser, nor was he forced to the margins of church life by an anti-ecclesiastical posture. Finally, Fraser was seemingly unaware of differences between Machen's confessional type of fundamentalism, which he admired, and the more moderate position of MacInnis. But in spite of such differences, MacInnis welcomed his support in the *Biblical Recorder,* claiming that he had found a true highlander.[163]

The strongest support that MacInnis received came from the moderate evangelical Presbyterians who looked to the leadership of Charles R. Erdman and Robert Speer in the Presbyterian controversies. MacInnis himself was a strong supporter of Erdman's position as moderator of the General Assembly, and he also supported Erdman's opposition to Machen at Princeton Seminary. The fact that MacInnis identified with Presbyterian moderates, who could at times make common cause with liberals, set MacInnis apart from most of his fundamentalist colleagues. Yet it is not surprising, given his close affinity for Erdman's theological views, that they would share a close bond of friendship and mutual support in the face of fundamentalist opposition.

Erdman and MacInnis had much more in common than balding heads. They were close in age, and with the exception of their educational histories, both followed similar career paths as Presbyterian ministers who reluctantly left the parish to become full-time educators. Both entered the premillennial conference movement. Both were deeply

---

[162] On Dickie cf. Davidson, "A Protesting Presbyterian," 207–13; for Fraser's view see P. B. Fraser to MacInnis, 25 July 1928, MacInnis Papers.

[163] MacInnis to P. B. Fraser, 10 July 1928, MacInnis Papers.

evangelical, supporting the foreign missions movement and popular revivalists like Billy Sunday. Both shared a common interest in that series of books called *The Fundamentals,* but unlike the well-connected Erdman, MacInnis' contribution to that endeavor was not accepted. Finally, both shared a common theological heritage, which is nicely characterized by Longfield as conservative in theology, tolerant in spirit, and evangelistic in purpose. In sum, MacInnis was closer to Erdman's spirit than to any other.[164]

Hence, it is no surprise that as Erdman and MacInnis passed together through the fires of fundamentalist opposition, that they also consoled each other along the way. Several of their letters between August and December reveal a profound sympathy for their mutual experience of suffering. But in MacInnis' opinion, in spite of the haranguing sounds of criticism, the position that he and Erdman were defending represented the majority of the church.

"We are receiving scores of letters from ministers all over the United States," he told Erdman confidently.

> Personally, I believe the way is wide open for the rallying of the interest and conscience of the Church of Jesus Christ to the New Testament conception of witness and life which is widely missed by the extreme group who are threatening the highest interests of the church.[165]

To be sure, not every minister that supported Erdman or MacInnis did so because they shared that "warm evangelical spirit." For MacInnis, outside of a Presbyterian institution, some simply responded to feelings of loyalty to a fellow Presbyterian minister, regardless of his views. Cleland McAffee, for example, who earlier had sharply criticized Bible schools in an article for the *Christian Century,* now praised MacInnis for bringing Biola into a cooperative relation with the Presbyterian church, reassuring him that he would succeed in spite of his difficult circumstances.[166] But MacInnis' optimism was fueled primarily by his perception that the "extreme fundamentalists," as he stated to Erdman, would not be able to "hold the field."

This hopeful letter MacInnis had written shortly before the beginning of the 1928/1929 school year. Although his problems had not diminished, it still seemed as though he might weather the storm. Bolstering his optimism were these "scores of letters" from fellow ministers around the United States. But this support had become in the context of a Bible school almost invisible. Though many prominent clergy had rallied to

---

[164] Longfield, *The Presbyterian Controversy,* 132.
[165] MacInnis to Charles Erdman, 17 August 1928, MacInnis Papers.
[166] Cleland B. McAfee to MacInnis, 31 July 1928, MacInnis Papers.

his defense, they were largely ignored by the increasingly radical and independently focused patrons of the Bible school movement. Hence, if the struggle was really about control of an institution and defining its goals and purposes, then it would not be resolved by appeals to leaders outside of the school's actual constituency. Instead, the future of Biola would lie with those who had a greater interest in preserving the school as a standard-bearer of radical fundamentalism.

The Final Days of the MacInnis Administration

During the summer of 1928, it became increasingly clear that the two sides of the conflict were intransigent. Militant fundamentalists, led mostly by W. B. Riley and Charles Trumbull, could not be persuaded to call off their attacks, and it appeared that the Biola Board of Directors was firmly resolved to defend MacInnis. Signs of separation between the sides were beginning to multiply. At the 10th annual gathering of the WCFA, the Southern California delegation was comprised of leaders from the anti-MacInnis group, and Biola was obtrusively absent. Philip Mauro was suddenly dropped from the WCFA program, providing another sign that "fundamentalism was being redefined," and that "scores of loyal ministers and teachers," including Biola itself, would be ostracized from the fundamentalist movement.[167] Charges of libel raised the specter of lawsuits between Keith Brooks and belligerent fundamentalist editors, revealing an intense personal acrimony. French Oliver's particularly pungent speech, describing *PFP* as "the most grotesque mixture of paganism, modernism and diluted orthodoxy . . . in thirty years," only exacerbated ill-will between the opponents. Finally, after his failure to reconcile with MacInnis, Charles Trumbull dropped Biola from his list of approved Bible schools.[168]

Also stoking the fire was G. Campbell Morgan, who candidly discussed the MacInnis controversy in the *British Weekly:* speaking of Torrey and "his friends," Morgan asserted that he found their attitudes "frankly impossible" and, therefore, he could not appear on their platforms. Morgan interpreted the controversy as a schism between an extreme fundamentalist movement, and "conservative evangelicals"; the latter, he claimed, do not separate from those who accept the evolution-

---

[167] For the WCFA delegation see the *Christian Fundamentalist,* June 1928, 11; for Mauro see "Is Fundamentalism Being Redefined," *The King's Business,* September 1928, 517.

[168] For Oliver's quote and threatened lawsuits see the *Christian Fundamentalist,* June 1928, 12–13; for the school list see the *Sunday School Times,* 11 August 1928, 469.

ary theory, nor from those who deny a literal inerrancy of scripture.[169] Riley, however, saw Morgan's candid admission in a different light. It was not, as Morgan construed it, a fight within the camp. Rather, Morgan's comments only showed that he and MacInnis were never in the fundamentalist camp at all! Seeing a good opportunity to press this point to the fundamentalist public, Riley now launched an assault on Morgan, who before this had not been a focus of attention.[170]

In Los Angeles, agitation continued. When a resolution of support was signed by the Biola student body near the end of the spring term, opponents countered with their own resolution calling for the immediate resignations of MacInnis and his staff and the repudiation and withdrawal of *PFP* from book stores.[171] Some of them also began to form new fundamentalist enterprises. Marion Reynolds started his "Fundamental Evangelistic Association," in which the principal speakers were well known opponents of MacInnis.[172] Rumors that Robert Hadden intended to start a rival Bible school once again began to circulate.[173] French E. Oliver, capitalizing on disaffection caused by McNeill's preaching impropriety, began the "First Fundamental Church of Los Angeles" with a cadre of about two hundred schismatic fundamentalists.[174] Given this spurt of independent activity, one observer was led to say: "Fundamentalism as a movement is destined to do what most ecclesiastical and theological reformations have had to do, namely quit the fellowship of apostates, originate another organization."[175]

---

[169] J.T.S., "Interview with Dr. G. Campbell Morgan," *British Weekly,* 5 July 1928, 295; for further discussions in the *British Weekly* see also "American Fundamentalists and Dr. Campbell Morgan," 2 August 1928, 378; "Dr. Campbell Morgan Resigns His Post at Los Angeles," 13 December 1928, 261.

[170] W. B. Riley, "Dr. Campbell Morgan and the Los Angeles Bible Institute," *Christian Fundamentalist,* August 1928, 12–15; also see "The Book Reviewers," February 1929, 56.

[171] W. B. Riley, "The MacInnis Book Again," *Christian Fundamentalist,* August 1928, 15–17. Riley reported that 112 students signed the petition, but it is unclear if his petition is the same as that recorded in the Biola Board Minutes, 1 June 1928. The latter reported that only 45 graduates signed a petition. Either way, the growing number was a sign of weakening support in the student body.

[172] Thomas C. Horton, "A New Bible Conference," *Christian Fundamentalist,* October 1928, 22.

[173] Robert Hadden to George B. Bell, 13 July 1928, MacInnis Papers. Hadden gave out this idea in the *Christian Fundamentals Magazine,* July 1928, 2.

[174] *The Presbyterian Banner,* 6 September 1928, 20.

[175] "The First Fundamentalist Church of Los Angeles," *Christian Fundamentalist,* November 1928, 26.

The acceleration of independent fundamentalist activity was primarily motivated by a perception that Biola would not alter its position. In Riley's opinion, Biola's board was refusing to heed fundamentalist complaints. Few expected any change in the board's position, in light of the determined stand that it was taking, and its attempts to project a positive, confident image.[176]

Just what prompted the board to reverse its position, therefore, is not known, and the board Minutes offer only slight indications. An entry on 13 November states: "Dr. MacInnis tendered his resignation as Dean of the Bible Institute." This entry also states that Biola's attorney, Nathan Newby, moved to accept his resignation, and that Mrs. Stewart seconded the motion.[177] But the records are confusing, for this date did not become the official date of his resignation. Ten days later, on 23 November, the board adopted a resolution that fixed the official date of his resignation on 16 November, and ended his services with the institute on 31 December.[178] This record also suggests that his resignation was accepted by a simple majority, because on 19 November, four members of the board resigned in protest of the board's action.[179]

The matter of his resignation itself became quite controversial. In an address before the entire institute, faculty and student body, MacInnis laid bare his feelings of betrayal. As far as he knew, claimed MacInnis, the board was standing by him. He was dismayed to find, therefore, that a committee of the board had decided to consider his resignation. MacInnis continued:

When I heard from the outside what was going on within the Board I asked for a hearing and an effort was made by the majority party in the Board to prevent me from making a statement, but the sense of justice prevailed and I was permitted to make the same. Even at that time nothing was said to me by the Board concerning the fact that my resignation was under consideration.[180]

This pained response to the board's action was somewhat affected, for MacInnis' wife had told her family as early as October 28 that his resig-

---

[176] Riley, "The MacInnis Controversy," 13. For Biola's image, see projections of a large enrollment: *The King's Business*, September 1928, 536; also "The Tide Turns," October 1928, 600–601.

[177] Biola Board Minutes, 13 November 1928.

[178] Biola Board Minutes, 23 November 1928.

[179] Biola Board Minutes, 19 November 1928; J. M, Irvine, J, M. Rust, William Hazlett, and Alexander MacKeigan to Nathan Newby, Letter of Resignation, 19 November 1928, MacInnis Papers.

[180] MacInnis, Statement of Resignation, Typed Document, n.d., MacInnis Papers.

nation was "on the table," and that Mrs. Lyman Stewart had turned against him.[181] He therefore must have at least expected that his resignation would possibly be requested. Even so, the circumstances of his resignation do not give much light on what prompted the board to change its position. More important are the explanations that gained wide circulation after MacInnis "went public" in early December. Initially the board had hoped to keep the matter somewhat quiet and free of controversy, by resolving that any severance pay be based on his maintaining an "attitude of fellowship" toward Biola.[182] But MacInnis felt constrained to give his side of the story, and so he presented his opinion of the board's decision before an assembly of students and faculty. After his public airing of the matter the board was deluged by criticism, only this time it came from friends and supporters of MacInnis.

One reason that the board changed its position, claimed MacInnis, was their belief that criticism of the institute was "introducing dissension, cutting down the student enrollment and drying up the financial resources."[183] Yet none of these supposed problems, he charged, were sufficient reasons for the board's action. In a point-by-point statement MacInnis disputed that there was any greater dissension within the institute or that enrollment had been hurt significantly by the controversy.[184] But his strongest remonstrance was against the charge that the controversy had caused a financial crisis at Biola, a charge that revealed his personal differences with Mrs. Lyman Stewart. "I am not the cause of the present financial stress," he exclaimed defiantly.

> Therefore, it was manifestly unjust to recommend the acceptance of my resignation on this basis. In the light of the facts it is also obvious that when the Trustee [Mrs. Stewart] makes my elimination a condition of relieving the serious financial condition of the Institute and insists upon it in the face of losing four of the most useful members of the Board and the support of some of the most generous contributors to our work, the real cause for this demand has not been frankly stated. My own conviction is that the real cause of this course is the desire of the Trustee to dictate to the Board of Directors and to dominate the whole life and activities of the Institute.[185]

---

[181] Ida MacInnis to Family, 28 October 1928, MacInnis Papers.

[182] Biola Board Minutes, 23 November 1928.

[183] MacInnis, Statement of Resignation.

[184] Enrollment statistics became a very contentious aspect of the dispute, but in general, it seems that the 1928 fall enrollment had declined by about 12% from the 1927 enrollment: "Facts Regarding Enrollment," *The King's Business,* May 1928, Special Insert.

[185] MacInnis, Statement of Resignation.

As previously noted, misunderstandings about the Bible Women and a belief that MacInnis was doing away with evangelistic programs had caused Mrs. Stewart considerable upset. But now MacInnis was pointing to an even deeper problem—a power struggle caused by Mrs. Stewart's alleged desire to dictate Biola policies. In his criticism, MacInnis made public a fiscal problem which had divided the board during his administration, and which caused, in part, the resignations of four board members. This issue requires additional explanation.

Lyman Stewart, prior to his death, had given Biola a deed of stock in a business enterprise called the Western Machinery Company. Unfortunately, during the mid twenties this company began to flounder, and so, in order to protect its interests, Biola borrowed large sums of money to keep the bereft company from failing. This, however, turned into a financial disaster for the school, because in spite of optimistic predictions from some board members the company continued to fail, leaving the school, according to MacInnis and the minority of the board, "hopelessly encumbered."[186]

As the financial situation worsened, and the school could not meet its financial obligations in a timely manner, MacInnis and several members of the board began to call on Mrs. Stewart to resolve the crisis by reducing the school's indebtedness. Prior to his death, Lyman Stewart had established a trust fund to protect Biola from financial calamity, and it was now evident to MacInnis and the minority of the board, that just such a crisis was at hand. Mrs. Stewart, however, who was the sole trustee of the fund, was not willing to liquidate it for the alleviation of the school's indebtedness.[187] Although the situation was complicated by personal pique, Mrs. Stewart's reluctance to use the trust fund was not just a "desire to dictate to the Board of Directors," as MacInnis bitterly complained, but also a desire to preserve the ministries such as the Bible Women, which she had supported from this fund for years. To spend it would have been to lose, in her view, a vital ministry of Biola.

The resignation of MacInnis, of the four board members, and his open statements before the school, precipitated a sudden backlash of criticism for the board. G. Campbell Morgan, by far the best known faculty member, had announced his resignation on November 23, and in the following four weeks the board considered at least nine more resignations. Although it is difficult to get an exact accounting, approximately twenty teachers and employees of Biola resigned. Out of the

---

[186] For a brief summary see Williams and Miller, *Chartered for His Glory*, 51; for MacInnis' view see his Statement of Resignation; for the minority opinion of the board see Irvine et al., Letter of Resignation.

[187] Irvine et. al., Letter of Resignation.

Bible faculty, slightly more than half resigned.[188] Although some of
them agreed to stay and complete the spring semester, the fact that so
many faculty submitted their resignations demonstrated a strong show
of support for MacInnis.

While the Biola board met on Friday night, December 7, to discuss
the repercussions of the crisis, local churches planned their own discussions, and leaders of the Los Angeles Presbytery called for a special
meeting to discuss if anything could be done on behalf of MacInnis.[189]
The Biola directors were caught off-guard by the flurry of protests and
failed to respond adequately to the spreading criticisms. Though Nathan
Newby, the new chairman of the board, addressed the student body on
December 7, the record indicates little else in the way of an organized
response. Not until after the special meeting of presbytery on December
19, did the board begin to defend its actions.[190]

The meeting of the Los Angeles Presbytery proved to be an important
event for MacInnis. It passed a unanimous resolution that upheld his
loyalty and devotion to Jesus Christ and ordered that the resolution be
sent to every Presbytery in the United States and Great Britain.[191] When
asked to speak, MacInnis received a lengthy ovation, after which he
thanked his friends and excoriated his critics for their "conscienceless,
unscrupulous and unchristian" attitudes. It seems that his victory in the

---

[188] Resignations from the Board were Irvine, MacKeigan, Rust, and Hazlett;
from the Biola Society, Thomas Holden, of the Los Angeles Presbytery, and
Mary Stewart, the second wife of Milton Stewart (Biola Society Minutes, 20
December 1928); Ford Canfield, ex-missionary and Biola alumnus, and Charles
Hurlburt (Biola Society Minutes, 14 June 1929); from the faculty, Morgan,
Brooks, Atkinson, Kelly, Davis, Walter, Chaffee (Board Minutes, 7, 12, 20 December 1928), and Alva McClain (Board Minutes, 5 April 1929); for evidence
of McClain's dissatisfaction see McClain to MacInnis, 11 June 1929, MacInnis
Papers: other staff resignations were Glasse, of Biola's radio station, Kurtz and
Jenkins; for Kurtz and Jenkins see Helen Kurtz to MacInnis, 12 June 1929; although John McNeill did not leave over the MacInnis crisis, his departure a
month earlier was also a loss of a MacInnis sympathizer. Finally, from the music faculty, Tovey submitted a resignation, but he was still at Biola a year later
(Executive Minutes, 4 December 1929).

[189] Discussions of the crisis were offered by Gus Briegleb, St. Paul's Pres-
byterian Church, Bob Shuler, Trinity Methodist Church, and J. Whitcomb
Brougher, First Baptist Church of Glendale; see "Row of Church Group Stirs
Interest," the Los Angeles *Evening Herald,* 10 December 1928, Section A, p.
16. For the presbytery call see "Bible Institute Rift Spreading," Los Angeles
Times, 8 December, 1928, Part II, pp. 1–2.

[190] For the Newby address see Biola Board Minutes, 7 December 1928.

[191] "Vote Backs Bible Teacher," Los Angeles *Times,* 20 December 1928,
Part II, 1; "Action of the Presbytery of Los Angeles Relating to Dr. John Mac-
Innis," *Presbyterian Banner,* 10 January 1929, 4.

Los Angeles Presbytery prompted the Biola board to write a detailed response to his accusations, which it then distributed to every member of the presbytery.[192]

In spite of this enthusiastic support that he received from his friends in the presbytery, it soon became apparent that there was almost nothing to be done about the situation. The board had determined its course, and even though the action of the board was widely perceived as political expedience, an unprincipled sacrifice of MacInnis for the sake of a radical minority, there was little more than verbal comforts to be offered. From the perspective of Biola, however, its reputation had been considerably damaged in the eyes of most churches. It will be remembered that MacInnis had taken great pains to build confidence in the institute among the denominational churches, and now, by his rejection, Biola feared that this would be lost.

To recover lost ground, Biola finally issued a statement on December 28. Interestingly, the board's statement tried to maintain a middle position that would appeal to its disintegrating denominational constituency, but at the same time adequately explain their rejection of MacInnis. This attempt failed to satisfy either fundamentalist radicals or denominational moderates, and the controversy that followed became the final chapter of the MacInnis saga.

Resolution of the Controversy

The board's statement, which W. B. Riley published in full, side by side with MacInnis' address before the Los Angeles Presbytery, offered a lengthy, but unsatisfactory explanation of MacInnis' resignation. First, it affirmed as always that MacInnis "had not departed at all from the fundamental truths declared in its 'Statement of Doctrine,' and, therefore, the claim that he was a modernist was 'erroneous.'"[193] This statement, which continued to absolve MacInnis of the most common fundamentalist charges, left the institute in a slippery position. On the one hand, how could the board justify its dismissal of MacInnis, if the accusations against him were all patently untrue? On the other hand, Riley also expressed disappointment: "The intelligent reader will suffer some disappointment at the Board's diagnosis of the case."[194]

As if needing a scapegoat, Biola then accused MacInnis of substituting an educational program primarily based on "scholastic, rather than spiritual" considerations. This might have impressed a few fundamen-

---

[192] Biola Board Minutes, 20 December 1928.

[193] Statement of the Board of Directors, quoted in, *The Christian Fundamentalist,* February 1929, 51.

[194] Ibid., 54.

talist critics, but fearing that this could also tarnish their educational reputation they went on to deny that this was the basic reason for his resignation. Once again, no one was satisfied.[195]

Finally, the board also denied that financial problems had anything to do with accepting his resignation. True, many had withdrawn their support, but it was also true, according to the statement, that "friends of Dr. MacInnis made substantial contributions to the Institute." Therefore, it concluded, "we do not wish to attempt . . . to balance the financial gains and losses." In its brief statement the board denied every charge that MacInnis had made regarding his resignation. But if none of these reasons were true, why was he let go?

In a very unusual admission, Nathan Newby, the author of the board's statement, allowed that no valid reason had existed! But, because MacInnis had afterward accused the institute of financial mismanagement, this was an acceptable reason to terminate his employment.

> If no valid reason existed prior to November 16, 1928, for the acceptance of the resignation of Dean MacInnis, certainly the false impression created by his statement on this financial question, which he read to the faculty and student body, and which has been the basis of criticism from at least one pulpit in the City of Los Angeles, would abundantly justify the irrevocable action taken by the Board of Directors to terminate his connection with the Institute on December 31, 1928.[196]

Finally, the board affirmed its basic commitment to the church, which had been, ironically, the very cornerstone of the MacInnis administration.

> It has been suggested that the acceptance of the resignation of Dean MacInnis involved a repudiation of Christian fellowship with the Evangelical Churches of the World, and we can not too strongly deny this charge, for it does not represent either the attitude or the spirit of the Directors.[197]

Biola's statement reveals the intense ambiguity of the board's position, stuck between a sectarian and militant fundamentalist movement on the one hand, and the MacInnis ideal of denominational cooperation on the other. It was a precarious position that failed to appease anyone, least of all MacInnis, who rapped the board for giving a "wrong impression of the facts."[198]

---

[195] Ibid., 51.

[196] Ibid., 53.

[197] Ibid.

[198] "M'Innis Raps Board in Reply," Los Angeles *Times,* 28 December 1928,

Although letters of praise soon arrived from eminent fundamentalists like William Pettinghill, James Gray, and William Biederwolf, the controversy did not end so quickly. Fundamentalists were displeased that the board had not repudiated *PFP*. To satisfy these critics, the board decided on January 21 to discontinue "publication, sale and circulation" of *PFP* and also issued a new statement asserting that the book did not represent the thinking of Biola.[199] Unfortunately, this repudiation of Biola's earlier statement caused even more dissension in the board, and so another attempt was made on January 28 to write a new statement that did not explicitly condemn *PFP*.[200]

For a brief while it may have seemed that the board found a workable compromise, but as they quickly discovered, their fundamentalist watchdogs were not satisfied. During a visit to Moody Bible Institute, Charles Fuller and Mrs. Stewart tried to rehabilitate their damaged relationships with Trumbull and Gray. Their meetings, however, proved more onerous than expected, for though they were warmly received, Trumbull demanded that they publish a statement repudiating *PFP*. This, of course, meant that the board would have to reverse its position again, and possibly suffer further criticism.[201]

The attempt to arrive at an adequate statement that would satisfy the "Eastern critics" proved troublesome. On March 18, T. T. Shields, the widely known Canadian fundamentalist, attended the board, and after some debate a statement was finally carried. But dissatisfaction haunted the proceedings, because only two days later another meeting was called. Finally, after much controversy, the board with the approval of T. T. Shields, agreed to repudiate MacInnis' book, stating that "its thought and teaching does not represent the thinking and teaching of the Bible Institute today." A demand that the board accept this statement unanimously forced the acting board chairman, Nathan Newby, to resign.[202]

With the publication of this final statement, Trumbull, Gray, and Riley welcomed the prodigal Biola back into fundamentalist arms. The "MacInnis dream," to bring the Bible institute back under the denominational umbrella, had failed. To secure its fundamentalist position, Biola asked T. T. Shields to return to Los Angeles as an advisor to the board, and copies of this invitation were sent to Gray, Riley, and

---

Part II, pp. 1–2.

[199] Biola Board Minutes, 21 January 1929.

[200] Biola Board Minutes, 28 January 1929.

[201] Biola Board Minutes, 7 March 1929.

[202] Biola Board Minutes, 20 March 1929. Newby's resignation must have been as board chairman, because he continued voting on the board after this date.

Trumbull.[203] But internally, Biola's atmosphere was bleak. Among the faculty deep resentments boiled beneath the surface, sometimes leading to open disagreements.[204] In Alva McClain's perspective, Shields became a disruptive presence in the affairs of the board and a public embarrassment, for while he was boasting about his victory at Biola, he also became widely discredited for certain improprieties and blunders associated with Des Moines University.[205] As McClain put it, the Biola statement was "a dead letter."

> Of course, the whole statement was merely a sop passed out to the Eastern critics. If I ever see Mr. Trumbull again, I intend to tell him that technically he won the "victory", but that his victory is a rather hollow thing. In spite of all the statements that have been passed, no one, so far as I know, has changed his mind. The Board of Directors remind me of Galileo who was compelled to recant but did not change his mind.[206]

The reversal of Biola's position deeply hurt MacInnis. Not only did the board state that it had erred in commending his book, but it further claimed that this was the reason for accepting his resignation. This last point elicited a vigorous denial from MacInnis.[207] More bitter than this, however, was the board's decision to destroy all the remaining copies of *PFP* including its type-forms. Dejected, he wrote: "For the Institute I have nothing but sincere pity, for obviously all honor has forsaken its tattered banners and its house is left desolate."[208]

The destruction of the book, however, attracted greater attention and sympathy for MacInnis. The Los Angeles *Times,* for example, announced in bold headline: "Bible Leaders Destroy Book," and the Syracuse *Post-Standard* declared with bold type: "Dr. M'Innis' Book First Destroyed in Modern Times." MacInnis was quoted, saying: "To the best of my knowledge, this is the first instance in over two hundred years in which a Protestant religious book has been destroyed on the grounds of a heresy."[209] Although he may have been led to overstatement, the sym-

---

[203] Biola Board Minutes, 17 April 1929.

[204] Helen Kurtz to MacInnis, 12 June 1929, MacInnis Papers.

[205] On the Des Moines incident see C. Allyn Russell, "Thomas Todhunter Shields: Canadian Fundamentalist," *Foundations* 24 (Jan–Mar 1981): 23–26; for a positive view of Shields' work at Biola see T. C. Horton to J. Frank Norris, 8 May 1929, Norris Papers.

[206] Alva J. McClain to MacInnis, 11 June 1929, MacInnis Papers.

[207] "Bible Leaders Destroy Book," Los Angeles *Times,* 28 March 1929, Part II, p. 2; for the official Biola statement see Charles E. Fuller, "The Director's Statement," *The King's Business,* April 1929, n.p.

[208] Quoted in "Bible Leaders Destroy Book," p. 2.

[209] "Dr. M'Innis Book First Destroyed In Modern Times," Syracuse *Post-*

bolism of the destruction was evident. Writing to Mrs. Lyman Stewart, MacInnis asserted that a Christian historian called it "one of the most outrageous acts of intolerance and oppression in American history."[210] Probably in response to publicity surrounding the book, Harper & Brothers decided to republish it in 1930, with some slight changes. It was ironic, however, that Harper was interested in *PFP,* because only three years before this Harper had purchased the book publishing division of Trumbull's Sunday School Times Company![211]

BIBLE LEADERS DESTROY BOOK

Directorate of Institute Issues Statement

Los Angeles Times

Thursday, March 28, 1929

Work of Dr. MacInnis New Cause of Rift

Former Dean Scores Action in Open Letter

Destruction by the board of directors of the Bible Institute of Los Angeles of "all remaining copies in their possession, together with type-forms," of a book on Christian philosophy objected to by so-called Fundamentalists, yesterday caused further widening of the rift in the ranks of the Bible Institute, which started last December. The acts of the board of directors related to a statement contained in the April issue of "The King's Business," official publication of the Institute, were the target of denunciation by Dr. John Murdoch MacInnes, former dean of the institute and author of "Peter, the Fisherman Philosopher," copies of which were destroyed.

SCORES ACT

"This country has not seen an act of such religious intolerance in 200 years," declared Dr. MacInnes, as he prepared a written criticism of the board of directors.

Dr. MacInnis resigned as dean of the institute last December when certain directors declared that there was widespread criticism of the book. The dean's resignation was followed by eleven other members of the institute organization, and the controversy grew so that a special meeting of the presbytery of Los Angeles was called and a resolution passed expressing confidence in Dr. MacInnis.

Shortly after the board of directors issued a statement declaring that in accepting the dean's resignation they did not intend to cause any reflection upon his doctrinal soundness, but that his book had caused criticism to be directed at the institution that they felt would die out if he resigned.

MacINNIS RESIGNED

Dr. MacInnis's resignation went into effect and the matter apparently had quieted down, until the following, headed "Directors' Statement," appearing in "The King's Business:"

"After much prayer and serious reflection concerning the book, 'Peter, the Fisherman Philosopher,' written by Dr. J. M. MacInnis, former dean of the Bible Institute of Los Angeles, the board of directors desires to make the following statement:

"We reaffirm our belief in the great fundamental doctrines of Christianity as set forth in the Statement of Doctrine of the Bible Institute.

ERROR RECOGNIZED

"Because we recognized that we were in error in commending the book, 'Peter,' the Fisherman Philosopher,' the board some time ago accepted the resignation of the author and he now has absolutely...

Figure 12: *Los Angeles Times* **Article**

A copy of part of the *Los Angeles Times* article documenting the destruction of MacInnis' book in 1929. The method of destruction is not mentioned. (Source: *Los Angeles Times,* March 28, 1929, Part II, p. 1.)

Standard 17 July 1929, 4; "Bible Leaders Destroy Book," Los Angeles *Times,* 28 March 1929, Part II, pp. 1–2.

[210] MacInnis to Mrs. Lyman Stewart, 25 April 1929, MacInnis Papers. MacInnis did not identify this "Christian historian."

[211] John M. MacInnis, *Peter the Fisherman Philosopher* (New York & London: Harper & Brothers, 1930). On Harper see "Old Publishing House Expands," *Presbyterian Magazine,* December 1927, 674–75.

Satisfied that the Biola board had "removed the leaven from its midst" Gray, Trumbull, and Riley happily declared their confidence in the institute. Gray hoped that, "the broken fellowships will thus be restored and the work brought back again to the place of its founders."[212] Trumbull restored Biola to his list of approved schools and *The King's Business* to his list of approved magazines.[213] Riley stated almost gleefully that professors "not in line with the clear faith of fundamentalists," had left, and "the Fundamentalist public of America" could once again heartily back the institute.[214]

Aftermath

For a brief time after his resignation, rumors spread that a new Bible school might be started with students who had left Biola, or more provocative, that the Los Angeles Presbytery would attempt to take over Biola and turn it into a Presbyterian seminary.[215] But neither of these fears became a reality. Unlike the Princeton Seminary division, which happened a few months later and led to the formation of a new seminary, the MacInnis departure resulted in no new independent organizations. This fact, along with the sudden onset of the Depression, led to the fading of the crisis from public attention.

Within the Presbytery of Los Angeles, however, a psychological divide had been crossed. The cooperative relationship between the presbytery and Biola, in which many assumed that the institute would train lay leaders, city evangelists, foreign missionaries, and in some cases, even ministers, had now broken down. To be sure, some ministers in the presbytery continued their close ties with the institute, such as Walter Edmonds of the Glendale Church, or Sam Sutherland of the Grace Presbyterian Church. It is also true that the Presbyterian pastors of the independent Church of the Open Door continued to be, at least in name, welcome in the presbytery until 1954. But, in spite of these ties, there was a new awareness for many Presbyterian clergy that the church needed to provide for its own lay leadership training.

---

[212] [James Gray], "The Bible Institute of Los Angeles," *Moody Bible Institute Monthly,* June 1929, 471.

[213] Charles Trumbull, "Bible Schools that are True to the Faith," *Sunday School Times,* 1 February 1930, 63; and "Are Your Lesson Helps Safe or Dangerous?" 7 February 1931, 72–73.

[214] W. B. Riley, "The Los Angeles Bible Institute," *Christian Fundamentalist,* May 1929, 179; for other words of confidence see June 1929, 209, and August 1929, 303.

[215] "Los Angeles Presbytery and Bible Institute," *The Christian Fundamentalist,* January 1929, 10; "The Los Angeles Bible Institute," February 1929, 55–56.

In his speech before presbytery, MacInnis had clearly stated that the church could no longer rely on independent Bible schools for lay leadership training. In a letter filled with pathos, MacInnis explained in more detail his new found conviction, and his disillusionment with the Bible school ideal.

> The fact of the matter is I have come to the conclusion that the Bible Institutes, as organized in America today, are subversive of the truest interests of the organized church of Jesus Christ. No one ever made a more honest and earnest endeavor to understand the Bible Institute movement and the independent activities associated with them, and no one ever made a more sincere endeavor to win over that activity in a constructive way to the life of the church. But after three years of study, and now three years of sweating blood, I am forced to the conclusion it is impossible to do it. We must get at the thing from inside the church itself.[216]

In retrospect, it seems that MacInnis, in trying to bring a Bible school back into the orbit of denominational cooperation, was swimming against the tide. Fundamentalist defeats in the anti-evolution struggles, and the failure to root out liberalism in the denominations, had led to an increasing reliance on the Bible schools to carry the fundamentalist banner. At the same time, sectarian tendencies were growing, as fundamentalists increasingly agitated for withdrawal from mainline denominations. MacInnis' goal, when seen in the perspective of these national trends, was impracticable if not impossible.

---

[216] MacInnis to Cleland B. McAfee, 11 December 1928, MacInnis Papers.

CHAPTER 7

Peter the Fisherman Philosopher:
Toward an Historical Interpretation

When fundamentalist Robert Shuler sarcastically suggested that Riley should get together with his fellow critics before attacking MacInnis, he was pointing to one of the most puzzling aspects of the controversy, namely, that few could agree on just how MacInnis had erred.[1] So widespread was this disagreement, that some fundamentalists walked away from the controversy simply because there was a lack of critical consensus. Others, however, took the lack of agreement as confirmation of a vague sentiment that "there must be something wrong with that man MacInnis, if so many fine fundamentalist pastors are against him." Why was there disagreement about the meaning of *Peter the Fisherman Philosopher*? Why did some fundamentalists defend it, and others vilify it? The answer to this question, which takes the discussion beyond the level of the historical particularities of the crisis, has hitherto not been addressed. Yet no understanding of the crisis would be complete, if one failed to probe deeper into the complex currents of intellectual life that gave rise to *Peter the Fisherman Philosopher*.

On the Origin of *Peter the Fisherman Philosopher*

MacInnis claimed that *PFP* grew out of a seminar that addressed the problems of the collapse of civilization represented by World War I.[2] This seminar probably took place in 1919 at Syracuse University, while MacInnis was a minister at the nearby South Presbyterian Church. While this seminar was in progress, MacInnis recalled that he was studying the writings of Peter in the New Testament, and this led to his idea of portraying Peter as a simple homespun philosopher.

The origins of *PFP,* however, are more complex than this simple story would indicate. MacInnis himself, for example, noted that he had

---

[1] Robert P. Shuler to W. B. Riley, 13 March 1928, MacInnis Papers.

[2] John M. MacInnis, *Peter the Fisherman Philosopher* (Los Angeles: Biola Book Room, 1927), Preface (hereafter *PFP*).

conceived of the book as early as 1914, in connection with a series of articles which he had written for *The King's Business.*[3] This statement is important, because it indicates that *PFP* was not originally conceived in relation to the problems of fundamentalism in the 1920s. This is significant because *PFP* actually had in view a wider audience and purpose than what fundamentalists were able to allow in 1928. MacInnis did not intend to write a book on Christian doctrine. Rather, he was concerned about the challenges of modern critical thought for traditional Christianity and the intellectual crisis occasioned by World War I.

The most prominent theme of *PFP* is its repeated emphasis that there is nothing in "the best of modern thinking" that renders Christianity obsolete. Peter's insights, declared MacInnis, "can stand the test of the most searching thinking of our day." With a blustery confidence he asserted that, "the plain fisherman of the first century" had arrived at many of the conclusions of the "accomplished scientist of the twentieth century."[4] This theme was rooted in MacInnis' earlier intellectual development.

The earliest published writings of MacInnis reveal his concern to show that modern thinking had not made Christianity outmoded or irrelevant. An article that he published in 1909, which may have been the gist of a doctoral seminar taken at Temple University Divinity School, discussed this theme. Interestingly, this early published work echoed two refrains common to *PFP:* first, an attempt to put philosophical language into common parlance: "What," he asked, "in the language of the plain man of the common walks of life does all this mean?" Second, he hoped to prove that Calvinism was not obsolete in the 20th century, but "was strangely abreast of the best modern thinking."[5]

His interest in this theme continued in 1914–1915, when he published a series of articles entitled "The Fundamental Principles of Christianity in the Light of Modern Thinking."[6] As this title suggests, these articles attempted to demonstrate that modern thinking was no enemy of the faith, and some of this material contributed to the content of *PFP,* as MacInnis himself asserted. It is important to observe that these articles,

---

[3] MacInnis to Torrey, 7 June 1928, MacInnis Papers.

[4] *PFP,* Preface, 47.

[5] John M. MacInnis, "Calvinism and Modern Thought," *The Book News Monthly,* December, 1909, 270–73; a note scribbled at the top of this article in his personal papers states, "S. T. D. work." MacInnis said in 1908 that he had "written considerably" toward an S. T. D. apparently in connection with Temple Divinity School, but this work was not completed; see MacInnis to James D. McGregor, 4 July 1908, MacInnis Papers.

[6] See all the following issues of *The King's Business:* December 1913, 565; January 1914, 13; February 1914, 137; March 1914, 267; April 1914, 318; May 1914, 434; June 1914, 495; July 1914, 599; August 1914, 687.

just as *PFP*, displayed an open attitude toward "modern thought." Like liberals, he gave positive value to modern thinking, but unlike them, he did not argue that traditional beliefs required any extensive modifications.

Vol. V   JANUARY, 1914   No. 1

The King's Business

The Incarnation Tested by the Temptation
By A. C. DIXON, D. D.

The Fundamental Principles of Christianity
in the Light of Modern Thinking
By JOHN MacINNIS, B. D.

Studies in the Gospel According to John
By R. A. TORREY, D. D.

How We Kept Christmas Day in Congo
By EDITH HARLAND

The Almighty, the All-Merciful--Poem
By J. H. SAMMIS

Published Once a Month by the
Bible Institute of Los Angeles
LOS ANGELES, CAL.

FIFTY CENTS A YEAR

Figure 13: Cover of *The King's Business*, January 1914

MacInnis claimed that his 1928 book went back to a series of articles published as early as 1914.

MacInnis not only wanted to demonstrate the contemporary relevance of Christian beliefs, but he also wanted to reconstruct the rational basis for a Christian faith in modern society. This aspect of MacInnis' thought stemmed from a single event, which shook the foundations of western civilization and led intellectuals to question the basis of modern society.

After the great war, few could look at human society or the human heart with the same ebullient optimism of the 19th century. In the short span of four years, the horrors of that world crisis challenged intellectuals to re-evaluate their assumptions on social progress and the superiority of western culture. *PFP* was conceived in the context of this intellectual crisis.

As MacInnis listened to the discussions about the collapse of western civilization, he realized that the principles of Christianity must be introduced once again as the moral basis of human society. Europe's abandonment of a spiritual interpretation of the world was partly responsible for the war, but, MacInnis asserted, the best thinkers of the day were returning to a spiritual view of history.[7] One consequence of this renewed spiritual interpretation was the recognition shared by many postwar intellectuals, that liberalism had been overly optimistic about human goodness and moral progress: there was a tendency to make light of sin, he noted, but the tragedy of the war has brought an awareness of "the unspeakable depravity of even highly cultured lives and the whole question has emerged in a most acute form."[8]

Throughout the book, MacInnis attempts to offer a philosophy of life that will provide a basis for a reconstructed order. The world must find its basic readjustments not in the mere restructuring of institutions, but in the very moral and spiritual ideals that drive human life. In this regard, the church lost sight of its social significance as an agent to transform society in its moral and spiritual conceptions. But only through the moral ideals of the Christian faith, such as disinterested social concern and the hope of triumph over evil, will democracy survive.[9]

To the extent that *PFP* reflected the problems of post-war intellectual disillusionment, it was a book well suited for an audience of 1919, worrying about Woodrow Wilson's efforts to form the League of Nations, and to "make the world safe for democracy." But by the time *PFP* was published in 1927, this context had largely been forgotten in a decade of American isolationism. To the discerning reader it was there, but not overtly so. One of the strange facts of the MacInnis controversy is that there was virtually no awareness of the post-war context which underlay much of the content of *PFP*. Few even noticed that MacInnis was concerned more about the beliefs and values that were necessary for the survival of democracy, than of any specific doctrinal questions.

But if fundamentalists in 1928 failed to note the sense of intellectual crisis that initially gave rise to *PFP*, they were not without cause. There was much that changed in America between 1919 and 1928, and the

---

[7] *PFP*, 172–75.
[8] *PFP*, 997.
[9] *PFP*, 154, 163–64.

fears of the collapse of civilization emanating from the war years soon gave way to other topics, one of which was the rise of militant fundamentalism. From his view, as a teacher in a fundamentalist Bible school, the Fundamentalist Modernist Controversy became the most compelling religious issue of the day. It was a crisis that could not be ignored. Hence, from 1920 to 1927, when battle lines were drawn in some Protestant denominations, MacInnis adapted his earlier material to the issues of that religious conflict.

We know very little about what happened with the manuscript of *PFP* after 1920. MacInnis claimed that a lecture series he presented at Biola and Moody Bible Institute in 1922 later became the basis for *PFP*. These lectures were entitled, "The Christian Religion in the Light of Philosophy, Science, and Criticism."[10] Less than a year later, he received a compliment from the wife of A. C. Dixon, who read with pleasure his manuscript called, "The Philosophy of Peter's Life."[11] There is no further mention of the manuscript until 1927, when it was published with its subtitle, "A Study in Higher Fundamentalism." The choice of this subtitle implies that MacInnis had modified the material to relate to issues of fundamentalism and modernism. Clearly, this subtitle was not part of the manuscript in 1920, because the term "fundamentalism" had not yet come into vogue.[12] Moreover, there is no indication that he had used it in his 1922 lectures or in the 1923 manuscript that Mrs. Dixon read. Most likely, the subtitle was chosen after MacInnis became dean of Biola, because the book itself ends with a sentence describing the author as a highly driven "teacher and executive."[13]

Although it is not known to what extent, if any, MacInnis modified his manuscript in order to frame it in relation to the fundamentalist movement, his desire to articulate a "higher fundamentalism" was probably awakened in 1925, when he himself became the victim of fundamentalist persecution. He had long expressed concern about the divide forming between conservatives and liberals in the church, and in the context of his own position at Biola, his greatest worry was that he would find himself outside of the interests of his church: "I do not wish to be looked upon as opposed to the church or outside of its vital interests."[14] This fear took on greater urgency with every passing year, as MacInnis watched the deterioration of Biola's standing with mainline

---

[10] Reynolds Transcript, 8.

[11] A. C. Dixon to MacInnis, 6 April 1923, MacInnis Papers.

[12] Note, for example, that Clarence Macartney had not even heard the term until 1922, when Fosdick preached his famous sermon; Macartney, *Making of a Minister*, 183.

[13] *PFP*, 214. This ending was omitted in the 1930 edition.

[14] MacInnis to Cleland B. McAfee, 19 January 1923, MacInnis Papers.

churches in Southern California. His desire to bridge the growing chasm with a mediating theological position emerged shortly after he arrived at Biola. In 1923, for example, he expressed the hope that all parties in the church might "unite on a gospel of grace through a divine redeemer," and this idea became even more pressing in 1925, when he again wrote to Robert Nichols, saying: "I feel increasingly the time has come when we should call a halt to extreme expressions and give ourselves to a definite constructive work."[15]

Perhaps MacInnis chose his subtitle in response to the extremism that so disturbed him. About this there can be no certainty. But that he intended "higher fundamentalism" to be an alternative to the militant fundamentalism of his critics can hardly be doubted. Not surprisingly, at least two reviewers of *PFP* agreed that MacInnis was trying to find a *via media* through the maze of religious controversy, but each reacted differently. In Charles Trumbull's view, MacInnis was simply trying to hold two contrary positions at once; but this effort was doomed to failure, because neither position could be joined to the other without destroying their essence. James Clarke, on the other hand, saw in *PFP* a middle ground where liberals and fundamentalists could unite. "This higher fundamentalism," he lauded, "provides a platform where all can stand together."[16] Predictably, while MacInnis strongly denied Trumbull's view of *PFP* there remains no record of any disagreement with Clarke.

On the Purpose of *Peter the Fisherman Philosopher*

The happenstance way that MacInnis arrived at his subject may lead one to question if he began his writing with a clear objective and a particular audience in mind. In a surprisingly casual manner, MacInnis explained that he "happened" to be giving special attention to Peter's speeches and epistles, when it "dawned" on him that they contained a comprehensive philosophy of life, expressed in the language of the "common people."[17] With such quixotic beginnings, it seems reasonable to ask for whom the book was written? This question was debated almost as soon as *PFP* was published.

MacInnis wrote with a populist zeal that *PFP* was a philosophy for the common person. As he stated it: "Realizing that the most of the people who make up society are plain men and women and not trained phi-

---

[15] Robert Hastings Nichols to MacInnis, 19 July 1923, and MacInnis to Nichols, 24 April 1925, MacInnis Papers.

[16] Charles Trumbull to MacInnis, 23 May 1928, MacInnis Papers; James E. Clarke, "Higher Fundamentalism," *Presbyterian Advance,* 16 August 1928, 1.

[17] *PFP,* Preface.

losophers, we wanted to take over the essential considerations and conclusions of these technical discussions into the world of the common
man and recast them in his language."[18] True, he avoided technical language; but his assertion that it was written for the common person was
scuttled rather quickly. One of the first attacks on MacInnis, that of fundamentalist Marion Reynolds, criticized this very point. Reynold's
charged that MacInnis made scholarly language a higher standard than
the Bible itself, thus making the Bible unscholarly and inferior.[19] Backing away from his "common man" theme, MacInnis retorted that he had
hoped to write for young people in the universities.[20] This point, however, though apparently a genuine expression of his early intentions, did
not appear in the book and seemed to contradict his own statements that
he wrote for common people without college training.

As the controversy progressed, the question became more acute, for it
was not easy to explain how a book, written for untrained ordinary citi-
zens, could confuse even the best leaders of evangelical religion. But the
"student defense" was commonly utilized for at least two reasons: first,
it offered his defenders an easy explanation as to why so many misunderstood the book—one simply needed a university background to understand it. Alva McClain, the official ministerial review committee,
and several other supporters gave up any notion that it was written for
common people, arguing instead that it was intended for college students with training.[21] Second, the idea that *PFP* was written for university students appealed to many Americans who were worried about the
so-called youth crisis.

The perception that the new generation of youth was leaving behind
traditional values and beliefs worried many Americans, conservative
and liberal alike. For some leaders, like Harry Emerson Fosdick, materialism and irreligion in the universities undermined the ideal of Christian
character and service.[22] For others, such as W. B. Riley, blame could be
placed squarely on the doorsteps of skeptical university professors, who
corrupted the ideals of young people. The very same year that Fosdick
was bemoaning materialism in university education, Riley was citing
statistics that more than half of the biology, geology, and history professors in the United States had abandoned belief in a personal God and
personal immortality. So what was the result of this unbelief? As he

---

[18] Ibid.

[19] Reynolds Manuscript, 33.

[20] Reynolds Transcript, 3.

[21] McClain, review of *Peter the Fisherman Philosopher;* "What Those Who
Know Say About the Bible Institute of Los Angeles."

[22] Harry Emerson Fosdick, *Christianity and Progress* (New York: The
Fleming H. Revell Co., 1922), 74–75.

viewed it, academic infidelity had led nearly half of the college graduates in America to forsake Christian truths.[23]

Saving the faith of young people, especially college students, became an extraordinary endeavor. Religious publishing houses multiplied books by the hundreds aimed at keeping college students from losing their moorings. Indeed, while conservatives published books trying to persuade students of the reasonableness of traditional Christian beliefs, Fosdick and other liberals conceived of their theological enterprise as the only means of preserving the faith of "our more intelligent young people."[24] It was quite fitting, therefore, that MacInnis should have written a book for perplexed university students. But, unfortunately, MacInnis had failed to place his book in that context.

Confusion about the intended audience of the book was magnified by another anomaly: just what kind of a book was it? On the one hand, it was promoted as a simple layman's philosophy. But on the other hand, it seemed to be a study of the apostle Peter, his sermons and letters. The juxtaposition of these two elements were, for many fundamentalists, a discordant melody. Charles Trumbull made this dissonance the centerpiece of his attack: "Simon Peter: Philosopher or Apostle?" he asked in bold headlines. Sam Sutherland, later a president of Biola University, made a similar observation: "Most of us just didn't think Peter was a philosopher," he recalled.[25]

In his portrayal of Peter as a simple homespun philosopher, MacInnis ran headlong into a variety of conflicting attitudes, ironies, and contradiction. Perhaps if he had chosen to portray Peter as something other than a popular philosopher, he would have encountered less opposition. But philosophy, for many fundamentalists, smacked of everything anti-Christian. Philosophers relied on human reason rather than the Bible. They scoffed at things sacred, corrupted the virtues of youthful innocence, and traded in unprofitable and foolish speculations. Some conservatives believed philosophy was a greater threat than evolution. George Frederick Wright, for example, wrote that "the fatalism of the philosophers is more to be dreaded than the materialism of any scientific men." But others, like Rowland Bingham, simply thought that philosophy was a waste of time.[26]

---

[23] Riley, "The Christian Fundamentals Movement," 16.

[24] Harry Emerson Fosdick, *The Modern Use of the Bible* (New York: Macmillan Co., 1942), 61.

[25] Charles Trumbull, "Simon Peter—Philosopher or Apostle?" *The Sunday School Times,* 5 May 1928, 277; Sam Sutherland, Interview by Author, 28 May 1993, Chicago, IL.

[26] George Frederick Wright, "The Passing of Evolution," in *The Fundamentals,* ed. R. A. Torrey, A. C. Dixon, et al., vol. 4 (Bible Institute of Los Angeles,

Reuben Torrey was probably the very personification of ambivalent fundamentalist attitudes about philosophy. Unlike most fundamentalists, he had received graduate training in philosophy. But his religious piety and a practical personal bent left little room for traditional philosophical pursuits. Surprisingly, however, he invited MacInnis to teach a full course in Christian philosophy at Biola in 1922. But if Torrey had once been open to philosophy, the MacInnis crisis changed his perspective. Lamenting the conflict in 1928, he expressed an entirely different view of philosophy.

> It spoiled Cornelius Woelfkin, and now it looks as if it had wrecked Mac-Innis, if not the Los Angeles Bible Institute. I think we would do wisely if we should leave it entirely out of the Bible Institute course. Philosophy is one branch of study that has never gotten anywhere.[27]

But not all fundamentalists disliked philosophy. Many of his staunch defenders and a few of his opponents argued that there was a need for the discussion of philosophy among Christian thinkers. One influential opponent of MacInnis, Leander Keyser, had himself published a book on philosophy in 1928 and appeared critical of his brethren that attacked philosophy. When Marion Reynolds sent his printed criticism of *PFP* to the *Bible Champion* for a review, Keyser wrote that he agreed with almost everything except that he did not "countenance the slam at philosophy."[28] Others, like Alva McClain or Gerald Winrod, repeatedly urged their fundamentalist colleagues to consider *PFP* as a philosophical rather than a doctrinal or biblical work, and therefore, not to judge it by the same standards.

Actually, the whole question of whether or not *PFP* was a "philosophy" was rather moot. Fundamentalist objections to philosophy were more a part of the symbolic rhetoric of fundamentalism, where philosophy was depicted in biblical ideas as "worldly wisdom," which is but "foolishness in light of the gospel." In this regard, MacInnis simply challenged the symbolic significance of philosophy as idle speculation, by arguing that everyone, even the apostle, had a "philosophy." Of course, he did not mean by "philosophy" the technical concepts of logic, metaphysics, and epistemology, but simply the assumptions that undergird Christian beliefs such as divine revelation and morality. This, thought MacInnis, was a common person's philosophy.

1917: Baker reprint, 1980), 87; [Rowland Bingham], "Biola," *Evangelical Christian*, June 1928, 227.

[27] Ibid.

[28] Leander Keyser, "Additional Book Notices," *Bible Champion*, June 1928, 299.

Ironically, MacInnis shared more in common with his fundamentalist critics than was at first apparent. His approach was typically pragmatic and anti-metaphysical. He eschewed discussions about "theological theories," and insisted on the "bare facts," which was typical of the fundamentalist common sense approach. Finally, his emphasis on the uneducated blustery fisherman struck a resonant chord among fundamentalists. In one sense, MacInnis was only expanding a familiar fundamentalist theme that James Gray had once stated, namely, that even "the Christian peasant is wiser than an unbelieving philosopher."[29] This was really what *PFP* was all about—the notion that the "philosophy" of an unschooled fisherman was as good as the best thinking of modern philosophy and science. But even this apparently benign concept of philosophy presented too great a challenge to the intellectual boundaries of fundamentalism.

On *Peter the Fisherman Philosopher* as Literature

Although MacInnis never expected that anyone would find modernism in his book, his literary methods were probably at least different enough to have raised some doubts. There were two general aspects of his method that engendered confusion and criticism. First, MacInnis displayed an unusually open attitude toward modern thought. Second, his literary style was obtuse. Although these factors were not key issues in the controversy, they affected how people perceived his work.

Attitudes

Almost everyone would have agreed with Charles Erdman's statement that *PFP* was an "unusual book."[30] But in what sense was *PFP* unusual? The attempt to relate traditional and biblical thought to the problems of modern intellectual life was a popular genre of literature, conservative or liberal. In that genre, *PFP* was anything but unusual. Moreover, MacInnis himself cited other evangelical writers, who had written similar books to his own. Indeed, one book entitled, *The Old Paths in the Light of Modern Thought,* was written by J. Russell Howden, a close colleague of Charles Trumbull. Why, wondered MacInnis, would Trumbull attack *PFP* so vehemently, and ignore the obvious similarities between

---

[29] James Gray, "Scholarship and Evangelical Christianity," *Moody Bible Institute Monthly,* October 1928, 53.

[30] Charles Erdman, review of *Peter the Fisherman Philosopher,* in *The Princeton Theological Review* 26 (March 1928): 163.

his work and Howden's, which also tried to compare the Bible to modern thought?[31]

But *PFP* differed from Howden's and most fundamentalist works of its genre, in its positive embrace of modern thinking. Few works coming from a Bible school publisher shared this viewpoint. Bible schools were much more likely to publish books defending traditional beliefs and attacking theological innovations. It was, therefore, unusual that Biola would have put out a book that celebrated notions of scientific, social, and theological progress. For *PFP*, modernity was a friend, not a foe; lacking an opposition attitude, it sought to establish common ground between modern religious thinking and traditional orthodoxy.

This welcome embrace of modern thinking disturbed his conservative critics. When MacInnis stated repeatedly that "the best of modern thinking" agreed with the simple insights of the fisherman philosopher,[32] it seemed to many fundamentalists that MacInnis had made modern thought the fulcrum of religious belief. This attitude ran against the basic instincts of most of his readership, who were used to hearing "the latest results of scholarship" held up to scorn rather than praise. Riley's attitude was typical of fundamentalist antipathy toward modern thinking: "It is a pathetic endeavor," he stated, "to hold to the Scripture with one hand and to the latest and most uncertain deliverance of so-called science with the other."[33] Charles Trumbull reflected a similar attitude, when he charged that MacInnis honored modern philosophy and science, but God condemns them.[34]

Literary Style

If there was a single thing that everyone agreed on about *PFP*, friend or foe, it was that it was written in a difficult and ambiguous style. Although many quotations could be offered to support this point, the assessment of W. Graham Scroggie was typical.

> I cannot but feel that a risk has been taken, and that, in places, your utterances are exposed to an interpretation which, I am quite sure, you never intended. . . .

---

[31] J. Russell Howden, *The Old Paths in the Light of Modern Thought* (London: The China Inland Mission, 1921); MacInnis to Trumbull, 14 June 1928, MacInnis Papers.

[32] *PFP*, 444, 48–49, 57, 58, 65, 87, 95, 126, 135, 139, 164, 169, 185, 187, 199, 213.

[33] W. B. Riley, "Stuart Holden and Campbell Morgan," *Christian Fundamentalist*, May 1930, 654.

[34] Trumbull, "Simon Peter—Philosopher or Apostle?" 278.

... I have found it difficult to give expression to the impression which your book has left on my mind. Had I not known you and what you stand for, I might have been left wondering what your attitude was on such questions as evolution and inspiration.[35]

An example of his difficult writing style is the following description of Peter's inspiration.

Peter related himself to the final source of stimulus in such a way as to make it possible for him to be stimulated to thoughts that he could not think apart from that special stimulus.[36]

This labored prose, which required a very attentive reading, left some of his readers confused. Although he wanted to write for the "common man," his style was not very easy for even well educated readers. Hence, with this problem clouding the issues, MacInnis found himself on the defensive. From the start, he labored intensely to explain himself, but with little success. His efforts were also complicated by fundamentalist suspicions, like that of W. B. Riley, that liberals wrote in obscure language in order to evade meaning.[37]

Actually, the problem of language was not merely a result of his style or writing ability, but the result of his methodology. Because MacInnis was addressing many theological questions in "philosophical language," his words sometimes appeared excessively abstract and unfamiliar. His explanation of revelation, for example, as a stimulation by a final source of stimulus, was an odd phraseology that seemed to go in circles. One critic mocked his abstract phraseology. Noting that it sounded a bit like Mother Goose, a writer penned this satirical piece.

Simon Peter experienced an insight into an interpretation, An insight into an interpretation Simon Peter experienced. If Simon Peter experienced the interpretation into the insight, What was the insight of the experience that Simon Peter interpreted?[38]

Even more unsettling than his ambiguous language, however, was his use of words or phrases characteristic of liberalism, that made even his

---

[35] W. Graham Scroggie to MacInnis, n.d., MacInnis Papers.

[36] *PFP,* 118.

[37] See e.g., William B. Riley, "The Great Divide, or Christ and the Present Crisis," in *God Hath Spoken,* 31.

[38] Author unknown, "Brer Jackson Elucidates the Inwardness of Peter the Fisherman Philosopher," Typed Document [11 February 1928], MacInnis Papers.

close friends shudder a little. When MacInnis wrote, for example, that the central thought in Peter's idea of God was fatherhood, one critic charged that he was simply repeating the popular liberal slogan of the "fatherhood of God."[39] The same objection emerged in connection with another quotation.

> One of our scientific theologians who appreciates the need of a "growing creed" in order to bring our religious thought abreast of the progress of science and philosophy says, "The wisdom of God will be the process by which the life of Fatherhood secures its end in creation."[40]

Several other liberal terms disturbed his critics. Torrey worried about his use of the word "proxy," asserting that its use was common by those who denied propitiation.[41] Alva McClain argued for the utility of the term "social gospel," but not many fundamentalists were willing to embrace that usage.[42] Louis Bauman, eager to defend his friend, admitted he used phrases common to modernist writings, but then argued that he did not give these phrases the same meanings that modernists did.[43] Ironically, Bauman's argument simply reversed a common complaint of fundamentalists, namely, that liberals gave orthodox doctrines a modernist meaning. Now, a conservative MacInnis was giving modernist phrases an orthodox meaning!

Another facet of his literary method that fundamentalists disliked was his habit of quoting scholars, which prompted the criticism that he reveled in scholarship. This was not an entirely gratuitous criticism, for in the space of a small book MacInnis quoted more than fifty authors, giving the impression even to his own friends that he was too beholden to scholars. Of course, if he meant to survey the "best of modern thinking," that large number is not so difficult to understand. But still, his friend at Western Theological Seminary, David Breed, stated that *PFP* displayed a very wide reading, but the display was overdone.[44]

But more troubling even than his dependence upon scholarly opinion, which fundamentalists had long ridiculed, were the citations of scholars who held positions inimical to fundamentalism. He must have been aware of this potential difficulty, because he wrote this disclaimer in his

---

[39] Unsigned Review of *Peter the Fisherman Philosopher*, in *The Moody Bible Institute Monthly*, March 1928, 346.

[40] *PFP*, 59. See Arthur Forest Wells, review of *Peter the Fisherman Philosopher*, in *Our Hope*, May 1928, 689.

[41] Torrey to MacInnis, 22 February 1928, MacInnis Papers.

[42] McClain, review of *Peter the Fisherman Philosopher*, MacInnis Papers.

[43] "What Those Who Know Say About the Bible Institute of Los Angeles."

[44] David R. Breed to MacInnis, 22 May 1928, MacInnis Papers.

preface: "The use of quotations from authors and books with which we quite radically differ on questions of theology does not mean an approval of these books."[45]

In spite of this disclaimer, fundamentalists found it incomprehensible that so many scholars, who held opinions opposite to fundamentalism, would be cited as authorities. But this objection was often superficial, because few bothered to examine his actual use of quotations. Although there were many admiring quotations from non-fundamentalist authors, occasionally MacInnis quoted these writers in order to criticize them. For example, he criticized the liberal Kemper Fullerton, at Oberlin School of Theology, as well as a favorite target of fundamentalist criticism, H. G. Wells.[46] Citations from Henry Sloane Coffin, Rudolph Eucken and Josiah Royce were used to criticize British atheist, Bertrand Russell and the materialism of Thomas Huxley. Nevertheless, in his admiring use of writers like Walter Rauschenbusch, MacInnis had breached a symbolic rule of discourse in the fundamentalist community: giving credence to "the enemy" was taboo. The *Bible Champion* made explicit mention of this rule when the same issue surfaced in connection with E. Stanley Jones.

> May we not suggest that if evangelical writers and speakers wish to quote something from a Modernist ... they should always indicate that they cannot endorse his general attitude, but that on this one matter, he has said something that can be approved even by evangelical believers.[47]

Of course, MacInnis had made this very disclaimer! But a general impression that he was sympathetic to modernist writers could not be overcome.

If quoting modernists was taboo, criticizing a fellow conservative was even more so, particularly if that conservative was a veritable icon of sound biblical scholarship. Hence, when MacInnis found B. B. Warfield's doctrine of inspiration lacking, Trumbull, Riley, and many other reviewers were greatly disturbed. How, they asked, could he read and quote from "modernists" with approval, but criticize a fellow conservative? In their perspective, this gave the impression that conservatives lacked any intellectual authority. Though his faultfinding of Warfield was mild, it, nevertheless, was conspicuous in its contrast to the admiring quotations from other writers. Once again, MacInnis had breached a rule of discourse in publicly nitpicking a fellow conservative.

---

[45] *PFP*, Preface.

[46] *PFP*, 992, 166.

[47] Frank Boyer, "Quoting from the Modernists," *Bible Champion,* September 1927.

The unfavorable impression created by his open attitudes, his difficult literary style, his fealty to scholarly opinion, his use of unacceptable writers, and his criticisms of a fellow conservative, combined to give an impression in his opponents' mind that he had stepped outside of the fundamentalist circle. A sympathetic David Breed observed a paradox in his strange situation. "You have certainly given some occasion for unfavorable comment," he noted. But "if you had not been the dean of Biola," the book most "probably would have passed with little unfavorable notice."[48]

Doctrinal Controversy

Although the literary style and methods of *PFP* were startling to many fundamentalists, these alone would not have become a significant problem, if fundamentalists had not also perceived that MacInnis was undermining or attacking several crucial doctrines of fundamentalism. Some objected that in his book he had failed to clearly state certain doctrines, and others balked at the fact that he ignored some doctrines altogether. Generally speaking, there were four areas of controversy: the basis of religious authority, the nature of Christ's atonement, divine revelation and inspiration, and the relationship of Christianity to culture.

Higher Fundamentalism: Truth Out There Or Truth Mediated Through Experience?

The meaning of "higher fundamentalism" escaped some of his readers and provoked many others. It seemed to invite the question, "What could be higher than fundamentalism?"[49] Not surprisingly, MacInnis began his study with a brief definition.

> The Higher Fundamentalism is that insight of a living experience which is the light of life. It does not ignore or set aside doctrine. On the contrary, it grows out of a sound doctrine, making possible true insights which provide a genuine and adequate philosophy of life.[50]

This definition of higher fundamentalism, like many other statements in his book, caused some confusion. When he stated that higher fundamentalism is an "insight of a living experience," he seemed to mean that an understanding of Christian truth is made possible by a spiritual expe-

---

[48] David R. Breed to MacInnis, 22 May 1928, MacInnis Papers.

[49] Keyser, review of *Peter the Fisherman Philosopher,* 237; Trumbull, "Simon Peter—Philosopher or Apostle?" 277.

[50] *PFP,* 115.

rience. In other words, Christian truth for the higher fundamentalist is not merely a doctrine that an individual can memorize, like an axiom of geometry, but an understanding of truth which is mediated through human experience. In MacInnis' view, the apostle Peter was a good example of the higher fundamentalist. When Peter confessed that "Jesus was the Christ, the son of the living God," his confession was an "insight" made possible by his experience of God. In other words, his experience of God allowed Peter to correctly interpret the identity of Jesus.[51]

MacInnis went on to offer an interpretation of the "rock," upon which Christ would build his church. Debunking two popular viewpoints, he argued that the rock was not Peter himself, nor was it his confession. Rather, it was "Peter's experience of God which interpreted the life and thought of God." To this experience of God, MacInnis contrasted a mere formalism in religion.

> The men were talking about something they were experiencing. It was something vitally and vastly more than just repeating something that had been told them by someone else. They did tell what Jesus began to do and to say but they told it after they had experienced it in their own lives.[52]

It was no accident that many of his opponents focused their criticisms on his experience based theology. To them, MacInnis sounded as though he affirmed the priority of experience over objectively revealed truth, and that Peter's confession was the result more of Peter's experience than God's act of revelation. Moreover, the implication that fundamentalism was closely akin to an empty religious formalism was too close to the surface to be missed by his critics. To those familiar with modernism, MacInnis almost sounded like the famous modernist Shailer Mathews, who wrote: "Our starting point is the experience of God which comes when men accept Jesus as Lord."[53]

Riley was one of the first to assert that this interpretation of the rock made MacInnis a modernist, because modernism bases all religious authority on experience. Leander Keyser suggested that MacInnis had been influenced by the German thinker, Albrecht Ritschl, because he made experience a test of doctrine. But MacInnis denied these accusations. In a letter to Keyser, he explained that higher fundamentalism was not the idea that religious beliefs derived only from experience, but that experience of God was a vital element of doctrine.[54]

---

[51] *PFP*, 17.

[52] *PFP*, 220.

[53] Shailer Mathews, *The Faith of Modernism* (New York: Macmillan, 1924), 143.

[54] W. B. Riley to J. M. Irvine, 30 January 1928; Keyser, review of *Peter the Fisherman Philosopher*, 237; MacInnis to Leander Keyser, 23 February 1928,

In his explanation of Peter's confession, MacInnis was trying to allow a place for human experience in God's revelation. "There was something in the experience of Peter," he said, "that put him in an attitude that made possible an insight that he could not get in the ordinary way."[55] In this conception, a higher fundamentalist would not think of revelation simply as the imposition of information "from above." Put another way, the church could not be built solely on Peter's confession—apart from his experience of God—because it is "impossible to interpret reality through a detached instrument."[56] Doctrines about Christ, however true, are an inadequate foundation of the church and, therefore, of our understanding of reality. Instead, the church must be built on both the experience of Peter and his confession of Christ, brought together in a supernatural relation.[57] MacInnis suggested that Peter's experience was a paradigm for the Christian church, because he wrote that it was "the source of fundamentalism," which was an implied critique of fundamentalism's over emphasis on doctrine and lack of spiritual vitality.[58]

Although his statements shared an affinity for liberal formulations of religious authority, he eschewed the concept that doctrines were merely the "transient phrasings of permanent convictions and experiences," a record of human religious aspirations.[59] Thus, if Peter's confession was made possible by a prior experience of God, its final cause was none other than God himself: "Jesus calls the final source of stimulus 'My Father who is in heaven.'"[60] This confession, Peter could not have achieved through the "ordinary processes of reasoning."[61] MacInnis seems, therefore, to have allowed that there actually was an objective revelation of truth. Scripture was not merely an accounting of human experience alone. But in his formulation of the problem, he failed to explain how scripture could be objectively true, if it were somehow based on the experience of a historical person.

Trumbull attacked his argument directly. In effect, he said, MacInnis had made revelation dependent on Peter's experience. But this contradicts a common pattern of revelation in scripture, where revelation often comes in a way contrary to one's experience, such as the radical conversion of Paul. To argue, therefore, that Peter's experience was somehow

---

MacInnis Papers.

[55] *PFP*, 17.

[56] *PFP*, 19.

[57] MacInnis to Leander Keyser, 23 February 1928, MacInnis Papers.

[58] *PFP*, 26.

[59] Fosdick, *The Modern Use of the Bible*, 103.

[60] *PFP*, 18.

[61] Ibid.

a necessary aspect of God's self revelation was not even biblical.[62] Yet Trumbull's point may have missed what MacInnis meant by the word "experience." His use of the word experience did not mean a specific type of experience: rather, revelation was mediated through human experience in general. In his argument, therefore, MacInnis was drawing at the well of historicism, namely, that truth is bound to history. It is unclear, however, to what extent this element of his thought was self-conscious, for his meaning was equivocal. Sometimes by experience he simply meant a practical notion of Christian holiness and God's indwelling. At other times, especially when describing the priority of Peter's experience, he seemed to be arguing for a concept of religious authority based in history. If his critics were confused, therefore, it may have been because he lacked a precise understanding of how the unique experience of Peter as the recipient of revelation related to his critique of a spiritually barren fundamentalism.

Atonement

Another point of severe criticism was MacInnis' understanding of the atonement. W. B. Riley, for example, exclaimed that MacInnis had made the atonement sacrificial but not substitutionary. Charles Trumbull said that he had diminished the uniqueness of the atonement. David Breed thought that MacInnis held a moral influence theory of the atonement. But no one was so vituperative as Torrey. For him, MacInnis' understanding of the atonement made *PFP* the *bete noire* of religious books. While others were attacking his views on evolution or the social gospel, Torrey tried to be an impartial judge: "It is charged that the book teaches evolution," he stated. "It certainly does not." Nor did Torrey assert that it rejected the second coming of Christ. But in spite of these misperceptions fostered by other critics, the book, according to Torrey, "utterly failed" to represent a biblical view of the atonement.[63] To this assessment, he added the stinging words:

> The eighth chapter of your book is one of the most vicious, pernicious and false assaults on the great Bible doctrine of Vicarious Atonement that I have ever read. If really believed, it would utterly undermine faith in the true Gospel and lead to one's eternal damnation.

---

[62] Trumbull, "Simon Peter—Philosopher or Apostle?" 278.

[63] Riley, "Breaking the Bible School Defense Line," 7; Trumbull, "Simon Peter—Philosopher or Apostle?" 282; David Breed to MacInnis, 22 May 1928; Reuben Torrey to MacInnis, 22 February 1928, MacInnis Papers.

The harshness of Torrey's criticism led to an anguished response from MacInnis. He bitterly decried Torrey's "cruelty." Torrey replied that he was not cruel but severe, like a father chastening an errant child. From his view, severity was needed, because MacInnis had struck the heart of the gospel.[64]

In retrospect, however, it seems that Torrey's criticisms were mostly pedantic. For example, Torrey quoted the statement that salvation "was not an easy and cheap thing that could be accomplished by proxy,"[65] and argued that MacInnis was denying Christ's vicarious sacrifice. Actually, the context of the passage reveals rather clearly that MacInnis meant no one other than God himself, in the person of Christ, could have offered a satisfaction for sin. In another pedantic criticism, Torrey charged that by comparing the death of Christ to the deaths of soldiers in World War I, MacInnis was mitigating the unique finality of the atonement. However weak the analogy, it is clear that MacInnis did not intend to diminish the exceptional nature of Christ's death, for he explicitly wrote that the death of Christ meant more than the death of soldiers in the war.[66] Ironically, if Torrey had been less fussy, he could have allowed, as did Machen, that there was at least a strand of legitimacy in that analogy.[67]

But Torrey's criticisms were not completely meretricious. MacInnis eschewed atonement language—nowhere did he use the words propitiation or substitution. Moreover, he stated that Christ's sufferings were not limited to a single historical moment, but a continuous process of God's redemptive purpose: the fact that he died once for sins, he wrote, "can not mean that the sorrow of the divine in Christ was just for the moment of the sublime stoop in the life of the historic Jesus."[68] This desire to play down the historical act of atonement was characteristic of liberalism and received severe criticism from conservatives.[69] In another paradigm shift, MacInnis preferred to use language of reconciliation, love, and healing, more than the Pauline language of justification. This subtle shift of metaphors became quite apparent when he contrasted a forensic understanding of the atonement with a metaphor of life change: "It is not an artificial reckoning of a man just, but a fundamental ad-

---

[64] MacInnis to Torrey, 1 March 1928, and also Torrey to MacInnis, 10 March 1928, MacInnis Papers.

[65] Torrey to MacInnis, 22 Feb 1928, MacInnis Papers; see *PFP*, 116.

[66] *PFP*, 123–24.

[67] J. Gresham Machen, *Christianity and Liberalism* (New York: Macmillan, 1923), 125.

[68] *PFP*, 120.

[69] Machen, *Christianity and Liberalism,* 120; for liberal views see Cauthen, *The Impact of American Religious Liberalism*, 82, 210–12.

justment of life through a vital change of attitude which puts the life in a new relationship in the moral universe."[70]

Not only did he avoid traditional interpretations of Christ's atonement, but he also argued that Peter himself gave no explanation for how the death of Christ healed sinners. In fifteen short pages he repeated seven times that Peter's idea of atonement had no theological explanation.

> In this death He carried up the sins of the people upon the tree. Here again we have a fact stated without any attempt at explanation. . . . The church has lost the full significance of this fact because it has allowed the actual thing that took place to be over-shadowed by . . . theological explanation which grew up around it.[71]

Perhaps, as many fundamentalists assumed, MacInnis believed that so-called "theories of the atonement" were "artificial reckonings," and could be ignored in favor of "simple facts" and "plain statements." To conclude, however, that Peter's idea contained no theory of the atonement was closely reminiscent of liberal sentiments, such as those expressed in that Presbyterian declaration known as the "Auburn Affirmation." Signers of this affirmation objected to a decision of the 1923 General Assembly which declared that there were five essential Presbyterian doctrines, including the substitutionary atonement of Christ. Important in the Auburn Affirmation was a notion that the "facts of scripture" and the creeds of the church permitted more than one "theory" of the atonement.[72]

Like most Presbyterian conservatives, MacInnis opposed the Auburn Affirmation, though it is not clear if he did so for theological reasons.[73] But for most conservatives, the notion that doctrines of inspiration or atonement were theories that could bear more than one evangelical interpretation was unacceptable. Machen, for example, tended to blur any distinctions between the facts of the gospel and the theological explanation of the facts: "Christian doctrine," he said, "is not merely connected with the gospel, but it is identical with the gospel."[74] Machen never hesitated to assert a bold contrast: "Is it a theory of the atonement," he

---

[70] *PFP*, 125.

[71] *PFP*, 118–19.

[72] "An Affirmation Designed to Safeguard the Unity and Liberty of the Presbyterian Church in the United States of America," 5 May 1924, Auburn, New York.

[73] In a letter to one of its authors MacInnis opposed it for judicial reasons rather than for theological reasons; MacInnis to George B. Stewart, 22 August 1923, and Stewart to MacInnis, 23 August 1923, MacInnis Papers.

[74] Quoted in Longfield, *The Presbyterian Controversy*, 132.

asked. "Or is it the very truth of God?"[75] Even more explicit was Torrey, who simply argued that substitutionary atonement was a definite, plain, unmistakable, and positive Bible doctrine.[76]

The fact that MacInnis accepted a distinction between "simple facts" of scripture and "doctrinal theories" did not make him a modernist. There were other conservatives, if not fundamentalists, who were willing to give a wider berth to explanations of how Christ's death atoned for sin. The conservative scholar, James Orr, for example, affirmed that no single interpretation of the atonement could satisfy the fullness of the divine reality.[77] James Findlay's comment that Dwight L. Moody followed the moral influence theory is hardly convincing, but, nevertheless, highlights the tendencies of a few evangelicals following in that tradition of Moody to emphasize love and reconciliation in contrast to forensic ideas of law and punishment.[78] Norman H. Maring, in his study of the founders of Eastern Baptist Seminary, noted that although many of them considered themselves fundamentalists, as members of the Northern Baptist Fundamentalist Fellowship, they excluded substitution language from Eastern's statement of doctrine.[79] It cannot be said, therefore, that his views on the atonement warranted accusations of modernism.

Clearly, however, the rules of theological discourse for conservatives were changing. Fundamentalist critics of MacInnis had forgotten the earlier latitude of Orr and Moody. Whereas it once seemed simple enough to affirm that "Jesus bore sin in his body on the tree," by 1928 that declaration in *PFP* was not enough—even a prominent liberal like Henry Sloane Coffin could say as much.[80] In an earlier attack on E. Stanley Jones, one fundamentalist saw the problem exactly. It was no longer possible to simply say, "Christ died for me."

A few years ago these words would have been received at their face value. But today, with many, the cross means something other than the substitutionary death of the Son of God for the sins of mankind.[81]

---

[75] Machen, *Christianity and Liberalism,* 128–29.

[76] Reuben Torrey, *The Christ of the Bible* (New York: George H. Doran, 1924), 98.

[77] James Orr, *Sidelights on Christian Doctrine* (New York: A. C. Armstrong & Son, 1909), 134–35.

[78] Findlay, *Dwight L. Moody,* 232–33; on this see Stanley N. Gundry, *Love Them In: The Proclamation Theology of D. L. Moody* (Chicago: Moody Press, 1976), 109–20.

[79] Maring, "Conservative But Progressive," 41.

[80] *PFP,* 118. On Coffin see Longfield, *The Presbyterian Controversy,* 92.

[81] George Boddis, "The Christ of the Indian Road," *Moody Bible Institute Monthly,* May–June 1927, 23.

Although this writer's point was not that there was an earlier latitude
about the meaning of Christ's death, he realized, nevertheless, that the
constraints of acceptable language about the atonement had changed.
The problem was who would define the acceptable limits of atonement
language? For a dean of a fundamentalist Bible school, MacInnis'
atonement language had already moved beyond the pale of fundamentalist rules of discourse.

Revelation and Inspiration

Just as important to fundamentalists as the doctrine of atonement was
the doctrine of biblical inerrancy, and on this question as well MacInnis
was suspected of liberal leanings. There was, perhaps, a sound reason to
suspect that he did not completely concur with his fundamentalist colleagues on the issue of inerrancy, because he had reserved his most
telling criticism not for any modernist enemy but for a giant of that
Princeton tradition, Benjamin B. Warfield. This fact, combined with his
repeated usage of the phrase "Peter's insight," convinced many that he
had abandoned belief in verbal inspiration and an inerrant revelation.

When describing statements of the apostle Peter, MacInnis frequently
called them "insights." This exercised his critics greatly, because it appeared that he did not regard Peter's words as revealed truths. W.
Graham Scroggie, for example, wrote: "Perhaps many will feel that the
emphasis which should be laid upon Divine revelation is laid upon
Peter's apprehension." In reality, almost every critical reviewer objected
to this usage. Trumbull, for example, vigorously objected to the word
"insight," because Christ had disallowed that human insight, as a mental
process, could discover the Deity. A reviewer for the Moody Bible
Institute also found the word "insight" objectionable. Peter "had no insights" he declared, only "Holy Ghost revelations of truth."[82]

Those who defended MacInnis, however, pointed out that he had said
clearly that Peter's insights were from God.

> He [Jesus] also laid bare the source of this insight. He said, "Flesh and
> blood hath not revealed it unto thee, but my Father who is in heaven."
> Whatever may be said concerning the method by which this insight was
> given . . . Jesus wanted Peter to understand that it did not come in the or-
> dinary processes of reasoning.[83]

---

[82] Scroggie to MacInnis, n.d., MacInnis Papers; Trumbull, "Simon Peter—
Philosopher or Apostle?" 278; Smith, review of *Peter the Fisherman
Philosopher*, 346.

[83] *PFP*, 17.

The debate, therefore, centered on the interpretation of statements which on their surface appeared to contradict one another. Either Peter had insights, or he had divine revelation, but he could not have both. To other reviewers, it was more evident that he was using the terms interchangeably, suggesting that God's revelation to Peter was itself an insight, in so far as the revelation, once revealed, became the intellectual property of Peter's mind.[84] But most could not allow such a subtle distinction.

Why did he use the word insight? Aside from the already considered fact that MacInnis intended to write in a philosophical idiom, it also appears that he wanted to avoid any implications of a mechanical view of inspiration in which the human agent is only a passive receptacle of divine information. In other words, the issue was not the fact of revelation, nor the inspiration of the apostle, but the role of the human Peter in the process of revelation. For MacInnis, the content of revelation was both an insight of Peter, in the sense that it was related to Peter's experiential awareness, and a word from God, in the sense that the content expressed the mind and will of God.

> The revelation here spoken of as prophecy did not originate with "the will of man." Man was not able to think out all its contents alone. It is no mere human speculation. That does not necessarily mean that it was not in any sense the product of human thought.[85]

MacInnis worried that overly facile statements about "revealed Bible doctrines" might encourage a "mechanical dictation theory" of revelation and inspiration, that would exclude human participation.

> I am anxious to make this clear because it is at this very point that many of the unnatural theories of revelation and inspiration . . . are introduced. The logic usually followed in such cases is, this message did not come by the will of man. It did not originate with him. Therefore his thinking and experience had nothing to do with it. It was a message that was simply dictated to him. If that idea is in the Scriptures it certainly is not here.[86]

Ironically, conservatives often objected to charges that they held to a mechanical or dictation theory of inspiration, and so they were bothered that liberal-minded theologians often linked biblical infallibilism to a

---

[84] See e.g., Louis Bauman's report in "What Those Who Know Say About the Bible Institute of Los Angeles."

[85] *PFP*, 76–77; also cf. "Correspondence from Dr. MacInnis," *Moody Bible Institute Monthly*, July 1929, 536.

[86] Ibid.

"mechanical dictation theory." To conservatives this was little more than a red-herring.[87] When MacInnis used a similar line of reasoning in his criticisms of Warfield, therefore, he seemed to be echoing a familiar liberal refrain.

MacInnis, however, disliked Warfield's interpretation of II Peter 1:21, which says that "men moved by the Holy Spirit spoke from God." According to Warfield, to say that men were "moved" by the Holy Spirit meant that the "things which they spoke under this operation of the Spirit were . . . His things, not theirs." But for MacInnis, this was wrong.

> The fallacy in this reasoning is found in the fact that the being "borne along" [i.e. moved] necessarily involves a passive personality. A figure of speech is pressed at the expense of fundamental facts. The winds drive the ship when its sails are set and the ship has nothing to say about the operation. The reason is obvious. It is a thing and therefore in the very nature of things is passive. But when this term involves personalities and personal relationships it is at once evident . . . that the being "borne along" may be quite different from the process which merely involves things.[88]

In his perspective, Warfield had erred by making the recipient of revelation a passive vehicle. This, in effect, was a subtle recrudescence of the dictation theory of inspiration.

Although his criticism of Warfield was rather minor, it jutted boldly in the minds of his critics. To Charles Trumbull, for example, it was particularly odious that MacInnis criticized the "giant theological intellect of Princeton."[89] To MacInnis, however, Trumbull's point was hypocritical, because he gave an impression that a true fundamentalist would not differ with Warfield, when actually Trumbull himself had suffered theological differences with Warfield over Keswick holiness views. Writing to Trumbull, he angrily pointed out the double standard.

> It is really pathetic that Dr. Riley and yourself would refer to this. . . . Do you mean to say, therefore, that disagreeing with Dr. Warfield is an indication of modernism? If so, Dr. Riley and yourself find yourselves in an embarrassing position.[90]

---

[87] Machen, *Christianity and Liberalism*, 73.

[88] *PFP*, 779.

[89] Trumbull, "Simon Peter—Philosopher or Apostle?" 282.

[90] MacInnis to Charles Trumbull, 10 May 1928, MacInnis Papers.

Here, as in his other theological opinions, MacInnis saw his doctrine of scripture from the perspective of a broader Protestant tradition which could still accommodate a hermeneutical pluralism in its understanding of biblical inspiration. MacInnis was deeply influenced by James Orr, who disliked the term "verbal inspiration" and argued that it was not needed to safeguard the authority of scripture.[91] Hence, rather than an infallible scripture, MacInnis preferred to state simply that the apostles "came to know the mind of God so that they could speak from Him."[92] His use of the word "insight," suggested a view similar to what has been called the "dynamic view of inspiration." This view held that God "vouchsafed to men certain basic insights into reality, and men communicated these in the context of their own human experience." He did not, however, deny that inspiration was verbal. Rather, he only held that "verbal inspiration" was an inadequate explanation of the complex reality of biblical revelation.[93]

MacInnis' reticence to espouse the Princeton idea of biblical inerrancy and verbal inspiration was rare among Bible school leaders and those loosely identified with the WCFA. Rather, his viewpoint was more commonly seen in mainline conservatives who dissented from militant fundamentalism, such as J. C. Massee, as well as others associated with the Fundamentalist Fellowship, some of whom founded Eastern Baptist Seminary in 1924.[94] There were also moderate evangelical Presbyterians who dissented from Princeton's doctrine of scripture, such as Charles Erdman and Robert Speer, who based their view of biblical authority on the inner witness of Christ, rather than the concept of inerrancy.[95] But unlike MacInnis, these leaders did not answer to the whims of a radical Bible school constituency.

Most discouraging to MacInnis, however, was the fact that his primary argument was ignored. His purpose was not to stir up an inter-

---

[91] On "hermeneutical pluralism" see Jaroslav Pelikan, "Fundamentalism and/or Orthodoxy? Toward an Understanding of the Fundamentalist Phenomenon," in *The Fundamentalist Phenomenon: A View from Within, a Response from Without,* ed. Norman J. Cohen (Grand Rapids: Eerdmans Co., 1990), 6–9; for Orr's influence see John MacInnis to William MacInnes, 2 July 1938, MacInnis Papers; also see Robert J. Hoefel, "The Doctrine of Inspiration in the Writings of James Orr and B. B. Warfield: A Study in Contrasting Approaches to Scripture" (Ph.D. diss., Fuller Theological Seminary, 1983), 293–98.

[92] *PFP*, 79.

[93] MacInnis to W. B. Riley, 27 January 1928, and Riley to MacInnis, 31 January 1928; also, MacInnis to Leander Keyser, 23 February 1928, MacInnis Papers.

[94] Russell, *Voices of American Fundamentalism,* 112; Maring, "Conservative But Progressive," 41.

[95] Longfield, *The Presbyterian Controversy,* 40, 203.

necine conflict over inspiration, but to offer an argument for the plausibility of supernatural revelation. "The whole book," said a defiant MacInnis, "is an argument in the interest of supernatural revelation."[96] But his critics were unwilling to admit even this point.

Christianity and Culture

When MacInnis started his book with the problem of how to build an "effective and abiding society," it was immediately obvious that his book did not follow a typical fundamentalist approach to society and its problems. To many fundamentalists, building an "effective society" was quite unimportant, because society was collapsing and could not endure. This attitude is seen in W. B. Riley's widely published address entitled, "Is Society Rotting," in which he derided "optimists" for their belief that society was improving. The sense that there was little time for social programs when lost souls were perishing was typical of Bible school education. The gospel was the power of salvation, not of social progress—so a typical Bible school student often assumed.[97]

The contrasting attitude of social concern evident in *PFP* was ridiculed by an unknown fundamentalist writer sometime in 1928.

> I is always suspicious of these Revs. that has so much to say 'bout improvin' this world an' keeps so mum 'bout the next world. . . . When you knows this old world is gwine to be burned up an' shaken down mos' any time, you aint gwine to waste much time tinkerin' with it. You better be gettin' ready to go, 'stead o' gettin' ready to stay.[98]

Gaebelein's magazine also made this criticism: "We get the impression," they said, "that it is somewhat akin to the world's tenets of social betterment and the general theory of evolution."[99] To others, it appeared that MacInnis had rejected the premillennial coming of Christ, and this lapse had caused him to advocate a postmillennial vision of social progress—so W. B. Riley charged, ridiculing MacInnis for his reliance on Walter Rauschenbusch.[100]

Such widespread criticisms led one historian to conclude that *PFP* was "too congenial to the social gospel" for anti-MacInnis fundamen-

---

[96] W. B. Riley to MacInnis, 31 January 1928, MacInnis Papers.

[97] Riley's sermon was reprinted in *The Fundamentalist,* 9 March 1928, 1.

[98] "Brer Jackson Elucidates the Inwardness of Peter the Fisherman Philosopher," Typed Document [11 February 1928], MacInnis Papers.

[99] Wells, review of *Peter the Fisherman Philosopher,* 693.

[100] Riley, "Breaking the Bible School Defence Line," 7.

talists.[101] For certain, MacInnis was deeply influenced by social gospel writers. He boldly quoted Rauschenbusch, defending his statement that the goal of history was "the social salvation of the race."[102] For some readers, this alone was enough to persuade them of his weakened commitment to the old-fashioned gospel of repentance, conversion, and salvation. But other fundamentalists, such as Alva McClain, argued that it was unfortunate that conservatives had opposed the term "social gospel," because it contained an element of truth.[103]

In spite of influences from the social gospel, however, this was not its primary theme. Rather, in a typical Progressive Era fashion, the question of its preface, seeking to discover the values of an effective and abiding society, was far more important. The last six chapters tried to argue that a Christian worldview provides the necessary ideals and motivations required to sustain a democracy. This point was ignored by anti-MacInnis radicals.

Chapter nine is the most theologically oriented of the last six chapters, because it discussed the need for an organization (i.e. the Christian church) to embody the ideals of a Christian ethic. If there were any implicit criticism of fundamentalism in this chapter, it was that revivalism had fostered a radical individualism, which had obscured the need for individuals to "'grow up' into salvation in a social relationship."[104] But if MacInnis seemed to be espousing a social gospel, he still followed a typical 19th century argument that society will change only as individuals are changed.[105] As this latter point suggests, MacInnis did not abandon his commitment to an individualistic ethic, but he combined it with familiar social gospel ideas of social sin and salvation.

The following four chapters attempt to show that Christianity provides the necessary motivations to undergird modern democratic society. First, a significant danger in modern democracy is the tendency of selfish exploiters to advance their own interests at the expense of the whole society. Christian faith, however, supplies an ethic in which self-interest is subordinated to the interests of others. Second, Christians affirm that all suffering in the present is but a temporary stage in the progress of God's purpose in history, and this hope enables people to suffer and sacrifice for the common welfare. Third, a doctrine of personal immortality is a necessary motivation for the survival of modern democracy.[106] Finally, MacInnis argued that the teaching of Christ's personal

---

[101] Edmondson, "Fundamentalist Sects of Los Angeles," 167.

[102] *PFP,* 204.

[103] McClain, review of *Peter the Fisherman Philosopher,* MacInnis Papers.

[104] *PFP,*131–33.

[105] *PFP,*141.

[106] *PFP,* 150–52, 164, 173–78.

return could also provide a needed value for democracy, and in this last point he again engendered fundamentalist opposition.

In his last two chapters, MacInnis argued that a future reign of God's righteousness inaugurated by the second coming of Christ provides a motive for optimism about the future of human civilization. This was established by Peter's confidence that righteousness would never be defeated. Hence, Peter was "intensely optimistic."[107] At this point, however, the concept of a crisis in history precipitated by Christ's entry into the world causes a difficulty for the modern mind, which is used to thinking in terms of gradual development and social evolution. The problem, then, was to resolve these two seemingly exclusive pictures of world history.

MacInnis was struggling with two streams of 19th century Protestant tradition: a postmillennial vision of continuing social development, versus the apocalyptic vision of premillennialism, which saw the second coming of Christ as a cataclysmic break in world history.[108] There were two problems that he hoped to resolve. First, he wanted to show that there was no contradiction between belief in historical progress and the premillennial coming of Christ. Second, he also wanted to argue as a corollary of the first point, that premillennialism was not inherently pessimistic.

MacInnis became acutely worried about these problems after Shirley Jackson Case and Shailer Mathews began to accuse premillennialists of being a "serious menace" to democracy with their pessimistic attitudes and denials of social progress.[109] Hence, at this time he began to formulate a response to the view that premillennialists were inherently pessimistic, which he put out at the 1918 Philadelphia Prophetic Conference.

> A modern writer contends that [the second coming of Christ] would be a contradiction of established scientific knowledge. . . . We are not opposed to a real evolution; that is, a progress that is carrying out the intelligent plan that is moving to a definite consummation. We are against an evolutionary theory that would limit God in His own universe.[110]

MacInnis continued to state this point of view in very similar ways in *PFP*. There is nothing in Peter's philosophy, he noted, that would in any way indicate a "break with the past." On the contrary, the coming of

---

[107] *PFP*, 190.

[108] James H. Moorhead, "The Erosion of Postmillennialism in American Religious Thought, 1865–1925," *Church History* 53 (March 1984): 76–77.

[109] Shirley Jackson Case, "The Premillenial Menace," *Biblical World* 52 (July 1918): 16–23.

[110] *Light on Prophecy*, 49.

Christ is only one step in that unfolding and unveiling[111] purpose of God in history. In a subtle twist of biblical interpretation, however, MacInnis placed some of his fundamentalist opponents in a company of Christ mockers. In II Peter 3:3–4, there are mockers who come and attack the notion of Christ's second coming. To most fundamentalists, these mockers would be identified with enemies of premillennialism. But MacInnis saw it differently. These mockers, he noted, believe that there is no change, that "everything continues as it was from the beginning of creation." The mockers, therefore, are not those who attack the second coming of Christ. Instead, they are radical fundamentalists who deny that there is progress in history!

In his argument for historical progress, MacInnis not only opposed the premillennial pessimism of some fundamentalists, but also the agnosticism of thinkers like Herbert Spenser, who believed in an inevitable social evolution as an independent law of the universe. Social development, he wrote, "is not the unfolding of a mechanical world but the carrying out of a program by an Experiencer who is greater than His world."[112] Here again, MacInnis was opposing naturalism in a fashion very similar to moderate conservatives like Curtis Lee Laws and E. Y. Mullins,[113] but also like Harry Emerson Fosdick. In his *Christianity and Progress,* Fosdick also asserted that the attempt to found civilization on materialism had totally failed, that a spiritual interpretation of history was needed, and that a Christian worldview could supply motives for character and service. "If ever a river ran out into a desert," he opined, "the river of progressive hopes, fed only from springs of materialistic philosophy, has done so here."[114] Ironically, although fundamentalists shared this ground of opposition to naturalism, they ignored this aspect of MacInnis' book.

Concluding Remarks

Peter the Fisherman Philosopher was not easily understood, because it represented the confluence of many streams of thought. A major task of the intellectual historian is to sift through these streams of thought and compare them to the social and intellectual milieu in which they have their origin and meaning. Often these streams are half-conscious impulses, hardly recognized by well defined ideological boundaries. What Charles Cashdollar observed of positivism is also true of "higher fundamentalism."

---

[111] *PFP*, 192, 195.

[112] *PFP*, 197.

[113] Szasz, "Three Fundamentalist Leaders," 362–63.

[114] Fosdick, *Christianity and Progress,* 36.

What we think is determined in part by what we choose to oppose and how we choose to oppose it. The results here were subtle and often unrecognized—"indirect, silent, and unconscious."[115]

In another relevant observation, Nathan Hatch has followed Edmund S. Morgan's useful perspective, that intellectual change may not be the result of a clash between radically discontinuous beliefs, but a matter of emphasis.

Change in Christian thought, as Edmund S. Morgan has suggested, is usually a matter of emphasis. Certain ideas are given greater weight than was previously accorded them, or one idea is carried to its logical conclusion at the expense of others. "One age slides into the next," he says, "and an intellectual revolution may be achieved by the expression of ideas that everyone had always professed to accept."[116]

The observations of Cashdollar and Hatch give valuable insights for an understanding of the MacInnis controversy. In his provocative concept of a "higher fundamentalism," MacInnis was opposing a philosophical materialism on one front, but more importantly for, this study, a militant and rationalistic fundamentalism on the other. These lines of opposition shaped the contours of his intellectual position, which, in the words of Cashdollar, were filled with "indirect, silent, and unconscious" impulses.

These impulses had deep and variegated roots in late 19th and early 20th century thought. MacInnis was no gadfly, irritating his fundamentalist friends for the sake of controversy. Rather, he was an idealist hoping to find in his own religious roots a vision of evangelical orthodoxy, which was lost in the shame of fundamentalist militancy. His "revolution in thought," a higher fundamentalism, would not come by any radical departures from evangelical religion, therefore, but by emphasizing certain ideas more than others.

One theme that MacInnis chose to emphasize was Christian experience. Here was a complex theme, deeply rooted in evangelical religion: revivalism, pietism, Keswick holiness, and pragmatism all contributed to his experiential theology. If, however, MacInnis sometimes sounded more like a liberal than his critics liked, it is well to remember, as Grant Wacker once stated: "liberal and evangelical stirrings were similar re-

---

[115] Charles D. Cashdollar, *The Transformation of Theology, 1830–1890: Positivism and Protestant Thought in Britain and America* (Princeton University Press, 1989), 14.

[116] Hatch, *The Democratization of American Christianity*, 182.

sponses to common problems."[117] A desire to renew the *elan vital* of Protestant religion encouraged both liberals and evangelicals to drink from the cup of spiritual experience. Though these streams of thought gradually diverged, there was always a cross-fertilization of ideas. Some leaders hardened their views and excluded a middle ground. Others, many denominational moderates, maintained a traditional orthodoxy, but emphasized aspects of evangelicalism that were coterminous with more liberalized formulations of theology. As the ideas and expressions coalesced, it was not always clear even to participants themselves from where all these ideas came. This is why considerable confusion surrounded *The Christ of the Indian Road* and *Peter the Fisherman Philosopher*. Were these books, in the words of Leander Keyser, "so orthodox that the Modernists, if they think the proposition through thoroughly, will find no comfort in it?" Or were they, in the perspective of James Clarke, so agreeable that any liberal could "heartily subscribe to higher fundamentalism." The truth is: they were neither. What Jones and MacInnis had done was to emphasize portions of evangelical truth that had been lost in fundamentalist criticisms of liberalism: a social concept of sin more than fallen human nature, nurture more than evangelism, human instrumentality more than divine intervention, progress more than decay: all of these themes had roots in evangelicalism that went unrecognized by most fundamentalist critics. But at what point did one step outside of the circle, as Winrod put it? This, as always, depended on who was drawing the circle.

---

[117] Wacker, "The Holy Spirit and the Spirit of the Age," 49.

CHAPTER 8

The MacInnis Controversy and American Protestant Fundamentalism: A Concluding Postscript

After MacInnis left Biola on December 31, 1928, some members of the Los Angeles Presbytery, angered by the breach over MacInnis, felt a need to provide their own lay Christian training. To this end, funds were raised from J. M. Irvine and Mrs. Milton Stewart among others to create a program of lay Christian training under the control of the presbytery. In September 1929, a proposal was approved to invite MacInnis and his former associate, Florence Chaffee, to lead this new training program. Not housed in a single building, it was a "training school on wheels," consisting in a wide variety of classes held throughout Southern California. MacInnis led this program until 1936, when due to failing health, he retired.[1] During this period he also published three books, one having to do with his belief—forged in the fires of fundamentalist criticism—that the church alone is the "most perfect educational instrument," and the others having to do with the role of the Presbyterian church trustee and deacon.[2] On May 6, 1940, at the age of sixty eight, MacInnis died from a stroke.

MacInnis lived long enough to witness the fundamentalist schisms of the 1930s. Although T. T. Shields and J. Frank Norris had experienced splits from their Baptist associations in the 1920s, and Machen had contemplated a withdrawal from the Presbyterian Church as early as 1925, by and large most fundamentalists during the 1920s remained within their denominations, and the major schisms did not occur until the 1930s and 40s. Nevertheless, it is important to note that during the 1920s many moderate conservatives were alienated from the funda-

---

[1] MacInnes, "Leadership Training in the Synod of California," 34–45, 78–81.
[2] John M. MacInnis. *The Church As Teacher* (Philadelphia: Westminster Press, 1936), 71; and two books for the Presbyterian Board of Christian Education: *The Trustee and the Church Today* and *The Deacon and the Church Today* (Philadelphia, 1939).

mentalist movement, some quietly and without any controversy, but others under severe circumstances. This fissioning process in the 1920s both weakened and strengthened the fundamentalist coalition: it weakened it because the movement became increasingly marginalized and hence lost a significant voice in the larger religious culture. It strengthened it, however, by purging the movement of disparate elements, thus making it more homogeneous and capable of united action. When similar conflicts rose in the 1930s, therefore, fundamentalists were able to finally take the step of separation that had been threatened at least since 1919.

Although Riley had tried to create an image of fundamentalist unity in his depiction of the movement as the sole heir of Bible conferences and Bible schools started in the late 19th century, it is significant that he neglected the role of that series of books which later passed its name to the movement, the *Fundamentals.*[3] Perhaps his unwillingness to place these books at the center of fundamentalist history had to do with an uneasy feeling that they did not actually represent his idea of a unified militant fundamentalist front. MacInnis also reflected this feeling, noting that the *Fundamentals* was not really representative of fundamentalism, because some contributors had since been accused of modernism.[4] It has since become commonplace to observe that the *Fundamentals* represented a rather diverse cross section of anti-modernist attitudes.

This early diversity became more truncated with the rise of organized fundamentalism in the 1920s. Torrey's failed hopes to include conservatives like John Timothy Stone in the WCFA, for example, was a sign that organized fundamentalism was beginning with a narrower self-conception than did the *Fundamentals.* Nevertheless, the movement continued to encompass a small amount of diversity, not so much in its theological positions as in its attitudes toward mainline denominationalism, anti-evolutionism, militancy, and a few other contested issues. Thus, some denominational conservatives who were also closely tied with the Bible conference movement and Bible schools could still find a somewhat comfortable home in the movement in 1920. But even this diversity could not long be maintained, and so many of these individuals were alienated from fundamentalism for one reason or another, resulting in a further narrowing of the movement.

The MacInnis controversy shared many affinities with other divisions that took place among fundamentalists. The division that occurred between leaders of the Fundamentalist Federation and the Baptist Bible Union showed many similar features: federation members were less

---

[3] Riley, "The Christian Fundamentals Movement," 8–9.
[4] MacInnis to Robert Hastings Nichols, 24 April 1925, MacInnis Papers.

militant, more tolerant regarding premillennialism and evolution, and more willing to cooperate with denominational moderates and liberals. Other controversies too followed the lines of conservative-inclusive versus fundamentalist-exclusive, such as the positions of E. Y. Mullins against J. Frank Norris, John T. MacNeill against T. T. Shields, and Charles Erdman against J. Gresham Machen. But these divisions occurred primarily within denominations. The MacInnis controversy, though fought mostly between Baptist and Presbyterian fundamentalists, took place on an interdenominational turf. Here there were fewer instances of inclusive versus exclusive divisions. Often leaders just quietly receded from visibility in the fundamentalist movement, thus never becoming the focus of criticism. G. Campbell Morgan, for example, seems to have gradually distanced himself from the movement during the 1920s, and it was primarily due to his public support of MacInnis that he experienced a breach with fundamentalism. But MacInnis did not gradually retreat from organized fundamentalism. Instead, he was severed from the movement in a manner that became a harbinger of later fundamentalist schisms.

Central to the crisis was the problem of authority: how would issues of faith and practice be settled among those who were no longer identified with one of the denominations? Actually, this problem had always been a part of the evangelical movement. The great George Whitefield, for example, relied on what one historian has called a "cult of personality" rather than a specific institutional authority.[5] Mark Noll's discussion of how religious communities exercise authority in the interpretation of the Bible may also be applicable to the MacInnis crisis. The most dominant mode of authority was what Noll has called the magisterium, the authority of official religious leadership.[6] When opponents lined up religious leaders against each other, they were appealing to an informal magisterium to settle their dispute over the interpretation of *Peter the Fisherman Philosopher*. Lacking an institutional base, however, the magisterial authority was based principally on the popularity of evangelical leaders and their credentials to speak for the fundamentalist community. In this regard, credentials were seldom academic, indeed, academic or technical expertise could actually be a hindrance. Rather, credentials were derived in a very practical way—by leading a very large congregation, which allowed a pastor the resources to extend his influence beyond the confines of his own church, or by controlling the means of communication through a widely read periodical. These

---

[5] Jon Butler, *Awash in a Sea of Faith: Christianizing the American People* (Cambridge, MA: Harvard University Press, 1990), 191.

[6] Mark A. Noll, *Between Faith and Criticism: Evangelicals, Scholarship, and the Bible in America* (San Francisco: Harper & Row, 1986), 150–51.

sources of authority, however, could be preserved only by a continuous display of the criteria by which one was identified as a member of the community. Hence, authority could be a fickle thing in the community of fundamentalists. As long as one used the correct religious vocabulary and displayed the requisite militancy, one could speak with authority. But there were many who lost this authority when they began to alter accepted terms or soften their militant rhetoric. Rowland Bingham, for example, had been a militant opponent of higher criticism at McMaster College in 1910, attacking the views of I. G. Matthews. In 1926, however, he confessed that his abusive tactics had been wrong. This confession, however, became the occasion for a militant assault on Bingham's fundamentalist credentials by T. T. Shields. In this way, one's authority in the fundamentalist community could be lost, and this happened to leaders better known than MacInnis or Bingham, such as G. Campbell Morgan and Philip Mauro.[7]

A study of the MacInnis controversy challenges simplistic definitions of fundamentalism. One searches in vain for a unifying theme by which one can neatly delineate the movement. Perhaps, as some have argued, "militant anti-modernism" best describes those who opposed MacInnis, but certainly a judicious estimate would allow that some fundamentalists opposed him, or at least expressed doubts about him, because they read his book and concluded that its arguments were lacking. On the other hand, those who defended him may well have done so because they were ignorant of liberalizing tendencies in his thought, or (as many anti-MacInnis fundamentalists believed) because they liked MacInnis and could not bear to see so gentle a man ruined. But if easy classifications are elusive, it is simply because fundamentalism was still undergoing transformation during the 1920s: many who began the decade as fundamentalists ended it outside of the movement; and many others, who at first had no connection to the movement, were later drawn into its orb. This reality merely reflected the fact that individuals themselves were malleable. MacInnis, for example, after leaving the movement, appeared to move into a closer association with the well-known liberal, Robert Freeman, of Pasadena Presbyterian Church, while Alva McClain, whose defenses of MacInnis might have suggested his gradual transition away from fundamentalism, moved in a more conservative direction instead. Probably even more symptomatic of this difficulty is the position of Charles Fuller. Though he opposed MacInnis, and although he later acquired a broad fundamentalist constituency through his nationwide radio program, he also helped to organize Fuller Seminary, an

---

[7] McKenzie, 204, 213; for Bingham's confession see "An Editor's Confession," The *Evangelical Christian*, January 1926, 8.

institution which led the charge in reforming fundamentalism after 1947.

It is tempting to draw certain parallels between the movement which became known as "neo-evangelicalism," and the "higher fundamentalism" of MacInnis. Although there does not appear to be any organic links, they shared a similar spirit and outlook. Like MacInnis, neo-evangelical intellectuals like Carl F. H. Henry turned a critical eye toward the individualistic social ethic of fundamentalism. George Ladd's work on the kingdom of God revived the old historical premillennialism and repudiated dispensationalism. Bernard Ramm advocated a new openness to science and evolution, which was not dissimilar to the views of MacInnis twenty-five years earlier. Perhaps most intriguing are the similarities between MacInnis and the preeminent intellectual of the movement, Edward Carnell. Although MacInnis lacked Carnell's rigorous and perspicacious intellect, they shared several important affinities: both wanted to restore intellectual respectability to orthodox Christianity, and both found in philosophy the tools of an effective apologetic against the materialism and secularism of modern culture on the one hand, and religious fundamentalism on the other, which earned them fundamentalist derision. Other similarities are also striking. Both men, for example, had scholarly temperaments that were ill-suited for their administrative responsibilities. Moreover, both men appeared to be on an intellectual trajectory leading further away from their conservative evangelical roots. It is certainly tempting to speculate whether or not Carnell would have encountered the kind of opposition that MacInnis did, had he not died prematurely. But this, of course, is impossible to say.[8]

Unlike many later neo-evangelicals, MacInnis developed his reforming vision from within the fundamentalist movement itself. Neo-evangelicalism, however, had to develop an alternative institutional framework to sustain its intellectual vision, such as the influential magazine *Christianity Today,* which became its primary voice, and Fuller Theological Seminary, which became its principal intellectual center. Ironically, in this regard, MacInnis came to hold a very different viewpoint than the neo-evangelicals, for after the demise of "higher fundamentalism" at Biola, MacInnis repudiated the usefulness of the para-church organization. Neo-evangelicalism, however, in spite of its hopes to achieve the respect of mainline denominations, still largely depended on para-church organizations. Although MacInnis was in no way an intellectual forebear of neo-evangelicalism, his message given in the 1920s

---

[8] For these observations see Rudolph Nelson, *The Making and Unmaking of an Evangelical Mind: The Case of Edward Carnell* (Cambridge: Cambridge University Press, 1988), 97–106, 204–6.

serves as an important reminder that reforming movements do not arise in a vacuum. A realization that there were evangelicals hoping to reform fundamentalism, to make it a "higher fundamentalism" in MacInnis' words, may dampen any overly enthusiastic suggestions that the development of neo-evangelicalism some twenty years later was unique and unprecedented.

Bibliography

Primary Sources

Special Collections

Billy Sunday Papers, Collection 61. Billy Graham Archives. Wheaton, Illinois.

John Franklyn Norris Collection. Southern Baptist Historical Library and Archives. Nashville, Tennessee.

John Murdoch MacInnis Papers. Presbyterian Historical Society. Philadelphia, Pennsylvania.

Lewis Sperry Chafer Papers. Dallas Theological Seminary. Dallas, Texas.

Lyman Stewart Papers. Biola University Archives. La Mirada, California.

Reuben Torrey and James Gray Correspondence Files. Moody Bible Institute Archives. Chicago, Illinois.

Miscellaneous Literature

Affirmation Designed to Safeguard the Unity and Liberty of the Presbyterian Church in the United States of America. Auburn Conference Committee, 1924.

The Biolan. Biola, 1927. Biola University Archives. La Mirada, California.

Brooks, Keith. "The Spirit of Truth and the Spirit of Error." Pamphlet. N.d. Biola University Archives. La Mirada, California.

Bulletin of the Bible Institute of Los Angeles. 1920, 1922, 1927, 1929. Biola University Archives. La Mirada, California.

Catalogue of the Bible Institute for Home and Foreign Missions of the Chicago Evangelization Society. 1897. Moody Bible Institute Archives.

Catalogue of the Bible Institute of Los Angeles [1913]. Church of the Open Door Archives. Glendora, California.

Catalogue of the Moody Bible Institute. 1911–1925. Moody Bible Institute Archives. Chicago, Illinois.

Fuller, Rebecca Harrison. Interview by Author, 5 June 1991. Sepulveda, California.

Fuller, Roy Harold. Handwritten Diary. 1927–1928. In Author's Possession. Montrose, California.

"John McNeill." Typed Document. N.d. Biola University Archives. La Mirada, California.

McGee, J. Vernon. "Why I Left the Presbyterian Church." Printed Sermon. N.d. Biola University Archives. La Mirada, California.

Minutes of Biola Faculty Meetings. 1924–1929. Biola University Archives.

Minutes of the Biola Board of Directors, Executive Committee of the Biola Board of Directors, and the Biola Evangelization Society. 1918–1929. Biola University President's Office. La Mirada, California.

Montrose Bible Conference 50th Jubilee, 1908–1958. Booklet. N.d. MacInnis Papers. Philadelphia, Pennsylvania.

Sutherland, Samuel. Interview by Author, 28 May 1993. Chicago, Illinois.

Temple University Catalog. 1912–1913. Temple University Archives.

Periodical Literature

Bible Champion. Reading, Pennsylvania.
Bible Witness. Hounslow, United Kingdom.
Biblical Recorder. Melbourne, Australia.
Biblical Review. New York, New York.
Biblical World. Chicago, Illinois.
Bibliotheca Sacra. Pittsburgh, Pennsylvania.
Bob Shuler's Magazine. Los Angeles, California.
Book News Monthly. Philadelphia, Pennsylvania.
British Weekly. London, England.
Christian Century. Chicago, Illinois.
Christian Fundamentalist. Minneapolis, Minnesota.
Christian Fundamentals Magazine. Los Angeles, California.
Defender. Wichita, Kansas.
Evangelical Christian & Missionary Witness. Toronto, Ontario.
Fundamentalist. Fort Worth, Texas.
Gospel Message. Kansas City, Missouri.
Gospel Witness. Toronto, Ontario.
Grace and Truth. Denver, Colorado.
King's Business. Los Angeles, California.
Literary Digest. New York, New York.
Moody Bible Institute Monthly. Chicago, Illinois.
Our Hope. New York, New York.
Presbyterian Advance. Nashville, Tennessee.
Presbyterian Banner. Pittsburgh, Pennsylvania.
Presbyterian Magazine. Philadelphia, Pennsylvania.
Princeton Theological Review. Princeton, New Jersey.
Record of Christian Work. Northfield, Massachusetts.
Review and Expositor. Louisville, Kentucky.
Searchlight. Virginia, Minnesota.
Serving and Waiting. Philadelphia, Pennsylvania.
Southern Baptist Trumpet. Oklahoma.
Sunday School Times. Philadelphia, Pennsylvania.
Watchman-Examiner. New York, New York.

Newspapers

Los Angeles *Evening Herald*
Los Angeles *Times*
Syracuse *Herald*
Syracuse *Post-Standard*

Books

Abbott, Lyman. *The Theology of an Evolutionist*. Boston: Houghton, Mifflin and Co., 1897.
Betts, Frederick W. *Billy Sunday: The Man and Method*. Boston: Murray Press, 1916.

————. *Forty Fruitful Years*. Boston: Murray Press, [1929].

Cameron, Robert. *Scriptural Truth About the Lord's Return*. New York: Fleming H. Revell Company, 1922.

Dixon, Amzi C., Louis Meyer, and Reuben A. Torrey, eds. *The Fundamentals: A Testimony to the Truth*. 12 Volumes. Los Angeles and Chicago, 1910–1915.

Erdman, Charles. *The Return of Christ*. New York: George H. Doran Co., 1922.

Fosdick, Harry Emerson. *Christianity and Progress*. New York: Fleming H. Revell Co., 1922.

————. *The Modern Use of the Bible*. New York: Macmillan, 1942.

God Hath Spoken: Twenty-Five Addresses Delivered at the World Conference on Christian Fundamentals, May 25 to June 1, 1919. Philadelphia: Bible Conference Committee, 1919.

Gordon, Ernest. *The Leaven of the Sadducees*. Chicago: Bible Institute Colportage Assn., 1926.

Hartzler, H. B. *Moody in Chicago or The World's Fair Gospel Campaign*. New York: Fleming H. Revell Co., 1894.

Horton, Thomas C. *Personal and Practical Christian Work*. Los Angeles: Biola Book Room, 1922.

Howden, J. Russell. *The Old Paths in the Light of Modern Thought*. London: The China Inland Mission, 1921.

Jones, E. Stanley. *The Christ of the Indian Road*. New York: Abingdon, 1925.

————. *Christ at the Round Table*. New York: Abingdon, 1928.

Light on Prophecy: Proceedings and Addresses at the Philadelphia Prophetic Conference, May 28–30, 1918. New York: The Christian Herald Bible House, 1918.

Macartney, Clarence E. *The Making of a Minister*. Great Neck, NY: Channel Press, 1961.

Machen, J. Gresham. *Christianity and Liberalism*. New York: MacMillan Co., 1923.

MacInnis, John Murdoch. *The Church As Teacher*. Philadelphia: Westminster Press, 1936.

————. *The Deacon and the Church Today*. Philadelphia: Presbyterian Board of Christian Education, 1939.

————. *Peter the Fisherman Philosopher*. Los Angeles: Biola Book Room, 1927.

————. *Peter the Fisherman Philosopher*. New York and London: Harper & Brothers, 1930.

————. *The Trustee and the Church Today*. Philadelphia: Presbyterian Board of Christian Education, 1939.

Macphail, Andrew. *The Master's Wife*. Toronto: McClelland and Stewart Ltd., 1939.

Mathews, Shailer. *The Faith of Modernism*. New York: Macmillan Co., 1924.

Mauro, Philip. *The Gospel of the Kingdom: With an Examination of Modern Dispensationalism*. Boston: Hamilton Brothers, 1928.

Minutes of the General Assembly of the Presbyterian Church in the United States of America. Philadelphia: Office of the General Assembly, 1884–1929.

Orr, James. *Sidelights on Christian Doctrine*. New York: A. C. Armstrong and Son, 1909.

Riley, William B. "The Christian Fundamentals Movement: Its Battles, Its Achievements, Its Certain Victory." In *Scriptural Inspiration versus Scientific Imagination: Messages Delivered at the Great Christian Fundamentals Conference at Los Angeles, California*, 7–23. Los Angeles, Biola Book Room [1922].

— — —. "The Great Divide, or Christ and the Present Crisis." In *God Hath Spoken: Twenty-Five Addresses Delivered at the World Conference on Christian Fundamentals, May 25 to June 1, 1919,* 27–45. Philadelphia: Bible Conference Committee, 1919.

Torrey, Reuben A. *What the Bible Teaches.* New York: Fleming H. Revell Co., 1898.

— — —. *The Christ of the Bible.* New York: George H. Doran Co., 1924.

Secondary Sources

Books

Ahlstrom, Sydney E. *A Religious History of the American People.* New Haven and London: Yale University Press, 1972.

Allen, Frederick Lewis. *Only Yesterday: An Informal History of the Nineteen Twenties.* New York: Harper & Brothers, 1931.

Ayer & Sons. *American Newspaper Annual and Directory.* Philadelphia: N. W. Ayer & Son, 1928.

Barr, James. *Fundamentalism.* London: SCM Press Ltd., 1977.

Beale, David O. *In Pursuit of Purity: American Fundamentalism Since 1850.* Greenville, South Carolina: Unusual Publications, 1986.

Bebbington, David W. *Evangelicalism in Modern Britain: A History from the 1730s to the 1980s.* London: Unwin Hyman, 1989.

Bledstein, Burton J. *The Culture of Professionalism: The Middle Class and the Development of Higher Education In America.* New York: W. W. Norton, 1976.

Blumhofer, Edith L. *Aimee Semple McPherson: Everybody's Sister.* Grand Rapids: Eerdmans, 1993.

Blumhofer, Edith L., and Randall Balmer, eds. *Modern Christian Revivals.* Urbana and Chicago: University of Illinois Press, 1993.

Blumhofer, Edith L., and Joel A. Carpenter, eds. *Twentieth Century Evangelicalism: A Guide to the Sources.* New York: Garland Publishers, 1990.

Boone, Kathleen C. *The Bible Tells Them So: The Discourse of Protestant Fundamentalism.* Albany: State University of New York, 1989.

Bozeman, Dwight. *Protestants in an Age of Science: The Baconian Ideal and Antebellum American Religious Thought.* Chapel Hill: University of North Carolina Press, 1977.

Brereton, Virginia Lieson. *Training God's Army: The American Bible School, 1880–1940.* Bloomington: Indiana University Press, 1990.

Brooks, Garland C. *Challenged to Be the Church in Unity: An Historical Review of the United Church of Canada on Prince Edward Island, 1925–1985.* Sherwood PEI: PEI United Church History Committee, 1988. Maritime Conference Archives, United Church of Canada. Halifax, Nova Scotia.

Burkinshaw, Robert K. *Pilgrims in Lotusland: Conservative Protestantism in British Columbia, 1917–1981.* Montreal and Kingston: McGill-Queen's University Press, 1995.

Butler, Jon. *Awash in a Sea of Faith: Christianizing the American People.* Cambridge, MA: Harvard University Press, 1990.

Cashdollar, Charles. *The Transformation of Theology, 1830–1890: Positivism and Protestant Thought in Britain and America.* Princeton: Princeton University Press, 1989.

Cauthen, Kenneth. *The Impact of American Religious Liberalism.* New York: Harper & Row, 1962.

Clark, A. H. *Three Centuries and the Island: A Historical Geography of Settlement and Agriculture in Prince Edward Island, Canada.* Toronto: University of Toronto Press, 1959.

Cleland, Robert. *The History of Occidental College, 1887–1937.* Los Angeles: Occidental College, 1937.

Clifford, N. Keith. *The Resistance to Church Union in Canada, 1904–1939.* Vancouver: University of British Columbia Press, 1985.

Cocoris, G. Michael. *70 Years on Hope Street: A History of the Church of the Open Door.* Los Angeles: Church of the Open Door, 1985.

Cohen, Norman J., ed. *The Fundamentalist Phenomenon: A View from Within, a Response from Without.* Grand Rapids: Eerdmans, 1990.

Cole, Stewart G. *The History of Fundamentalism.* New York: Harper & Row, 1931; repr., Hamden, CT: Archon Books, 1963.

Cremin, Lawrence. *American Education: The Metropolitan Experience, 1876–1980.* New York: Harper & Row, 1988.

Crutchfield, Larry V. *The Origins of Dispensationalism: The Darby Factor.* Lanham, MD: University Press of America, 1992.

Dayton, Donald W., and Robert K. Johnston, eds. *The Variety of American Evangelicalism.* Downers Grove, IL: InterVarsity Press, 1991.

Dolan, Jay P., and James P. Wind, eds. *New Dimensions in American Religious History: Essays in Honor of Martin E. Marty.* Grand Rapids: Eerdmans, 1993.

Dollar, George. *A History of Fundamentalism in America.* Greenville, SC: Bob Jones University, 1973.

Dorsett, Lyle W. *Billy Sunday and the Redemption of Urban America.* Grand Rapids: Eerdmans, 1991.

Draper, Virginia, and Jesse Heath McClendon. *Virginia Draper: An Autobiography.* Pasadena, CA: Welsh Graphics, 1977.

Ferrier, William Warren. *Ninety Years of Education in California, 1846–1936.* Sather Gate Book Shop: Berkeley, CA, 1936.

Findlay, James F., Jr. *Dwight L. Moody: American Evangelist, 1837–1899.* Chicago: University of Chicago Press, 1969.

Fogelson, Robert M. *The Fragmented Metropolis: Los Angeles, 1850–1930.* Cambridge, MA: Harvard University Press, 1967.

Frank, Douglas W. *Less Than Conquerors: How Evangelicals Entered the Twentieth Century.* Grand Rapids: Eerdmans, 1986.

Frankiel, Sandra Sizer. *California's Spiritual Frontiers: Religious Alternatives in Anglo-Protestantism, 1850–1910.* Berkeley: University of California Press, 1988.

Fuller, Daniel. *Give the Winds a Mighty Voice: The Story of Charles E. Fuller.* Waco, TX: Word Books, 1972.

Furniss, Norman. *The Fundamentalist Controversy, 1918–1931.* New Haven: Yale University Press, 1954.

Gaddis, Vincent, and John Huffman. *The Winona Lake Story.* Winona Lake, IN: Winona Lake Assembly, 1960.

Gaebelein, Frank E. *Christian Education in a Democracy: The Report of the N.A.E. Committee.* New York: Oxford University Press, 1951.

Gardiner, Gordon P. *Champion of the Kingdom: The Story of Philip Mauro*. Brooklyn, New York: Bread of Life, 1961.

Gaspar, Louis. *The Fundamentalist Movement*. The Hague, Paris: Mouton & Co, 1963.

Gatewood, Willard B., ed. *Controversy in the Twenties: Fundamentalism, Modernism, and Evolution*. Nashville, TN: Vanderbilt University Press, 1969.

Getz, Gene. *MBI: The Story of Moody Bible Institute*. Chicago: Moody Press, 1969.

Ginger, Ray. *Altgeld's America: The Lincoln Ideal Versus Changing Realities*. New York: Funk & Wagnalls Co., 1958; reprint, Chicago: Quadrangle Books, 1965.

Guarneri, Carl, and David Alvarez, eds. *Religion and Society in the American West: Historical Essays*. Lanham, MD: University Press of America, 1987.

Gundry, Stanley N. *Love Them In: The Proclamation Theology of D. L. Moody*. Chicago: Moody Press, 1976.

Harkness, Robert. *Reuben Archer Torrey: The Man. His Message*. Chicago: The Bible Institute Colportage Association, 1929.

Harries, John. *G. Campbell Morgan: The Man and His Ministry*. New York: Fleming H. Revell Co., 1930.

Hart, Darryl G. *Defending the Faith: J. Gresham Machen and the Crisis of Conservative Protestantism in Modern America*. Baltimore: Johns Hopkins University Press, 1994.

Hatch, Nathan. *The Democratization of American Christianity*. New Haven: Yale University Press, 1989.

Hedge, Manoah. *Past and Present of Mahaska County, Iowa*. Chicago: S. J. Clarke, 1906.

Henry, Helga Bender. *Mission on Main Street*. Boston: W. A. Wilde Co., 1955.

Henry, James O. *For Such a Time as This: A History of the Independent Fundamental Churches of America*. Westchester, IL: The Independent Fundamental Churches of America, 1983.

Hill, Laurance L., ed. *Six Collegiate Decades: The Growth of Higher Education in Southern California*. Security First National Bank of Los Angeles, 1929.

Hine, Leland D. *Baptists in Southern California*. Valley Forge, PA: Judson Press, 1966.

Hofstadter, Richard. *Anti-Intellectualism in American Life*. New York: Alfred A. Knopf, 1963.

Hopkins, C. Howard. *History of the Y.M.C.A. in North America*. New York: Association Press, 1951.

Howard, Phillip. *Charles Gallaudet Trumbull: Apostle of the Victorious Life*. Philadelphia: The Sunday School Times Co., 1944.

Hutchison, William R. *The Modernist Impulse in American Protestantism*. New York: Oxford University Press, 1976.

Kirkemo, Ronald B. *For Zion's Sake: A History of Pasadena/Point Loma College*. San Diego, CA: Point Loma Press, 1992.

Kraus, C. Norman. *Dispensationalism in America: Its Rise and Development*. Richmond, VA: John Knox Press, 1958.

Leuchtenburg, William E. *The Perils of Prosperity, 1914–32*. University of Chicago Press, 1958.

Lippy, Charles H., ed. *Twentieth Century Shapers of American Popular Religion*. New York: Greenwood Press, 1989.

Livingstone, David N. *Darwin's Forgotten Defenders: The Encounter Between Evangelical Theology and Evolutionary Thought*. Grand Rapids, MI: Eerdmans, 1987.

Loetscher, Lefferts A. *The Broadening Church: A Study of Theological Issues in the Presbyterian Church Since 1869*. Philadelphia: University of Pennsylvania Press, 1954.

Longfield, Bradley. *The Presbyterian Controversy: Fundamentalists, Modernists, and Moderates*. Religion in America Series. New York: Oxford University Press, 1991.

Macleod, John. *History of Presbyterianism on Prince Edward Island*. Chicago: Winona Publishing Company, 1904.

Magnuson, Norris A., and William G. Travis. *American Evangelicalism: An Annotated Bibliography*. West Cornwall, CT: Locust Hill Press, 1990.

Marsden, George M., ed. *Evangelicalism and Modern America*. Grand Rapids: Eerdmans, 1984.

Marsden, George M. *Fundamentalism and American Culture: The Shaping of Twentieth-Century Evangelicalism, 1870–1925*. New York: Oxford University Press, 1980.

―――. *Reforming Fundamentalism: Fuller Seminary and the New Evangelicalism*. Grand Rapids: Eerdmans, 1987.

―――. *The Soul of the American University: From Protestant Establishment to Established Nonbelief*. New York: Oxford University Press, 1994.

―――. *Understanding Fundamentalism and Evangelicalism*. Grand Rapids: Eerdmans, 1991.

Martin, Roger. *R. A. Torrey: Apostle of Certainty*. Murfreesboro, TN: Sword of the Lord Publishers, 1976.

Marty, Martin E., and R. Scott Appleby eds. *Fundamentalisms Observed*. The Fundamentalism Project 1. Chicago: University of Chicago Press, 1991.

Marty, Martin E. *Modern American Religion*. Volume 2, *The Noise of Conflict, 1919–1941*. Chicago: University of Chicago Press, 1991.

McLoughlin, William G. *Billy Sunday Was His Real Name*. Chicago: University of Chicago Press, 1955.

―――. *Modern Revivalism: Charles Grandison Finney to Billy Graham*. New York: Ronald Press, 1959.

McWilliams, Carey. *Southern California: An Island on the Land*. Santa Barbara, CA, and Salt Lake City, UT: Peregrine Smith, Inc., 1973; first ed., 1946.

Moberg, David O. *The Great Reversal: Evangelism versus Social Concern*. Philadelphia: J. B. Lippincott Co., 1972.

Montgomery, G. H. *Gerald Burton Winrod*. Wichita KS: Mertmont, 1965.

Morgan, Jill. *A Man of the Word: Life of G. Campbell Morgan*. London: Pickering & Inglis, 1951.

Nelson, Rudolph. *The Making and Unmaking of an Evangelical Mind: The Case of Edward Carnell*. Cambridge: Cambridge University Press, 1988.

Noll, Mark A. *Between Faith and Criticism: Evangelicals, Scholarship, and the Bible in America*. San Francisco: Harper & Row, 1986.

Numbers, Ronald L. *The Creationists*. New York: Alfred A. Knopf, Inc., 1992.

Petersen, Paul D., ed. *Evangelicalism and Fundamentalism: A Bibliography Selected from the ATLA Religion Database*. November 1983. American Theological Library Association, Religion Indexes 1983. Chicago: ATLA, 1983.

Pierson, George Wilson. *Yale College: An Educational History, 1871–1921*. New Haven: Yale University Press, 1952.

Rausch, David A. *Arno C. Gaebelein, 1861–1945, Irenic Fundamentalist and Scholar: Including Conversations with Dr. Frank E. Gaebelein.* New York: Edwin Mellen Press, 1983.

———. *Zionism Within Early American Fundamentalism, 1878–1918: A Convergence of Two Traditions.* New York: Edwin Mellen Press, 1979.

Rawlyk, George A., and Mark Noll, eds. *Amazing Grace: Evangelicalism in Australia. Britain, Canada, and the United States.* Grand Rapids: Baker Books, 1993.

Reid, Daniel G., Robert D. Linder, Bruce L. Shelley, and Harry S. Stout, eds. *Dictionary of Christianity in America.* Downers Grove, IL: InterVarsity Press, 1990.

Renich, Jill Torrey. *A Dream That Refused To Fade: The Montrose Bible Conference Story.* Montrose PA: Montrose Bible Conference, 1978.

Ribuffo, Leo P. *The Old Christian Right: The Protestant Far Right from the Great Depression to the Cold War.* Philadelphia: Temple University Press, 1983.

Ringenberg, William C. *The Christian College: A History of Protestant Higher Education in America.* Grand Rapids: Eerdmans, 1984.

Robertson, Darrel M. *The Chicago Revival, 1876: Society and Revivalism in a Nineteenth-Century City.* Metuchen, NJ: Scarecrow Press, 1989.

Rolle, Andrew. *Occidental College: The First Seventy-Five Years, 1887–1962.* Occidental College, 1962.

Runyan, William M. *Dr. Gray at Moody Bible Institute.* New York: Oxford University Press, 1935.

Russell, C. Allyn. *Voices of American Fundamentalism.* Philadelphia: Westminster Press, 1976.

Ryan, Halford R. *Harry Emerson Fosdick: Persuasive Preacher.* New York: Greenwood Press, 1989.

Sandeen, Ernest R. *The Origins of Fundamentalism: Toward a Historical Interpretation.* Edited by Richard C. Wolf. Facet Books Historical Series (American Church). Philadelphia: Fortress Press, 1968.

———. *The Roots of Fundamentalism: British and American Millenarianism, 1800–1930.* Chicago: University of Chicago Press, 1970; reprint, Grand Rapids: Baker Books, 1978.

Schlesinger, Arthur M. *A Critical Period in American Religion, 1875–1900.* Edited by Richard C. Wolf. Facet Books Historical Series (American Church). Philadelphia: Fortress Press, 1967.

Schuster, Robert D., James Stambaugh, and Ferne Weimer. *Researching Modern Evangelicalism: A Guide to the Holdings of the Billy Graham Center, with Information on Other Collections.* Bibliographies and Indexes in Religious Studies. Westport, CT: Greenwood Press, 1990.

Selden, William. *Princeton Theological Seminary: a Narrative History, 1812–1992.* Princeton, NJ: Princeton University Press, 1992.

Singleton, Gregory H. *Religion in the City of Angels: American Protestant Culture and Urbanization. Los Angeles, 1850–1930.* Ann Arbor, MI: UMI Research, 1979.

Sizer, Sandra S. *Gospel Hymns and Social Religion: The Rhetoric of Nineteenth-Century Revivalism.* Philadelphia: Temple University Press, 1978.

Spring, Joel. *The American School, 1642–1985: Varieties of Historical Interpretation of the Foundations and Development of American Education.* New York: Longman, 1986.

Stackhouse, John G. *Canadian Evangelicalism in the Twentieth Century: An Introduction to Its Character.* Toronto: University of Toronto Press, 1993.

Starr, Kevin. *Material Dreams: Southern California Through the 1920's.* New York: Oxford University Press, 1990.

Stevenson, Louise. *Scholarly Means to Evangelical Ends: The New Haven Scholars and the Transformation of Higher Learning in America.* Baltimore: Johns Hopkins University Press, 1986.

Sweet, Leonard I., ed. *The Evangelical Tradition in America.* Macon, GA: Mercer University Press, 1984.

Szasz, Ferenc M. *The Divided Mind of Protestant America, 1880–1930.* University: University of Alabama Press, 1982.

Thaman, Mary Patricia. *Manners and Morals of the 1920s: A Survey of the Religious Press.* New York: Bookman Associates, 1954.

Trollinger, William V. *God's Empire: William Bell Riley and Midwestern Fundamentalism.* Madison: University of Wisconsin Press, 1990.

Wacker, Grant. *Augustus H. Strong and the Dilemma of Historical Consciousness.* Macon, GA: Mercer University Press, 1985.

Weber, Timothy P. *Living in the Shadow of the Second Coming: American Premillennialism, 1875–1982.* Chicago: University of Chicago Press, 1979.

Weisberger, Bernard. *They Gathered at the River: The Story of the Great Revivalists and their Impact upon Religion in America.* Boston: Little, Brown and Co., 1958.

Williams, Peter W. *Popular Religion in America: Symbolic Change and the Modernization Process in Historical Perspective.* Urbana: University of Illinois Press, 1989.

Williams, Robert, Marilyn Miller. *Chartered for His Glory: Biola University, 1908–1983.* La Mirada, CA: Associated Students of Biola University, 1983.

Young, Arthur P., and E. Jens Holley, eds. *Religion and the American Experience, The Twentieth Century: A Bibliography of Doctoral Dissertations.* In Bibliographies and Indexes in Religious Studies, Volume 31. Westport, CT, and London: Greenwood Press, 1994.

Young, Nellie May. *William Stewart Young: Builder of California Institutions.* Glendale: The Arthur H. Clark Co., 1967.

Articles

Ahlstrom, Sydney E. "Continental Influence on American Christian Thought Since World War I." *Church History* 27 (September 1958): 256–273.

Anderson, Douglas F. "San Francisco Evangelicalism, Regional Religious Identity, and the Revivalism of D. L. Moody." *Fides et Historia* 15 (Spring/Summer 1983): 44–66.

Bassett, Paul M. "The Theological Identity of the North American Holiness Movement: Its Understanding of the Nature and Role of the Bible." In *The Variety of American Evangelicalism.* Edited by Donald W. Dayton and Robert K. Johnston, 72–108. Downers Grove, IL: InterVarsity Press, 1991.

Bebbington, D. W. "Baptists and Fundamentalism in Inter-War Britain." In *Protestant Evangelicalism: Britain, Ireland. Germany and America: Essays in Honor of W. R. Ward.* Edited by Keith Robbins, 297–326. Studies in Church History, Subsidia, 7. Oxford: Basil Blackwell Publishers, 1990.

— — —. "Martyrs for the Truth: Fundamentalists in Britain." In *Martyrs and Martyrologies: Papers Read at the 1992 Summer Meeting and the 1993 Winter Meeting of the*

Ecclesiastical History Society. Edited by Diana Wood, 417–51, Volume 30, Studies in Church History. Oxford: Basil Blackwell Publishers, 1993.

Brereton, Virginia L. "The Bible Schools and Conservative Evangelical Higher Education, 1880–1940." In *Making Higher Education Christian.* Edited by Joel A. Carpenter and Kenneth W. Shipps, 110–36. Grand Rapids: Eerdmans, 1987.

Bundy, David. "Keswick and the Experience of Evangelical Piety." In *Modern Christian Revivals.* Edited by Edith Blumhofer and Randall Balmer. Urbana: University of Illinois Press, 1993.

Burkinshaw, Robert K. "Conservative Evangelicalism in the Twentieth-Century 'West': British Columbia and the United States." In *Amazing Grace: Evangelicalism in Australia, Britain, Canada, and the United States.* 317–48. Grand Rapids: Baker Books, 1993.

Carpenter, Joel A. "From Fundamentalism to the New Evangelical Coalition." In *Evangelicalism and Modern America.* Edited by George M. Marsden, 3–16. Grand Rapids: Eerdmans, 1984.

— — —. "Fundamentalist Institutions and the Rise of Conservative Protestantism, 1929–1942." *Church History* 49 (March 1980): 62–75.

— — —. "The Fundamentalist Leaven and the Rise of an Evangelical United Front." In *The Evangelical Tradition in America.* Edited by Leonard I. Sweet, 257–88. Macon GA: Mercer University Press, 1984.

— — —. "The Scope of American Evangelicalism: Some Comments on the Dayton-Marsden Exchange." *Christian Scholar's Review* 23 (September 1993): 53–61.

Carter, Paul A. "The Fundamentalist Defense of the Faith." In *Change and Continuity in Twentieth Century America: The 1920s.* Edited by John Braeman, 179–214. Columbus: Ohio State University Press, 1968.

Coale, James J. "Influence of the Automobile on the City Church." In *The Automobile: Its Province and Its Problems.* Edited by Clyde L. King, 80–82, Annals of the American Academy of Political and Social Science, Vol. 116. Philadelphia: American Academy of Political and Social Science, 1924.

Davidson, Allan K. "A Protesting Presbyterian: The Reverend P. B. Fraser and New Zealand Presbyterianism, 1892–1940." *Journal of Religious History* 14 (December 1986): 193–217.

Dayton, Donald. "Rejoinder to Historiography Discussion." *Christian Scholar's Review* 23 (September 1993): 62–71.

— — —. "'The Search for the Historical Evangelicalism'; George Marsden's History of Fuller Seminary as a Case Study." *Christian Scholar's Review* 23 (September 1993): 12–33.

Ellis, William E. "Edgar Young Mullins and the Crisis of Moderate Southern Baptist Leadership." *Foundations* 19 (1976): 171–85.

— — —. "Evolution, Fundamentalism, and the Historians: An Historiographical Review." *The Historian* 44 (November 1981): 15–35.

Ernst, Eldon G. "American Religious History from a Pacific Coast Perspective." In *Religion and Society in the American West.* Edited by Carl Guarneri and David Alvarez, 3–39. Lanham, MD: University Press of America, 1987.

Findlay, James F., Jr. "Moody, 'Gapmen,' and the Gospel: The Early Days of Moody Bible Institute." *Church History* 31 (September 1962): 322–35.

Funk, Robert W. "The Watershed of American Biblical Tradition." *Journal of Biblical Literature* 95 (1976): 4–22.

Handy, Robert T. "The American Religious Depression, 1925–1935." *Church History* 29 (March 1960): 3–16.

———. "Fundamentalism and Modernism in Perspective." *Religion in Life* 24 (Summer 1955): 381–94.

———. "Protestant Patterns in Canada and the United States: Similarities and Differences." In *In the Great Tradition: In Honor of Winthrop S. Hudson: Essays on Pluralism. Voluntarism, and Revivalism*. Eds. Joseph Ban and Paul Dekar, 33–51. Valley Forge, PA: Judson Press, 1982.

Hays, Samuel P. "The Social Analysis of American Political History, 1880–1920." *Political Science Quarterly* 80 (September 1965): 373–94.

Heidebrecht, Paul H. "Chicago Presbyterians and the Businessman's Religion." *American Presbyterians: Journal of Presbyterian History* 64, no. 1 (Spring 1986): 39–48.

Henry, James. "Black Oil and Souls to Save." *BIOLA Broadcaster* 3 (December 1973): 4–28.

Hunter, James Davison. "Fundamentalism in Its Global Contours." In *The Fundamentalist Phenomenon: A View from Within. A Response from Without*. Edited by Norman J. Cohen, 56–72. Grand Rapids: Eerdmans, 1990.

Hutchison, William R. "Cultural Strain and Protestant Liberalism." *American Historical Review* 76 (April 1971): 386–411.

Jacobsen, Douglas, and William Vance Trollinger Jr. "Historiography of American Protestantism: The Two-Party Paradigm and Beyond." *Fides et Historia* 25 (Fall 1993): 4–15.

Livingstone, David N. "B. B. Warfield, the Theory of Evolution and Early Fundamentalism." *Evangelical Quarterly* 58 (January 1986): 69–83.

Maring, Norman H. "Baptists and Changing Views of the Bible, 1865–1918 (Part II)." *Foundations* 1 (October 1958): 30–61.

———. "Conservative But Progressive." In *What God Hath Wrought*. Edited by Gilbert L Guffin. Chicago: Judson Press, 1960.

Marsden, George M. "Defining American Fundamentalism." In *The Fundamentalist Phenomenon: A View from Within, A Response from Without*. Edited by Norman J. Cohen, 22–37. Grand Rapids: Eerdmans, 1990.

———. "Defining Fundamentalism." *Christian Scholar's Review* 1 (Winter 1971): 141–51.

———. "Fundamentalism and American Evangelicalism." In *The Variety of American Evangelicalism*. Edited by Donald W. Dayton and Robert K. Johnston, 22–35. Downers Grove, IL: InterVarsity Press, 1991.

———. "The Gospel of Wealth, The Social Gospel, and the Salvation of Souls in Nineteenth-Century America." *Fides et Historia* 5 (Fall and Spring 1972–1973): 10–21.

———. "Understanding Fundamentalist Views of Science." In *Science and Creationism*. Edited by Ashley Montagu, 95–116. New York: Oxford University Press, 1984.

Meehan, Brenda M. "A. C. Dixon: An Early Fundamentalist." *Foundations* 10 (January–March 1967): 50–63.

Moore, LeRoy. "Another Look at Fundamentalism: A Response to Ernest R. Sandeen." *Church History* 37 (June 1968): 195–202.

Moorhead, James H. "The Erosion of Postmillennialism in American Religious Thought, 1865–1925." *Church History* 53 (March 1984): 61–77.

Mouly, Ruth, and Roland Robertson. "Zionism in American Premillenarian Fundamentalism." *American Journal of Theological Philosophy* 5 (September 1983): 96–109.

Murphy, Terrence. "The Religious History of Atlantic Canada: The State of the Art." *Acadiensis* 15 (1985): 152–71.

Niebuhr, H. Richard. "Fundamentalism." In *Encyclopedia of Social Sciences,* 6:526–27. New York: Macmillan Company, 1931.

Noll, Mark A. "The University Arrives in America, 1870–1930: Christian Traditionalism During the Academic Revolution." In *Making Higher Education Christian.* Edited by Joel A. Carpenter and Kenneth Shipps, 98–109. St. Paul, MN: Christian University Press, 1987.

Pelikan, Jaroslav. "Fundamentalism and/or Orthodoxy? Toward an Understanding of the Fundamentalist Phenomenon." In *The Fundamentalist Phenomenon: A View from Within, a Response from Without.* Edited by Norman J. Cohen, 3–21. Grand Rapids: Eerdmans, 1990.

Pierard, Richard V. "The New Religious Right in American Politics." In *Evangelicalism and Modern America.* Edited by George M. Marsden, 161–74. Grand Rapids: Eerdmans, 1984.

Randall, Ian. "A Christian Cosmopolitan: F. B. Meyer in Britain." In *Amazing Grace: Evangelicalism in Australia, Britain, Canada, and the United States.* Edited by George A. Rawlyk and Mark A. Noll, 157–82. Grand Rapids: Baker Books, 1993.

Robertson, Ian R. "Historical Writing on Prince Edward Island Since 1975." *Acadiensis* 18 (Autumn 1988): 157–83.

Russell, C. Allyn. "Thomas Todhunter Shields: Canadian Fundamentalist." *Foundations* 24 (Jan–Mar 1981): 15–31.

Sandeen, Ernest. "Defining Fundamentalism: A Reply to Professor Marsden." *Christian Scholar's Review* 1 (Spring 1971): 227–32.

Shelley, Bruce. "A. J. Gordon and Biblical Criticism." *Foundations* 14 (January 1971): 69–77.

— — —. "Sources of Pietistic Fundamentalism." *Fides et Historia* 5 (Spring 1973): 68–78.

Singleton, Gregory H. "Fundamentalism and Urbanization: A Quantitative Critique of Impressionistic Interpretations." In *The New Urban History: Quantitative Explorations by American Historians.* Edited by Leo F. Schnore, 205–27. Princeton: Princeton University Press, 1975.

Smith, Gary Scott. "Conservative Presbyterians: The Gospel, Social Reform, and the Church in the Progressive Era." *American Presbyterians: Journal of Presbyterian History* 70 (Summer 1992): 93–110.

Smith, Timothy L. "The Evangelical Kaleidoscope and the Call to Christian Unity." *Christian Scholar's Review* 15 (1986): 125–40.

— — —. "Historical Fundamentalism." *Fides et Historia* 14 (Fall–Winter 1981): 68–72.

Soden, Dale E. "In Quest of a City on a Hill: Seattle Minister Mark Matthews and the Moral Leadership of the Middle Class." In *Religion and Society in the American West.* Edited by Carl Guarneri and David Alvarez, 355–73. Lanham, MD: University Press of America, 1987.

"The Stewarts as Christian Stewards, the Story of Milton and Lyman Stewart." *Missionary Review of the World* 47 (August 1924): 595–602.

Sweet, Leonard I. "Wise as Serpents, Innocent as Doves: The New Evangelical Historiography." *Journal of the American Academy of Religion* 56 (Fall 1988): 397–416.

Wacker, Grant. "The Holy Spirit and the Spirit of the Age in American Protestantism, 1880–1910." *Journal of American History* 72 (June 1985): 45–62.

— — —. "Searching for Norman Rockwell: Popular Evangelicalism in Contemporary America." In *The Evangelical Tradition in America*. Edited by Leonard I. Sweet, 289–315. Macon, GA: Mercer University Press, 1984.

Weale, David. "The Time Is Come! Millenarianism in Colonial Prince Edward Island." *Acadiensis* 7 (No. 1 1977): 35–48.

Weber, Timothy P. "Fundamentalism Twice Removed: The Emergence and Shape of Progressive Evangelicalism." In *New Dimensions in American Religious History: Essays in Honor of Martin E. Marty*. Edited by Jay P. Dolan and James P. Wind, 261–87. Grand Rapids: Eerdmans, 1993.

— — —. "The Two-Edged Sword: The Fundamentalist Use of the Bible." In *The Bible in America: Essays in Cultural History*. Edited by Nathan O. Hatch and Mark A. Noll. New York: Oxford, 1982.

Weeks, Louis. "The Incorporation of American Religion: The Case of the Presbyterians." *Religion and American Culture: A Journal of Interpretation* 1, no. 1 (Winter 1991): 101–18.

Thesis Literature

Anderson, Douglas F. "California Protestantism, 1848–1935: Historiographical Explorations and Regional Method for a Nascent Field." Unpublished Manuscript, 1983. Graduate Theological Union Library, Berkeley, CA.

Brackett, Charles. "The History of Azusa College and the Friends, 1900–1965." M. A. Thesis, University of Southern California, 1967.

Brooks, Alan. "The Exodus: Migration from the Maritime Provinces to Boston During the Second Half of the 19th Century." Ph.D. diss., University of New Brunswick, 1978.

Cameron, James Donald. "The Garden Distressed: Church Union and Dissent on Prince Edward Island, 1904–1947." Ph.D. diss., Queens University, 1989.

Dugan, Richard Pierce. "The Theory of Education Within the Bible Institute Movement." Ph.D. diss., New York University, 1977.

Edmondson, William. "Fundamentalist Sects of Los Angeles, 1900–1930." Ph.D. diss., Claremont University, 1969.

Hannah, John David. "James Martin Gray, 1851–1935." Th.D. diss., Dallas Theological Seminary, 1974.

— — —. "The Social and Intellectual History of the Origins of the Evangelical Theological College." Ph.D. diss., University of Texas, Dallas, 1988.

Harrington, Carroll Edwin. "The Fundamentalist Movement in America, 1870–1920." Ph.D. diss., University of California, Berkeley, 1959.

Hart, Nelson Hodges. "The True and the False: The Worlds of an Emerging Evangelical Protestant Fundamentalism in America." Ph.D. diss., Michigan State University, 1976.

Herman, Douglas E. "Flooding the Kingdom: The Intellectual Development of Fundamentalism, 1930–1941." Ph.D. diss., Ohio University, 1980.

Hoefel, Robert J. "The Doctrine of Inspiration in the Writings of James Orr and B. B. Warfield: A Study in Contrasting Approaches to Scripture." Ph.D. diss., Fuller Theological Seminary, 1983.

Kim, Ki Hong. "Presbyterian Conflict in the Early Twentieth Century: Ecclesiology in the Princeton Tradition and the Emergence of Presbyterian Fundamentalism." Ph.D. diss., Drew University, 1983.

Lewis, James. "An Historical Survey of Radical Sectarianism in Los Angeles." M.A. Thesis, Occidental College, 1950.

MacInnes, Donald. "Leadership Training in the Synod of California, Southern Area: Inception, Formative Years, the Present." M.A. Thesis, San Francisco Theological Seminary, 1960.

McKenzie, Brian A. "Fundamentalism, Christian Unity, and Premillennialism in the Thought of Rowland Victor Bingham (1872–1942): A Study of Anti-Modernism in Canada." Ph.D. diss., University of Toronto, 1985.

Moncher, Gary. "The Bible College and American Moral Culture." Ph.D. diss., University of California, Berkeley, 1987.

Staggers, Kermit. "Reuben A. Torrey: American Fundamentalist." Ph.D. diss., Claremont Graduate School, 1986.

Still, Mark Sumner. "'Fighting Bob' Shuler: Fundamentalist and Reformer." Ph.D. diss., Claremont Graduate School, 1988.

Szasz, Ferenc M. "Three Fundamentalist Leaders: The Roles of William Bell Riley, John Roach Straton, and William Jennings Bryan in the Fundamentalist-Modernist Controversy." Ph.D. diss., University of Rochester, 1969.

Wenger, Robert. "Social Thought in American Fundamentalism, 1918–1933." Ph.D. diss., University of Nebraska, 1973.

Wilt, Paul. "Pre-Millennialism in America, 1865–1918, With Special Reference to Attitudes Toward Social Reform." Ph.D. diss., American University, 1970.

Miscellaneous Literature

Henry, James O. A Manuscript History of the Bible Institute of Los Angeles. N.d. Biola University, La Mirada, California.

MacInnes, William. "A Son's Appreciation." Typed Document. November, 1957. MacInnis Papers. Philadelphia, Pennsylvania.

MacKinnon, Suzanne. *History of the Zion Presbyterian Church, 1860–1985.* Privately Printed Pamphlet by the Author, 1985. Robertson Library, University of Prince Edward Island, Prince Edward Island, Canada.

Marquis, Neeta. *Immanuel and the Fifty Years, 1888–1938.* Los Angeles: Immanuel Presbyterian Church, 1938.

Matheson, W. H., et al. *History of St. John's United Church, Halifax, Nova Scotia, 1793–1975.* St. John's United Church Historical Committee, [1975]. Maritime Conference Archives, United Church of Canada. Halifax, Nova Scotia.

Prichard, William H. "A. B. Prichard." Typed Document. N.d. Presbyterian Historical Society, Philadelphia, Pennsylvania.

San Gabriel Union Church 75th Anniversary, 1919–1994. Printed Booklet. Alhambra, CA: San Gabriel Union Church [1994].

Index of Persons and Subjects

Studies in Evangelical History and Thought
(All titles uniform with this volume)
Dates in bold are of projected publication

Andrew Atherstone
Oxford's Protestant Spy
The Controversial Career of Charles Golightly
Charles Golightly (1807–85) was a notorious Protestant polemicist. His life was dedicated to resisting the spread of ritualism and liberalism within the Church of England and the University of Oxford. For half a century he led many memorable campaigns, such as building a martyr's memorial and attempting to close a theological college. John Henry Newman, Samuel Wilberforce and Benjamin Jowett were among his adversaries. This is the first study of Golightly's controversial career.
__2006__ / 1-84227-364-7 / approx. 324pp

Clyde Binfield
Victorian Nonconformity in Eastern England
Studies of Victorian religion and society often concentrate on cities, suburbs, and industrialisation. This study provides a contrast. Victorian Eastern England—Essex, Suffolk, Norfolk, Cambridgeshire, and Huntingdonshire—was rural, traditional, relatively unchanging. That is nonetheless a caricature which discounts the industry in Norwich and Ipswich (as well as in Haverhill, Stowmarket and Leiston) and ignores the impact of London on Essex, of railways throughout the region, and of an ancient but changing university (Cambridge) on the county town which housed it. It also entirely ignores the political implications of such changes in a region noted for the variety of its religious Dissent since the seventeenth century. This book explores Victorian Eastern England and its Nonconformity. It brings to a wider readership a pioneering thesis which has made a major contribution to a fresh evolution of English religion and society.
__2006__ / 1-84227-216-0 / approx. 274pp

John Brencher
Martyn Lloyd-Jones (1899–1981) and Twentieth-Century Evangelicalism
This study critically demonstrates the significance of the life and ministry of Martyn Lloyd-Jones for post-war British evangelicalism and demonstrates that his preaching was his greatest influence on twentieth-century Christianity. The factors which shaped his view of the church are examined, as is the way his reformed evangelicalism led to a separatist ecclesiology which divided evangelicals.
2002 / 1-84227-051-6 / xvi + 268pp

Jonathan D. Burnham
A Story of Conflict
The Controversial Relationship between Benjamin Wills Newton and
John Nelson Darby
Burnham explores the controversial relationship between the two principal
leaders of the early Brethren movement. In many ways Newton and Darby were
products of their times, and this study of their relationship provides insight not
only into the dynamics of early Brethrenism, but also into the progress of
nineteenth-century English and Irish evangelicalism.
2004 / 1-84227-191-1 / xxiv + 268pp

Grayson Carter
Anglican Evangelicals
Protestant Secessions from the Via Media, c.1800–1850
This study examines, within a chronological framework, the major themes and
personalities which influenced the outbreak of a number of Evangelical clerical
and lay secessions from the Church of England and Ireland during the first half
of the nineteenth century. Though the number of secessions was relatively
small—between a hundred and two hundred of the 'Gospel' clergy abandoned
the Church during this period—their influence was considerable, especially in
highlighting in embarrassing fashion the tensions between the evangelical
conversionist imperative and the principles of a national religious establishment.
Moreover, through much of this period there remained, just beneath the surface,
the potential threat of a large Evangelical disruption similar to that which
occurred in Scotland in 1843. Consequently, these secessions provoked great
consternation within the Church and within Evangelicalism itself, they
contributed to the outbreak of millennial speculation following the
'constitutional revolution' of 1828–32, they led to the formation of several new
denominations, and they sparked off a major Church–State crisis over the legal
right of a clergyman to secede and begin a new ministry within Protestant
Dissent.
2007 / 1-84227-401-5 / xvi + 470pp

J.N. Ian Dickson
Beyond Religious Discourse
Sermons, Preaching and Evangelical Protestants in Nineteenth-Century
Irish Society
Drawing extensively on primary sources, this pioneer work in modern religious
history explores the training of preachers, the construction of sermons and how
Irish evangelicalism and the wider movement in Great Britain and the United
States shaped the preaching event. Evangelical preaching and politics,
sectarianism, denominations, education, class, social reform, gender, and revival
are examined to advance the argument that evangelical sermons and preaching
went significantly beyond religious discourse. The result is a book for those with
interests in Irish history, culture and belief, popular religion and society,
evangelicalism, preaching and communication.
2005 / 1-84227-217-9 / approx. 324pp

Neil T.R. Dickson
Brethren in Scotland 1838–2000
A Social Study of an Evangelical Movement
The Brethren were remarkably pervasive throughout Scottish society. This study
of the Open Brethren in Scotland places them in their social context and
examines their growth, development and relationship to society.
2003 / 1-84227-113-X / xxviii + 510pp

Crawford Gribben and Timothy C.F. Stunt (eds)
Prisoners of Hope?
Aspects of Evangelical Millennialism in Britain and Ireland, 1800–1880
This volume of essays offers a comprehensive account of the impact of
evangelical millennialism in nineteenth-century Britain and Ireland.
2004 / 1-84227-224-1 / xiv + 208pp

Khim Harris
Evangelicals and Education
Evangelical Anglicans and Middle-Class Education in
Nineteenth-Century England
This ground breaking study investigates the history of English public schools
founded by nineteenth-century Evangelicals. It documents the rise of middle-
class education and Evangelical societies such as the influential Church
Association, and includes a useful biographical survey of prominent
Evangelicals of the period.
2004 / 1-84227-250-0 / xviii + 422pp

Mark Hopkins
Nonconformity's Romantic Generation
Evangelical and Liberal Theologies in Victorian England
A study of the theological development of key leaders of the Baptist and
Congregational denominations at their period of greatest influence, including
C.H. Spurgeon and R.W. Dale, and of the controversies in which those among
them who embraced and rejected the liberal transformation of their evangelical
heritage opposed each other.
2004 / 1-84227-150-4 / xvi + 284pp

Don Horrocks
Laws of the Spiritual Order
*Innovation and Reconstruction in the Soteriology of Thomas Erskine
of Linlathen*
Don Horrocks argues that Thomas Erskine's unique historical and theological
significance as a soteriological innovator has been neglected. This timely
reassessment reveals Erskine as a creative, radical theologian of central and
enduring importance in Scottish nineteenth-century theology, perhaps equivalent
in significance to that of S.T. Coleridge in England.
2004 / 1-84227-192-X / xx + 362pp

Kenneth S. Jeffrey
When the Lord Walked the Land
The 1858–62 Revival in the North East of Scotland
Previous studies of revivals have tended to approach religious movements from
either a broad, national or a strictly local level. This study of the multifaceted
nature of the 1859 revival as it appeared in three distinct social contexts within a
single region reveals the heterogeneous nature of simultaneous religious
movements in the same vicinity.
2002 / 1-84227-057-5 / xxiv + 304pp

John Kenneth Lander
Itinerant Temples
Tent Methodism, 1814–1832
Tent preaching began in 1814 and the Tent Methodist sect resulted from
disputes with Bristol Wesleyan Methodists in 1820. The movement spread to
parts of Gloucestershire, Wiltshire, London and Liverpool, among other places.
Its demise started in 1826 after which one leader returned to the Wesleyans and
others became ministers in the Congregational and Baptist denominations.
2003 / 1-84227-151-2 / xx + 268pp

Donald M. Lewis
Lighten Their Darkness
The Evangelical Mission to Working-Class London, 1828–1860
This is a comprehensive and compelling study of the Church and the complexities of nineteenth-century London. Challenging our understanding of the culture in working London at this time, Lewis presents a well-structured and illustrated work that contributes substantially to the study of evangelicalism and mission in nineteenth-century Britain.

2001 / 1-84227-074-5 / xviii + 372pp

Herbert McGonigle
'Sufficient Saving Grace'
John Wesley's Evangelical Arminianism
A thorough investigation of the theological roots of John Wesley's evangelical Arminianism and how these convictions were hammered out in controversies on predestination, limited atonement and the perseverance of the saints.

2001 / 1-84227-045-1 / xvi + 350pp

Lisa S. Nolland
A Victorian Feminist Christian
Josephine Butler, the Prostitutes and God
Josephine Butler was an unlikely candidate for taking up the cause of prostitutes, as she did, with a fierce and self-disregarding passion. This book explores the particular mix of perspectives and experiences that came together to envision and empower her remarkable achievements. It highlights the vital role of her spirituality and the tragic loss of her daughter.

2004 / 1-84227-225-X / xxiv + 328pp

Don J. Payne
The Theology of the Christian Life in J.I. Packer's Thought
Theological Anthropology, Theological Method, and the Doctrine of Sanctification
J.I. Packer has wielded widespread influence on evangelicalism for more than three decades. This study pursues a nuanced understanding of Packer's theology of sanctification by tracing the development of his thought, showing how he reflects a particular version of Reformed theology, and examining the unique influence of theological anthropology and theological method on this area of his theology.

2005 / 1-84227-397-3 / approx. 374pp

Ian M. Randall
Evangelical Experiences
A Study in the Spirituality of English Evangelicalism 1918–1939
This book makes a detailed historical examination of evangelical spirituality
between the First and Second World Wars. It shows how patterns of devotion
led to tensions and divisions. In a wide-ranging study, Anglican, Wesleyan,
Reformed and Pentecostal-charismatic spiritualities are analysed.
1999 / 0-85364-919-7 / xii + 310pp

Ian M. Randall
Spirituality and Social Change
The Contribution of F.B. Meyer (1847–1929)
This is a fresh appraisal of F.B. Meyer (1847–1929), a leading Free Church
minister. Having been deeply affected by holiness spirituality, Meyer became
the Keswick Convention's foremost international speaker. He combined
spirituality with effective evangelism and socio-political activity. This study
shows Meyer's significant contribution to spiritual renewal and social change.
2003 / 1-84227-195-4 / xx + 184pp

James Robinson
Pentecostal Origins
Early Pentecostalism in Ireland in the Context of the British Isles
Harvey Cox describes Pentecostalism as 'the fascinating spiritual child of our
time' that has the potential, at the global scale, to contribute to the 'reshaping of
religion in the twenty-first century'. This study grounds such sentiments by
examining at the local scale the origin, development and nature of
Pentecostalism in Ireland in its first twenty years. Illustrative, in a paradigmatic
way, of how Pentecostalism became established within one region of the British
Isles, it sets the story within the wider context of formative influences emanating
from America, Europe and, in particular, other parts of the British Isles. As a
synoptic regional study in Pentecostal history it is the first survey of its kind.
2005 / 1-84227-329-1 / xxviii + 378pp

Geoffrey Robson
Dark Satanic Mills?
Religion and Irreligion in Birmingham and the Black Country
This book analyses and interprets the nature and extent of popular Christian
belief and practice in Birmingham and the Black Country during the first half of
the nineteenth century, with particular reference to the impact of cholera
epidemics and evangelism on church extension programmes.
2002 / 1-84227-102-4 / xiv + 294pp

Roger Shuff
Searching for the True Church
Brethren and Evangelicals in Mid-Twentieth-Century England
Roger Shuff holds that the influence of the Brethren movement on wider evangelical life in England in the twentieth century is often underrated. This book records and accounts for the fact that Brethren reached the peak of their strength at the time when evangelicalism was at it lowest ebb, immediately before World War II. However, the movement then moved into persistent decline as evangelicalism regained ground in the post war period. Accompanying this downward trend has been a sharp accentuation of the contrast between Brethren congregations who engage constructively with the non-Brethren scene and, at the other end of the spectrum, the isolationist group commonly referred to as 'Exclusive Brethren'.
2005 / 1-84227-254-3 / xviii+ 296pp

James H.S. Steven
Worship in the Spirit
Charismatic Worship in the Church of England
This book explores the nature and function of worship in six Church of England churches influenced by the Charismatic Movement, focusing on congregational singing and public prayer ministry. The theological adequacy of such ritual is discussed in relation to pneumatological and christological understandings in Christian worship.
2002 / 1-84227-103-2 / xvi + 238pp

Peter K. Stevenson
God in Our Nature
The Incarnational Theology of John McLeod Campbell
This radical reassessment of Campbell's thought arises from a comprehensive study of his preaching and theology. Previous accounts have overlooked both his sermons and his Christology. This study examines the distinctive Christology evident in his sermons and shows that it sheds new light on Campbell's much debated views about atonement.
2004 / 1-84227-218-7 / xxiv + 458pp

Kenneth J. Stewart
Restoring the Reformation
British Evangelicalism and the Réveil at Geneva 1816–1849
Restoring the Reformation traces British missionary initiative in post-Revolutionary Francophone Europe from the genesis of the London Missionary Society, the visits of Robert Haldane and Henry Drummond, and the founding of the Continental Society. While British Evangelicals aimed at the reviving of a foreign Protestant cause of momentous legend, they received unforeseen reciprocating emphases from the Continent which forced self-reflection on Evangelicalism's own relationship to the Reformation.
2006 / 1-84227-392-2 / approx. 190pp

Martin Wellings
Evangelicals Embattled
Responses of Evangelicals in the Church of England to Ritualism, Darwinism and Theological Liberalism 1890–1930
In the closing years of the nineteenth century and the first decades of the twentieth century Anglican Evangelicals faced a series of challenges. In responding to Anglo-Catholicism, liberal theology, Darwinism and biblical criticism, the unity and identity of the Evangelical school were severely tested.
2003 / 1-84227-049-4 / xviii + 352pp

James Whisenant
A Fragile Unity
Anti-Ritualism and the Division of Anglican Evangelicalism in the Nineteenth Century
This book deals with the ritualist controversy (approximately 1850–1900) from the perspective of its evangelical participants and considers the divisive effects it had on the party.
2003 / 1-84227-105-9 / xvi + 530pp

Haddon Willmer
Evangelicalism 1785–1835: An Essay (1962) and Reflections (2004)
Awarded the Hulsean Prize in the University of Cambridge in 1962, this interpretation of a classic period of English Evangelicalism, by a young church historian, is now supplemented by reflections on Evangelicalism from the vantage point of a retired Professor of Theology.
2006 / 1-84227-219-5 / approx. 350pp

Linda Wilson
Constrained by Zeal
Female Spirituality amongst Nonconformists 1825–1875
Constrained by Zeal investigates the neglected area of Nonconformist female spirituality. Against the background of separate spheres, it analyses the experience of women from four denominations, and argues that the churches provided a 'third sphere' in which they could find opportunities for participation.

2000 / 0-85364-972-3 / xvi + 294pp

Paternoster
9 Holdom Avenue,
Bletchley,
Milton Keynes MK1 1QR,
United Kingdom
Web: www.authenticmedia.co.uk/paternoster

July 2005